CW00433722

Progressive Creation and the Struggles of Humanity in the Bible

7/1/2020

To Carmody,
with very best
wishes,

Zoltán

Progressive Creation and the Struggles of Humanity in the Bible

A Canonical Narrative Interpretation

Zoltán Dörnyei

FOREWORD BY
Karen Kilby

☞PICKWICK *Publications* · Eugene, Oregon

PROGRESSIVE CREATION AND THE STRUGGLES OF HUMANITY
IN THE BIBLE
A Canonical Narrative Interpretation

Copyright © 2018 Zoltán Dörnyei. All rights reserved. Except for brief quotations in critical publications or reviews, no part of this book may be reproduced in any manner without prior written permission from the publisher. Write: Permissions, Wipf and Stock Publishers, 199 W. 8th Ave., Suite 3, Eugene, OR 97401.

Pickwick Publications
An Imprint of Wipf and Stock Publishers
199 W. 8th Ave., Suite 3
Eugene, OR 97401

www.wipfandstock.com

PAPERBACK ISBN: 978-1-5326-3389-8
HARDCOVER ISBN: 978-1-5326-3391-1
EBOOK ISBN: 978-1-5326-3390-4

Cataloguing-in-Publication data:

Names: Dörnyei, Zoltán, author | Kilby, Karen, foreword.

Title: Progressive creation and the struggles of humanity in the Bible : a canonical narrative interpretation / Zoltán Dörnyei ; foreword by Karen Kilby.

Description: Eugene, OR: Pickwick Publications, 2018. | Includes bibliographical references and indexes.

Identifiers: ISBN 978-1-5326-3389-8 (paperback). | ISBN 978-1-5326-3391-1 (hardcover). | ISBN 978-1-5326-3390-4 (ebook).

Subjects: LCSH: Creation—Biblical teaching | Bible. Genesis, I–II, 4—Criticism, interpretation, etc. | Spiritual warfare.

Classification: BS652 D66 2018 2018 (print). | BS652 (epub).

Manufactured in the U.S.A.

Unless otherwise noted, or except when quoting from other writers' works, Scripture quotations are from the New Revised Standard Version Bible, copyright 1989, Division of Christian Education of the National Council of the Churches of Christ in the United States of America. Used by permission. All rights reserved.

Scripture quotations marked (NIV) are taken from the Holy Bible, New International Version®, NIV®. Copyright © 1973, 1978, 1984, 2011 by Biblica, Inc.™ Used by permission of Zondervan. All rights reserved worldwide. www.zondervan.com The "NIV" and "New International Version" are trademarks registered in the United States Patent and Trademark Office by Biblica, Inc.™

Scripture quotations marked (NKJV) are from the New King James Version®. Copyright © 1982 by Thomas Nelson. Used by permission. All rights reserved.

Scripture quotations marked (ESV) are from The ESV® Bible (The Holy Bible, English Standard Version®), copyright © 2001 by Crossway, a publishing ministry of Good News Publishers. Used by permission. All rights reserved.

03/15/18

Contents

Foreword

PICK UP THIS BOOK and read a paragraph or two, and you may not notice how unusual it is. Even a quick browse of the introduction or the conclusion will not reveal the distinctiveness, because Zoltán Dörnyei's style is modest, often understated—he does not shout at the reader about his originality.

A first thing to note is that it is a book which does not fit into familiar theological genres. Is it systematic theology? It deals with broad themes (creation and what we might normally speak of in terms of sin and evil) but there is far too much exegesis, far too much focused engagement with particular biblical texts, for this to look like any kind of standard work in systematics. It must, then, be biblical studies? But it ranges more widely and freely across the canon than any work in biblical studies that I can call to mind.

Zoltán Dörnyei came late to the study of theology, but he came already formed as a scholar, an established figure in another discipline. Both of these things were necessary to make this book possible. On the one hand, I suspect no one who had been shaped early in life by the conventions of contemporary academic theology would attempt something quite as bold as is found between these covers. On the other, because Zoltán brought to the project such a prodigious scholarly capacity, he has been able rapidly and gracefully to find his way around a really extraordinary range of literature, all the while working out his own quite unique proposal.

Zoltán offers in this book, then, something like a new paradigm. He offers a new canonical narrative, which draws lines of connection between Genesis and Job and the New Testament in unfamiliar ways; and at the same time, almost without trying, he offers a new way of escaping the divide between systematics and biblical studies (something which many theologians lament even as they instruct new generations of students in the difference between the two and train them to follow the conventions of one or the other).

What should one anticipate, then, when one reads a book so bold as this, a book which offers a new paradigm? Two things, I think—one about the book, and one about its reader. The book, one should expect, won't be perfect: in something so ambitious, new, and wide-ranging, there will surely be some lacunae, some loose ends, something to which we can object. And from ourselves, as readers, on the other hand, we should anticipate resistance, a resistance which arises quite apart from any actual problems in the book: when something does not fit long established patterns, it is surprisingly hard to take in, and nearly impossible to get beyond an instinctive feeling that "you just can't do it like that."

For those who can put aside their resistance, there is a great deal to learn here: a rich theological proposal, intriguing in every chapter, and overall an enormous stimulus and provocation to thought. It is undoubtedly a fascinating piece of work.

Karen Kilby

Bede Professor of Catholic Theology
Durham University

Preface

THE ORIGINAL MOTIVATION BEHIND this work has been a broad desire to explore the biblical basis of the fundamental challenges that humanity has been confronted with throughout its history, which has resulted in a state of affairs in the world that few would consider optimal. It was hoped that such an exploration would offer guidelines about Christian conduct in the current age, particularly with respect to spiritual challenges and how to respond to them. Accordingly, I set out to examine the theology of spiritual warfare, but as the investigation progressed, this initial focus underwent a considerable transformation largely due to the recognition of three important issues.

First, I realized that rigorous academic discussions of the topic already exist,[1] but at the same time, it also became clear that even works meeting the highest scholarly standards in this area tended not to reach the theological mainstream. One reason for this, I came to believe, was the fact that while the scriptural references to various heavenly beings and spiritual forces have been subjected to extensive scrutiny in biblical studies, the resulting proposals usually remained somewhat "localized," that is, did not add up to an overarching theological argument that was sufficiently integrated with the central themes of the Bible, such as atonement and salvation through Jesus Christ. This observation shifted the focus of my project toward adopting a broader perspective that could potentially bring together the relevant episodic insights into a coherent and comprehensive construal (hence the adoption of a canonical narrative analysis, as discussed in chapter 1).

Second, and related to the first point, it also became apparent that human tribulations cannot be fully understood from a theological perspective without examining their origins in the biblical description of creation; it

1. E.g., Page, *Powers of Evil*; C. E. Arnold, *Three Questions About Spiritual Warfare*; Moses, *Practices of Power*; for a recent overview, see Beilby and Eddy, *Understanding Spiritual Warfare*.

was felt that, regardless of the complexity, subtlety, or abstraction of the analysis, the fundamental question of why God's creation accommodates evil and suffering would inevitably emerge at some time. This point was driven home to me during the study of the book of Job: As we shall see in chapter 5, this book offers arguably the most elaborate insights into spiritual opposition to God's work and the resulting human struggles and suffering, and yet the conclusion of the text—God's response in the final divine speeches to Job's pleas and complaints—almost entirely concerns creational issues. Therefore, the current, final version of the book starts out with the presentation of a progressive view of divine creation that spans the biblical canon from the beginning of Genesis to the eschatological completion of new creation at the end of Revelation.

Third, over the course of the analysis, I came to realize that while spiritual challenges remain an important aspect of understanding humanity's struggles as portrayed in the canon, they are presented in the Bible as part of a wider discourse that is centered around the inherent imperfections of human corporeality and creatureliness. An obvious illustration of this point (to be elaborated on in chapter 3) is the fact that while the serpent of the Fall did play an active role in leading Adam and Eve astray, the ultimate reason for the first human couple's failure to obey God's command lay not so much in the power of the serpent's deception as in the fact that they *could* be deceived because of their human failings. Consequently, the scope of the enquiry has been extended to include a description of the wide range of corporeal, societal, and spiritual vulnerabilities and temptations of humankind, and the original focal issue, the biblical basis of spiritual warfare, will be addressed directly only in the final chapter (chapter 7) in a consideration of the various practical implications for the Christian believer's conduct.

The discussion in the following chapters draws on extensive biblical interpretation, and given the basic tenet of hermeneutics that the subjective preconceptions of the interpreter will inevitably shape the nature of any interpretation, let me conclude this Preface by addressing some relevant aspects of my personal background and the overall tenor of the interpretive approach adopted in this book. Having been christened as a Catholic, I grew up in a non-believing family in Communist Hungary and became a Christian in a Baptist church only when approaching forty. Since then I have attended churches of three different Christian strands, and while I adhere to the Ecumenical Creeds, I have been impacted by a socio-ecclesiastic context in the UK that is often described as post-denominational, and have not developed as a result a strongly partisan denominational identity. From a hermeneutical perspective, such an "undefined" spiritual background might carry both possible benefits (e.g., fewer constraints on drawing on a wide variety of Christian interpretations and images) and potential risks (e.g., eclectic mixing of views that are not necessarily compatible). Given, however, that a nondenominational position is relatively untested in biblical scholarship, it is fair to conclude that its implicit presuppositions are not as yet always clear. For the purpose of exegesis I use the Protestant canon of the Bible, partly because this collection of biblical books can be seen as a "common denominator" among the various versions of the canon, shared by all mainstream Christian strands.[2]

My academic background also represents a somewhat nonstandard history regarding biblical scholarship. Although I have undertaken both undergraduate and graduate studies in theology (leading to an MA in biblical interpretation and a PhD in theology), the formative aspect of my academic career has been three decades of working in the social sciences as a psycholinguist specializing in research on second-language acquisition. In this position, I have gained broad experience of engaging with textual and linguistic information (including issues of translation and intercultural communication), both at the discourse and micro-linguistic levels, and this experience has prepared me in some measure for the systematic handling of biblical texts and for anticipating some of the challenges of scriptural analysis that an interpreter may encounter. At the same time, the ingrained norms of empirical research in the social sciences carry the ongoing risk of generating a proclivity to identify "optimal" solutions and, in doing so, to underplay the hermeneutical inevitability of the pluralism of potential biblical interpretations.

Regarding the interpretive approach adopted, the current book follows the hermeneutic tradition that views the biblical corpus as a *canon*, that is, a textual whole in which the individual elements are not only mutually inter-pretive but are to be understood in relation to the whole of which they form parts.[3] Within this framework, I will be working alongside the Christian tradition that maintains that the biblical corpus is a divinely inspired set of texts; that is, regardless of the extensive human involvement of authors, redactors, scribe copiers, and church authorities in shaping the biblical texts, it is assumed that ultimately it was God who—to use Wolterstorff's terminology[4]—"authorized" the resultant biblical canon. Having said that, I am aware of many subtle and less subtle challenges to biblical interpretation

2. Thus, as John Peckham (*Canonical Theology*, 44) rightly points out, in the canon debates the concern is not that the sixty-six books of the Protestant Bible are canonical, but rather whether there are other books that should be viewed as canonical.

3. See e.g., Peckham, *Canonical Theology*; Webster, "Canon." Chapter 1 of this book offers further discussion of this topic.

4. Wolterstorff, "Unity behind the Canon," 228.

concerning biblical authorship, divine inspiration, the canonization process, historical accuracy, and internal textual contradictions—to name but a
few—and the material in the following chapters is not blind to such matters;
in this sense the approach is in accordance with Kevin Vanhoozer's notion
of "critical biblicism" concerning interpretive authority.[5]

Besides my personal conviction, there was also an academic rationale
for giving such a high status to Scripture in the hermeneutic analysis. This
was related to the fact that the Ecumenical Creeds of the patristic era, which
have served as a compass for Christian believers over the past millennia,
make no mention of matters concerning human struggles, tribulations, or
the assaults of agents of evil, including those of the devil. The silence of the
Creeds in these complex and highly loaded matters has left Christian believers with a great deal of uncertainty and has been partly responsible for the
development of diverse explanations, proposals, and strategies in these areas
over the centuries, with little consensus on some key issues across different
church communities and denominations. This uncertainty has been palpa-
ble, for example, in the wake of salient tragic events of the past two decades
such as the 9/11 attacks or the 2004 tsunami, when many people—believers
and nonbelievers alike—were groping for an answer to the question of how
such things could be allowed to happen. A less dramatic but equally pertinent example of the same issue concerns *human temptation*, a recurrent
biblical theme which is also one of the most frequent sources of struggle
within everyday Christian life. There is an absence of creedal guidance on
this matter and, as will be argued in chapter 7, while the literature contains
many useful, practically oriented works on the topic, there is currently no
fully articulated Christian theology of human temptation—indeed, there is
a marked paucity of reference in the scholarly literature to matters of temptation and, more generally, on how to handle spiritual challenges. This can
be seen to considerably reduce the effectiveness of the church in helping
believers to stand firm amid their struggles.

With no realistic prospect in the near future of an Ecumenical Synod
laying down guidelines to fill these gaps, one may argue that the biblical
corpus remains the most solid basis for theologians to build on when seeking further understanding of such contested issues. The current work is an
attempt to examine what lessons would emerge from the Scriptures in these
areas if a conscious effort was made to focus on the biblical text as the primary source of analysis, with as few preconceptions as possible, and it will
be argued in chapter 1 that the "low-inference" and relatively open-ended
nature of the specific hermeneutical approach adopted—a canonical narrative interpretation—is consonant with this goal.

5. Vanhoozer, *Biblical Authority*, 145.

Acknowledgments

THIS BOOK IS BASED on my PhD research conducted at the University of Durham, UK. I would like to express my sincere gratitude to my supervisors, Professor Karen Kilby and Dr. T. J. Lang, for their guidance and support, as well as for their invaluable feedback on this work that helped to sharpen the arguments and reduce the inaccuracies. Thank you also, Karen, for writing the foreword of this book. I am thankful to the two examiners of the dissertation, Professor Paul Murray and Dr. Nathan Eubank, for their constructive comments and suggestions that helped to shape the final form of the work. I owe a debt of gratitude to my wife, Sarah, who has not only stood by me throughout the years and provided a loving environment for me to work in, but has also done a thorough reading of the manuscript and offered many valuable comments and insights. Finally, I would like to thank the entire Wipf and Stock team for their interest in publishing this work and for all their helpful assistance in making it a reality.

Abbreviations

AB	Anchor Bible
ABRL	Anchor Bible Reference Library
BDB	Francis Brown, S. R. Driver, and Charles A. Briggs, *Hebrew and English Lexicon of the Old Testament*. Oxford: Clarendon, 1907
BECNT	Baker Exegetical Commentary on the New Testament
BZNW	Beihefte zur Zeitschrift für die neutestamentliche Wissenschaft
CD	Karl Barth, *Church Dogmatics*. Translated by G. T. Thomson et al. Edinburgh: T. & T. Clark, 1936–77
NICNT	New International Commentary on the New Testament
NICOT	New International Commentary on the Old Testament
NIGTC	New International Greek Testament Commentary
NIVAC	NIV Application Commentary
NTS	*New Testament Studies*
PNTC	Pillar New Testament Commentary
TDNT	*Theological Dictionary of the New Testament*. 10 vols. Edited by Gerhard Kittel and Gerhard Friedrich. Translated by Geoffrey W. Bromiley. Grand Rapids: Eerdmans, 1964–76
WBC	Word Biblical Commentary

1

Setting the Scene

Hermeneutical Approach, the Christian Doctrine of Creation,
and Different Conceptions of Spiritual Warfare

THE MAIN ARGUMENTS AND claims of this book have largely been derived from exegesis that employs a canonical narrative interpretation of Scripture, and the following chapters will present a canonical narrative of progressive creation that overarches the whole biblical canon from the beginning of Genesis to the end of Revelation. In order to set the scene for the forthcoming discussion, the current chapter provides an overview of the broader scholarly context of three central topics, the hermeneutical approach adopted for the study, the Christian doctrine of creation, and the main conceptions of spiritual warfare in contemporary theology. These summaries are intended to situate the primary themes of the book in existing theological paradigms, and they also provide a backdrop against which the new elements of the work can be appraised.

The discussion of the first topic, the characterization of the hermeneutical approach employed in this work, will address the origins and the distinctive features of the canonical narrative analysis, and it will also include a synopsis of the specific narrative presented in the following chapters. The overview of the Christian doctrine of creation has been warranted by the substantial role that creational issues have assumed in the overall discussion as well as by the fact that the creational perspective taken in this book is non-traditional in its emphasis on the unfolding *process* rather than the origins of creation. Finally, as was explained in the Preface, although the study of spiritual warfare, which constituted the initial focal issue of the investigation, has been integrated into a wider construal concerning the inherent imperfections of human creatureliness and the ensuing struggles of humankind, the role of spiritual forces opposing God's creative work remains an important element in the discussion; a summary of different understandings of spiritual warfare is also necessitated by the controversial and often misunderstood nature of this subject both in theology and in church circles.

1.1 Hermeneutical Approach

The hermeneutical approach adopted for the analysis of Scripture—a canonical narrative interpretation—has been inspired and modelled by Kendall Soulen book on *The God of Israel and Christian Theology*,[1] even though the actual canonical narrative proposed by Soulen has a different focus to the current work: He was primarily concerned with the continuing theological importance of Judaism for Christianity and what he saw as doctrinal supersessionism rooted in an inadequate reading of the canon, whereas—as was explained in the Preface—the current book explores the creational implications on humanity's plight. Let us start the examination of the specifics of this hermeneutical method by first considering two concepts that are central to the perspective taken in this book, "canon" and "composition."

Canon and Composition

The current book follows the hermeneutic tradition whereby the full *canonical message* of the Bible is taken to be delivered by the constituent texts in concert, and this unifying principle applies not only to the books within the two Testaments but also across them. The perception of a unified biblical testimony can be traced back to the traditional doctrine of the "harmony of Scripture," which posits that because the various parts of the biblical canon have all originated from God, they represent different forms of expression of the same divine purpose,[2] a unity acknowledged by most Christian denominations.[3] Regarding the much debated question of which biblical books comprise the canonical corpus, the current work takes an unmarked position and considers—as mentioned briefly in the Preface—only the sixty-six books of the Protestant canon. There is virtually complete agreement in contemporary Christianity about the canonical status of these books, and this

---

1. Soulen, *God of Israel.*

2. See e.g., Barr, *Holy Scripture,* 3; Greer, "Christian Bible," 200–201.

3. For example, the *Catechism of the Catholic Church* states: "The Second Vatican Council indicates three criteria for interpreting Scripture in accordance with the Spirit who inspired it. §112: 1. Be especially attentive 'to the content and unity of the whole Scripture.' Different as the books which compose it may be, Scripture is a unity by reason of the unity of God's plan . . ."

is hoped to limit the vulnerability of the exegesis of this corpus. The specific canonical analysis follows a "final-form approach," which takes into account the findings of textual criticism but which stops short of attending to any "non-manuscript-based reconstruction of the text"[4] (Peckham).

One useful way of understanding the interrelated and interdependent nature of the assembled texts within the whole of the canon is to see them forming parts of an overall biblical *composition*. The term "composition" has been most commonly used in visual arts and music, where it refers to the different aspects of a work of art that combine to produce a harmonious whole. The analogy between artistic and biblical compositions was first highlighted by Irenaeus of Lyons in a famous passage from *Against Heresies* in which he discusses how Gnostic heresy falsified the biblical truth.[5] He compared the Bible to a beautiful image of a king, constructed by a skillful artist out of precious stones, and likened the Gnostic practice of choosing biblical passages and putting them together in a way that they seemingly supported their nonbiblical scheme to the act of rearranging the gems "into the form of a dog or of a fox, and even that but poorly executed." The remarkable aspect of Irenaeus's point is that the false images are constructed from the same components as the true ones and it is only the *order* of the components that was falsified to create deception. This foregrounding of the significance of the individual parts' position in relation to the whole constitutes a genuinely compositional approach.[6] Matthew Emerson argues that sequencing principles also play a role at the macro-level of the canon,[7] which is prominently illustrated, for example, by the different ordering of the books of the Hebrew Bible and the Old Testament: The former ends with 2 Chronicles, whereas the Old Testament ends with Malachi, which provides a smooth link with the New Testament.[8]

Adopting a compositional perspective on how the textual elements within the biblical canon relate to each other can help to deal with instances when the assumed harmony of Scripture is seemingly broken. As Robert Alter, among others, points out, there are certain biblical passages that "seem

---

4. Peckham, *Canonical Theology*, 200.

5. Irenaeus, *Against Heresies*, 1:8:1.

6. For a relevant discussion adopting a Gestalt-perspective, see Fischer, "Revelation as Gestalt," 79.

7. Emerson, *Christ and the New Creation*, 28

8. Emerson cites the Introduction of the Jewish Bible published by The Jewish Publication Society, which explicitly states, "The ordering matters because it alters the context in which we understand the text; a book's meaning can shift depending on which books we read before and after it" (ibid.).

to resist any harmonizing interpretation,"[9] for example when the narratives contain some obvious contradictions. A common response in historical-critical scholarship to such "difficult" texts has been to assume that they are the outcome of some human error or distortion that occurred after the specific text was authored (e.g., copying mistake, redactional inconsistency, questionable editorial "clarification" or "improvement," etc.). However, Alter argues that some of the textual conflicts are so glaring that one cannot realistically believe that the original authors/redactors were so unperceptive as to simply miss them unless we risk falling into the "modem provincialism of assuming that ancient writers must be simple because they are ancient."[10] Instead, he suggests, such inconsistencies are better seen as examples of a compositional technique applied in the Scriptures whereby biblical authors and redactors expressed complex meanings that were resistant to linear delineation by placing not-fully-compatible passages in juxtaposition. As he explains, "A writer in another tradition might have tried somehow to combine the different aspects of the story in a single narrative event; the biblical author, dealing as he often did in the editing and splicing and artful montage of antecedent literary materials, would appear to have reached for this effect of multifaceted truth by setting in sequence two different versions that brought into focus two different dimensions of his subject."[11]

A famous example of this practice, cited by Alter,[12] is Gen 1:27—"So God created man in his own image, in the image of God he created him; male and female he created them"—where the montage technique is applied within a single verse. Interestingly, the splicing technique of placing together, and thus uniting, different components or ingredients is well known in modern art; it is employed, for example, in film montages or Cubist paintings to achieve visual impact through the dynamic interplay of irreconcilable presentations (e.g., two juxtaposed or superimposed perspectives of the same face in a picture).[13] It may not be farfetched to find the same montage principle also at work in the Bible at the level of larger blocks of material, for example in the interrelationship of the four Gospels, or perhaps even in the co-existence of the two Testaments, with all the well-documented continuities and discontinuities between them.[14] If we look at the biblical composition through

9. Alter, *Biblical Narrative*, 133.

10. Ibid., 145.

11. Ibid., 140.

12. Ibid., 146.

13. Ibid.

14. A case in point is the interrelationship of the four Gospels. As Watson emphasizes, modern scholarship has increasingly rejected attempts to harmonize the seemingly incompatible aspects of the different gospel narratives, because the resulting discourse

such a dynamic lens, it can be likened to a rich, dramatic landscape in which different segments co-occur sometimes in a harmonious and complementary manner, sometimes in tense juxtaposition.

An important corollary of a compositional approach is the understanding that the complex interrelationship of the elements allows for multiple parallel readings. Any intricate—multi-layered and multi-genre—textual composition offers several avenues for meaningful reflection, depending on which aspects of the design the exploration starts with, what elements it focuses on, and what external background information it brings to the process. In other words, a textual composition such as the Bible is open to various valid interpretations, and indeed, there is ample evidence of this plurality of compositional meaning in the bewildering diversity of construals produced by biblical interpretation over the past two millennia.

Narratives and Narrative Interpretation

A compositional perspective on the canon raises the fundamental questions of how the multiple components of a written composition are held together to form a whole, and how the composition, in turn, is digested or "beheld" by the reader. Pictorial analogies are of limited value in this respect, because unlike visual images where the visual Gestalt can be experienced at a glance, written texts reveal their content only incrementally through progressive reading, and therefore they necessitate some kind of temporal or chronological scaffolding. This is an area where literary criticism has much to offer to theology, because a great deal of scholarship in this field has focused on *narratives* as effective tools for providing extended written works with a temporal framework to link events into a plot and to weave characters into a unique narrative world.[15] Inspired by analyses of chronological continuity in literary texts as well as by the undeniable fact that the Bible

---

is seen to destroy the integrity of the individual stories. Watson, "Fourfold Gospel," 48. However, Watson also underlines "a genuine theological concern . . . to articulate the oneness of the fourfold gospel in its testimony to the one God and the one Lord Jesus Christ." He therefore argues that viewing the fourfold gospel only in terms of "a plurality of diverging images of Jesus, with no principle of coherence, is totally at odds with the canonical form" (ibid.). A compositional perspective that adopts Alter's principles is in agreement with Watson's argument in that it seeks to read the Gospels as being complementary, rather than mutually antagonistic, within their canonical context in the sense that they are seen to be witnessing to the same truth through distinct voices.

15. See e.g., Griffiths, "Limits of Narrative Theology," 219; Robinson, "Narrative Theology," 689; Vanhoozer, *Drama of Doctrine*, 93.

contains a substantial number of narratives of various length and kinds,[16] the 1970s saw a new movement emerging in theology which highlighted the significance of biblical narratives for theological reflection.[17] This loose but influential theological orientation—often referred to as *narrative theology*— drew attention to the compositional role played by the network of narrative ties within the biblical canon, arguing that the intricate narrative structure underlying the texture of Scripture is instrumental in creating coherence in the patchwork of constituent biblical genres, discourse types, and voices. In George Lindbeck's words, "What holds together the diverse materials it contains: poetic, prophetic, legal, liturgical, sapiential, mythical, legendary, and historical? These are all embraced, it would seem, in an overarching story that has the specific literary features of realistic narrative . . ."[18]

The recognition of the theoretical significance of narratives at the end of the twentieth century was not restricted to the humanities but also occurred in the social sciences,[19] where scholars' primary interest in the topic concerned the relationship between narrative formation and human identity.[20] This latter topic has also been seen as a significant factor in theology[21] because of the recognition that the narrative as a fundamental human interpretive schema allows one to relate to scriptural stories in an immediate and personal way—in Vanhoozer and Treier's words, stories "*configure* characters and events, thereby *making sense* of what happened."[22] And once people are caught up in the world that the narrative proposes, they can perceive biblical meaning that may otherwise have been lost on them if those

16. McGrath, for example, states that narrative "dominates Scripture" (*Christian Theology,* 128).

17. See, e.g., Bauckham, "Reading Scripture as a Coherent Story"; Frei, *Eclipse of Biblical Narrative*; Goldingay, "Biblical Narrative and Systematic Theology"; Hauerwas and Jones, "Why Narrative?"; Jones, "Narrative Theology."

18. Lindbeck, *The Nature of Doctrine,* 120.

19. See e.g., the seminal paper by Jerome Bruner, which is often seen as one of the main instigators of the narrative turn in the social sciences. Bruner, "Life as Narrative."

20. E.g., Bruner argued that people "seem to have no other way of describing 'lived time' save in the form of a narrative" ("Life as Narrative," 12). Therefore, he went on, a life is not "how it was" but rather how it is interpreted, told and retold; in short: "a life as led is inseparable from a life as told" (ibid., 31). Accordingly, he concluded that "In the end, we *become* the autobiographical narratives by which we 'tell about' our lives" (ibid., 19).

21. E.g., Vanhoozer concludes, "No other literary form is better suited to describe a person's identity than narrative" (*Drama of Doctrine,* 273). An influential paper on this subject has been Crites, "Narrative Quality of Experience."

22. Vanhoozer and Treier, *Theology and the Mirror of Scripture,* 95.

had been conveyed in a propositional form.[23] In addition to the recognition of the explanatory power of the notions of narrative meaning and narrative identity, certain hermeneutical considerations have also played an important part in facilitating the narrative turn in theology. The originator of the movement, Hans Frei, for example, recounted that one of his main concerns in developing his narrative approach was to offer a *postliberal alternative* to the biblical interpretation of liberal scholars that, in his view, had the tendency to show too much flexibility in adjusting the biblical message to their particular world views.[24] Indeed, one compelling attraction of the narrative perspective over the past three decades has been its capacity to open up a new avenue for engaging in biblically-based theological analysis without having to be controlled by the various critical approaches advocated in the post-Enlightenment era. In Hunsinger's summary, "Frei has nothing less far-reaching in view than to break with the entire modern liberal tradition in theology, while still remaining within the purview of that tradition to the extent that he does not wish merely to relapse into the pitfalls of the older orthodoxy. He wishes to accept and yet subvert the liberal tradition by simultaneously correcting and outbidding it."[25]

Thus, the foregrounding of narratives was expected to "redress the balance and correct the lopsidedness resulting from overemphasis on historical criticism"[26] (Wiles), and in this sense, narrative hermeneutics fitted well into the postliberal zeitgeist of renewing biblical interpretation in the last quarter of the twentieth century: It shifted the main thrust of analysis from distinct facts, historical details, and textual fragments to larger blocks of biblical discourse that represent more holistic meaning (a theme that we shall revisit below).

Metanarratives

To reiterate, when the biblical corpus is regarded as a compositional whole, the narrative elements in the texts assume increased importance, because they comprise the cohesive ties that hold the diverse textual segments

23. Home, "Theology in the Narrative Mode," 967.

24. In a response to a lecture by Carl Henry at Yale University, Frei stated: "When I wrote *The Eclipse of Biblical Narrative* I had liberals much more than conservatives in mind. And what I had in mind was the fact that if something didn't seem to suit the world view of the day, the liberals quickly reinterpreted it, or as we say today, 'revised' it. And my sense of the matter though I'm not antiliberal, was that you can revise the text to suit yourself only just so far" ("Response," 22).

25. Hunsinger, "Hans Frei as Theologian," 236.

26. Wiles, "Scriptural Authority and Theological Construction," 45.

together. Within this narrative structure, the primary axes are provided by temporal frames that link events and characters to form plot lines, while also generating movement and direction within and across the biblical books that make up the canon. Given the non-reductionist orientation of the post-critical era, identifying such overarching narrative threads has received increasing attention over the past decades—as manifested, for example, by multiple attempts to produce biblical interpretation in a purely narrative vein, portraying the Bible as a "story," "novel," or "drama"[27]—and the unifying narrative axes have been referred to under various labels such as "grand narratives," "master narratives," or "metanarratives." Within the biblical composition, several possible metanarrative plots can be identified, with the most widely known storyline that spans the canon from the description of the Fall in Genesis to the Day of Judgment in Revelation usually referred to as *salvation history*. It is centered around the seminal biblical theme of redemption, that is, how God reconciles to himself rebellious humanity, who were alienated from him after the disobedience of Adam and Eve, by sending his son, Jesus Christ to redeem the world through his incarnation, death, and resurrection. Thus, the focus in salvation history is on the unfolding of God's rescue plan to restore creation to its original goodness.[28]

A second grand narrative of the biblical cannon can be presented from the perspective of the *mission* to extend God's glory to all the nations. As Christopher Wright argues in his comprehensive volume on this subject, a missional hermeneutic begins "with the Bible's very existence,"[29] because starting with Genesis 12, where God calls Abraham to bless the nations through him, the biblical canon can be read as a witness to the "story of God's mission through God's people in their engagement with God's world for the sake of the whole of God's creation."[30] In some books of the Bible this missionary purpose is made explicit (e.g., in John 20:30–31), while other books can be seen, in Howard Marshall's words, as "the documents of a mission."[31]

A third coherent thread that runs through the entire canon concerns the notion of *warfare* between God's people and their enemies, whether on the actual battlefield (as so often in the Old Testament) or at the personal level

27. E.g., Alexander, *From Eden to New Jerusalem*; Bartholomew and Goheen, *The Drama of Scripture*; Jackson, *The Eden Project*; Kurz, *Reading the Bible as God's Own Story*; Wangerin, *The Bible as a Novel*.

28. See e.g., Henri Blocher, *Original Sin*, 128; Goldingay, "Salvation History," 204–5; Green, "Narrative Theology," 531.

29. C. Wright, *The Mission of God*, 48.

30. Ibid., 51.

31. Marshall, *New Testament Theology*, 34.

of resisting temptation and maintaining righteousness (as in the New Testament). Although Soulen's work does not in general fall under the warfare rubric, he captures the essence of this approach well in his explanation that Genesis 3 can be read as a "calamitous setback" in God's scheme, "whereby the first parents through their disobedience unleashed the destructive powers of sin, death, and evil upon themselves and the good creation."[32] Indeed, hostile forces and agents are presented in the Bible often and in many forms,[33] and accordingly, Gregory Boyd sees a dominant motif running throughout Scripture "that depicts God as warring against human and angelic opponents who are able in some measure to thwart his will."[34] As Boyd concludes, "The ultimate canvas against which the unfolding drama of world history is played out is, for biblical authors, a warfare worldview."[35]

Finally, a metanarrative frame that spans the whole biblical corpus between the two bookends of the beginning of Genesis and the end of Revelation is *divine creation*. Because of its prominence in the Bible, creation is seen to play some part in any biblical metanarrative, but a specifically creational perspective can be viewed as distinct in that the focus is not so much on the "Paradise lost, Paradise regained" motif but rather on the gradual process whereby creation becomes ready to accommodate the eschatological Paradise. In other words, a creational story line assumes that the initial creation described in Genesis 1–2 is, as David Fergusson puts it, "incomplete and unfulfilled. The making of the world is only the first of God's works."[36] This perspective will be central to the current book.

The common denominator among the above readings is the identification of progression within the biblical story rather than viewing the Bible solely as an anthology of divinely inspired oracles and messages. Significantly in this respect, establishing overarching narrative frames is not alien to the biblical texts themselves, as Scripture also contains several plot summaries of varying scope,[37] including one, in Acts 13:17–41, where Paul's

32. Soulen, *God of Israel*, 15.

33. For a systematic, scholarly overview of the biblical references to the spiritual opponents of God's will, see Page, *Powers of Evil*.

34. Boyd, *Satan and the Problem of Evil*, 15.

35. Boyd, *God at War*, 14.

36. Fergusson, "Creation," 78. Adopting a similar perspective, Beale describes the primary story of the Bible as one in which "God . . . progressively re-establishes his new-creational kingdom out of chaos over a sinful people by his word and spirit through promise, covenant, and redemption, resulting in worldwide commission to the faithful to advance this kingdom and judgment (defeat or exile) for the unfaithful, unto his glory" (*New Testament Biblical Theology*, 62).

37. Bauckham lists the following summaries: Deut 6:20–24 (exodus to occupation of the land); Deut 26:5–9 (settlement in Egypt to occupation of the land); Josh 24:2–13

speech spans both Testaments as it recounts events starting in Egypt and concludes with Jesus' ministry. Richard Bauckham rightly points out that these summaries are "themselves part of the story and even contribute to the story's own development."[38] Thus, we may conclude that noticing or generating foundational narratives when reading the canon in order to process and appropriate its complex compositional meaning is in keeping with the nature of the Scriptures.

There is, however, a limit to how much clarity a focus on narratives can bring to the biblical composition. Bauckham offers an insightful summary of the multiple facets of this limitation:

> the Bible does not have a carefully plotted single storyline, like, for example, a conventional novel. It is a sprawling collection of narratives along with much non-narrative material that stands in a variety of relationships to the narratives. . . . Then there is the profusion and sheer untidiness of the narrative materials: the proliferation of little stories within the larger ones, the narrative directions left unfinished, the narrative hints that enlist readers' imagination, the ambiguity of stories that leave their meanings open, the narrative fragments of the stories of prophets or apostles in their books, the references to stories external to Scripture, as well as non-narrative materials that challenge the adequacy of the narratives. All this makes any sort of finality in summarizing the biblical story inconceivable.[39]

Bauckham's conclusion is that "the biblical story refuses to be summed up in a finally adequate interpretation that would never need to be revised or replaced,"[40] and Vanhoozer represents a similar stance when he points out that "narrative is not the only biblical genre. To elevate narrative over all other literary genres is to succumb to the same temptation that besets the propositionalist, namely, of reducing the many canonical forms into one kind only."[41] This position is consistent with the compositional perspective of the canon outlined earlier, namely that the complex, multi-layered meaning of the Scriptures sometimes resists linear delineation: Even if one

---

(Abraham to occupation of the land); Neh 9:6–37 (creation + Abraham to return from exile); Ps 78 (exodus to David); Ps 105 (Abraham to occupation of the land) and 106 (exodus to exile), cf. 1 Chr 16:8–36; Ps 135:8–12 (exodus to occupation of the land); Ps 136 (creation + exodus to occupation of the land); Acts 7:2–50 (Abraham to Solomon). Bauckham, *Bible and Mission*, 41.

38. Ibid., 42.

39. Ibid., 92–93.

40. Ibid., 93.

41. Vanhoozer, *Drama of Doctrine*, 273.

follows the canonical hermeneutical principle of understanding the parts in the light of the whole, focusing on a specific plotline will inevitably deemphasize—or as we saw in Alter's analysis, in some cases even disaffirm—some scriptural elements and possibly even whole biblical themes. Therefore, although metanarratives are undoubtedly useful tools for orientating the reader through the canon, they still represent a somewhat reductionist effort as they offer linear interpretations of complex compositional meaning. In the end, the full biblical story is revealed only by the whole biblical text and, accordingly, not even a close alignment of biblical interpretation with an overarching biblical metanarrative will guarantee a fully unified, comprehensive reading.

A Canonical Narrative Approach

In an overview of theological hermeneutics, Charles Wood has argued that any attempt to use the canon as a whole for biblical interpretation must involve a "canonical construal" for the purpose of orientation.[42] Consistent with the previous discussion of compositional meaning and metanarratives, Wood maintains that many different construals of the canon are possible, each giving rise to its own set of questions and problems. This being the case, the success of a construal can be gauged by the extent to which it can highlight aspects of narrative and theological unity in the biblical composition—an effective construal, therefore, offers a coherent and productive understanding of the canon from a specific angle. In his book, Wood did not provide any detailed illustration of a canonical construal, and his conceptualization was largely along doctrinal lines. This aspect of the concept was further developed by Kendall Soulen, whose training at Yale University—the primary theological hub both for narrative theology and canonical analysis (see below)—placed him in an ideal position to broaden Wood's notion of a canonical construal by strengthening its narrative dimension. As Soulen explains, "I prefer to speak of a canonical narrative rather than construal because the term narrative identifies the particular kind of construal upon which Christians have in fact traditionally relied. The interpretive framework that Christians commonly use to read the Bible has the basic character of a story. This is hardly surprising in view of the prominent role that narrative plays in the biblical text itself."[43]

We must note here that in the light of the Bible's narrative character discussed earlier no canonical construal is conceivable without any

42. Wood, *Theological Hermeneutics*, 99.
43. Soulen, *God of Israel*, 14.

narrative elements and, therefore, the distinction between a canonical construal and a canonical narrative is not so much a matter of quality as of degree. In that sense, a canonical narrative might be viewed as being on a continuum between a canonical construal, which represents a doctrinal emphasis, and a metanarrative, which is primarily a descriptive unit, offering a concise summary or an extended plot that cuts through the episodic and historical details of a complex story. A canonical narrative aims to provide an analytical framework for reading the Bible *both* as a theological and a narrative unity by bringing into focus central theological messages as well as overarching narrative moves within Scripture.[44] This said, the distinction between the concepts of canonical construal, canonical narrative, and metanarrative is by no means clear-cut, as they all concern the interpreter's decision about how the components of the canon "hang together." Indeed, these conceptual frameworks with different hermeneutical starting points tend to converge when they are being applied, which is illustrated in the following characterization of canonical narratives by Soulen: "In effect, a canonical narrative is a *story* that permits Christians to read the multiplicity of biblical stories (and legal codes, genealogies, letters, etc.) in reasonably coherent and consistent terms."[45]

Related Hermeneutical Approaches

Besides the narrative roots of the canonical narrative framework adopted in this book, it also shares certain characteristics with a number of contemporary interpretive approaches. Providing a comprehensive overview of these would go beyond the scope of this book, but a brief description of the most salient parallels is informative about how a canonical narrative analysis fits into the current hermeneutical zeitgeist:

Canonical analysis: We have seen above that narrative theology has shifted the focus of hermeneutical exegesis toward taking as its textual base larger blocks of biblical discourse that represent more holistic meaning, and this desire to expand the scriptural foundation of biblical interpretation shares much in common with the approach of "canonical analysis," proposed by Brevard Child, a colleague of Frei at Yale University. Its central premise is that the books of the Bible should be interpreted as wholes in their final, "canonical" form, with the various parts heard in concert rather

44. Ibid., 13.
45. Ibid., 15; emphasis added.

than seen as fragmented texts representing conflicting voices, distinct layers, and individual editors with private agendas.[46]

Canonical-linguistic approach: This approach has been advocated by Kevin Vanhoozer as a "postconservative theology" that "roots theology more firmly in Scripture while preserving Lindbeck's emphasis on practice."[47] That is, while acknowledging the relevance of ecclesial culture in biblical interpretation, the approach takes its primary bearings from the Scriptures themselves and assigns normative power to the biblical canon. In putting the approach into practice, Vanhoozer employs a broad metaphor of "theo-drama" and, similar to the canonical narrative approach, he allots an important place in the system to doctrine, seeing it as a bridge between the "biblically scripted theo-drama" and "theology as gospel performance."[48]

Theological interpretation: Closely related to the canonical-linguistic approach and also associated with Vanhoozer as one of its main proponents, this movement is not so much a well-defined hermeneutic method as a broad family of interpretive approaches with a shared theological concern.[49] "Theological interpretation" has become the banner for a relatively wide range of scholars—evangelicals and non-evangelicals alike[50]—whose exegetical approach can be broadly described as "pragmatic orthodoxy" as they pursue the postliberal intention of renewing biblical interpretation by providing rigorous alternatives to critical historicism. In doing so, their emphasis has been on offering a viable substitute to the liberal tenor of historical criticism: Vanhoozer, for example, describes theological interpretation as a deeply "spiritual affair"[51] and Richard Hays argues that "faith is the epistemological precondition for reading Scripture well."[52] Thus, what is highlighted here is the required harmony between the process and the target of biblical interpretation; Vanhoozer writes in this respect, "to serve the text is not only to witness to its good news but also to embody it,"[53] but

---

46. Childs, *Isaiah*, 4.

47. Vanhoozer, *Drama of Doctrine*, xiii.

48. As Vanhoozer argues, "Canonical-linguistic theology gives scriptural direction for one's fitting participation in the drama of redemption today" (ibid., 22).

49. For overviews, see e.g., Hays, "Practice of Theological Exegesis," 5–22; Moberly, "What Is Theological Interpretation?" 162; Vanhoozer, "What Is Theological Interpretation?" 20; Vanhoozer and Treier, *Theology and the Mirror of Scripture*, 158–91.

50. See e.g., Wellum, "Theological Interpretation of Scripture," 3.

51. Vanhoozer, "Imprisoned or Free" 92.

52. Hays, "Practice of Theological Exegesis," 5.

53. Vanhoozer, "Imprisoned or Free," 64.

he also admits that no one model of theological interpretation of the Bible currently "holds sway in the church."[54]

Critical traditioning: This approach, proposed by Ellen Davis, is centered around the crucial issue in exegesis of how to deal with "difficult" biblical passages (i.e., ones that appear uncongenial or internally contradictory) without attempting to "reduce the scriptural base available for theological reflection to a relatively small 'canon within the canon.'"[55] Davis proposes to follow an interpretive approach of "artful negotiation of difficulty" within the biblical tradition in the same way as she perceives "the biblical writers themselves dealt with difficult texts, that is, how they handled elements of the tradition that they could no longer accept as ethical or edifying."[56] This practice involves working from within the tradition toward achieving a new understanding, while also allowing for the existence of some unresolved tension, not unlike Alter's suggestion (described earlier) that the canon may contain inconsistencies as a deliberate compositional technique to convey multifaceted truth. Indeed, Davis remarks in this respect that "Negotiation of difficulty was, moreover, a primary element in the formation of the canon as a whole."[57]

1.2 The Canonical Narrative of the Book

A common feature of the above approaches, also shared by Wood's notion of canonical construal and Soulen's concept of canonical narrative, is that they do not prescribe a concrete set of hermeneutical mechanisms or strategies to be applied to the biblical discourse, but formulate, instead, broad guiding principles. Therefore, in the absence of specific interpretive templates, exegetes need to develop their own interpretive practices within the broad paradigm they have adopted. This being the case, let us consider the central features of the specific method utilized in the following chapters, to be followed by the outline of the actual canonical narrative presented in the current work.

---

54. Vanhoozer, "What Is Theological Interpretation?" 23.
55. Davis, "Critical Traditioning," 164.
56. Ibid., 166.
57. Ibid.

Central Features of the Canonical Narrative Approach

The canonical narrative approach utilized in this book displays the following main characteristics:

Limited level of abstraction. Differing strands of theology vary considerably in the extent to which they distil abstract principles and doctrines from the biblical canon. At one end of this hermeneutical continuum are "high-inference" approaches such as philosophical and systematic theology, as they often make statements that are perceived to be consistent with the overall spirit of the Bible or the character of God without pointing explicitly or in detail to Scriptural warrants. The canonical narrative approach may be considered to be at the other, "low-inference" end of the theological continuum, since it is not suited to deviating far from the textual reality of the biblical discourse, and the interpreter's creativity is contained by the specific text. Having said that, it must be recognized that there is always some degree of inference involved in any biblical interpretation, and although low-inference approaches often sit more comfortably with ecclesial communities, while high-inference approaches are more commonly applied in theology, both in their own way are needed to control each other and add to the collective wisdom of biblical interpretation.

Dependence on the narrative's lead. The canonical narrative approach attempts to interpret Scripture on its own terms, abiding as far as possible by the biblical discourse's own indicators and rationalizations. The Bible is seen as a unique interface between the transcendental divine and the earthly human, and the alignment of interpretation with the text is a means of "following Scripture's lead" in maintaining the balance between the two spheres. Accordingly, in order to achieve a coherent reading of the canon, this approach aims to identify narrative moves and metanarrative components within the text, and then present a theological interpretation that is intended to reflect these narrative aspects.

Awareness of the dangers of excessive anthropomorphism. Wolfhart Pannenberg cautions that in discussing divine creation there is an inherent danger of excessive anthropomorphism in the description of the relationship between the Creator and creature, because there is a proclivity to conceive of God "as if standing at the beginning of the process of the universe and looking ahead to its future while choosing aims and means to execute through his creative action."[58] This, Pannenberg warns, is incompatible with the eternity of God. The danger is even stronger in the low-inference, Scripture-led approach taken in this book, because references to God in the

---

58. Pannenberg, "God the Creator," 459.

Bible are often quite personal, frequently making use of anthropomorphic language.[59] The dilemma is, therefore, how much to follow the Scriptures' lead in conceptualizing God's personality and actions in human terms, particularly in view of the fact that the human perception of the absolute and transcendental nature of God is always somewhat "analogical,"[60] that is, it is comprehensible only inasmuch as a person can draw parallels with his/her own experience. For this reason, some commentators argue that a certain amount of anthropomorphism is inescapable and that, in fact, Scripture's own use of anthropomorphism might be seen to make this practice "within the biblical limit justifiable."[61] The interpreter's challenge is, according to Vanhoozer, to know "when, and how far, to take anthropomorphisms, like other metaphors, as 'reality depicting.'"[62] The low-inference approach of the current canonical narrative interpretation retains some of the anthropomorphic style of the Scriptures for the sake of presenting a constructive theological account without, however, ultimately being committed to claims about the nature of God which would be equally anthropomorphic.[63]

Non-polemical tenor. It was argued earlier that the compositional complexity of the biblical canon allows for multiple parallel readings. With this in mind, the purpose of the current interpretation is not so much to enter into a critical or polemical dialogue with alternative explications but rather to sketch a coherent canonical narrative as one possible reading, providing worked examples and fleshing it out at certain key points in order to show that it is consistent both with Scripture and scholarship, and that it can enrich biblical interpretation.

Depth and breadth of analysis. The scope of this book spans both Testaments and touches upon a number of major theological themes, ranging from creation to the Atonement and the Great Commission. Such a broad sweep is consistent with the canonical narrative perspective applied, but, at the same time, length limitations have necessitated rather selective discussion of the topics covered. It is hoped, however, that this will be offset by the

---

59. E.g., Clines explains that God is recurrently referred to in the Old Testament as if he were a man attributing to him parts of the human body (e.g., hands, eyes, and ears), human behaviors (e.g., sitting, laughing, and walking) and human emotions (e.g., anger, joy, and regret). Clines, "Image of God in Man," 70.

60. Culver, "Anthropomorphism," 117.

61. Bromiley, "Anthropomorphism," 138.

62. Vanhoozer, *Remythologizing Theology*, 62.

63. Peckham makes an interesting suggestion with regard to scriptural language that ascribes emotions to God: He argues that because humans were created in the image of God, one should perhaps view the canon's treatment of humans as being theomorphic and theopathic rather considering certain descriptions of God anthropopathic. Peckham, *Canonical Theology*, 244.

potential strength of the canonical narrative genre, namely that the parts come together into a coherent whole and display a high level of intertextuality across the canon as well as new links among the biblical texts.

The novelty of the discussion. It is highly unlikely that any new theological insight worthy of consideration has not already been proposed by somebody before. Indeed, although the current book intends to take a fresh look at a number of theological topics and biblical texts, it will be made clear in the following chapters that most of the insights have been noted, one way or another, by some scholars in the past (even when the specific idea expressed in the current text did not originate from them). The novelty of the discussion therefore lies not so much in the new interpretation of individual details as in the way these details are woven together into a coherent understanding: The canonical narrative presented in the book links a wide range of themes—including the *Chaoskampf,* the Fall, the raising of the nation of Israel, Jesus Christ's incarnation, the Atonement, the Eucharist, the Lord's Prayer, the Great Commission, human temptation, spiritual warfare, and new creation—as part of an ongoing transformation process (see below for a brief summary). As a result, the emerging reading of the canon relates humanity's plight back to the initial making of the world as well as forward to the realization of God's eschatological kingdom, thereby offering a unique biblical perspective.

The Specific Canonical Narrative Presented in This Book

The first half of the book in centered around the presentation of primal material creation from a progressive perspective, arguing in chapter 2 that the Genesis accounts of creation describe the making of the world as an incremental process that did not result in a finished and finite product after the first six days. Rather, the initial creational phase described in Genesis 1–2 can be seen to have set up an evolving, living ecosystem that was to mature and reach completion in new creation and the eschatological fulfilment of the kingdom of God. This being the case, it will be proposed that in its initial form the material world suffered from incompleteness, and its stewards—humankind—from the imperfections of their corporeal creatureliness. Even so, God stated unequivocally that the original creation was "very good" (Gen 1:31), which was an expression of his trust that "the creation itself will be set free from its bondage to decay and will obtain the freedom of the glory of the children of God" (Rom 8:21). The main thesis of the book is the understanding that the process of aligning material creation fully with divine purpose is described in the Bible as a long, turbulent, and multi-phased progression, riddled with individual, social, and spiritual challenges for humanity.

There are indications in the Genesis accounts that the transformation of the world would have taken a steadier course had the boundaries of the Garden of Eden been progressively expanded until they embraced the whole earth. However, as discussed in chapter 3, Gen 2:18 marked a turning point in the process, as we read there that for some reason the steward of the earth, Adam, was insufficient on his own and needed a helper. Although the companion whom God eventually made for Adam—Eve—was fully compatible with him and thus allowed for the generation of a succession of stewards in the form of the human species, the first human couple lacked sufficient moral integrity and social maturity, and their incompleteness was further aggregated by the deliberate interference of opposing spiritual powers that were intent on disrupting God's creative purpose. As a result, the supposedly harmonious progression of creation was derailed by the Fall, and Adam and Eve were expelled from the Garden.

Chapter 4 describes how the course of progress outside Eden deteriorated rapidly and deviated from its original, God-ordained path, with the first human offspring committing murder and the human race eventually reaching a social crisis and complete moral breakdown. God responded to the burgeoning "wickedness of humankind" (Gen 6:5) by means of setting in motion the "un-creation" of the Flood, followed by a new beginning—or a "re-creation"—through Noah. This initiated a second phase of creation whose main purpose has been the social transformation of humanity into citizens of God's eschatological kingdom, with the process driven forward by a series of divine interventions—most notably the raising of the nation of Israel—toward the decisive point of the incarnation and Jesus Christ's inauguration of the new creation.

Chapter 5 accounts for the ensuing spiritual confrontation between Jesus and Satan, who had established by the time of the incarnation—as evidenced by the NT canon—a powerful dominion of darkness on earth. However, despite Satan's repeated attempts to divert Jesus from God's purpose, Jesus remained "obedient to the point of death—even death on a cross" (Phil 2:8), and demonstrated thereby that a corporeal being can have sufficient integrity to resist corruption and to fulfil the role of being God's steward. It will be argued, then, that Jesus' victory and subsequent resurrection led to a cosmic shift in the spiritual realm, whereby the heavenly host finally committed themselves fully to humanity and the Holy Spirit was released onto the earth to act as the ultimate changing agent who transfigures believers by dwelling within them.

While Calvary and Pentecost successfully launched the final, un-stoppable phase of progressive creation, these events did not complete in themselves the transformation of humanity into God's image and did not eradicate Satan's dominion of darkness; consequently, during the current, transitional era, Christian believers are still to play a proactive role in bring-ing creation to fulfilment. Chapter 6 presents three assignments that Jesus gave to his future followers: celebrating the Eucharist to foster the believers' communion with the living God; praying the Lord's Prayer to align them-selves with God's creative purpose and to receive cleansing and protection; and fulfilling the Great Commission to ensure a lasting succession of disci-ples, who are the new stewards on earth. The NT canon also contains a rich collection of pastoral exhortations and advice on how Christians should conduct their everyday lives to become active agents and full beneficiaries of the ongoing transformation process, and chapter 7 offers an overview of this pastoral teaching: After surveying the range of human weaknesses and temptations that underlie humanity's plight, it considers practical strategies presented in the canon for the purpose of helping Christian believers to "fight the good fight of the faith" (1 Tim 6:12) in the face of the difficulties they are bound to encounter in order to inherit eternal life in God's escha-tological kingdom (Rev 21:7).

1.3 The Christian Doctrine of Creation

The biblical canon starts with the declaration that "God created the heavens and the earth." Although scholars have been divided on how this verse is linked to the next verse (to be discussed in section 2.1), this dispute does not affect the profound theological statement made at the opening of Scripture, namely that the entire universe is God's work. This confession is reiterated in the biblical canon many times,[64] and there is no mention in the Scriptures of an alternative source in the cosmos, or of any forces, whether spiritual or corporeal, that are outside the bounds of God's sovereignty. Accordingly, the church has been uniform in adopting this understanding as the bedrock of the Christian faith and the Niceno-Constantinopolitan Creed begins by declaring, "We believe in one God, the Father Almighty, Maker of heaven and earth, and of all things visible and invisible."

While there may be unanimity about the sovereignty of the Creator, this does not extend to the specific *process* of creation, and several different creational theories have been proposed over the centuries;[65] indeed, in one

---

64. E.g., Neh 9:6; Isa 48:12–13; Jer 10:12; Acts 14:14, 17:24; Rev 4:11.

65. For a concise overview, see, e.g., the Appendix of Wilkinson, *Creation*; for two

of the most comprehensive analyses of the Christian doctrine of creation, Gerhard May concludes that even when definitive dogmatic formulations had already been established about Christology and the Trinity in the patristic era, the theme of creation "could still be handled with a certain speculative freedom."[66] We find a similarly undefined situation in Judaism, where, according to Shalom M. Paul and his colleagues' summary in the *Encyclopedia Judaica,* the act of creation was regarded by many rabbis in the Talmudic period as belonging to "esoteric lore" that was "not to be expounded,"[67] and even today "there is no uniform or binding belief as to how the world was created."[68] In fairness, the knowledge that God is the sole Creator of heaven and earth is sufficient for most believers—after all, the Book of Hebrews clearly states that "By faith we understand that the world was created by the word of God" (11:3)—and cosmogonical questions have come to the forefront of theology primarily during periods when external factors precipitated a need to develop explicit doctrines regarding certain aspects of the divine creative process. The most prominent period of this kind occurred around the middle of the second century AD, when influential Neoplatonist and Gnostic teachings concerning the ontology of matter started to undermine the theological foundations of the Christian faith, thereby forcing Christian thinkers to crystallize their views about the creation of matter, resulting in the doctrine of *creatio ex nihilo.*

Although the doctrine of "creation out of nothing" has been the best known aspect of God's creative work in theology, and indeed many scholars have, explicitly or implicitly, equated it with the Christian doctrine of creation in general, there has also been a second, less salient strand in the theological tradition, going back to the Middle Ages but having its roots in the patristic era, which concerned the *preservation* of the created order and has sometimes been referred to as *creatio continua.*[69] Recently, there has been a surge of interest in this aspect of creation in contemporary Christian theology, partly due to the appearance of a formidable new external challenge on the scene, the advent of various evolutionary theories in modern sci-

---

recent book-length discussions of the doctrine of creation, see Fergusson, *Creation*; McFarland, *From Nothing.*

66. May, *Creatio ex Nihilo*, 25.

67. Paul et al, "Creation and Cosmogony in the Bible," 275.

68. Ibid., 276.

69. As Haught summarizes, "The concept of continuing creation, which portrays creation not simply as the world's initial coming into being but also as an ongoing process of creation, has long been part of Christian teaching, but it has not usually been a theme of great significance" ("In Praise of Imperfection," 174). For concise overviews, see e.g., Pannenberg, "Doctrine of Creation"; Pannenberg, "God the Creator."

ence. The quest for ways of harmonizing these scientific developments with aspects of divine creation gave birth to various proposals of continuing/continuous/progressive creation that, as we shall see below, went beyond the original meaning of *creatio continua* in that they not only involved the conservation and maintenance of the created order but also the emergence of *new* forms. Let us have a look at these two strands of creation in more detail; because of its specific relevance to the canonical narrative of this book, emphasis will be given to describing continuing creation and how it complements the traditional doctrine of creation out of nothing.

Creatio ex nihilo

The doctrine of *creatio ex nihilo* addresses the specific nature of creation by declaring that it happened "out of nothing". There is no conclusive scriptural information in the Bible about *how* creation took place,[70] and even scholars who consider *creatio ex nihilo* to be a true reflection of the biblical revelation of divine creation—or indeed a necessary interpretation to align creation with other biblical themes—acknowledge that the doctrine is not a straightforward conclusion based purely on exegetical grounds.[71] Neither was the notion of creation out of nothing given a normative status in the Creeds, but rather it emerged as the outcome of theological inference that Christian scholars were compelled to make in response to the challenges of Greek philosophy and Gnostic influences within the Church in the patristic era. Gerhard May explains that the key concern in this respect was related to the ontology of matter: If matter was *not* created out of nothing then it had to be either unoriginate—that is, eternal as the Platonists believed—or associated with an alternative creative source, which implies the kind of dualism that is at the heart of Gnostic thinking. The issue assumed particular acuteness when matter was linked to the evil found in the world: Platonists derived evil directly from the imperfection of matter in an attempt to solve the problem of theodicy, whereas Gnostics suggested that creating the world out of deficient sources was a sign of the imperfection of the creator himself.[72] There existed several Gnostic variations on how exactly evil was conceived

70. E.g., already Irenaeus stated: "For we have learned from the Scriptures that God holds the supremacy over all things. But whence or in what way He produced it, neither has Scripture anywhere declared" (*Adversus Haereses*, II 28,7).

71. See e.g., Barth, *CD* III/1, 103; Fergusson, "Creation," 73; Fergusson, *Cosmos and the Creator*, 12–13; May, *Creatio ex Nihilo*, xi; Osborn, "Creation," 430; McFarland, *From Nothing*, 5.

72. May, *Creatio ex Nihilo*, 57.

to be related to matter, but all these world views shared in common the fact that they set limits on God's creative power.[73]

In contrast, the theologians of the early Church came to realize that the overall tenor of the Scriptures in presenting an all-powerful Creator was contrary to any such limits; as McFarland summarizes, "For these theologians the claim that the ontological autonomy marked a fundamental limit on God's sovereignty was inconsistent with God's power to save."[74] Consequently, Christian scholars, and most notably Theophilus and Irenaeus in the second century AD, gradually arrived at the conviction that the best means of "ring-fencing" God's unique divinity as the sole Creator was a doctrine that categorically excluded eternal matter and disallowed any form of dualism linked to the making of the physical world. Their solution, a parsimonious yet robust theory of the divine creation of matter out of nothing, was one of the central themes of Irenaeus's major theological work, *Against Heresies* (c. AD 180), whose full title explicitly states the author's agenda: *On the Detection and Overthrow of the So-Called Gnosis*. In this book the doctrine of *creatio ex nihilo* reached its mature form, and this then prevailed throughout the centuries and was also embraced by Jewish and Islamic medieval thinkers.[75]

Curiously, therefore, the most powerful argument in favor of the doctrine of *creatio ex nihilo* has been an indirect one, namely that the opposite of the doctrine—that God's creative act described in Genesis used some primordial matter as "raw material"—would raise the difficult question of the "ownership" of this matter: If God stepped into the creation process *in medias res*, who or what had been responsible for the primordial material? Since Judeo-Christian belief does not recognize any agency outside the bounds of God's sovereignty, it was taken for granted that any form of matter was "owned"—and therefore created—by the God of Abraham.[76] Accordingly, while Barth, for example, freely admits that *creatio ex nihilo* is not explicit in the Scriptures, he still supports the doctrine, because "its antithesis—the mythological acceptance of a primeval reality independent of God—is excluded in practice by the general tenor of the passage [Gen 1–2] as well as its position within the biblical context."[77] Westermann is thus

73. McMullin, "Creation *ex Nihilo*," 20.

74. McFarland, *From Nothing*, 19.

75. See Cogliati, "Introduction," 7–8; Samuelson, *Judaism and the Doctrine of Creation*, 82.

76. In McFarland's words, "To say that God creates the world *from nothing* is in the first instance to say that the existence of the world is to be ascribed to *nothing but God*" (*From Nothing*, 87).

77. Barth, *CD* III/1, 103.

right to conclude that scholars would often subscribe to the doctrine simply because "this is the only appropriate way in which to speak of creation."[78]

The Need for a Complementary Doctrine of Creation

Thus, the doctrine of *creatio ex nihilo* offers an unambiguous declaration that there is no creative agency other than God and therefore everything within the universe is to be interpreted through him; in David Kelsey's summary, it is a "claim that God is related to all that is not God in a continuously active 'productive' way."[79] There is nothing about the substance of this claim that would invite theological disagreement, but with a doctrine of such a high profile as *creatio ex nihilo* what also becomes important is what it does *not* cover or what it inadvertently *implies*. From the perspective of the focus of the current book—humankind's struggles—a significant gap in the doctrine is the absence of any obvious opening for explaining problematic issues with the created order of the world. The logic of the doctrine suggests that if God started out with a clean slate—that is, "nothing"—without any preexisting constraints whatsoever, the outcome of this unconstrained act of divine creation should not be expected to show any sign of imperfection. After all, where would the imperfections derive from? Or, as Fergusson puts it, "If God freely called the universe into being from out of nothing, then why not produce a better universe than the actual one with all its suffering and flaws?"[80] This logic is not conducive to understanding the very real problems that humanity does experience in God's world, many of which are also reflected in Biblical texts, beginning with Genesis 3; indeed, Fergusson adds that the doctrine of creation out of nothing, which he calls the classical tradition, "appears to intensify the problem of evil,"[81] Jon Levenson argues forcefully in a similar vein:

> First, although it is now generally recognized that *creatio ex nihilo*, the doctrine that God produced the physical world out of nothing, is not an adequate characterization of creation in the Hebrew Bible, the legacy of this dogmatic or propositional understanding lives on and continues to distort the perceptions of scholars and laypersons alike. In particular, a false finality or definitiveness is ascribed to God's act of creation, and, consequently, the fragility of the created order and its vulnerability to

78. Westermann, *Genesis*, 108.
79. Kelsey, "Doctrine of Creation from Nothing," 48.
80. Fergusson, *Creation*, 34.
81. Ibid.

chaos tend to be played down. Or, to put the point differently, the formidability and resilience of the forces counteracting creation are usually not given their due, so that the drama of God's exercise of omnipotence is lost, and a static idea of creation then becomes the cornerstone of an overly optimistic understanding of the theology of the Hebrew Bible.[82]

Regarding any unintended implications of the doctrine, Levinson's critique mentions a key issue in this respect, the "static idea of creation." Because of its ontological focus, the doctrine proposes an act of creation with no temporal resolution; as Ernan McMullin's explains, "from our perspective, the creation *ex nihilo* took place at the moment of cosmic origination."[83] This being the case, *creatio ex nihilo* tends to suggest, even if it does not logically require, the making of a finite, finished product: one moment there was nothing, the next moment there was a new thing. This understanding—which is curiously reminiscent of the popular image of creation at the wave of a magic wand—is at odds with the process of creation as described in the Bible. This will be explored in detail in the next chapter, but to make a preliminary point here, if material creation was indeed a forthright, something-out-of-nothing act, why is it presented as the work of six days rather than just one moment? Furthermore, the unnuanced nature of the creative act as suggested by the doctrine conceals—or at least downplays—the fact that the Bible speaks of several different creative processes besides creating by fiat, for example (as will be shown later), separation, transformation, the fashioning of animals out of clay, blessing living organisms and making them fertile, and breathing life into Adam's nostrils.[84]

We may therefore conclude that the doctrine of *creatio ex nihilo* is fundamentally an ontological rather than a temporal claim, and it is, ultimately, "a proposal of the character of God's relationship to the world"[85] (McFarland). However, despite the fact that the doctrine is related to creation's ontological relationship with God rather than the temporal framework of creation, the articulation of the doctrine is often at risk of taken to be about the beginnings—that is, temporal origination—of things, thereby

82. Levenson, *Creation*, xxix.

83. McMullin, "Creation," 22.

84. The static conception of creation is illustrated well by the following quote by Moltmann: "The divine act of creation is never described in differentiated terms. Nor is it dissected into a number of different processes. It is unified and unique. This means among other things that time is excluded from the act of creation, for time always requires duration, and creation takes place suddenly, as it were—in a moment" (*God in Creation*, 73).

85. McFarland, *From Nothing*, xiv.

adding a fundamentally time-specific element. The contention of this book is that the essence of the doctrine is not related to the time dimension, and neither does it suggest an original, perfected, and immutable creation. It would follow from this contention, then, that taking *creatio ex nihilo* as the sole doctrine of creation carries a real danger of capturing our imagination in the wrong way, in the sense that by doing so we risk missing or downplaying certain essential points about the *process* of divine creation that are given emphasis in the Bible in the Genesis accounts and elsewhere. This has recently been highlighted by Sean McDonough in his discussion of creation and new creation when he concluded: "There is no question that creatio continua needs to be an integral part of the doctrine of creation. Indeed, . . . the idea that the Father is 'always working' has been a feature of theological tradition from the beginning. It may even be the case that the relative weights of fixity versus process need to be recalculated."[86]

All these considerations underline the need for another component of the overall doctrine of creation that supplements *creatio ex nihilo* by specifying how creation unfolds in time, and as we shall see in the following overview, several contemporary scholars have turned to the traditional doctrine of *creatio continua* for this purpose.

Creatio continua

In an overview of the doctrine of creation, Wolfhart Pannenberg explains that the traditional understanding of the creative act of God has involved a close correspondence between initial creation and conservation: "The world was not just placed into existence once, at the beginning of all things, in such a way that it would have been left on its own afterwards. Rather, every creature is in need of conservation of its existence in every moment, and according to theological tradition such conservation is nothing else but a continuous creation."[87]

The notion of *creatio continua* has originally been understood to concern this preservational aspect of God's providence, and because this process exerts its influence in the course of an already existing world, it was perceived to be distinct from *creatio ex nihilo*, which concerns the initial creation of the world. Yet, as Timothy Miller emphasizes, the "divine conservation" of all contingent reality was seen to amount to a *continuation* of the act of creation by several theistic scholars such as Descartes, Leibniz,

86. McDonough, *Creation and New Creation*, 155.
87. Pannenberg, "Doctrine of Creation," 8.

Berkeley, and Jonathan Edwards.[88] Such theistic views received considerable support in the final quarter of the twentieth century as a result of the work of Christian theologians, many of them with a background in science, who were seeking to harmonize the high-profile evolutionary theories emerging in modern science with biblical principles. We shall start our overview of modern theological reflections on continuous creation with this paradigm of *theistic evolution*.

Theistic Evolution

In his book titled *God after Darwin: A Theology of Evolution*, John Haught clearly summarizes the evolutionary agenda underlying the recognition of continuous creation: "the fact of evolution now allows theology to realize more palpably than ever that creation is not just an 'original' but also an ongoing and constantly new reality. In an evolving cosmos creation is still happening, no less in the present than 'in the beginning.' . . . evolution has allowed theology to acknowledge at last that the notion of an originally and instantaneously completed creation is theologically unthinkable in any case."[89]

The resulting notion of "theistic evolution" contends that God used biological evolution as a vehicle to create diversity of life,[90] and that he interacts with his material creation through his presence "in, with, under and through many levels of the fabric of the natural and human world woven by its entities, structures and processes,"[91] to quote Arthur Peacocke's oft-cited formulation. Accordingly, Peacocke concludes, the "perennial sustaining in existence of the entities, structures, and dynamic processes of the world . . . is properly regarded as 'continuous,' an aspect of God as *semper Creator* with respect to the *creatio continua*."[92]

Although the conceptions of theistic evolution proposed by different scholars form a wide spectrum, they converge in the assumption that God works through some form of "divine manipulation" of the laws of nature, not unlike "an improvising choreographer or composer"[93] (Barbour). Indeed, developments in the natural sciences such as quantum mechanics and nonlinear systems theories (e.g., complexity theory, chaos theory, and dynamic systems theory) shifted the scientific perspective from a deterministic model

---

88. Miller, "Creation and Conservation," 471–72.

89. Haught, *God after Darwin*, 40–41.

90. E.g., Russell, "Evolution," 174.

91. Peacocke, *Theology for a Scientific Age*, 211.

92. Peacocke, *Evolution*, 16.

93. Barbour, *When Science Meets Religion*, 115.

of mono-causality (i.e., from assuming a linear relationship between cause and effect) to one in which cause does not necessarily determine outcome in a proportionate manner, and only probabilities rather than certainties can be assigned to particular expected outcomes. Such dynamic frameworks, in turn, have allowed for the perception of God's ongoing creative work in a "scientifically sound" manner, through the changing of the probabilities involved in the operation of the elements rather than through setting aside the laws of nature.[94]

The science-conscious views of theistic evolution have reinforced the creational dimension of *creatio continua* in the sense that processes such as self-organization and emergence emphasize the ongoing formation of qualitatively *new* entities, thereby suggesting an understanding which goes beyond the traditional meaning of preservation;[95] for example, Ted Peters points out in this respect that the "degree of unpredictable newness" of structures and emerging realities in the world involves a transformation that is more profound than what the original notion of conservation entailed,[96] and Ian Barbour states with passion, "Surely the coming-to-be of life from matter can represent divine creativity as suitably as any postulated primeval production of matter 'out of nothing.'"[97] This view, then, is echoed in Pannenberg's conclusion: "The continuous creative activity of God involves more than the conservation of what was created in the beginning. Each individual life is the immediate object of the creative action of God, and not only a case of conserving the species."[98]

Other Support for creatio continua *in Modern Theology*

Although theistic evolution offers the most consistent endorsement of *creatio continua* in modern theology, there have also been other influential voices outside this paradigm to support the notion. Jürgen Moltmann, for example, has articulated the complex relationship between creation and conservation particularly clearly: On the one hand, he fully acknowledges the distinction between original and continuous creation on the basis that

94. See e.g., Barbour, *Science and Religion*, 283–305; Barbour, *When Science Meets Religion*, 90–119; Brodrick, "From Divine Action to Divine Presence," 6; Russell, "Quantum Physics," 355–56; Russell, "Evolution," 175–77; Gregersen, "Anthropic Design and Complexity," 207–8; Pannenberg, "Science and Theology," 110–11; Peacocke, *Evolution*, 45.

95. Peters, "On Creating the Cosmos," 296.

96. Ibid., 292; for a similar view, see Peacocke, *Creation and the World of Science*, 79.

97. Barbour, *Science and Religion*, 385.

98. Pannenberg, "God the Creator," 456.

the former act established time itself, while the latter process takes place *within* the dimension of time and is, as such, "God's influence on time";[99] on the other hand, he underlines the fact that this influence not only preserves but also "renews the world," and this renewal "takes place through anticipations of the new creation of all things through rebirth to life."[100] Consequently, his conclusion is that "'Creation' as the quintessence of God's creative activity . . . embraces the initial creative activity, creative activity in history, and the eschatological consummation."[101] Interestingly, Moltmann's argument echoes Emil Brunner's reflection from several decades earlier on the fact that—as already mentioned briefly above—the initial creation is represented biblically in six days:

> If we indulge in a little mild allegory we may interpret the creation of the world in six days thus: the series of creative acts of God, which has been planned in a clear succession of periods (whether of days or of millions of years) contains at least one aspect of the doctrine of a *creatio continua*, plurality in Time, the ordered series of acts of creation. The more we take into account the fact that the various forms of life did not all arise at the same time, as we certainly must do on the basis of our present knowledge, the more unavoidably are we led to this thought. God did not create everything at once; He is continually creating something afresh. This idea is not alien to the Bible.[102]

Ian McFarland has recently expressed a similar understanding regarding the continuity between original creation and preservation: Although he, too, emphasizes the "real difference" between origination and preservation (the latter concerning "maintaining in existence the being of a creature already originated"[103]), he sees the two acts as "sequential aspects of a single divine project: the flourishing of creatures."[104] Finally, an analogous progressive understanding of creation can also be found in Jewish scholarship; in an insightful article in the journal *Judaism*, Bernard Och asserts, "Creation is not a self-contained, once-upon-a-time event but an ongoing dynamic reality which affects God's relationship to humanity throughout history."[105] His subsequent conclusion is consistent with the Christian views presented

99. Moltmann, "Reflections on Chaos," 209.

100. Ibid.

101. Moltmann, *Future of Creation*, 118.

102. Brunner, *Christian Doctrine of Creation*, 34.

103. McFarland, *From Nothing*, 141.

104. Ibid.

105. Och, "Creation," 241.

in this chapter: "God rests on the seventh day, but He, by no means, with-draws from His creative activity. The goodness of creation and the underly-ing Divine intention to bring into being and to fruition all aspects of life presuppose a kind of continuous creativity: it is a *creatio continua*, which is directed not only toward the preservation of what was once created, but also toward the fulfilment of that promise which original creation represents in its very self."[106]

Eschatological Directionality

While agreeing with the theistic evolutionary approach on the key points of the ongoing aspect of creation, Moltmann's position also diverges from it in one important aspect: Rather than merely emphasizing the non-static and evolving nature of the continuously changing cosmos, it also highlights an overt eschatological end-point for the ongoing creational process, and links to it the biblical concept of "new creation" (see chapter 4). As Moltmann summarizes, the beginning of creation "is at the same time the condition for its history and its completion. Creation at the beginning is the creation of conditions for the potentialities of creation's history."[107] In other words, "The initial creation points toward salvation history, and both point beyond themselves to the kingdom of glory."[108] This is a marked deviation from sci-entific theories of evolution, which tend to deny that biological evolution is purposive or goal-oriented, and understand "progress" primarily in terms of the increasing but non-teleological sophistication of living systems.[109]

In his book on *Creation and Redemption,* Gabriel Daly further un-derlines the redemptive direction of continuing creation; as he argues, in Western Christian tradition "salvation" and "sin" tend to be so closely linked to each other that salvation is not seen as a "condition desirable in its own right" but rather as a "merciful expedient designed by an offended God"[110] to save the human species from perdition. This understanding, however, has had significant implications for creation:

> One effect of this penal view of salvation was the separation
> of the theology of creation from the theology of salvation. Al-
> though creation was regarded as good, coming as it does from

106. Ibid., 230.
107. Moltmann, *Future of Creation,* 120.
108. Ibid., 119.
109. For a summary, see Schloss, "Spirit and the Ordering of Creation," 43–47.
110. Daly, *Creation and Redemption,* 4.

the hands of God, this fact was coupled with the implicit and highly questionable premise that what is good is in no need of salvation . . . I wish to contend that the scope of salvation includes, but far exceeds, the scope of sin . . . The prospect of salvation is built into the very concept of a creation which flowers in intelligence and freedom.[111]

Accordingly, Daly concludes, "Salvation is not an afterthought: it is implicit in the creation of a truly free being."[112] Continuous creation's potential to lead to redemption is also underlined by Haught when he explores the theological implications of the *unfinished* nature of the universe: "An evolutionary universe is an unfinished universe, and an unfinished universe is by definition imperfect. But the good news that comes with an unfinished universe is that future redemption is still possible. My point then . . . is that the world's being unfinished is the cosmic condition for tragedy and sin. But it is also the condition for hope, redemption, and reconciliation."[113]

The question of the unfinished nature of the created order is an important matter with considerable theological implications, and therefore we shall return to it at the end of chapter 2. We should, however, also note here that aligning biological evolution with the redemptive directionality of creation might raise issues. David Fergusson, for example, highlights two potential problems related to identifying the evolutionary process too closely with God's purpose (which he succinctly calls "baptizing" the evolutionary process):[114] First, it may lead to an "underestimation of the problems posed by suffering and evil," particularly because God's purpose in Scripture is achieved by "often working against the grain of nature and history."[115] This point, as we shall see, is highly relevant to the canonical narrative of the current book, and so is his second point that warns about the danger of a reductionist angle that can be presented by a theistic evolutionary perception: "divine action can be narrowed by an exclusive preoccupation with the laws of natural science, and so determined only by what seems most consistent with patterns of natural explanation. The danger here is that theology simply becomes a gloss on the prevailing scientific worldview. By contrast, the different types of divine action that characterize the central themes of Scripture and tradition require a differentiated approach that employs a variety

---

111. Ibid., 4–5.

112. Ibid., 54.

113. Haught, "In Praise of Imperfection," 175.

114. Fergusson, *Creation*, 85.

115. Ibid.

of models to understand divine involvement in creation, incarnation, and eschatological fulfillment."[116]

Creatio continua *and Metaphysics*

The main focus of the science-inspired paradigm of continuing creation has been on the material world—that is, on non-human creation and biological evolution—and the tone of the discussion has typically been characterized by a rather abstract theism that utilized a mixture of the conceptual toolkits of metaphysics and the natural sciences. At the end of his seminal book on the topic, *Creation and the World of Science*, Peacocke reflected on the potential risk of this abstract stance leading to a detachment from the concerns of Christian life: "I would not like to leave the impression that the doctrine of creation is merely an arid formulation of the abstracting intellect for making coherent a number of otherwise unintelligible features of the world and of our lives in it. It is, or rather should be, I believe, one of the throbbing arteries of the Christian life."[117]

Although theistic evolution offers a viable compatibility of the theological and scientific worldviews and can therefore remove possible objections that would prevent some scientifically-oriented people from turning to God, one would be hard pressed to find many specific points in the works representing the concept of continuous creation thus conceptualized that could have a direct bearing on believers' lives. This detachment is undoubtedly related to the fact that the movement is rooted in the natural sciences, which focus on the laws of nature rather than the human stewards of nature, and indeed, in his pioneering publication that played an important role in launching the field, *Issues in Science and Religion*, Barbour confirms that "No systematic analysis of the social sciences or humanities is here attempted."[118] Interestingly, Barbour does emphasize in the concluding section of the book that "In the biblical tradition, faith in God as Redeemer is *more important* than faith in God as Creator,"[119] and he even adds that "statements about nature do have an important though *always secondary* place in theology."[120] Nonetheless, the notion of redemption does not feature in the discussion,[121] and Barbour

---

116. Ibid., 86.

117. Peacocke, *Creation and Science*, 358.

118. Barbour, *Science and Religion*, 175.

119. Ibid., 453 (italics added).

120. Ibid., 454 (italics added).

121. The term "redemption" does not appear in the Subject Index of Barbour's *Science and Religion*, and nor do other related concepts such as salvation or eschatology.

reiterates in the conclusion that "while theology must start from historical revelation and personal experience, it must also include a *theology of nature* which does not disparage or neglect the natural order."[122]

Barbour's case is relevant because his influential book exemplified, and in many ways set the tone for, the style and approach of the subsequent line of scholarly work on the interface between science and religion. Therefore, it is noteworthy that in the concluding section he defends the role of metaphysics in theological discussions of evolution, arguing that it provides the bridge between the discordant perspectives of theology and science.[123] He concludes by expressing the desire for an ideal—and perhaps idealistic—synthesis not unlike the one Peacocke called for (cited above): "It may be objected that reference to God in metaphysics serves very different functions from reference to God in worship, and this is indeed the case . . . a theistic metaphysics is detached and speculative and its modes of thought are abstract and general—a long way from personal reorientation or the worshiping community . . . The position we are defending would employ metaphysical categories within the expression of the Christian message."[124]

The Distinctiveness of the Current Approach

The approach of the current book is congruent with the view that *creatio ex nihilo* and *creatio continua* are two compatible facets of divine creation. At the same time, the proposed canonical narrative runs counter to the understanding of the notion of continuing creation as anchored in modern scientific consciousness in that it takes a different starting point, the biblical canon. It is noteworthy that none of the modern proponents of *creatio continua*—not even non-scientists such as Daly, Moltmann, or Pannenberg—have engaged with a systematic exegesis of the Scriptures to examine the extent to which their proposed views on creation are reflected there, and the theological arguments tend to be presented at a rather abstract level. That is, apart from the occasional citing of Bible verses, little work has been done in modern scholarship to identify broader scriptural segments and

---

122. Ibid., 454 (italics original).

123. Barbour states that "the absence of philosophical concepts as a bridge between theology and science hinders communication between these realms of discourse; there are simply no common terms between scientific language about electrons and biblical language about God" (ibid., 459). By means of illustration, he adds, "Because Barth tries to avoid metaphysics and relies entirely on the language of grace, providential action as he presents it seems to have no connection with nature as understood by the scientist" (ibid.).

124. Ibid., 460–61.

themes in the biblical narrative that are in keeping with the notion of continuing creation, even though, as Barbour pointed out over half a century ago, "Continuing creation is a biblical idea. Almost every chapter of the Old Testament witnesses to the conviction of God's continuing sovereignty over history and nature."[125]

The canonical narrative interpretation employed in this book seeks to fill this gap by offering an analytical approach guided by exegesis, which makes the creational perspective presented in the following chapters different from other proposals of *creatio continua* in two distinctive ways: First, it exhibits a process of ongoing creative transformation as deduced from the Scriptures rather than emerging as an abstract conjecture. Second, in its portrayal of creation it seeks to utilize as much as possible Scripture's own concepts, metaphors, and characterizations rather than metaphysical categories. John Haught has recently argued that "Science's fresh picture of nature-as-narrative invites theology to transplant the central biblical motif of divine promise onto a cosmological terrain that can give new breadth, nourishment, and vitality to our spiritual and ethical lives."[126] The current book is resonant with this call in its contention that a progressive creational narrative is inherent to the biblical canon itself.

1.4 Conceptions of Spiritual Warfare

The final petition of the Lord's Prayer concerns a plea to be delivered from *ponēros* (Matt 6:13), which can be translated as either "evil" (e.g., ESV and KJV) or "the evil one" (e.g., NRSV and NIV), since the original Greek text allows for both renderings (see chapter 6 for a discussion). The difference between the two translations is not insignificant, because while most Christian believers would probably agree that some sort of "evil" does exist in the world, fewer would accept that it is appropriate to personalize this evil into an "evil one," that is, the devil. This dilemma taps into a deep-seated uncertainty in contemporary Christian circles surrounding the reality of hostile spiritual forces and how to handle them, a subject that is often discussed in the literature under the rubric of "spiritual warfare." As Paul Eddy and James Beilby summarize in the introduction to a recent edited volume on the subject, this is an area which has been characterized by "a long-running intra-Christian dialogue and debate about the nature and extent, the biblical and theological moorings, and the rational, experiential, and practical

---

125. Ibid., 383.
126. Haught, *Resting on the Future*, 2.

implications" of the topic.[127] Indeed, contested questions about spiritual warfare abound, ranging from the existence and nature of demonic entities to strategies on whether and how to combat spiritual opposition.

Beilby and Eddy have offered a useful overview of the diverse approaches to the subject by inviting four representatives of high-profile contemporary models of spiritual warfare—Walter Wink, David Powlison, Gregory Boyd, and Peter Wagner (with Rebecca Greenwood)—to present their own positions and to comment on the other contributors' views.[128] The principal difference between the four perspectives lies in the degree of reality they attribute to forces of evil and the specific approaches they propose for contending with them. On a continuum of indirect to direct engagement with the subject, Wink's influential work[129]—presented in detail in his "Powers" trilogy[130]—represents one end as it focuses on the notion of "Principalities and Powers" at a somewhat abstract, societal level,[131] conceptualizing the Powers as "institutional evil" without personalizing them. Wink argues that the "Powers possess an outer, physical manifestation (buildings, portfolios, personnel, trucks, fax machines) and an inner spirituality, or corporate culture, or collective personality,"[132] and in *Naming the Powers* he elaborates on these two facets as follows: "As the inner aspect they are the spirituality of institutions, the 'within' of corporate structures and systems, the inner essence of outer organizations of power. As the outer aspect they are political systems, appointed officials, the 'chair' of an organization, laws—in short, all the tangible manifestations which power takes."[133]

Wink therefore does not perceive demonic entities to be individual spiritual beings and, consistent with this view, he submits that the "image of Satan is the archetypal representation of the collective weight of human fallenness, which constrains us toward evil without our even being aware of it."[134] This perception therefore shares some common ground with other proposals in theology (e.g., by Rudolf Bultmann) that offer a demythologized understanding of spiritual forces rather than a belief in literal spirit beings

---

127. Eddy and Beilby, "Introducing Spiritual Warfare," 1.

128. Beilby and Eddy, *Understanding Spiritual Warfare*.

129. Wink, "World Systems Model."

130. Wink, *Naming the Powers*; Wink, *Unmasking the Powers*; Wink, *Engaging the Powers*.

131. As Wink states, "It is my conviction that any attempt to face the problem of evil in society from a New Testament perspective must be bound up with an understanding of what the Bible calls the "Principalities and Powers" (*Engaging the Powers*, 3).

132. Ibid., 3.

133. Wink, *Naming the Powers*, 5.

134. Wink, "World Systems Model," 57.

such as a "personal devil."[135] Within this framework, Wink suggests that the
Christian believer's most powerful weapon against the "great socio-spiritual
forces that preside over so much of reality"[136] is intercessory prayer, as well as
the "weapons of the Spirit: love, peace, nonviolence, and forgiveness."[137]

In what Beilby and Eddy call the "classical model" of spiritual warfare, Powlison[138] goes beyond Wink's understanding of institutional evil
by accepting "the real existence of diabolical agents operating within the
fog of war and behind the scenes in human affairs,"[139] as well as the reality
of "the world, the flesh, and the devil" as interdependent but ontologically
distinct sources of temptation and deceit (see chapter 7 of this book for a
detailed discussion). This model represents another established position in
Christian thinking, as exemplified by, for example, Gerald Bonner's book
on *The Warfare of Christ*[140] from the early 1960s. In this work, the author
acknowledges the actuality of demonic forces, partly because, as he argues, they are evidenced by the New Testament itself,[141] and partly because
of his conviction that when one considers the traditional notion of the
temptations of the world, the flesh, and the devil, "there was a class which
could fairly be described as devilish since it came outside the limits of the
World and the Flesh."[142] In other words, Bonner—along with Powlison and
many other scholars—contends that some experiences of temptation do
not originate in personal or societal shortcomings but reflect the distinct
contribution of spiritual agency.

135. Vanhoozer concludes that Bultmann's demythologizing approach is characteristic of much of Protestant liberalism in the twentieth century. Vanhoozer, *Remythologizing Theology*, 13; see also, e.g., Moses, *Practices and* Powers, 4. Wink states in this
respect: "Rudolf Bultmann's program of demythologizing the Bible was a move in the
right direction but from the wrong foundation. He defined myth as a falsifying objecti-
fication of reality and sought to dispense with it through existential interpretation. Had
he worked with a more positive understanding of myth, such as we find in the work of
Carl Jung, Mircea Eliade, or Paul Ricoeur, his quite proper concern for making the text
intelligible and existentially meaningful could have been achieved without sacrificing
the myth to the interpretation" (*Naming the Powers*, 143).

136. Wink, "World Systems Model," 68.

137. Wink and Hardin, "Response to Gregory Boyd," 159.

138. Powlison, "Classical Model."

139. Powlison, "Response to Wagner and Greenwood."

140. Bonner, *Warfare of Christ*.

141. Bonner contends that "There can be no doubt that our Lord, His disciples,
and the writers of the New Testament accepted the contemporary belief in Satan and
the devils . . . The point is that our Lord Himself plainly believed in demons and held
converse with them when He cast them out. This fact can be explained away, but only
by considerable feats of intellectual legerdemain" (*Warfare of Christ*, 96).

142. Ibid.

On the other hand, although the classical model acknowledges Satan and his forces as realities, this acknowledgement does not mean that the model envisages spiritual warfare as involving a direct confrontation with these beings. Robert Moses's argument exemplifies the justification of this common Christian stance:

> To attribute too much significance to the powers is to fail to come to grips with the power of our baptism, for in baptism believers are mapped onto Christ's life, death, burial, and resurrection. Participation in Christ's career means that believers have been rescued from the domain of the powers. The powers are still at work in the world, but to affirm our Christian baptism is to live in light of the victory over the powers that took place at the cross, when Christ dealt a fatal blow to the powers, thereby foreshadowing their ultimate destruction (1 Cor 15:24–26).[143]

Powlison emphasizes the inextricable link between the personal, societal, and spiritual levels of human sinfulness, and recommends a response to this "triumvirate" by means of "normal ministry methods"[144]—that is, methods designed for every form of sin—such as repentance, prayer, the reading of Scripture, and the striving for righteousness in the face of temptation.

Bonner offers an interesting, and perhaps somewhat unexpected, illustration of the indirect handling of spiritual assaults in the case of the desert fathers and mothers: According to various records of the sayings and actions of these spiritual warriors,[145] struggling with demonic temptation and deceit constituted a salient part of their everyday lives, and yet Bonner argues that it was primarily an unyielding striving for holy living that formed the basis of their resistance.[146] Interestingly, at the beginning of this new millennium, the leaders of the Catholic and the Anglican churches independently highlighted the lessons offered by the desert fathers on how to stand firm in various predicaments, and they, too, emphasized indirect measures of warfare that would fall under the rubric of the classical model (even though both denominations also recognize more direct strategies of spiritual warfare such as exorcism[147]). In an address given at the Bulgarian

---

143. Moses, *Practices of Power*, 233

144. Powlison, "Classical Model," 103.

145. E.g., Chryssavgis, *In the Heart of the Desert*; Ward, "Introduction."

146. As Bonner concludes, "it is this training in sanctity, this *ascesis*, which is a feature of the monks of the desert in their campaign against the demons" (*Warfare of Christ*, 114).

147. See, e.g., §1673 of the *Catechism of the Catholic Church* and https://www.churchofengland.org/media/1734117/guidelines%20on%20deliverance%20ministry.pdf.

Monastery of Rila,[148] Pope John Paul II underlined the significance of the monks' "spiritual combat" as an "element of monastic life which needs to be taught anew and proposed once more to all Christians today." This combat, as he summarized, "is a secret and interior art, an invisible struggle in which monks engage every day against the temptations, the evil suggestions that the demon tries to plant in their hearts; it is a combat that becomes crucifixion in the arena of solitude in the quest for the purity of heart."[149]

The then Archbishop of Canterbury, Rowan Williams, highlighted the desert fathers and mothers' "quest for the truth of oneself"[150] and their ability to face up to their problems and "stay in touch with the reality of who I am as a limited creature, as someone who is not in control of everything, whether inner or outer, as an unfinished being in the hands of the maker."[151] That is, Williams underscored the "relentlessly prosaic element in the journey to holiness. Never mind the ecstasies and the feats of self-denial, never mind the heroics: the essential task is whatever is there to be done next."[152] As he concluded, "our life and death is with the neighbor, the actual here and now context in which we live—including that unique neighbor who is my own embodied self and whom I must confront truthfully as I confront all the rest truthfully."[153]

Undeniably, the rich records of the desert fathers could also have inspired summaries of a different nature, elaborating more on the interaction and confrontation of the material and the spiritual realms, but it is noteworthy that these respected church leaders chose to concentrate on the indirect features as transferrable lessons for contemporary believers.

Occupying a place on the direct side of the continuum in Beilby and Eddy's division of spiritual warfare are two models, by Boyd[154] and Wagner,[155] which go beyond the "classic" position described above in that they not only perceive demonic forces as real, but also endorse direct confrontation, or "power encounters," with them, through healing

---

148. Delivered on 25th May, 2002; see http://w2.vatican.va/content/john-paul-ii/ en/speeches/2002/may/ documents/hf_jp-ii_spe_20020525_rila-bulgaria.pdf.

149. The internal, private characters of spiritual warfare is reiterated once again in the address: "the art of spiritual combat, the discernment of spirits, . . . the invocation of the Holy Name of Jesus and of his mercy must once more become a part of the inner life of the disciple of the Lord" (ibid.).

150. Williams, *Where God Happens*, 11.

151. Ibid., 101.

152. Ibid., 102.

153. Ibid., 117.

154. Boyd, "Ground-Level Deliverance Model."

155. Wagner and Greenwood, "Strategic-Level Deliverance Model."

and deliverance ministry, as well as strategic warfare prayers—it should be noted that in the popular Christian literature it is these two models that are usually referred to as spiritual warfare proper.[156] For Boyd the primary battle-ground is at the individual level, and the main weaponry involves a mixture of personal deliverance and counselling, while Wagner promotes, in addition, what he calls "strategic-level spiritual warfare,"[157] which targets "territorial spirits" that occupy spiritual strongholds in certain geographical territories and social networks. Wagner also supports the offering of "identification repentance," that is, repentance on behalf of various people groups for sins committed in the past. There is a great variety of recommended methods by which such direct warfare principles may be applied,[158] but some of these have been contested not only by followers of less direct approaches but also by different schools of direct spiritual warfare (e.g., regarding the question as to whether territorial spirits need to be engaged with).[159]

While these four models cannot be considered exhaustive or fully representative of the whole spectrum of beliefs and practices of spiritual warfare in various denominational contexts throughout the world,[160] they are useful for outlining the wide array of contemporary understanding in the area. As was mentioned in the Preface, the current book originally set out to provide a systematic exploration of the biblical basis of spiritual warfare issues, and although this subject was eventually subsumed into a wider-range narrative of humanity's struggles, key elements of it remain important themes in the discussion: Drawing primarily on the Book of Job, chapter 5 examines spiritual opposition to God's work—from the devil in particular—and in chapter

156. As C. E. Arnold writes in the Preface of his overview on spiritual warfare, "Ninety-seven books on the topic of 'spiritual warfare' line one of the shelves of my office. All but a dozen of these have been published in the last ten years. Most of them present some form of 'deliverance ministry' and are full of dramatic and triumphant stories" (*Three Crucial Questions*, 13).

157. Wagner and Greenwood, "Strategic-Level Deliverance Model," 179.

158. E.g., one of the most detailed summaries of the spectrum, Murphy's *Handbook for Spiritual Warfare*, is over 600 pages long, covering topics from "the believer's warfare with the flesh" to "demonization and mental health issues."

159. See e.g., Powlison, "Response to Wagner and Greenwood"; and Wink and Hardin, "Response to Boyd." For a balanced and well-researched summary of some of the key issues, see C. E. Arnold, *Three Crucial Questions*.

160. E.g., Robert Moses outlines a somewhat different division of dispositions to spiritual warfare, which also includes Wink's work but adds three other alternative positions, ranging from Bultmann's "demythologized" view of the spiritual realm as one extreme to Arnold's "attempts to recover the traditional premodern Christian belief in the existence of evil supernatural beings" as the other, with Berkhof and Wink's work placed in between the two. Moses, *Practices and* Powers, 4.

7 the theme of "fighting the good fight of the faith" (1 Tim 6:12) is developed, which includes various warfare components. However, the contention of the current canonical narrative—following the Apostle Paul's teaching (e.g., in Rom 8:5–6)—is that the principal element of the "good fight of the faith" in the biblical canon is an *internal* battle between two warring human "mindsets"—one centered around the indwelling Spirit, the other around the constraints and diversions of corporeal creatureliness—and it will be argued that the Scriptures present three broad strategies to achieve victory in this Christian warfare: adopting a Spirit-centered mindset, resisting influences that would divert one away from this mindset, and consolidating the mindset through conducive action. The third strategy underlines the fact that although the primary battlefront in the Christian struggle tends to be described in the Scriptures as being internal to the believers, the call to be also "doers of the word" (Jas 1:22) is an important element of fighting the good fight of the faith, involving as it does proactive ministry to people in physical or spiritual destitution/bondage who would not be able to avoid their—often tragic—destiny without the intervention of Christian helpers.

2

The Accounts of Creation in Genesis 1–2

AN EXAMINATION OF HUMANITY's plight immediately raises the question of
why God's creation accommodates imperfection, sin, and even forces that
are openly hostile to God's work—a question that has been a central issue
underlying the "problem of evil" in theology and philosophy. According
to the canonical narrative proposed in this book, the origins of "those
things which are contrary to God"[1] (Waltke) ultimately lie in the nature
of creation seen as an ongoing "work in progress" which moves through
a multi-phased evolution, encompassing human history from its beginnings to the completion of new creation. This chapter begins to develop this
theme through the exegesis of Genesis 1–2, and it will be shown that the
Scriptures present a perspective on primal creation that involves a gradually and incrementally unfolding *process*. It will also be argued that the
newly created material world was pronounced "very good" at the end of the
sixth day not necessarily because it was complete and perfected but rather
because it contained all that was needed to set into motion a progression
that will eventually culminate in the realization of the kingdom of God on
earth. As we shall see below, such an understanding of the incompleteness
of the initial created order has been voiced by several influential theologians
since the patristic era, suggesting that creation was intended to go through a
gradual maturation process. However, these proposals have never yet been
assembled into a coherent and overarching biblical theory of progressive
creation; as an attempt to go some way toward filling this gap, this chapter first explores the biblical account in Genesis 1 of how a series of divine
creational acts transform an initial "formless void" into a fully functioning global ecosystem, and then examines the second creation account in
Genesis 2, which concentrates on one key aspect of this process in detail,
the making of humankind.

1. Waltke, "Creation Account IV," 339.

2.1 "In the beginning . . ."—The Exegetical Debate about Genesis 1:1–2

In the beginning when God created the heavens and the earth, the earth was a formless void and darkness covered the face of the deep, while a wind from God swept over the face of the waters. (Gen 1:1–2)

Because of the scant scriptural basis of the doctrine of *creatio ex nihilo*, the first two verses of the Bible—which have been regarded as potentially enlightening in this respect—have been subject to extensive scrutiny over the past two millennia, making this passage one of the most intensively analyzed texts in biblical scholarship. The vast majority of exegetical effort has been centered around the inherent grammatical ambiguity of how the two verses are related to each other, because it was hoped that a definitive solution to this question would shed light on the starting point of creation. From a linguistic perspective, the exegetical debate boils down to one key question of syntax: Is the initial verse (a) an independent superscription or principal clause to be translated as "In the beginning God created the heavens and the earth" (NIV) or (b) a subordinate temporal clause to be translated "In the beginning *when* God created the heavens and the earth" (NRSV, emphasis added)?[2] The former would lend support to *creatio ex nihilo*, because it declares that God is the Creator of everything, whereas the latter could be read as an indication that the first creative act reported in the Bible was linked to some sort of preexistent matter described in v. 2—"the earth was a formless void . . ."—that provided the "raw material" for subsequent divine creation. The discussion has been wide-ranging and has utilized a full armory of biblical scholarship: Besides exploring various issues of discourse analysis concerning highly subtle and elusive points—about which Childs and Kelsey, among others, have probably rightly concluded that no definitive resolution is ever likely to be reached solely on the basis of grammar[3]—scholars have also been considering a wide array of contextual and circumstantial evidence that might be relevant to understanding the originally intended meaning of the passage.[4]

---

2. For a representative selection of summaries from different perspectives, see Barth, *CD* III/1, 100–105: Blocher, *In the Beginning*, 62; Giere, *A New Glimpse of Day One*, 21; Levenson, *Creation*, 121; Löning and Zenger, *To Begin With*, 21; Paul et al., "Creation and Cosmogony," 273; Speiser, *Genesis*, 12–13; Westermann, *Genesis*, 93–94.

3. Childs, *Biblical Theology*, 111; Kelsey, "Doctrine of Creation from Nothing," 58.

4. These included ancient renderings of the passage in translations (particularly in the Septuagint, the Vulgate, and various Targums), parallels to Near Eastern conventional formulae used for initial temporal phrases (e.g., Childs, *Biblical Theology*,

Curiously, however, the temporal link between the two verses does not make a huge difference in the overall understanding of the main thrust of the Genesis passage. The first verse clearly states that God is the creator of everything and the second describes the starting point of a creative sequence, the creation of the earth—or, as Barth further specifies, "the lower, visible part of the universe"[5]—that is the subject of the rest of the Genesis chapter. This is the sole content of the two verses; they do not give any further details about how the initial state of the creational sequence came into being. Westermann is therefore right that the passage does not intend to reveal anything specific about the ontology of matter or the beginning of the creation of the universe in general.[6] This lack of intentionality is fully consistent with the general reticence of Genesis 1 about disclosing details of the creation of the heavenly sphere of the angels.[7]

Thus, the initial verses of Genesis do not specify the origin of the formless void,[8] whether because it is something beyond human understanding or because it is simply the product of a previous stage of divine creation that is irrelevant to the process described in the rest of Genesis 1. This latter view—termed the *two-stage solution*—was already suggested by Theophilus in the second century, and the understanding that the formless void in Gen 1:2 was the fruit of God's first creative act was also shared by Thomas Aquinas and the Reformers.[9] This solution also mirrors the potter metaphor that recurs several times in the Bible,[10] in the sense that it distinguishes two separate phases in the making of something: first having the raw material and then giving form to it. Not only is this view compatible with the notion of creation out of nothing but also with that

---

111), the clear parallel with the prologue of the Gospel of John, the traditional manner of reading out the text in synagogues (e.g., Blocher, *In the Beginning*, 62), as well as changes in the emerging scholarly consensus about the passage throughout the ages, which initially supported seeing the first verse as an independent sentence but which has recently shifted toward the subordinate clause solution (e.g., Osborn, "Creation," 430; McMullin, "Creation," 14).

5. Barth, *CD* III/1, 104.

6. Westermann, *Genesis*, 109–10.

7. A passage in Job 38:4–7 indicates that this realm had been in place when the foundations of the earth were laid, because "all the heavenly beings" witnessed this act and "shouted for joy" (v. 7).

8. Consistent with this conclusion, McFarland states, "it is important to insist that the proper content of the Christian doctrine of creation cannot be decided on the basis of a narrow focus on the Hebrew of Genesis 1:1" (*From Nothing*, 21).

9. See e.g., Blocher, *In the Beginning*, 64; Fergusson, *Cosmos and the Creator*, 25–26.

10. Isa 29:16, 45:9, 64:8; Jer 18:1–6; Rom 9:20–21.

of a progressive, step by step creational process, which—as we shall see below—is at the heart of the two Genesis accounts.

2.2 The First Account of Creation

If the account of creation in Genesis 1 had wanted to emphasize the "something out of nothing" nature of divine creation, it could have taken us straight to the outcome of Day Six, describing the "something" element in detail. However, what we find in the actual text is a step-by-step unfolding of an incremental process whereby the dark, formless, watery void that is presented at the beginning of the account is gradually transformed into an ordered world that is fertile and accommodates life. The main focus is therefore on presenting a *transformation sequence* that produces created order, and although the description is somewhat sketchy, indeed hardly more than shorthand, it succeeds in conveying four central ideas concerning material creation: (a) progression, (b) creation as multi-faceted transformation, (c) the world as a living system, and (d) the contrast between the initial and the end states of the six-day creation process. Each of these facets of creation will be discussed separately below, while a fifth important point made in the Genesis account, the centrality of humanity within the created order, will be explored later in connection to the second account of creation (Genesis 2).

Progression

The creation account in Genesis 1 presents a multi-phased process whose progression is punctuated by prominent sequence markers such as the division of the process into six consecutive units ("days"), as well as the use of the recurring phrases "And God said, 'Let there be . . .'" and "And there was evening and there was morning . . ." The process is incremental in nature, because every new phase builds on, and thus adds to, the state of the created order achieved in the previous stage. The first three creative acts produce the fundamental parameters of the material world as we know it, adding to the originally dark, formless, and watery void (a) *light* and through the temporal alternation of day and night: *time*; (b) *shape*, that is, a *spatial dimension*; and (c) *solid matter*. The dry land is then made fertile so that it can produce vegetation, and regular cycles of plant life are ensured through the addition of permanent sources of light to the sky. By the beginning of the fifth day the world has been made ready to support living creatures, and God populates first the seas, then the skies, and finally the land, concluding the process by the making of humankind as the pinnacle of creation (i.e., as having "dominion" over all the living creatures on earth). This outline shows that although the Genesis account describes the development of the world with broad strokes, the process presents logical and cumulative progression.[11]

Creation as Multi-faceted Transformation

The recurring framing of the creational acts ("And God said . . .") suggests a largely uniform process—creation by fiat—but a closer look at the nature of the process reveals that the act of "creation" subsumes several distinct subprocesses that contribute jointly to the overall transformation sequence:

- The first divine engagement with the primeval substrate we are told about (in v. 2) is through the "wind from God" (NRSV) or "Spirit of God" (NIV) that "swept over the face of the waters." Commentators have been divided about which meaning of the Hebrew word *rûaḥ* best fits the particular context,[12] but given that the attribute accompanying *rûaḥ* is *'ĕlōhîm*, which means "of God" or "divine,"[13] it is safe to conclude that this verse does not concern a meteorological phenomenon but rather a direct, targeted intervention by God.[14]

- The first divine "Let there be . . ." utterance concerns light (v. 3), and given that 1 John 1:5 pronounces that "God is light and in him there is no darkness at all," this creative act involves the emanating of the very core of the Creator. The transformational capacity of the divine light of Gen 1:3–4 is also highlighted in 2 Cor 4:6, where Paul specifically

11. Pannenberg points out that the sequence of creative forms presented in Genesis 1 displays "substantial analogies" with our contemporary ideas about the development of creation: "the sequence of steps appears from a modern perspective as an evolutionary process leading from primitive to more complex or higher organized forms" ("The doctrine of creation," 19).

12. For arguments supporting "wind," see e.g., Speiser, *Genesis*, 5 and Westermann, *Genesis*, 107–8; for Spirit, see e.g., Waltke, "Creation Account IV," 339 and Blocher, *In the Beginning*, 69, with the latter concluding that rendering *rûaḥ* into "wind" is a "minority interpretation [that] has lost all credibility . . ."

13. Although some scholars believe that it is simply a superlative form, as in "mighty wind," the dominant scholarly opinion is in favor of "divine"; for a review, see Westermann, *Genesis*, 107.

14. The verb following *rûaḥ* in Gen 1:2 is used in the Bible only once, in Deut 32:11, for describing a bird fluttering over its young, which suggests a nurturing function, and this connotation of *rûaḥ* is consistent with Ps 104:30: "When you send forth your spirit [*rûaḥ*], they are created; and you renew the face of the ground." See also, e.g., Grudem, *Systematic Theology*, 267.

relates it to the believers' transformation as well as to the Transfiguration of Jesus (Mark 9:2–8 and parallels): "For it is the God who said, 'Let light shine out of darkness,' who has shone in our hearts to give the light of the knowledge of the glory of God in the face of Jesus Christ."

- Light was then used to begin the transformation of the dark formless void though the process of *separation*: "God separated the light from the darkness. God called the light Day, and the darkness he called Night" (vv. 4–5). The separated light functioned as a counterbalance to darkness, which is further underscored by the reiteration of "there was evening and there was morning" for each of the six days of creation (in vv. 5, 8, 13, 19, 23 and 31). Through the alternation of day and night, darkness became contained and the primeval world came to be regularly exposed to God's transfiguring light.

- *Separation* was also applied in the next act (Gen 1:6–8) when God separated the primordial waters into waters on the earth and waters in the heavens by creating a solid dome—called Sky—between them. Samuel Giere points out that the common factor in this and the previous act of separation is the establishment of cosmic boundaries between certain elements[15]—as Psalm 148 sums up the essence of the process, "he fixed their bounds, which cannot be passed" (v. 6). It seems therefore that separation on both days involved ring-fencing—through establishing "the basic categories of existence, namely time and space"[16] (Westermann)—certain key components of the world—light and water—that God pronounced to be "good," thereby indicating that they were essential for the creational process. The fact that these elements needed to be "separated" also suggests that they were originally in some ways endangered, which reveals a menacing aspect of the primeval substrate of pervasive darkness and the watery deep. This menacing quality might explain why so many commentators have referred to the initial primeval condition outlined in Gen 1:2 as "chaos,"[17] even though it would be hard to pinpoint anything specifically "chaotic" in the description of this primordial reality (this question will be further explored in the next chapter).

---

15. Giere, *A New Glimpse of Day One*, 283.

16. Westermann, *Genesis*, 121.

17. E.g., Barth, *CD* III/1, 103; Blocher, *In the Beginning*, 71; Boyd, "Evolution as Cosmic Warfare," 141; Fergusson, *Cosmos and the Creator*, 7; Griffin, "Creation out of Nothing," 109; Levenson, *Creation*, 127; Löning and Zenger, *To Begin With*, 18: Moltmann, "Creation and Redemption," 125; Westermann, *Genesis*, 121.

- Once the primeval waters had been sufficiently "tamed" through separation, they could be further processed by *parting the Seas and the Earth*, thereby creating dry land that could host flora and fauna. It is interesting that the term "separate" (*bdl*) is not used in the description of this act, even though the literal meaning of the verb would be fitting for the division of sea and land. This adds weight to the suggestion above that the notion of "separation" in Genesis 1 is reserved for the safeguarding of precious ingredients—light and water—that had a pronounced role in the process.

- The *creation of vegetation* brought about the first living organisms in the world, but verses 11–12 point out twice that it was the earth that put forth the various plants and trees rather than God fashioning them himself. This can be seen as the cumulative impact of the ongoing transformation of the original dark, formless void: As a result of God's Spirit brooding over it and the subsequent regular exposure to divine light, the inert primordial substrate had been turned into fertile soil that could bring forth plants. In Genesis 2 we are given further details about this transformation process: First "a stream would rise from the earth, and water the whole face of the ground" (v. 6) and the outset of plant life was also mediated by the rain (". . . when no plant of the field was yet in the earth and no herb of the field had yet sprung up—for the LORD God had not caused it to rain upon the earth" v. 5). Thus, the creation of vegetation involved the preparation of appropriate conditions: fertile soil, light, and water.

- On the fourth day (vv. 14–19), God introduced *permanent sources of light* into the world: He made the sun, the moon, and the stars "to rule over the day and over the night and to separate the light from the darkness" (v. 18), and also to establish the rhythm of plant life through the cycles of seasons and years. Of all the creational acts described in the first six days, this act comes closest to the "summoning-something-into-existence" aspect of creation by fiat.

- The *creation of animate life* seems at first glance to be similar to that of vegetation in that the text states that the waters and the earth brought forth living creatures (vv. 20, 24); however, it is later pointed out that God made them directly (vv. 21, 25), and in 2:19 this is further explained: "So out of the ground the LORD God formed every animal of the field and every bird of the air." Thus, the raw material for the making of animals was the same impregnated, productive soil that brought forth vegetation, only in the case of animals God gave them shape individually.

- Westermann points out that the *blessing* of the first animals introduced a new element to the creational process, thereby suggesting that the creation of living beings involved a two-step scheme, with the pronouncement of a blessing added to the initial creational act.[18] Because the divine blessing is linked to the subsequent instruction "Be fruitful and multiply . . . ," it seems also to have inaugurated the reproductive cycle of animate life and, therefore, blessing can be seen as a potent act of empowering living creatures.

- The *creation of humans* will be the central issue in the discussion of the second creation account below, but it is important to note here that their making is both similar and different to the creation of other living beings. On the one hand, man was also formed by God himself from "the dust of the ground" (2:7), and the act was accompanied by a blessing that also included the instruction "Be fruitful and multiply, and fill the earth" (1:28). On the other hand, the making of humans also involved new elements: (a) they were made in God's image and likeness; (b) the blessing included the instruction to subdue the earth and have dominion over all the animals; and (c) the act of forming man also included breathing into his nostrils the "breath of life" (2:7).

In taking stock of the various processes involved in establishing the ecosystem of the earth, it is clear that referring to creation simply as "creation by fiat" de-emphasizes a defining aspect of the creation account, because by distinguishing a number of central creational processes, the Genesis text offers a broader understanding than merely declaring that the universe is God's work. Furthermore, the listing of the distinct creative acts has particular significance in the light of the fact that, as we shall see in chapter 4, several of the processes reoccur at later stages in the biblical narrative concerning the transformation of humankind.

The World as a Living System

An important feature of the emerging world in the Genesis account is that it is described as an evolving, living and self-sustaining system. As Bonhoeffer sums up, "The Creator wills that his creation itself should affirm and continue his work, he wills that created things should live and create further life."[19] This representation is in accordance with the progressive conception of creation, because it describes a continuous, ongoing process that does

18. Westermann, *Genesis*, 134.
19. Bonhoeffer, *Creation and Temptation*, 32.

not necessarily conclude at the end of the sixth day (a question that will be further discussed in a separate section below). Indeed, the short passage concerning vegetation (1:11–12) mentions "seeds" no fewer than four times, and the command to "multiply" is also a central part of God's blessing of the living creatures. Regarding humankind, it is specifically mentioned that God has created them male and female, thus highlighting the human sexuality that underlies procreation, that is, the human species' life-sustaining and reproductive potential. In this respect, Blocher asks an important (rhetorical) question: "Might there be in procreation—that mysterious gift granted to the man and the woman, of bringing into the world a being who is the image of God—a reflection of divine creation?"[20]

The Contrasting Poles of the Six-Day Creation Process

Although the account in Genesis 1 does not offer any detail about the origins of matter, and the creational acts are described in a highly condensed, almost stylized manner, the vivid contrast between the initial stages and the end-state of the six-day sequence provides a definite sense of God's creative purpose. The initial state of affairs is described in only a handful of content words within a single verse, with the key element of the image presented by the enigmatic Hebrew phrase *tōhû wābōhû* (v. 2), translated "formless void" by the NRSV. The two components of the phrase constitute a "hendiadys," that is, a figure of speech in which two words are joined with "and" to express a single idea more powerfully than they would have done individually, and the combined phrase links up "unformed" and "void" to describe "a formless waste."[21] It occurs in only two other passages in the Bible, in Isa 34:11 and Jer 4:23, the former referring to Isaiah's prophecy about the desolation in Edom after the Lord's day of vengeance, the second to Jeremiah's vision of the disintegration of the world under God's "fierce anger" (v. 26). Thus, both cases describe the devastating condition of the world after some divine act of destruction, as if creation had been reversed and the earth had returned to the state in which it was before the first creative utterance. Accordingly, in Gen 1:2 *tōhû wābōhû* represents inert, lifeless matter which is not yet aligned

---

20. Blocher, *In the Beginning*, 93.

21. According to the BDB *tōhû* is used in the Bible in the sense of "formlessness" and "empty, trackless waste," and Isaiah (24:10), for example, speaks about the "city of chaos [*tōhû*]" as part of his extended vision of God's judgement to "lay waste the earth and make it desolate" (Isa 24:1). *Wābōhû*, suggests an Arabic verb, "to be empty," and only occurs in conjunction with *tōhû* as a rhyming pair to augment its meaning; for analyses, see e.g., Blocher, *In the Beginning*, 65–66; Speiser, *Genesis*, 5.

with God's life-giving scheme; in Fergusson's words, this surd element embodies the "antithesis of order" that precedes the act of creation.[22]

Following the phrase *tōhû wābōhû*, Gen 1:2 continues with a second striking picture: "darkness covered the face of the deep." The Hebrew word translated as "deep" (*tĕhôm*) refers to a deep abyss or a surging mass of water, suggesting to Goldingay the "tumultuous and threatening dynamic energy of waters in flood (cf. Gen 7:11; 8:2)"[23] In the same vein, Barth points out that the same word is used in Pss 33:7 and 104:6 to refer to some primordial flood, and the image of water is further strengthened by the reference to the "face of the waters" at the end of v. 2. This picture combined with the pervasive darkness offers, according to Barth, "a second and different view of this desolate state of the world,"[24] and thus Gen 1:2 as a whole evokes the sense of a dark, empty, and disorderly reality, a lifeless, amorphous substrate that carries considerable negative resonances.

At the latter end of the six-day creation sequence is a fertile world populated by living creatures, and the climax of the process is the creation of humankind, who is given the explicit task of subduing the earth, using the flora for food, and having dominion over the fauna. Importantly, besides highlighting the life-giving potential of humans (see above), Genesis 1 presents a further key characteristic of humanity that may be seen as an explanation for their privileged status: Humans were created in God's image (v. 26), a point given strong scriptural emphasis by its reiteration several times.[25] However, despite the great amount of interest that this idea—often referred to as "*imago Dei*"—has generated over the past two millennia, no scholarly consensus has emerged about what exactly the phrase might mean.[26] Genesis 1:26 foregrounds a functional dimension of the divine-human interface when it pronounces that humans will have "dominion" over all the animals of the earth;[27] this amounts to a *de facto* delegation by God of some of his

22. Fergusson, *Cosmos and the Creator*, 12.

23. Goldingay, *Old Testament Theology*, 81.

24. Barth, *CD* III/1, 105.

25. It is paraphrased in the same verse as "according to our likeness," then repeated twice in v. 27 and two more times in 5:1 and 9:6.

26. E.g., Childs explains that the tantalizing expectation to decipher the meaning of *imago Dei* has been "continually frustrated by the uncertainty of the text's interpretation. The history of modern exegesis demonstrates convincingly how a consensus regarding its meaning only momentarily emerges which is then shortly dissolved into newer forms of dissension" (*Biblical Theology*, 567). For overviews, see Barth, *CD* III/1, 192; Childs, *Biblical Theology*, 567–69; Clines, "Image of God in Man"; Westermann, *Genesis*, 148.

27. See e.g., Fergusson, "Creation," 74–75: "This more functional or relational account of the divine image makes better sense of the succeeding verses that speak of the

authority by appointing humankind to act as his representatives in his name, that is, in his functional likeness,[28] and consistent with this, Ps 8:5–6 declares about humans that God "crowned them with glory and honor" as he gave them "dominion over the works of your hands."[29]

In sum, the examination of the two ends of the six-day creation sequence in Genesis 1 reveals a vivid contrast between the image of dark, inert, disorderly, and lifeless matter and a thriving, living system under the dominion of humankind, who have been created in God's own image. Genesis 1 therefore outlines a transformation process whose main drive concerns aligning the initially inimical matter with the principles of divine created order, or in Goldingay's words, "turning empty void into meaningful whole."[30] This is consistent with a summary in Isaiah 45:18 of God's creation of the earth: "he established it; he did not create it a chaos, he formed it to be inhabited!"

2.3 The Second Account of Creation

The second account of creation in Genesis 2 represents a markedly different perspective to the first account, with the emphasis being not so much on how the initially inert matter became populated with living things as on just one prominent aspect of this process, the creation of humankind. We shall look at this account in detail in chapter 3 and here only the *progression* aspect of the account is examined. In this respect it can be observed that notwithstanding some discrepancies in the order of creation (see below), the overall portrayal conveys a similar sense of progression to that of the first account. It begins with an image of the world being desolate and inimical to life (v. 5), and proceeds by stating that the "whole face of the ground" (v. 6) was exposed to watering by a stream rising from the earth. The account than relates the beginning of the population of the earth by first describing the making of man

roles of human beings in the world already made."

28. As von Rad expounds, "Just as powerful earthly kings, to indicate their claim to dominion, erect an image of themselves in the provinces of their empire where they do not personally appear, so man is placed upon earth in God's image as God's sovereign emblem. He is really only God s representative, summoned to maintain and enforce God's claim to dominion over the earth. The decisive thing about man's similarity to God, therefore, is his function in the non-human world" (*Genesis*, 60).

29. It is also of note in this respect that Genesis 5 draws an analogy between God making humankind in the likeness of God (v. 1) and Adam becoming "the father of a son in his likeness, according to his image" (v. 3), particularly because in Luke 3:38 Adam is listed in Jesus' genealogy as "son of God," and Paul declares in Acts 17:29 that "we are God's offspring."

30. Goldingay, *Old Testament Theology*, 81.

from the "dust of the ground" (v. 7), then the creation of vegetation (Garden of Eden) in a similar manner to how it is described in the first account—by making it grow "out of the ground" (v. 9)—and finally the formation of the various animal species again "out of the ground" (v. 19).

The order of the creational phases deviates from the succession found in Genesis 1 in that the making of the man is mentioned as the first appearance of life. Chronological sequencing, however, does not appear to be the main concern for this account, as the description of the creation of both flora and fauna is within the context of how these life forms were related to humanity, which may be explained by the priority given to the making of man. For example, the creation of the Garden of Eden is mentioned only after the forming of Adam, and yet he seems to have been placed in the garden straight away with instructions on how to feed himself (implying established vegetation); what the text emphasizes is the *functional* link between the man and the Garden of Eden (to be discussed in the next chapter) and not the order of their creation. In the same way, the making of animal life is also presented in relation to the man, as an intended means to provide him with a helper to share the burden of his work. Despite these differences, the conclusion of the second creation account in Genesis 2 is exactly the same as the last creative act in Genesis 1: the launching of humankind as a species that can multiply and thereby populate the earth.

In sum, the second creation account is not concerned with systematically depicting the sequence of the different phases of the emerging created order, but rather it foregrounds the making of the human species and presents the other elements of creation in relation to it. As such, its presence adjacent to the first creation account can be seen as an example of the "montage method" highlighted by Alter[31] (discussed in chapter 1), but, at the same time, the overall thrust of the creational sequence is compatible with the framework outlined in Genesis 1.

2.4 Two Crucial Questions about the Progressive Nature of Creation in the Genesis Accounts

In his overview of *creatio continua*, Christian Link submits that the Genesis account "does not mention a permanent divine activity of maintenance. It assumes that the very first establishment of the world itself guarantees the permanent existence of the world on the basis of God's commandments."[32] It is indeed the case that in the Genesis accounts the seventh day is de-

31. Alter, *Biblical Narrative*, 145.
32. Link, "Creatio Continua," para. 1.

scribed to have brought a closure to the preceding creational process without any indication that the created order was to be subjected to any subsequent divine maintenance; moreover, at this point God also evaluated his work as being "very good," which would again support the implication that no further development was needed. These points, then, raise two critical questions about the proposed canonical narrative of progressive creation: Does the closure on the seventh day stipulate unequivocally that creation was permanently finished, and what aspect of creation was appraised to be "very good"?

Was Creation Finished on the Seventh Day?

The seventh day is described in Genesis 2 as a closure to the preceding creational process; v. 1 states unequivocally, "Thus the heavens and the earth were *finished*, and all their multitude" (italics added). The next verse adds further emphasis to this closure: "And on the seventh day God finished the work that he had done, and he rested on the seventh day from all the work that he had done" (2:2), and God's rest is reiterated in v. 3: "God rested from all the work that he had done in creation." These verses leave no doubt about the fact that God completed the work he intended to accomplish in the first six days, and when he had conducted a final survey of everything that he had made, his overall verdict was "very good" (Gen 1:31). From the progressive perspective, the fundamental question is whether the creation process had finished on the seventh day.

God's "activity" on the seventh day is repeatedly described as "resting." Although the Hebrew verb for resting (*šbt*) can mean "cease" (as in Josh 5:12: "The manna ceased on the day they ate the produce of the land"), it is also used to mean the taking of a temporary break as in Leviticus 25:2, where it is part of God's instruction to the Israelites for the land to "rest" every seventh year. Similarly, the noun "*šabbāt*" (Sabbath)—derived from the same verb—refers to a temporary abstinence from labor for relief and refreshment every seventh day (e.g., Exod 23:12), and indeed, this refreshment aspect is directly linked to divine creation in Exod 31:16–17: "Therefore the Israelites shall keep the sabbath, observing the sabbath throughout their generations, as a perpetual covenant. It is a sign forever between me and the people of Israel that in six days the LORD made heaven and earth, and on the seventh day he rested, and was refreshed."

This would suggest that the rest on the seventh day can be understood as an *interval* in divine creation rather than as a full closure. If this is the case, however, what does Gen 2:1 refer to as being "finished"? As we saw earlier, the six-day creation in Genesis 1 may be seen as a creational sequence which set up a living, self-supporting ecosystem, and in this sense "finished" can be taken to mean that all the necessary elements and conditions for the system had been put into place and, thus, the system was ready to be set into motion. Significantly, this understanding does not exclude any further acts of creation, because a living system can evolve and can receive input that will help it to reach new operational levels. Accordingly, divine creation is conceived in this book to include a potential for continuity by means of further transformation, and the reality of this potential is illustrated in both Testaments by multiple references to a "new creation" (2 Cor 5:17; Gal 6:15), the making of "a new heaven and a new earth" (Isa 65:17; 66:22; 2 Pet 3:13; Rev 21:1), and the descent of New Jerusalem (Rev 3:12; 21:2; 21:9–27). Indeed, the next two chapters will demonstrate that the biblical canon presents a consistent pattern of transformational acts leading up to the completion of new creation, often using the same terminology to characterize these acts as was used in the first two Genesis accounts of creation.

What Was "very good"?

Was the pronouncement at the end of the sixth day that the created order "was very good" an indication of the fact that creation had reached its optimal form and did not therefore require any follow-up or refinement, as suggested by several commentators?[33] The answer to this question depends largely on what aspect of creation the "very good" appraisal refers to. A key consideration in this respect is that the biblical narrative that follows the creation accounts does not present the picture of a well-functioning system: As we shall see in more detail in chapter 3, Genesis 3 describes the Fall and Adam and Eve's subsequent expulsion from the Garden of Eden, followed by the account of how the first ever child born on earth, Cain, murders his brother (Genesis 4). The ensuing deterioration of human affairs is summarized in the shocking revelation of Gen 6:5: "The LORD saw that the wickedness of humankind was great in the earth, and that every inclination of the thoughts of their hearts was only evil continually. And the LORD was sorry that he had made humankind on the earth, and it grieved him to his heart."

The first sentence of this passage expresses unequivocally that humankind has become utterly corrupt (note the adverbs "every" and "continually"), and the second sentence conveys God's profound disappointment with

---

33. E.g., Childs has argued, "God pronounced his workmanship good and blessed it. The creation rested in its perfection; no further work was needed" (*Biblical Theology*, 385).

how things have turned out; in Wilkinson's words, the "'out of jointedness of creation' is testimony that it was not always intended to be like this."[34] As a result, the Genesis narrative describes that God decides to purge the earth through the Flood, and his dramatic response not only reflects the gravity of the crisis but also renders it highly implausible that God's earlier positive appraisal in Gen 1:31 referred to the state of the created order as it was manifested in the short run (since this would imply that God got something terribly wrong). A more likely scenario is that the "very good" pronouncement concerned the *long-term potential* of creation; that is, rather than viewing the initial created order as the final product, God's assessment considered it the launching pad of a process that would in due time reach its successful conclusion, regardless of any interim setbacks on the way. This inherent potential of the system receives confirmation in Paul's famous declaration in Romans 8 concerning the eschatological *hope* that creation will be able to shed its constraints in due course: "for the creation was subjected to futility, not of its own will but by the will of the one who subjected it, in hope that the creation itself will be set free from its bondage to decay and will obtain the freedom of the glory of the children of God" (vv. 20–21).

The perceived capability of the initial ecosystem to fulfil its creational potential is further corroborated by the next verse in Romans 8—"We know that the whole creation has been groaning in labor pains until now" (v. 22)—in which the phrase "labor pains" connotes the hope of birth and, as such, of future new life.[35] This creational potential is not unlike how a seed can be seen as an embryonic plant that one day will come into full existence, an understanding which is, in fact, consistent with the fact that the Flood did not eradicate the living system of the material world completely but merely "re-booted" it (to use Bill Jackson's fitting metaphor[36]): Plant seeds are known to be able to survive short-term flooding and Noah's ark carried "prototypes" of all living creatures to repopulate the world after the cleansing waters had receded.

We shall examine the possible reasons for the short-term futility of the created order in chapter 3, and the postdiluvian "re-booting" and

34. Wilkinson, *Creation*, 240. Goldingay also emphasizes that the biblical narrative sees in the ongoing conflict in the world "a frustrating of God's creative purpose" (*Old Testament Theology*, 74).

35. As Wright explains, "Part of the point of the image is that the coming new world will involve, not the abolition of the present one, but its transformation: Birth (particularly in the culture of Paul's day, both Jewish and pagan) speaks of new life that is at the same time the mother's own life, delighting her, despite the pain of labor, with a fresh fulfilment" ("The Letter to the Romans," 597).

36. Jackson, *Eden Project*, 46.

"re-creation" will be explored in chapter 4; the important point for our current purpose is that God's "very good" verdict may rightfully have an eschatological interpretation instead of taking it to concern the state of the world after the first six days. Proposals for such an understanding in theology can be traced back as far as the origins of the Christian doctrine of creation in the patristic era (e.g., in the work of Irenaeus and Augustine), and the perception of a world that is incomplete but has the creational potentiality to reach eschatological fulfilment was then endorsed both by the Reformers (e.g., Martin Luther) and several modern theologians (e.g., Brunner, Pannenberg, Moltmann, Haught). Let us conclude this chapter by briefly considering their views.

2.5 Incomplete Creation and Creational Potentiality

It was the same theologians who developed the concept of *creatio ex nihilo*—Theophilus and Irenaeus—who first proposed that humans were not created perfect but were intended to go through a gradual maturation process that mirrors the developmental cycle of human beings in general.[37] For example, in chapter 38 of Book 4 of *Against Heresies*—titled "Why man was not made perfect from the beginning"—Irenaeus states that humankind is created in "an infantile stage of existence"[38] and has to go through a long-term process before "being glorified": "man [is] making progress day by day, and ascending toward the perfect, that is, approximating to the uncreated One. For the Uncreated is perfect, that is, God. Now it was necessary that man should in the first instance be created; and having been created, should receive growth; and having received growth, should be strengthened; and having been strengthened, should abound; and having abounded, should recover [from the disease of sin]; and having recovered, should be glorified; and being glorified, should see his Lord."[39]

This and other similar passages draw a parallel between human history in general and the specific development of an individual human being from infancy to adult maturity, and as Rowan Greer summarizes, this theological framework remained constant throughout the patristic era: "The story moves from the immaturity or the unstable perfection of Adam in paradise to the maturity or stable perfection of the resurrection life in

37. E.g., *Theophilus to Autolycus* II.24, 25; Irenaeus, *Against Heresies* 4.38. An overview of the relevant patristic literature is offered in Hick's presentation of his theory of theodicy. Hick, *Evil and the God of Love*.

38. Irenaeus, *Against Heresies* 4.38.2.

39. Ibid., 4.38.1, 3.

the heavenly city."[40] During the Reformation, Martin Luther extended the human developmental metaphor to include the whole of creation (i.e., not just the making of humanity) when he likened the making of the world to the creation of a child:

> the Almighty God has not created the world in a day but taken time for this purpose, as when He now creates a child. He first creates the rudiments of heaven and earth, but these as yet unfashioned, and waste and void, with no life or growth or shape or form. . . . Just as originally the infant, although it is not nothing in its mother's womb, is not yet formed as a perfect child is to be; and just as smoke is not nothing, but has neither light nor radiance, so the earth was [in Gen 1:2] as yet unfashioned and had no dimensions either of breadth or length, neither was there any seed or trees or grass on it, but poor and barren earth like an uninhabited land or desert where nothing grows. And similarly heaven was without form, although it was not nothing.[41]

The advantage of using the metaphor of a child's maturation when talking about creation is that it helps to reconcile the originally declared goodness of creation with the subsequent setbacks, as the latter can be seen as inevitable concomitants of the process of coming to age. However, this reading also raises some difficult questions concerning the Fall, because one could equally argue that the inherent imperfection in humankind led unavoidably to stumbling and therefore an infant may be expected to have "diminished responsibility" when it comes to sinning.[42] Or, to go one step further, if human history is, in Greer's words, "a story of the growth from innocence to experience,"[43] one might even submit that the Fall was a *necessary* stage in the human maturation process. We shall come back to this and related questions when we discuss the futility of creation in the next chapter, but here it is important to note that the maturing child metaphor has not been the only way to try to capture the progressive aspect of creation. Augustine used a related image, a seed growing into a plant, which has fewer moral implications than the maturing child analogy; in *The Literal Meaning of Genesis* he made an extensive comparison between the created world and a beautiful tree, and as part of this he stated:

40. Greer, "Christian Bible," 185.

41. Luther, *Sermon on Genesis* (cited in Barth, *CD* III/1, 103).

42. Irenaeus himself does not make this connection consistently, because elsewhere in the same book (4.22.1) he reiterates the Pauline teaching of sin and death entering the world through the first man; see Greer, "Christian Bible," 168; Soulen, *God of Israel*, 43.

43. Greer, "Christian Bible," 168.

This tree surely did not spring forth suddenly in this size and form, but rather went through a process of growth . . . from a seed, and therefore in the seed all those parts existed primordially, not in the dimensions of bodily mass but as a force and causal power. The bodily mass was built up by an accumulation of earth and moisture. But there exists in that tiny grain the power more wonderful and excellent by which moisture was mingled with earth forming a matter capable of being changed into wood, into spreading branches, into green leaves of appropriate shape, into beautiful and luxurious fruits, with all parts developed into a well-ordered whole.[44]

Therefore, he concluded,

In the seed, then, there was invisibly present all that would develop in time into a tree. And in this same way we must picture the world, when God made all things together, as having had all things together which were made in it and with it when day was made. This includes not only heaven with sun, moon and stars, whose splendor remains unchanged as they move in a circular motion; and earth and the deep waters, which are in almost unceasing motion, and which, placed below the sky, make up the lower part of the world; but it includes also the beings which water and earth produced in potency and in their causes before they came forth in the course of time as they have been known to us in the works which God even now produces.[45]

Thus, while Christian theology was in the process of developing and solidifying the doctrine of *creatio ex nihilo*, there was also a parallel line of thinking that did not conceive the emerging created order as being finite and perfected but rather as one that was intended to undergo further transformation. This is consistent with the earlier discussion of the complementary nature of *creatio ex nihilo* and *creatio continua*: The idea of a cosmic origination that underlies the "biblically inspired metaphysics of creation *ex nihilo*"[46] accounts for how the timeless Creator brings into being the whole cosmos, including time, whereas theorizing that takes as its starting point the Genesis narrative of creation—which deals almost exclusively with the process of the "maturing of the seed"—considers the steps that have been molding, shaping, and transforming the original matter and the pinnacle of material creation, humanity.

44. Augustine, *Literal Meaning of Genesis*, V/44, 174–75.
45. Ibid., IV/45, 175.
46. McMullin, "Creation," 22.

Moltmann captured this aspect of creation when he called it *"creatio mutabilis,"* that is, "perfectible, not perfect, for it is open for the history of both disaster and salvation, for both destruction and consummation,"[47] and elsewhere he further argues that if we read Genesis 1 in the light of Revelation 21, we find that "Genesis 1 does not describe a perfect world, but only the beginning of a creation which just arrives at its true nature in the 'new creation.'"[48] Accordingly, he concludes, "Genesis I describes only Act I of creation, the beginning of a creation history which arrives at its goal and its perfecting in the kingdom of God's glory. . . . In this respect, the 'new creation' will bring not only redemption from sin, death, and chaos, but also the completion and perfecting of the first act of creation, and the fulfillment of its initial promise."[49]

In his *Systematic Theology*, Pannenberg acknowledges that "a Christian theology of creation does not have to insist on a perfect state at the first,"[50] but at the same time he also voices the other side of the dilemma: "But the authoritative statements of the biblical creation story concerning the goodness of creation force it in this direction."[51] Reflecting on this issue further, Pannenberg arrives at the same crucial question that has been at the heart of our current discussion: If the initial acts of creation resulted in an unfinished product, what was "very good" about it? His answer concurs with the response that emerged from the current analysis, namely that God's positive appraisal concerned the inherent potentiality of the created order to run its course and achieve completion:

> Only in the light of the eschatological consummation is the verdict justified that in the first creation story the Creator pronounced at the end of the sixth day when he had created the first human pair: "And God saw everything that he had made, and behold, it was very good" (Gen. 1:31). Only in the light of the eschatological consummation may this be said of our world as it is in all its confusion and pain . . . The verdict "very good" does not apply simply to the world of creation in its state at any given time.[52]

In sum, a strong case can be made for a reading of the Genesis narrative that supports a progressive creational perspective, conceiving of creation as

47. Moltmann, *Future of Creation,* 120.

48. Moltmann, "Spirit of Life," 68.

49. Ibid.

50. Pannenberg, *Systematic Theology,* vol. 2, 163.

51. Ibid.

52. Pannenberg, *Systematic Theology,* vol. 3, 645.

a process that did not conclude on the sixth day. Admittedly, the various views presented above diverge in how they explain the specific reasons for, and nature of, the incompleteness of the created order and how this incompleteness was to be offset by further maturation (which will be explored further in chapter 3); however, they do converge in their assumption that the originally created ecosystem was not the final product but rather an interim state that needed to undergo further transformation to reach its full creational potential, a view that is aptly summarized by David Fergusson in the passage that was already partially cited in chapter 1: "Creation is imperfect in the sense that it is incomplete and unfulfilled. The making of the world is only the first of God's works. As the beginning of a history, it sets in motion a narrative that has a focal point in the coming of Jesus."[53]

2.6 Summary

The first two chapters of Genesis foreground a perspective on creation that centers around the gradually and incrementally unfolding nature of the process. The essence of this progression is the transformation of the initially lifeless, formless, dark void into a habitable and indeed inhabited world, under the dominion of humankind, who were made in God's image and likeness. A defining aspect of the portrayal of how the world was made is the variety of creative acts involved in it, and referring to divine creation exclusively as "creation by fiat" fails to do justice not only to this richness of the process but also to the fact that the Genesis accounts characterize creation primarily not as the summoning of new things into existence but rather as a series of multi-faceted transformational acts. It was argued that the identification of these distinct creative acts is also of significance to our understanding because it helps us to realize that several of these acts reoccur later in the biblical narrative in connection with the transformation of humankind (see chapters 3 and 4).

The created order that has emerged by the end of the sixth day is a self-supporting, living ecosystem, in which created things are to create further life. Vegetation was originally put forward by the impregnated earth and is to be sustained through seeds, and the command to multiply is a central part of God's blessing for all the living creatures; indeed, it is specifically mentioned that God has created human beings male and female, thereby highlighting procreation. All this is in accordance with the principles of continuing creation as discussed earlier, and the progressive nature of the transformation process is further affirmed by the fact that, as

53. Fergusson, "Creation," 78.

was proposed in this chapter, it did not necessarily finish on the seventh day when God rested. Although God pronounced the initial creation to be "very good," it was suggested that his appraisal concerned the material world's inherent potential to achieve perfection in the future rather than its actual, current functioning.

In sum, the reading offered in this chapter outlines a picture of creation that involves a process of progressive transformation as well as an initial created order that is unfinished. It was shown that aspects of such an understanding have been shared by several renowned theologians both in the past and in modern times, but that the various proposals have not as yet been assembled into a comprehensive scheme that is integrated with other major biblical themes. In an article entitled "In Praise of Imperfection," John Haught points out that although the observation that the universe we live in is still unfinished "may not sound terribly consequential initially, . . . the theological implications are enormous";[54] indeed, it follows from the unfinished state of the world that "we cannot justifiably expect it here and now to be the full embodiment of perfect 'design.'"[55] This realization offers a viable starting point for the exploration of the origins of humanity's struggles, and in keeping with this interpretation, the next chapter focuses on examining the futility of the initial created order.

---

54. Haught, "In Praise of Imperfection," 174. In his recent book, Haught explores these implications further for the purpose of expanding Catholic theology by answering the question of "what Catholic faith might mean if we take fully into account the fact that our universe is still on the move" (*Resting on the Future*, 1).

55. Haught, "In Praise of Imperfection," 174.

3

The Futility of Creation and the Fall

WE SAW BRIEFLY IN the previous chapter that the biblical narrative that follows the creation accounts in Genesis presents humankind as being on a deteriorating course that led to a complete moral breakdown before the Flood. This dire predicament is consistent with Paul's assertion in Romans that creation was "subjected to futility" (8:20) and was in "bondage to decay" (v. 21). The deficiency of the material world is also signaled in the various canonical descriptions of new creation, which hold up a mirror to the current, imperfect state of affairs and which give a glimpse of the changes that God's fully realized creative purpose will bring about: Isa 65:17–25, for example, depicts a future without any "sound of weeping" or "cries of distress," with no people who "labor in vain" or "bear children for calamity," and without "an infant that lives but a few days, or an old person who does not live out a lifetime." Similarly, Revelation 21:4 foretells that in new creation "Death will be no more; mourning and crying and pain will be no more, for the first things have passed away."

The Bible offers no direct explanation of the origins of the futility of creation, and in the absence of any scriptural—or creedal—teaching on this matter, scholars have been divided about why and how things could go so wrong. Some would simply acknowledge that "the fact of wickedness and evil in the world remains an insoluble riddle and offense,"[1] while others have sought answers by drawing on disciplines such as philosophy[2] or evolutionary biology.[3] In trying to offer a theological response, two

---

1. Pannenberg, *Systematic Theology,* vol. 2, 164.

2. See, e.g., the studies in McBrayer and Howard-Snyder, *Problem of Evil*; and in Rowe, *God and the Problem of Evil.*

3. E.g., Southgate, *The Groaning Creation.* As Haught submits, "we may speculate that the evolutionary character of life inevitably gives the universe a dark side that is capable of harboring tragedy and moral evil" (*God after Darwin,* 175).

approaches have been prominent in the literature. The first concerns the infrequent but undeniable occurrence of biblical passages that describe a sinister or dark side of primordial matter that needed to be actively contained and gradually "tamed" by God, a theme that is usually linked to the motif of *Chaoskampf* ("chaos fight") against primordial powers of waters or sea monsters and the like. The second and more common proposal for the source of the corruption of the created order is connected to Adam and Eve's disobedience in the Garden of Eden, with some blame also being placed on the serpent for orchestrating the events. As we shall see below, both explanations have scriptural support, but they also leave open some important questions that warrant further reflection. The canonical narrative interpretation applied in this chapter creates a link between these two themes and then offers a new perspective on the Fall and on Adam and Eve's subsequent banishment from Eden.

3.1 The Dark Side of Matter

As seen in chapter 2, the creative act of "separation" involved setting up boundaries to protect two key components of the emerging world—light and "good" water—and it was pointed out that the very fact that these elements needed to be protected against the forces of darkness and primordial waters was evidence of a sinister undertone: Clearly, darkness signified something more than merely a lack of luminescence, and the potential destructive power of the primeval waters was later demonstrated in the Flood when God removed the protection and "the fountains of the great deep burst forth, and the windows of the heavens were opened" (Gen 7:11). Recall also that the Hebrew phrase for "formless void" in Gen 1:2, *tōhû wābōhû*, occurs in two other places in the Bible (Isa 34:11; Jer 4:23), both times within an oracle of doom to describe the devastating conditions of a desolate wasteland, leading Fergusson to conclude that this surd element embodies the "antithesis of order."[4] In a detailed discussion of creation, Barth called the primeval substrate "nothingness"[5] and argued that it represents an "entire sinister system of elements"[6] that offer opposition and resistance to God's purposes. Thus, commentators are in agreement that some aspect of the primordial matter as portrayed in the Scriptures was

---

4. Fergusson, *Cosmos and the Creator*, 12.
5. Karl Barth, *CD* III/3, 289.
6. Ibid.

antagonistic to the created order and represented "a state of existence contrary to the character of God"[7] (Waltke).

Given the allusive quality of the relevant biblical references, it is difficult to go beyond such admittedly rather vague characterizations, and in his analysis Barth also comes to an impasse: On the one hand, he argues that it is not right to assume that nothingness "derives from the positive will and work of God"[8] because that would shift all responsibility of sin onto God; on the other hand, he admits that the other side of the argument—namely that nothingness "derives solely from the activity of the creature"[9]—is also inadequate, because that would deny God's "unlimited majesty over every sphere."[10] Accordingly, he submits that "we have here an extraordinarily clear demonstration of the necessary brokenness of all theological thought and utterance,"[11] while still insisting that it is inappropriate to think of nothingness as an active agent, that is, as a "form of a monster which, vested with demonic qualities, inspires fear and respect."[12] However, as we shall see below, there is mention in the Scriptures of God actively crushing certain opposition, which does suggest the existence of some form of conscious antagonistic agency; indeed, even Barth acknowledges, "It is clear enough that there is a chaos; that creation is 'somehow' related to it; that it plays its part even in the later history which begins with creation; and that there too there are definite encounters between it and God."[13]

Barth was not alone with the above views; in his influential book on *Creation and the Persistence of Evil* Jon Levenson takes a similar position when he states that some things in the created world "exist that ought not to, and these deserve to be blasted from the world. Not everything that exists in nature is good or conforms to God's highest intentions. Some of what is, is not yet good."[14] Although, as said above, the Bible does not offer an explicit depiction of this sinister dimension of the world, we can get a sense of the issues involved from considering three relevant biblical threads: ongoing references to the two primeval elements, *darkness* and *primordial waters*,

7. Waltke, "Creation Account IV," 339.

8. Barth, *CD* III/3, 292.

9. Ibid.

10. Ibid.

11. Ibid., 293.

12. Ibid.

13. Barth, *CD* III/1, 103.

14. Levenson, *Creation*, xxiv.

and passages alluding to what has been called the *Chaoskampf,* that is, "the battle of the warrior god with the monstrous forces of chaos"[15] (Angel).

Darkness

Although Isa 45:7 describes darkness as having been originally created by God, it is portrayed in Gen 1:2 as a primordial element whose containment was the first step in the creational sequence of the material world, and the canon then presents a series of divine acts that eventually lead to the complete elimination of primeval darkness. Through the initial separation of light, darkness was first "confined to its place through alternation with light"[16] (Levenson), and Waltke argues that naming of the darkness "Night" constituted a second step of pronouncing lordship over it and integrating it into the created order of the world.[17] On the fourth day, darkness was further domesticated through the creation of two permanent sources of light, "the greater light to rule the day and the lesser light to rule the night" (v. 16), and the significance of this act is underlined by the subsequent repeated reference to control over darkness: "God set them in the dome of the sky to give light upon the earth, to rule over the day and over the night, and to separate the light from the darkness" (vv. 17–18). It was only after setting up this permanent safeguard that God finally declared the position of darkness in the created order to be "good" (v. 18).

In the New Testament, the Prologue of John's Gospel uses explicit creational language that associates the creative Word with the light of life (1:4), and, significantly, the text continues as follows: "The light shines in the darkness, and the darkness did not overcome it" (v. 5). Then in vv. 6–7, the incarnate Word, Jesus Christ, is declared to be the "true light, which enlightens everyone" (v. 9), which is famously reinforced twice in the Gospels: first during the Transfiguration, where divine light shines from Jesus' face and clothes (Matt 17:2), and then in John 8:12, where Jesus affirms that "I am the light of the world. Whoever follows me will never walk in darkness but will have the light of life" (a statement reiterated in 9:5). The light/darkness contrast is further advanced in several other places in John's Gospel to outline a dualistic cosmos in which light battles with darkness (e.g., 3:19–21; 9:4–5; 11:9–10; 12:35–36),[18] and in Revelation we are given the promise that the completion of new creation will eliminate darkness

---

15. Angel, *Chaos,* 1.

16. Levenson, *Creation,* 123.

17. Waltke, "Creation Account IV," 341.

18. See, e.g., Neyrey, *Gospel of John,* 43.

altogether when New Jerusalem descends from heaven: "and there will be no night there" (Rev 21:25) because "the glory of God is its light, and its lamp is the Lamb" (v. 23). This promise is reiterated two verses later—"And there will be no more night . . . for the Lord God will be their light" (22:5)—and the same message is also expressed in two prophetic visions in the Old Testament, by Zechariah[19] and Isaiah.[20]

Primordial Waters

The treatment of primordial waters shows a similar pattern to that of the gradual containment and elimination of darkness. These waters are also described as having been originally created by God (Ps 148:5) and they, too, form part of the primeval substrate. A portion of them was first separated by the "firm dome" under the sky, and then God gathered—that is, confined to finite places—these separated waters and named them "Seas." After this twofold containment process, the secured waters were pronounced good; however, several OT passages suggest that the relationship between God and the domesticated waters retained a certain amount of underlying tension,[21] because the seas continued to pose a menace that had to be constantly kept at bay to forestall the destruction of the created order.[22]

In the New Testament, Jesus is presented as light in opposition to darkness, and similarly, he is also associated with *living water:* When he met the Samaritan woman at the well, he told her, "The water that I will give will become in them a spring of water gushing up to eternal life" (John 4:14), and later in Jerusalem, on the very same day as he declared that he was the light of the world, Jesus invited people to partake in this water: "Let anyone who is thirsty come to me, and let the one who believes in me drink'" (John 7:37–38). In Revelation we are told that in New Jerusalem there will

19. "And there shall be continuous day (it is known to the LORD), not day and not night, for at evening time there shall be light" (Zech 14:7).

20. "The sun shall no longer be your light by day, nor for brightness shall the moon give light to you by night; but the LORD will be your everlasting light, and your God will be your glory. Your sun shall no more go down, or your moon withdraw itself; for the LORD will be your everlasting light, and your days of mourning shall be ended" (Isa 60:19–20).

21. E.g., Ps 77:17: "when the waters saw you, they were afraid; the very deep trembled."

22. E.g., in Jer 5:22 the sea is said to produce waves that test its boundaries, and in several passages God is described as exercising control over it (e.g., "You rule over the surging sea; when its waves mount up, you still them" Ps 89:9) or rebuking it (e.g., "At your rebuke they [the waters] flee; at the sound of your thunder they take to flight" Ps 104:7); see also Levenson, *Creation*, 15.

be a "river of the water of life, bright as crystal, flowing from the throne of God and of the Lamb" (Rev 22:1), a vision also confirmed by Zechariah's prophecy (that occurs immediately after the promise that "at evening time there shall be light" 14:7): "On that day living waters shall flow out from Jerusalem" (14:8). Finally, similar to the cessation of darkness, it is declared in Revelation that ultimately "the sea was no more" (21:1).

Representing a Jewish perspective and thus drawing only on the testimony of the Hebrew Bible, Levenson concludes that "God has not annihilated the primordial chaos. He has only limited it."[23] However, in Isaiah and Zechariah's prophesies (cited earlier) there is the suggestion of more than mere controlling the dark side of primeval matter, and later, as we saw above, the New Testament not only affirms the containment process but concludes with the anticipation of the full abolition of both darkness and primordial waters from the new created order. Accordingly, Mark Stephens rightly states about the riddance of the sea: "Its vanishing connotes the final elimination from the earth of all evil powers, symbolically indicating the inauguration of an entirely new quality of existence, in which creation is made eternally secure. It is therefore deliberately coordinated (through verbal linkages) with the removal of death, mourning, crying and pain."[24]

Chaoskampf

The previous two sections have pointed to the existence of some conflict between the primordial elements and God's purpose for the world, and in some verses of Scripture we find this conflict being described as a full-scale confrontation in which God actively reins in certain hostile forces. The language of these passages is often military, evoking a sense of a battle, which explains why this biblical theme has been labelled *Chaoskampf*. As Andrew Angel summarizes,[25] the hostile forces are variously referred to either by some water-related name (e.g., sea,[26] river,[27] waters,[28] and various combinations of these[29]) or as serpent-related monsters (e.g., serpent,[30] dragon,[31]

23. Levenson, *Creation*, 123.

24. Stephens, *Annihilation or Renewal*, 236–37.

25. Angel, *Chaos*, 1.

26. E.g., Nah 1:4; Hab 3:15

27. E.g., Ps 93:3; Hab 3:8

28. E.g., Isa 17:12–13; Hab 3:15

29. E.g., Isa 8:7; Exod 15:8, 10; Prov 8:29

30. E.g., Job 26:13; Isa 27:1

31. E.g., Ps 74:13; Isa 27:1, 51:9

Leviathan,[32] and Rahab[33]). They all share in common the fact that they are described as agents whom God physically conquers, and while it is true that nowhere in the Bible are they portrayed as an ultimate threat to God, Levenson correctly questions that if they never pose a *serious* challenge to God's purpose, then "why the ecstatic jubilation at the thought of his vanquishing them? Indeed, why must they be vanquished at all?"[34]

The following extract from Psalm 74 provides a good illustration not only of the use of divine force in containing various antagonistic agents but also how closely the *Chaoskampf* motif is related to creation.[35]

> Yet God my King is from of old,
> > working salvation in the earth.
> You divided [or "broke"[36]] the sea by your might;
> > you broke the heads of the dragons in the waters.
> You crushed the heads of Leviathan;
> > you gave him as food for the creatures of the wilderness.
> You cut openings for springs and torrents;
> > you dried up ever-flowing streams.
> Yours is the day, yours also the night;
> > you established the luminaries and the sun.
> You have fixed all the bounds of the earth;
> > you made summer and winter. (Ps 74:12–17)

The biblical references to the *Chaoskampf* motif are admittedly infrequent—indeed, are altogether absent in the Pentateuch—and are often hardly more than fragments that appear in poetic or hymnic passages.[37] Yet they constitute a discernible scriptural thread that has attracted considerable attention in biblical scholarship after various archaeological discoveries in the Near East between the mid-nineteenth and mid-twentieth centuries found written records of ancient non-Jewish—most notably Babylonian and Ugaritic[38]—mythologies that displayed close parallels with these scattered biblical references, both in terms of imagery and philology.[39] Since

32. E.g., Job 3:8; Ps 74:14; Isa 27:1

33. E.g., Job 26:12; Isa 51:9; Ps 89:10

34. Levenson, *Creation*, xxi–xxii.

35. As Levenson sums up, Ps 74:12–17 is "the *locus classicus* of the idea that the God of Israel not only defeated the Sea and its monsters, but also dismembered Leviathan altogether and then created the familiar world" (*Creation*, 18).

36. Goldingay, *Old Testament Theology*, 66.

37. Levenson, *Creation*, 8; Waltke, "Creation Account I," 35.

38. But other mythologies also display similar themes; see Goldingay, *Old Testament Theology*, 43.

39. For a summary, see Angel, *Chaos*, 3–6.

then—perhaps understandably—much of the *Chaoskampf* research has focused on identifying the extent of the biblical versus non-biblical commonalities, speculating about the nature of and the reason for these links. However, from the canonical narrative perspective of this book such historical parallels are not necessarily helpful, particularly because they suggest militant polytheist cosmogonies that portray the creator as something equivalent to the "last god standing," which is alien to the Scriptures taken as a whole. For example, the Babylonian myth Enuma Elish describes a war between two factions of gods, where the champion of one side, Marduk, creates the world out of the monster-like body of the sea-goddess, Tiamat, whom he has slain in a fierce battle. Interestingly, the divine sea also plays an important role in the Ugaritic Baal Cycle: A key component of the myth is Baal's fight with Yamm, the god of the sea, and perhaps the best illustration of the parallel between the Ugaritic and biblical texts is the fact that the Hebrew word for sea is *yam*.

The Bible presents a perspective that is very different from the main thrust of ancient Near Eastern mythologies: If the biblical passages related to *Chaoskampf*—including those which contain imagery that is similar to that found in ancient pagan sources—are read canonically, it is evident that God is not contending with other gods or rivals of any sort but rather with elements and creatures of the world that he himself has created. It is significant in this respect that the only specific animals mentioned in the creation accounts of Genesis 1–2 are the "great sea monsters" (*tannîyn*), which are closely related to the other aquatic beasts, Leviathan and Rahab,[40] and in Gen 1:21 God calls this group of animals that includes sea monsters "good."[41] Also, as we shall see in chapter 5 discussing the Book of Job, while God describes the Leviathan as an undaunted, untamed, and irresistible force in the wild, this portrayal does not suggest any kind of enmity between God and this beast but rather a hint of affectionate appreciation.[42]

These considerations suggest that contrary to what other contemporary Middle Eastern sources imply, the *Chaoskampf* material in the Bible is better understood to refer to the internal/inherent resistance of some

---

40. E.g., *tannîyn* are juxtaposed with Leviathan in Isaiah 27:1 and with Rahab in Isaiah 51:9; for a detailed intertextual analysis, see Giere, *New Glimpse of Day One*, 63–64.

41. Waltke, "Creation Account IV," 333.

42. Angel also draws attention to the puzzling co-existence of passages in which the personifications of chaos are the enemies of Yahweh (e.g., Ps 74:12–17; Isa 27:1; 51:9–11) and ones where they are under his control or even in his service (e.g., Ps 104:26; Isa 8:7; 51:15; Jer 31:35), and indeed, even the Flood involved the utilization or primordial waters to execute God's purpose. Angel, *Chaos*, 17.

aspects of the created world to aligning with God's purposes, rather than to some cosmic conflict associated with creation in general, as is sometimes stated.[43] The primordial elements and forces are at times described as being subjugated and at other times domesticated or captivated by their Maker, with the most prominent example of this offered by the second divine speech in the Book of Job, which devotes the whole of chapter 41 to describing Leviathan (see chapter 5). Having said that, one may still ask that in the absence of a potent enemy, what explains the significance attached to containing or overcoming the various primordial elements in several verses of Scripture? After all, Levenson rightly states that "it is no great accomplishment to have triumphed over a non-entity or proven superior to one's own handiwork";[44] furthermore, he goes on, the act of creating and maintaining boundaries also becomes "unimportant, in fact silly" if "on the far side of the boundary there lies either nothing or something just as good as that which lies on this side."[45] Indeed, in Psalm 74, for example, the Psalmist reminds God of how he used to "bring salvation on the earth" (v. 12; NIV) exactly through the various acts of containing primordial elements discussed above, and if no viable opposition or cosmic victory was involved, what does "salvation" refer to in that case?

It may therefore not be too farfetched to conclude that the making of the material world involved unleashing and then taking control of formidable forces, some inimical to creation, and Levenson is right that downplaying the significance of these antagonistic powers may result in a skewed perception: "the fragility of the created order and its vulnerability to chaos tend to be played down. Or, to put the point differently, the formidability and resilience of the forces counteracting creation are usually not given their due, so that the drama of God's exercise of omnipotence is lost, and a static idea of creation then becomes the cornerstone of an overly optimistic understanding of the theology of the Hebrew Bible."[46]

The current book goes beyond Levenson's reading of the Hebrew Bible in suggesting that the complete Christian canon offers a progressive creational understanding in which, as will be argued in the next chapter, Jesus Christ plays a vital role in bringing about new creation. However, the sheer fact that primal creation needed to be followed by a long process of transformation that will only be concluded in the eschatological future does

43. Examples of the latter view include Boyd, "Evolution as Cosmic Warfare," 135; Goldingay, *Old Testament Theology*, 64–66; Levenson, *Creation*, 106.

44. Levenson, *Creation*, xxv.

45. Ibid., xxv.

46. Ibid., xxix.

underscore Levenson's argument about the potency and resilience of the "forces counteracting creation." Let us now turn to the Genesis account of Adam and Eve to examine how such inimical forces were manifested in relation to the fall of humankind, which constitutes the most common explanation offered in theology for the woeful predicament of the world.

3.2 Human Failing

Positioned immediately after the two creation accounts in Genesis is a narrative that describes how the first human couple disobeyed God's explicit instruction. This action led to their expulsion from the Garden of Eden, and the divine Curse (Gen 3:14–19) that followed explicitly states that the result of Adam and Eve's disobedience would be a different, harder course than originally planned. Christians usually refer to this episode as the Fall, and it is widely seen as the origin of corruption in the world—as Fergusson summarizes, from Origen onwards this has become the standard method in attempting to resolve the problem of evil.[47] Besides the prime position of the Fall in the Genesis narrative, seeing it as the principal reason for the sinful state of the world is supported by two further factors. First, as Pannenberg points out, "Since an original perfection is ascribed to creation, the evil that is present in the world had to come later,"[48] and the Fall has been seen by many as the best candidate for this "late entry." Second, the Christian reading of Genesis 3 has been profoundly shaped by the Apostle Paul's well-known interpretation of the passage in Rom 5:12–21, in which he contrasts Adam and Jesus' respective roles as bringing about condemnation and death versus justification and life. Let us begin the discussion by examining this latter interpretation.

Paul's Interpretation of Genesis 3 in Romans 5

One reason for starting the exploration of Genesis 3 with Paul's interpretation in Romans 5 is that without the latter there would be a danger of missing the essential significance of the former. Although the Fall is presented in a prominent position in the Scriptures—immediately after the creation accounts—and although it contains the very first example recorded in the Bible of a creature going against the Creator's will, the canon then describes such a large number of sinful human acts that Adam and Eve's disobedience

47. Fergusson, *Cosmos and the Creator*, 78.
48. Pannenberg, *Systematic Theology*, vol. 2, 163.

could easily be seen merely as one of many. Such a view would also be justifiable in the light of the surprising disregard of Genesis 3 in the rest of the canon with Adam being hardly referred to beyond Genesis 5:[49] he is virtually not mentioned in the Old Testament[50] and only three times in the New Testament.[51] Accordingly, Westermann, for example, describes the Fall narrative as "an exceedingly marginal text"[52] and Barr concludes, "Clearly, the emphasis on the sin of Eve and Adam as the means by which death came into the world was not considered a universal necessity in New Testament Christianity: whole books were written which took no notice of it."[53] It is against this backdrop that Paul's analysis in Rom 5:12–21 gains special significance, as this passage has played a decisive role in making the Fall a centerpiece of Christian theology.

Although there are well-documented exegetical difficulties concerning the text[54] and scholars do not agree on some crucial details in it (e.g., the extent to which the various terms referring to sin express different or synonymous meaning),[55] there can be no doubt about the central thrust of Paul's message: Adam is juxtaposed with Jesus as two archetypal figures representing two alternatives for humankind, a contrast that Dunn describes

49. See e.g., Barr, *Garden of Eden*, 5–6; Brueggemann, *Genesis*, 41; Childs, *Biblical Theology*, 570; Soulen, *God of Israel*, 142; Westermann, *Genesis*, 276.

50. Adam as a proper name is referred to only in genealogies and possibly in two brief references (Hos 6:7; Job 31:33) that can be translated "like Adam" with regard to breaking the covenant. As Barr points out, even in a statement which specifically mentions ancestral sin such as Isaiah 43:27 ("Your first ancestor sinned"), the reference is not to Adam, but "to Jacob or some other pioneer of the people of Israel" (*The Garden of Eden*, 6).

51. Romans 5; 1 Corinthians 15; 1 Timothy 2.

52. Westermann, *Genesis*, 276.

53. Barr, *Garden of Eden*, 5.

54. E.g., Schreiner concludes, "Romans 5:12–21 is one of the most difficult and controversial passages to interpret in all of Pauline literature" (*Romans*, 267). This is partly caused by the fact that the passage is very short and dense relative to the number of major themes discussed in it (e.g., death, sin, grace, Law, dominions of sin and grace), and partly by the somewhat disjointed grammar; e.g., Paul begins v. 12 with a comparison ("just as . . .") that he does not fully complete but becomes involved in a number of 'asides' before returning to the full comparison in vv. 18–19.

55. Along with several scholars, Dunn offers an elaborate distinction between "sin" (*hamartia*), "overstepping, transgression" (*parabasis*), "false step, transgression" (*paraptōma*), and "disobedience" (*parakoē*), even though he comments that the "fact that Paul continues to use the verb *hamartanō* as equivalent to the noun *parabasis/ paraptōma* in 5.14 and 16 does not help." Dunn, *Paul*, 96. On the other hand, Wright concludes, "There are no doubt fine distinctions between these terms, but there is also broad overlap and flexibility; we may assume that part of Paul's reason for choosing different words, in some cases at least, is to avoid repetition" ("Romans," 524).

as Paul's version of the "epochal choice between death and life laid before Israel in the climax to the Deuteronomic covenant."[56] This primary theme is also confirmed by linguistic considerations, because the backbone of the discourse structure of Rom 5:12–21 is the contrast between the power of Christ's act of obedience and Adam's act of disobedience: It emerges as many as five times in "just as/so also" and "not as/so is" comparisons,[57] and in vv. 15–19 the outcomes of Adam and Jesus' action are reiterated five times each[58]—it is thus clear that Paul was at pains to get through the message about the Adam/Christ contrast by applying parallel structures and repetitions. The two human archetypes are particularly relevant from a creational perspective because they can be seen to define two developmental trajectories; as Arland Hultgren summarizes, "Each of these two persons is head of a humanity, either that of the old aeon (leading to sin and death) or of the new (leading to righteousness and life)."[59] The trajectory leading to sin and death can be perceived as one that *deviates from* God's creative purpose, whereas the one leading to righteousness and life resets the direction of creation onto a gradually *converging* course. As will be argued in chapter 4, this latter trajectory coincides with biblical references to an ongoing "new creation" starting with Jesus' incarnation and earthly ministry.[60]

The fully developed Adam/Jesus comparison in Rom 5:12–21 is in stark contrast to the vagueness of the same passage with regard to *how* sin and death entered the world. Beyond making it clear that "Adam gave sin its foothold within the human race"[61] (Ziesler), there is no explanation of how Adam's disobedience created this universal foothold.[62] In fact, Dunn

56. Dunn, *Paul*, 94.

57. Vv. 12, 18, 19, 21 and vv. 15–17, respectively; see Moo, *Romans*, 315.

58. As a result of Adam's disobedience, "many died" (v. 15); his sin "brought condemnation" (v. 16); "death exercised dominion" (v. 17); sin "led to condemnation" (v. 18); and "many were made sinners" (v. 19). In contrast, as a result of the work of Christ more "have the grace of God" (v. 15), which "brings justification" (v. 16) so that believers can "exercise dominion in life" (v. 17); Jesus' righteousness "leads to justification and life for all" (v. 18); and through Christ's obedience "the many will be made righteous" (v. 19); see Schreiner, *Romans*, 268.

59. Hultgren, *Romans*, 221. In a similar vein, Dunn also submits that "Adam is the pattern, or 'prototype' of Christ in that each begins an epoch and the character of each epoch is established by their action" (*Romans 1–8*, 277).

60. In this respect John Ziesler states, "Paul's vision of Christ is not just of someone who can release men and women from guilt and give them a new and fruitful relationship to God. More than that, he sees Christ as inaugurating a new way of being human (his being the new Adam must mean at least that)" (*Romans*, 144–45).

61. Ziesler, *Romans*, 145.

62. There is reasonable consensus about this view; see e.g., Barrett, *Romans*, 105; Dunn, *Romans*, 272; Jewett, *Romans*, 374; Moo, *Romans*, 322–23.

points out that Paul is *unlike* most of his contemporaries in that he does *not* speculate about the way in which sin entered the world,[63] and Cranfield is likely to be right when he states that Paul's "restraint and sobriety of his own references to Adam" are related to the fact that his attention is firmly centered on Christ, with Adam only mentioned "to bring out more clearly the nature of the work of Christ."[64] Paul's consistency in avoiding any ontological discussion of this topic is also manifest in the absence of any explanations—or even clues—about the nature of the link between sin and death beyond affirming that a causal nexus exists. Thus, the curious fact is that although Rom 5:12–21 is the key biblical passage associated with the doctrine of original sin[65] (see further below), Jewett has a point in concluding that Paul's primary goal was "not to set forth a doctrine of Adam's sin but to demonstrate the scope of the overflowing dominion of grace."[66]

What Paul does say about the interlinked notions of sin and death is twofold: (a) they entered the world through Adam's action and were therefore not part of the original created order; and (b) after their entry they spread through creation, affecting all the descendants of Adam, thereby becoming universal. Paul thus unambiguously marks the Fall as the initiation point of a dramatic shift in creation with far-reaching consequences, although at the same time he leaves unspecified the nature of this shift and how one man's disobedience has impacted "the many" (i.e., all the successive generations).[67] With these considerations in mind, let us return to the Genesis narrative to examine the textual suggestions of how Adam's act diverted the trajectory of creation from its divinely set course and how the universal inevitability or necessity of sin and death started to spread irresistibly among humankind.

---

63. Dunn, *Romans*, 272; for a similar point, see Jewett, *Romans*, 374.

64. Cranfield, *Romans*, vol. 1, 281.

65. See e.g., Mann, "Augustine on Evil and Original Sin."

66. Jewett, *Romans*, 370.

67. Dunn summarizes this issue as follows: "However much Paul wants to stress the universality of the effects of Adam's sin (vv 13–14, 18–19), the fact remains that he begins with (v 12) and maintains throughout (vv 15–19) a distinction between 'one' and 'all'/'the many'. The link between the 'one' and the 'all' is not explained, but the distinction is clear: The 'one' is not the 'all,' and the 'all' are not simply subsumed within the 'one.' What comes to expression is rather . . . the tension between the inescapableness of human sin operating as a compelling power from within or without." Dunn, *Romans*, 273. For a similar conclusion, see Wright, *Romans*, 527.

Disobedience and Expulsion

The story of the "Fall," recounting how a talking serpent successfully enticed the first human couple to disobey God's explicit instruction, is well known and, as discussed above, the consequences of this sin of Adam and Eve set creation on a new, deviant course. Indeed, this episode has taken a central place in the Christian understanding of salvation history, because it allowed for the reconciliation of the goodness of God and the perfection of all his work with the imperfect state of the world. In theology, relevant discussions often take place under the rubric of "original sin," which refers to a set of proposals linking the source of all human imperfection to the Fall, most closely associated with—but not limited to—the influential work of Augustine of Hippo.[68] Although there have been ongoing debates about the validity and usefulness of the concept, Fergusson is right to emphasize that "We should not underestimate the significance of this doctrine and its hold over Christian imagination, at least in the Latin West,"[69] because by laying the blame "at the door of Adam and in him all humanity" it offers a straightforward explanation for the degradation of the created order: "The moral disorder of the human species was a consequence of Adam's fall from grace."[70] This message, which is part of the core beliefs of most Western Christian denominations,[71] was clearly expressed, for example, in the following passage of Augustine's major work, *The City of God*:

> For God, the author of natures, not of vices, created man upright; but man, being of his own will corrupted, and justly condemned, begot corrupted and condemned children. For we all were in that one man, since we all were that one man, who fell into sin by the woman who was made from him before the sin. . . . And thus, from the bad use of free will, there originated the whole train of evil, which, with its concatenation of miseries, conveys the human race from its depraved origin, as from a corrupt root, on to the destruction of the second death, which has no end, those only being excepted who are freed by the grace of God.[72]

68. See, e.g., Mann, "Augustine on Evil and Original Sin"; Nelson, *Sin*.

69. Fergusson, *Cosmos and the Creator*, 77.

70. Ibid., 77–78.

71. E.g., §390 of the *Catechism of the Catholic Church* states, "Revelation gives us the certainty of faith that the whole of human history is marked by the original fault freely committed by our first parents."

72. Augustine. *City of God* 13.14

The doctrine of an initial, catastrophic Fall does indeed offer a possible account of the roots of humanity's undeniable propensity to sin, and the perception of sin as a congenital feature of the human species receives some confirmation in a verse in the Psalms—in King David's famous outcry of repentance in Psalm 51: "Indeed, I was born guilty, a sinner when my mother conceived me" (v. 5)—where the suggestion is that sin is not something that we acquire over time but rather the product of an inherited fallen state that humans are born into. Perhaps the strongest support for the doctrine of original sin is the universal perception of this "fallen state," which Blocher sums up clearly in his observation: "That a bent toward sinning does affect all humankind, and that it cannot be isolated as belonging to any one part of the person, has been agreed on all sides, or nearly so, in the twentieth century."[73] In fact, he continues, "It would be hard to close one's eyes to the data of experience."[74] Moo concurs that the doctrine "appears to explain the data of history and experience as well as, or better than, any rival theory."[75]

On the other hand, John Hick among others rightly points out that the "Augustinian picture is so familiar that it is commonly thought of as the Christian view of man and his sinful plight. Nevertheless it is only *a* Christian view"[76] (emphasis in the original). Indeed, while some tenets of original sin are present in Rom 5:12–21 (as discussed above), the doctrine is not stated explicitly anywhere in the canon or the Creeds, and it also raises certain issues. First, it does not address the question of how the created order could *allow* things to go so wrong that God needed to wipe out humanity by means of the Flood. Second, there is no clear-cut uniform understanding about *how* Adam and Eve's one-off disobedience could result in the universal corruption of humankind, turning all the descendants of the first couple into sinners. Third, when we try to map the doctrine of the Fall onto the actual biblical narrative of the Fall, we do not find an exact match: The Genesis account contains several important elements that the doctrine does not address, most notably the creational role of the Garden of Eden, Adam's task "to till it and keep it" (Gen 2:15), and the specific implications of humankind's expulsion from Eden. Accordingly, the rest of this chapter will offer a re-reading of the Genesis narrative within the framework of progressive creation that attempts to harmonize the details of the text with relevant doctrinal considerations as well as with aspects of the understanding of the dark side of the matter discussed earlier.

73. Blocher, *Original Sin*, 19–20.

74. Ibid., 20.

75. Moo, *Romans*, 329.

76. Hick, *Evil and the God of Love*, 201–2.

3.3 Expulsion from Eden: Causes and Consequences

It was stated in chapter 1 that complex compositions offer multiple layers of meaning depending on the particular approach and emphasis of the interpreter, and this could not be more true in the case of such a fundamental issue as the Fall. The current re-narration of the events will first consider a number of key factors foregrounded by the Genesis narrative that contributed either directly or indirectly to Adam and Eve's expulsion from Eden, and then examine the creational consequences of the Fall. Let us begin the discussion by looking at the actual stage of the drama, the Garden itself.

The Garden of Eden

The Garden of Eden is described in Genesis as God's enclosed arboreal sanctuary separated from the rest of creation[77] that hosted "every tree that is pleasant to the sight" (Gen 2:9). It is usually considered merely as the idyllic setting for the initially unspoiled, paradisiacal phase of human existence, but the actual text suggests that it was more than a pleasant botanical garden: On the one hand, we are told that God spent time "walking in the Garden" (Gen 3:8), and indeed, elsewhere in the Bible it is referred to as "the garden of the LORD" (Isa 51:3) and "the garden of God" (Ezek 28:13); on the other hand, the Garden also represented the heart of life on earth, as in the middle of it stood the "tree of life" (Gen 2:9), and the Genesis account offers an unusually detailed description of how the water source of the Garden, a river flowing from Eden, divided and formed four branches when leaving the enclave, thus fertilizing the outside region.[78] The prominence of this passage (vv. 10–14; it is over three times as long as, for example, the description of the creation of Adam in v. 7) highlights the nurturing and life-giving significance of the enclave, and the overall description of the rivers forms a strong link with two powerful visions of rivers of vitality flowing out of holy ground described later in the Bible. In the first, Ezekiel saw a welling river flowing from the Temple (Ezek 47:1–12) and he was told by an angel guid-

---

77. The Hebrew word for "garden" (*gan*) comes from the Hebrew root meaning "to be enclosed, fenced off, protected," and therefore Waltke explains that "garden" probably denotes an "enclosed, protected area where the flora flourishes" (*Genesis*, 85).

78. Although it is outside the canonical reading of the text, it is of note that the immediate region fertilized by the rivers coincides with the geographical area that would be known as the "cradle of civilization" in human history: While the subsequent Flood will have altered the initial topography of the landscape, as Hamilton summarizes, geographical and other considerations point to the conclusion that Genesis 1–11 is set against the background of Mesopotamia. Hamilton, *Genesis*, 202.

ing him that "everything will live where the river goes" (v. 9). Interestingly, there were "all kinds of trees" alongside this river with unique qualities: "On the banks, on both sides of the river, there will grow all kinds of trees for food. Their leaves will not wither nor their fruit fail, but they will bear fresh fruit every month, because the water for them flows from the sanctuary. Their fruit will be for food, and their leaves for healing" (v. 12).

The second vision concerns the "river of the water of life" flowing from the throne of God in the heart of New Jerusalem (Rev 22:1–2), with the tree of life on its banks: "On either side of the river is the tree of life with its twelve kinds of fruit, producing its fruit each month; and the leaves of the tree are for the healing of the nations" (v. 2). The three scenes are undoubtedly related,[79] suggesting that the Garden of Eden had a prominent spiritual dimension, which in turn explains why Waltke, among others, refers to it as a "temple."[80] Thus, the central locus for creation-related action in Genesis 2, the Garden of Eden, represented a sanctuary with concentrated life-giving potential that can be thought of as God's laboratory producing the "yeast" or "divine leaven" that was to gradually permeate the whole earth by means of the outflowing rivers of life. This impregnating function of the Garden is consistent with the main thrust of material creation described in the previous chapter, namely with the gradual alignment of initially inert matter with the principles of divine created order.

Having called the Garden of Eden a "temple," Waltke also adds that "its priest is the man with the woman to help him."[81] We shall consider below whether this in an appropriate label for the stewards of the Garden, but Waltke is certainly right in establishing a strong link between the Garden and the first humans: After God created Adam, he immediately placed him in the Garden to look after it, and as we shall see below, it was partly Adam's need of support in this job that led to the creation of Eve. Indeed, in the Genesis 2 account, the Garden of Eden and its stewards play an interwoven part in the process of creation, which is well illustrated by the fact that Adam and Eve's expulsion from Eden not only profoundly shaped the future of humankind but also had an impact on the Garden

79. Significantly, there is also a fourth important mention of a water of life in the Bible, in Jesus' dialogue with the Samaritan woman, when Jesus said, "whoever drinks the water I give them will never thirst. Indeed, the water I give them will become in them a spring of water welling up to eternal life" (John 4:14, NIV); this is repeated in Revelation when Jesus declares, "I am the Alpha and the Omega, the beginning and the end. To the thirsty I will give water as a gift from the spring of the water of life" (Rev 21:6).

80. Waltke, *Genesis*, 81.

81. Ibid.

itself: After the loss of its stewards, it completely disappeared from the biblical records of human history, which can be understood—within the current reading—as a sign of its bondedness to humans. Eden only reappears—as seen in the Revelation quotation above—in a transformed but recognizable form as part of new creation.

The Stewards of the Garden

Genesis 2:5 describes the early, primeval state of the earth and explains the inhospitability of the environment by the fact that "the LORD God had not caused it to rain upon the earth, and *there was no one to till the ground*" (emphasis added). The importance of this verse from the current perspective is that it creates a direct link between the desolate state of the world and the absence of a human being to cultivate it. The significance of this is reinforced by the subsequent creation of Adam (v. 7), whom God promptly placed in the Garden of Eden (v. 8) for a specific purpose: "to till it and keep it" (v. 15). The two Hebrew verbs describing Adam's commission literally mean "to serve" and "to exercise great care over" to the point of guarding it,[82] and the same pair of words is used in Num 3:7 and 3:8 to describe the duties of the Levites in tending and looking after the tabernacle. Thus, tilling and keeping the Garden was not so much an agricultural duty as a spiritual function, and Bill Arnold rightly concludes from this that God put Adam in the Garden for a distinct purpose, "as the representative of Yahweh God to cultivate the earth and as the one responsible for keeping or protecting it."[83] This reading is consistent with the understating of *imago Dei* as referring to God's appointment of humankind to act as representatives in his name and functional likeness, and it is also in line with God's mandate to humanity in Gen 1:28 to fill the earth, subdue it, and to rule over the whole of creation. Walter Moberly makes this analogy explicit when he states: "Yahweh's setting the human in the garden with responsibility over it (2:15) is conceptually similar to God's gift of dominion over creation to humanity in the overture account of creation (1:26–28); the human is given the dignity of responsibility under God."[84]

It may be concluded therefore that humankind was created to be not only an important but an *indispensable* agent in the progress of material creation, and the assertion at the beginning of the second creation account that without the service of human agency the inert matter could not

---

82. See e.g., Hamilton, *Genesis*, 171.

83. B. T. Arnold, *Genesis*, 59.

84. Moberly, *Genesis*, 78.

be domesticated is further strengthened by the fact that even the Lord's garden, the Garden of Eden, *required* the attention of human stewards. This points to the interdependence of human and nonhuman creation, a connection reinforced in several places in the canon where the deviant moral state of humans is linked directly to the pollution of the land (e.g., Isa 24:5–6; Lev 18:24–28). We shall return to this issue below in the discussion of the Curse as a consequence of the Fall—since God declares, "cursed is the ground because of you" (Gen 3:17)—but it is important to reiterate that even *before* the Fall, the created order needed humans to steward it, that is, to keep and protect it.

The Bible does not specify what aspects of the land needed to be thus contained—or, using the language of Gen 1:28, to "subdued"—but the fact that this issue was relevant even *before* sin had entered the world at the Fall suggests a link with the dark side of primordial matter discussed at the beginning of this chapter; in Boyd's words, "The term ["subdue"] . . . may suggest that, even prior to the human 'fall' there was something in creation that needed to be conquered."[85] As was shown earlier, several biblical passages highlight aspects of the primeval substrate that were antagonistic to the divine creative order, an inherent resistance of the "sinister system of elements"[86] that had to be gradually overcome. The charges to "subdue" the earth and to "till" and "keep" the Garden of Eden are consistent with the need to contain and subjugate this inimical aspect of material creation.

"It is not good that the man should be alone . . ."

In Gen 2:18, the creation account takes a dramatic turn when after repeated positive appraisals of the various stages of the creation process God declares: "It is not good that the man should be alone; I will make him a helper as his partner." In Genesis 1, the recurring "it is good" evaluations invariably referred to fundamental aspects of the creation process and served as the validation of the overall soundness of the created order; therefore, when God declares the opposite in relation to the pinnacle of creation, the first human being, it is to be understood as a very strong statement signifying a substantial issue. As Wenham submits, "Against the sevenfold refrain of 'and God saw that it was (very) good' in chap. 1, the divine observation that something was not right with man's situation is startling,"[87] and Blocher concurs: "The remark amazes us. It is the only negative assessment in the

85. Boyd, "Evolution as Cosmic Warfare," 142.
86. Barth, *CD* III/1, 289.
87. Wenham, *Genesis*, 68.

creation narrative, and it is emphatically negative."[88] What Gen 2:18 states, in effect, is that at one point during the process of the creation of the universe, God declared that a crucial component was "not good" and, as we shall see below, the first attempt to rectify the problem through searching for suitable support for Adam among the animals did not achieve its purpose. This episode therefore constitutes the first documented case in the Bible when the divine creational process had run into a problem.

We are not given any details about the exact nature of the issue highlighted in Gen 2:18 beyond the fact that for some reason Adam alone was insufficient and was in need of "a helper as his partner." The Hebrew word for "helper" ('ēzer) occurs in the Bible 21 times and, remarkably, every occurrence is associated with the Lord in some way;[89] therefore, the semantic domain of the word involves more than a mere helper/partner/companion/ aid—Alter translates it "sustainer" because, as he states, "'Help' is too weak because it suggests a merely auxiliary function."[90] This deeper, sustaining type of "help" is also emphasized by the fact that the word is used within a compound prepositional phase ('ēzer keneḡeḏ hû')—which only occurs here and in Gen 2:20—whose literal meaning is "in front of/opposite/alongside him," and thus the phrase refers to a "corresponding, complementary helper/sustainer", who is a "counterpart."[91]

Commentators invariably connect the meaning of the phrase 'ēzer keneḡeḏ hû' with the fact that in the end a woman was made to be the helper, whereas this is surprising, because—as we shall see below—Eve was not God's first choice for the role and the Hebrew noun for "helper" in Gen 2:18 is masculine. Nevertheless, scholars usually seek to understand the reason for why it is not good for Adam to be alone in his psychological needs, imagining the "existential loneliness of the first man"[92] (Reno) and typically arguing along the line that "Solitude 'is not good'; man is created for sociability"[93] (von Rad). Although this may well be true, the biblical text

88. Blocher, In the Beginning, 96.

89. In thirteen occasions it refers to God himself, in seven occasions it occurs in a verse that delivers a direct message from God and in one occasion it is used by a messenger of God (to Daniel).

90. Alter, Genesis, 9.

91. See e.g., B. T. Arnold, Genesis, 60; Hamilton, Genesis, 175; Speiser, Genesis, 17; Wenham, Genesis, 68.

92. Reno, Genesis, 72.

93. So von Rad, Genesis, 82; see also Blocher, In the Beginning, 96; Wenham, Genesis, 68. De la Torre expresses the solitude argument fully: "God noticed that man was alone, and it was not good. In the idyllic garden of perfection; God was not enough. Man needed more than just a relationship with his Creator; man needed a partner, someone with whom there could be intimacy. Humans are social creatures. From the

does not offer any indications to this effect. In fact, given that the Genesis narrative suggests that in the Garden of Eden Adam had fellowship with God himself, it is difficult to see how this relationship could have left Adam psychologically unfulfilled. Furthermore, a rarely discussed aspect of the text also implies that Adam's needs involved something more than filling a gap in his personal life with a female companion: After Gen 2:18, the narrative goes on to state that God's first attempt to offer a solution involved the animal world, that is, other living creatures that he had already formed from out of the ground (v. 19). However, after Adam duly examined and named each of the species, "for the man there was not found a *helper as his partner*" (v. 20; emphasis added; the same prepositional phrase used here as in Gen 2:18). That is, God's initial response to the realization that Adam could not find sufficiency alone did *not* involve the making of the woman to keep him company. Instead, the phrase "helper as his partner" (vv. 18, 20) implies that Adam's problem was functional and was related to a need for support in order to be able to accomplish something.

But what is the "something" that needed to be accomplished? Up to this point in the Genesis narrative, only one task has been mentioned with regard to Adam, the commission to attend to the Garden, "to till it and keep it." The fundamental creational significance of this stewardship task (discussed earlier) would fully explain the dramatic statement of "It is not good . . ." if the outcome was in danger: If the steward faltered in this pivotal role, any setback in this area could potentially bring the ongoing process of creation to a halt. This suggestion gains further traction if we consider the possibility that Adam's insufficiency was related to the broader process of domesticating the world: As some commentators have proposed,[94] Adam's task may not have been limited to attending to the Garden but ultimately also to *extending* it beyond its original boundaries. John Walton for example explains, "It is necessary, however, to move beyond the 'serving and preserving' role. If people were going to fill the earth, we must conclude that they were not intended to stay in the garden in a static situation. Yet moving out of the garden would appear a hardship since the land outside the garden was not as hospitable as that inside the garden (otherwise the garden would not be distinguishable). Perhaps, then, we should surmise that people were gradually supposed to extend the garden as they went about subduing and ruling."[95]

---

beginning, humans, as relational beings, are meant to be in community, to exist with and for others" (*Genesis*, 50–51).

94. E.g., Walton, *Genesis*, 186; Heiser, *Unseen Realm*, 51.

95. Walton, *Genesis*, 186.

Thus, given the prominence attached to the life-giving role of the enclave in relation to the four rivers flowing from it, it might well be the case that Adam alone proved insufficient to extend the Garden beyond its boundaries, and the special nature of God's response to this issue corresponds to the gravity of the issue. Until that point in the narrative every living creature had been fashioned from the fertile soil (including Adam, who also received the "breath of life"), but the text now presents the Creator turning to a novel method of creation and performing what could easily be redescribed in the language of a medical operation as follows: He first gave Adam a general anesthetic and then removed one of his ribs so that it could be used to form Eve through organism/reproductive cloning.[96] It is curious how much detail is offered in the Genesis account about this particular procedure relative to other mechanisms of creation, where Scripture is largely silent about the specific method[97]—it is as if the account wanted to emphasize the unique nature of the creative process involved here. As we know, this intervention did indeed achieve a perfect match for Adam, as evidenced by Adam's exclamation, "This at last is bone of my bones and flesh of my flesh" (Gen 2:23), and it also offered a permanent solution to the lack of helpers, because it enabled husband and wife to "cling" to each other and "become one flesh" (v. 24), thereby producing a succession of stewards who could successfully populate the earth.

The Stewards' Moral and Social Vulnerability

Both creation accounts in Genesis (Genesis 1 and 2) conclude at the same point, with God launching humankind as a species, blessing them and—as we know from Genesis 1—declaring the created ecosystem to be "very good." This positive portrayal, however, is in stark contrast with the immediate follow-up to these accounts in Genesis 3, in which Adam and Eve are enticed by a talking serpent to disobey God, thereby forcing the Creator to intervene in the course of creation and orchestrate their expulsion from Eden. The obvious question is how the initial "very good" created order could prove to be so fragile as to allow a seemingly insubstantial challenge (*Did God really say so? Come on, surely not . . .*) to produce such dramatic

---

96. While at first reading this procedure may sound peculiar, extracting a small part of an organism and growing it into another one is not at all alien to contemporary bioscience, for example when utilizing the capability of embryonic stem cells to differentiate into multiple cell lineages.

97. E.g., the creation of the woman is described in roughly twice as many words as the making of the man.

results? Or, to put it in another way, how could it happen that two creatures who were formed by God's own hands and who were in regular conversation with God were so easily misguided by another, lesser creature to go against the will of their Maker? It will be suggested below that the serpent's "seemingly insubstantial" challenge can in fact be read as part of a sophisticated, skillfully timed and executed scheme that capitalized on Adam and Eve's moral and social vulnerability.

Moral Vulnerability

The concluding verse of the second creation account—"the man and his wife were both naked, and were not ashamed" (Gen 2:25)—is a unique description of Adam and Eve, as it is the only scriptural reference to the first couple's existence *before* the Fall.[98] In the absence of other relevant details, the unashamed nakedness of Adam and Eve has been interpreted in two different ways. One common view has taken it as an expression of an unspoiled, pristine condition[99] and marital bliss[100] that reflect creation's ultimate perfection, an understanding which has given rise to the image of the "Paradise" that was then lost at the Fall.[101] However, following Irenaeus's interpretation already mentioned briefly at the end of the previous chapter, Adam and Eve's innocence can also be understood as mirroring their "childlike mind"[102] on the analogy of little children who tend to be oblivious—or at least not fully conscious—of sexual and moral constraints at the early stages of their development. Indeed, developing an awareness of nakedness and the personal/social inhibitions attached to it is a significant aspect of

98. Perhaps because this verse is wedged in between two high-profile passages, the statement about husband and wife becoming one flesh (Gen 2:24) and the description of the Fall (3:1–7), the significance of its content is often overlooked; for example, it is not commented on at all by Brueggemann, *Genesis;* McKeown, *Genesis;* Reno, *Genesis;* or Speiser, *Genesis;* and several scholars treat it merely as a counterpoint for Gen 3:7, which describes how the humans' eyes were opened and they saw their nakedness, e.g., B. T. Arnold, *Genesis,* 61; von Rad, *Genesis,* 85; Wenham, *Genesis,* 71; Westermann, *Genesis,* 234.

99. E.g., Collins, *Genesis,* 102, 173.

100. E.g., De La Torre, *Genesis,* 84; Ferguson, *Genesis,* 39; Hamilton, *Genesis,* 181; Waltke, *Genesis,* 90.

101. Haught calls this the Church's "nostalgia for a lost original perfection" and a longing "for union with an eternal present untouched by time and history" (*Resting on the Future,* 1). Interestingly, as he critically adds, this "ageless inclination to restore the idyllic past or take flight into eternity, has bridled the spirit of Abrahamic adventure and dampened the sense of a new future for the whole of creation" (ibid.).

102. Irenaeus, *Demonstration of the Apostolic Preaching,* 14.

human maturation in childhood,[103] and although this analogy is of course from the post-Fall world, it is noteworthy that the Genesis narrative links the mindset of not being ashamed of nudity to the fact that Adam and Eve had not yet eaten of the fruit of the tree of the knowledge of good and evil: After the Fall, the first effect of eating of this fruit was an embarrassed realization of their nudity (Gen 3:7, 10). The knowledge of good and evil can be perceived as a sense of moral awareness—or, in Wright's words, "moral autonomy"[104]—and, significantly, acquiring moral awareness is another important developmental process in early childhood, roughly coinciding with the development of sexual awareness.[105]

Because the serpent's deception interrupted Adam and Eve's original way of existence, we cannot know for certain whether their state of naked innocence was intended to last indefinitely—which would be consistent with the "innocence-as-perfection" interpretation—or whether even without the Fall it would have only been a transitional stage in the newly created couple's life. In his theory of an "Irenaean type of theodicy,"[106] John Hick takes the latter view: "There is thus to be found in Irenaeus the outline of an approach to the problem of evil which stands in important respects in contrast to the Augustinian type of theodicy. Instead of the doctrine that man was created finitely perfect and then incomprehensibly destroyed his own perfection and plunged into sin and misery, Irenaeus suggests that man was created as an imperfect, immature creature who was to undergo moral development and growth and finally be brought to the perfection intended for him by his Maker."[107]

The Genesis narrative does indeed offer a reading that is consistent with Irenaeus' interpretation foregrounding the progressive-maturational perspective, particularly with regard to a key component of the story, the *tree of the knowledge of good and evil*. The existence of this tree *before* the making of Adam suggests that some awareness of evil was part of the original created order, and the fact that the knowledge of evil was represented in the form of an accessible tree with attractive, edible fruit does point to a

---

103. We usually do not find any inhibitions of nudity in preschool children; they develop an awareness of nakedness between the ages of 4 and 8 unless they are desensitized to this issue. Furthermore, although gender identity typically forms by the age of 3, preschoolers tend not to be aware of sexual taboos yet. For reviews, see de Graaf and Rademakers, "Childhood Sexual Development," 122; and DeLamater and Friedrich, "Human Sexual Development," 10.

104. Wright, *Romans*, 164.

105. Lapsley and Carlo, "Moral Development," 3–4.

106. Hick, *Evil and the God of Love*, 215.

107. Ibid., 214.

possible interpretation of the narrative that this fruit was not meant to be ignored forever but at a later point human eyes were intended to be opened to the knowledge of good and evil. Several biblical parallels substantiate this assumption: Heb 5:14 states that "solid food is for the mature, for those whose faculties have been *trained* by practice to *distinguish good from evil*" (emphasis added), implying that it requires preparation to become ready to deal with the issues of good and evil, and the maturation of a child and the faculty to respond to good and evil are also linked together in Isa 7:14–16: "Look, the young woman is with child and shall bear a son, and shall name him Immanuel. He shall eat curds and honey by the time he knows how to *refuse the evil and choose the good*. For before the child knows how to *refuse the evil and choose the good*, the land before whose two kings you are in dread will be deserted" (emphasis added).

Accordingly, Moberly points out that the knowledge or discernment of good and evil in the Bible is characteristic of "maturity and adult life, and is lacking in small children (Deut. 1:39; 1 Kgs 3:7, 9)"[108] and then concludes: "On the assumption that this usage is a genuine parallel to that in Gen. 3, it is these references to adult awareness that have provided much of the exegetical basis for the widespread modern reinterpretation of Gen. 3 whereby the story portrays the painful but necessary transition from childish innocence and transparence to adult awareness and experience which is marked by profound ambiguity—a 'fall upwards.'"[109]

In the light of the above considerations, we can see the serpent's approach as an attempt to instigate the Fall to be timed at a stage of the first humans' development when their knowledge of, and thus conscious resistance to, evil was limited, not unlike children who can disobey their parents but without quite knowing yet what is wrong or right. Adam and Eve's moral naivety must have profoundly affected how they perceived the serpent's scheme; after all, this had been their very first encounter with deception, at a time when they did not even know that evil existed. Bonhoeffer characterized this undefined state as follows:

> How can Adam understand the serpent's promise that he shall be like God? At any rate, not as the devilish promise of death and revolt against the Creator. He does not in any way know of the possibility of evil, and cannot understand it except as the possibility of being more devout, of being more obedient than he is in his *imago dei* structure. For Adam *sicut deus* can only be a new possibility within the given possibility of the

---

108. Moberly, "Serpent," 22. For a similar view, see Heiser, *Unseen Realm*, 62–63.

109. Moberly, "Serpent," 22; see also Collins, *Genesis*, 116.

imago dei creature. It can only signify a new, a deeper kind of creaturely being.[110]

The biblical text does not offer any details that would help to ascertain how closely Bonhoeffer's construal coincided with Adam's understanding, but it is noteworthy, as Barr emphasizes, that the narrative of Genesis 3 does *not* include any of the terms usually understood as "sin," "evil," "rebellion," "transgression," or "guilt."[111] It seems therefore that although God clearly conveyed his anger about the act of disobedience and expelled the humans from the Garden as a consequence, the text does not present the event as a moral crisis,[112] which may well be related to Bonhoeffer's suggestion that "Before the Fall there was no conscience."[113] Also, we shall see below that, contrary to common claims, there did not appear to be a dramatic breakdown in the relationship between humans and the Creator after the Fall.[114]

In summary, having had to respond to the serpent's deceptive initiative without any previous knowledge of evil undoubtedly put the first humans in a difficult, morally vulnerable position, particularly so because their moral naivety was augmented by their *social vulnerability*. Let us now consider how this latter weakness was exploited by the serpent.

Social Vulnerability

Most commentators highlight Adam and Eve's *free will* as a key component in explaining how things could go so wrong at the Fall; indeed, the sheer fact that God had given Adam an instruction on what to eat and what not to (2:16) demonstrates that the man had independent volitional control, because, as Blenkinsopp rightly points out, giving a command implies "the capacity to disobey it."[115] However, it is important here to emphasize a point rarely mentioned in commentaries, namely that as long as Adam was the

---

110. Bonhoeffer, *Creation and Temptation*, 71.

111. Barr, *Garden of Eden*, 6.

112. It must be noted that elsewhere in the canon the behavior of Adam and Eve *is* interpreted in sinful terms—e.g., in Rom 5:12–21 (discussed earlier) and 1 Tim 2:13—which is consistent with God's anger about the disobedience and the severity of the punishment of expelling the couple from Eden. Yet, it is noteworthy that at this point in the biblical narrative the notion of sin is not foregrounded. This complex matter is further discussed in the section on "Understanding 'Sin' and 'Death' from a Progressive Creational Perspective" at the end of this chapter.

113. Bonhoeffer, *Creation and Temptation*, 81.

114. See, e.g., Barr, *Garden of Eden*, 11; Goldingay, *Old Testament Theology*, 146.

115. Blenkinsopp, *Creation*, 80.

sole human being on earth he *did indeed exercise* his free will appropriately and *did remain* obedient to God's instruction. This indicates that his capability of sinning did not automatically mean that sin would follow. In the Genesis accounts of creation, complications arise only *after* God's realization that it was not good for Adam to be alone: The serpent was created as part of the animals among which God searched for a potential helper for the man, and it will be shown below that the making of a female companion for Adam—and thus turning God's single representative on earth into a *social being*—played a central part in the events leading to his disobedience as it created an opening for the serpent to make its (successful) move.

If we consider the details of the biblical description of the serpent's act, the relevance of the human social dimension becomes pronounced. To start with, the serpent did not tempt Adam directly,[116] but only through his wife, a point also underlined by God's statement to Adam afterwards, "Because you have listened to the voice of your wife . . ." (Gen 3:17). Why did this indirect approach weaken Adam's resistance? The text offers two relevant points about Adam and Eve's relationship: First, when answering God's initial rebuke, Adam referred to Eve as the "woman whom you gave to be with me" (v. 12), and while this is generally recognized as part of an attempt to shift the blame, one also has the sense that the way Adam distanced himself from his wife reflects the absence of a sufficiently established bond within the couple.[117] That this observation might be valid is supported by the second pertinent point, namely that at the time of the serpent's temptation, Adam had not as yet given the woman a *personal name* ("Eve")—this only happens later in the narrative, in v. 20.[118] The text, in other words, presents

---

116. It is assumed here that Adam was the serpent's main target, because in the Genesis narrative Adam has a central place relative to Eve: He is created first; God addresses him after the couple have eaten of the fruit; within the Curse the part said to him is the longest; within the Curse God states that he will rule over Eve; and finally, God drives him out of Eden: "the Lord God sent him forth from the garden of Eden, to till the ground from which he was taken. He drove out the man . . ." (Gen 3:23–24).

117. The same sense is also conveyed by the first person singular Adam used after the Fall when God asked him where he was: "I heard the sound of you in the garden, and I was afraid, because I was naked; and I hid myself" (Gen 3:10).

118. Genesis describes two instances when Adam names his wife, in 2:23 and 3:20. The first one follows the process of naming the animals, and therefore it can be seen as the initial identification of a new life form; as the text explains, "this one shall be called Woman, for out of Man this one was taken," indicating that the focus here is on an initial, broad categorization. In contrast, in 3:20 we are told that "The man named his wife Eve, because she was the mother of all living," emphasizing that this name concerns the relationship between the man and the woman by highlighting procreation; thus, the second naming involved giving Eve a personal name within her marriage.

the serpent approaching the couple at an early stage of their relationship when strong bonds had not as yet been established.

The serpent's specific strategy made conscious use of social factors: He directed his communication entirely to Eve, who did not appear to discuss the matter with Adam but took a unilateral decision to follow the serpent's leading (to be considered later). Consequently, Adam's first decision in this case was not whether to eat of the fruit or not—as it is often portrayed—but rather whether to *stop Eve from eating of it or not.*[119] Refraining from doing something oneself and not allowing someone else to do it are two different matters, as the latter involves a social aspect involving interpersonal conflict. Such loaded social interaction is never without complications, but here it would have been particularly problematic for Adam because his original instruction from God only concerned himself, and it was only *after* the Fall that God directly addressed the question of authority between the two humans when he declared to Eve that "he [Adam] shall rule over you" (v. 16).

In the absence of established relational norms—especially concerning power relations and authority structures—it is difficult to gauge whether Adam did at that stage have responsibility over his wife's actions, and it is noteworthy that God is not shown to reproach him afterwards for not stopping Eve from eating of the fruit. Adam's lack of action, however, resulted in a situation that is not often considered in analyses of the Fall: When Eve offered him the fruit, she had already eaten of it and thus Adam could see that contrary to God's warning, *she had not died as a result.* The fact that the fruit appeared to be harmless just as the serpent had predicted must have given some weight to the deceiver's second claim that eating the fruit would increase the humans' wisdom, and a combination of this consideration and the moral uncertainties described earlier may well have resulted in a confusing dilemma for Adam: Should he follow Eve's example and receive wisdom the same way she must have already done or should he say no and risk being "left behind" as a potentially lesser person? A phrase God later used in the Curse—"listen to the voice of [your wife]" (Gen 3:17)—is particularly revealing in this respect, as this is an idiom that means not simply to "hear" but rather to "obey" or to "follow the recommendation of" (as in Gen 16:2;

119. This of course assumes that Adam was there when the serpent approached Eve. Given that the Bible treats the couple as companions with no mention of any occasion when they were alone, this is the unmarked assumption, further reinforced by the fact that Gen 3:6 does mention that Adam was *with* Eve. However, even if Adam did not witness the exchange between Eve and the serpent (e.g., he was asleep) and was not aware of Eve's eating of the fruit, it does not change the subsequent sequence substantially, because when Eve offered Adam the fruit, he would have still seen that Eve had not died as a result of eating of it.

Exod 18:24; 2 Kgs 10:6).[120] The suggestion is, therefore, that Eve did not just quietly hand over the fruit to Adam but also applied some degree of persuasion. We can thus see how, by manipulating the social situation, the serpent managed to twist around the originally straightforward message of obedience to God.

To summarize, on this reading the serpent's act of tempting involved the precisely timed outworking of a shrewd scheme, and the decision Adam had to make was not a clear-cut choice between obedience and rebellion. Instead, it involved being put on the spot and having to respond to Eve's initiatives on the basis of a somewhat unformed moral norm system (as his eyes had not yet been opened to the knowledge of good and evil yet) and within the confines of an equally hazy social situation (as the relational norms of their marriage had not been fully established). The serpent's scheme did achieve its purpose in causing Adam and Eve to disobey God and to eat of the fruit, thereby initiating the time of their "coming of age" *prematurely*: Although the opening of their eyes provided the human couple with the very thing—an awareness of good and evil—whose absence was one of the main sources of their initial vulnerability, because their loss of innocence did not happen according to God's timing, not only did it not make them "wiser" in the way they had hoped for, but it also precluded them from continuing with their maturation process in the Garden of Eden in the way God originally intended. Of course, the serpent's success in derailing the progress of creation in this way depended on two fundamental factors not yet discussed: (a) some sort of willingness on the part of Adam and Eve, and (b) some active, antagonistic agency behind the scheme. We shall now turn to considering these vital components.

Human Weaknesses

Along with many others, Moberly highlights the important fact that the serpent never specifically told Eve to transgress, but left her to draw her own conclusions,[121] and we may add about Adam that in spite of all the social and moral confusion detailed above, it was ultimately his own decision to accept the fruit from Eve and eat it. That is, it was within the power of both human beings to say no, and Bonhoeffer is right in emphasizing that "We would be simplifying and completely distorting the biblical narrative if we were simply to involve the devil, who, as God's enemy, caused all this.

120. Wenham, *Genesis*, 82.
121. Moberly, *Genesis*, 86.

This is just what the Bible does not say, for very definite reasons."[122] It does, however, raise the bewildering question of what motivated the creatures to go against the explicit order of their Creator. The identification of motives that distance people from God is closely related to the plight of human-kind and will be a prominent theme in chapter 7, but we must note here that Adam and Eve's case was different in two key respects from that of *all* their descendants: First, they *had not* sinned before they ate of the fruit and therefore their act was not affected in any way by possible corrupting influences of the past; second, Adam and Eve were living in the idyllic en-vironment of the Garden of Eden, in perfect peace, and therefore all their corporeal needs were met and their lives were in complete harmony with God's original plan for them. This being the case, the motivation to disobey God must have been rooted within themselves, that is, within some weak-ness at the core of their creatureliness.

Genesis 3 does not directly address Adam's motives for going against God's will, but the narrative does list three specific reasons why Eve ate of the fruit: "the woman saw that the tree was good for food, and that it was a delight to the eyes, and that the tree was to be desired to make one wise" (v. 6). These three sources of attraction correspond to the desire to satisfy one's *physical* (alimentary), *aesthetic,* and *intellectual needs*, and thus they display a close parallel with a similar list in 1 John 2:16—"the desire of the flesh, the desire of the eyes, the pride in riches"—with the first two desires being common to both lists and the third being similar in that it refers to the lure of augmenting human resources. In Eve's case, particularly this third motive—the wish to be endowed with wisdom—was powerful, because Gen 2:9 stated earlier that *every* tree planted in the Garden was pleasant to the sight and good for food (and thus the tree of the knowledge of good and evil did not stand out in these two respects).[123] So, what was it that made the desire to become wise so irresistible to humans? We may find a clue in the text if we look closely at the serpent's promise: It did not actually include the word "wise" but stated instead, "your eyes will be opened, and you will be like God, knowing good and evil" (v. 5), meaning that it was Eve who interpreted this as "to make one wise" (v. 6). That is, Eve equated "wisdom" with the striving for increased personal potential, coupled with the ability to make decisions for herself, which is a mixture that has often been associated with the notion of "pride" in Christian thinking.[124] Vanhoozer refers to Eve's

---

122. Bonhoeffer, *Creation and Temptation,* 64.

123. Blenkinsopp, *Creation,* 76.

124. See e.g., Mann ("Augustine on Evil and Original Sin," 46–47), who traces back this association to Augustine's influential discussion of the motive of *superbia*.

desire as "the quest for cognitive enhancement" and points out—consistent with the earlier discussion—that this desire was sinful "primarily because of its means and motivation—not necessarily the knowledge itself, but the manner in which she sought it."[125]

We shall discuss this question further along with the range of other desires that can divert humans away from God's purpose in chapter 7, but the point to underline here is that the pull of these inherently human motives was strong enough to dislodge humanity from their God-ordained trajectory: Even though Adam and Eve had everything their Creator deemed necessary for their existence in the idyllic environment of Eden, deep down they aspired for more. We are thus presented with the bewildering situation, to use the potter-and-clay metaphor, of the clay developing an urge to disalign from the potter, a painful recognition that is echoed in the following words from the very beginning of the book of Isaiah: "Hear, O heavens, and listen, O earth; for the LORD has spoken: I reared children and brought them up, but they have rebelled against me" (1:2). The Fall is thus the first and purest instance of the human tendency to follow creaturely desires and go against the Maker's purpose, suggesting that this is an inherent human weakness.

The Serpent

The opening of the Curse (Gen 3:14) makes it evident that what the serpent did was contrary to God's will. This demonstrates the fact that besides humankind, which God created in his image with free will, there exist further agents in the universe with independent volitional control, some of which actively resist their Creator's work. Such willful agency is not characteristic of the animal world—2 Pet 2:12, for example, describes sinful people as being "like irrational animals, mere creatures of instinct, born to be caught and killed." There is one notable biblical exception to this, the "sea monsters" (tannînim, Gen 1:21), which, as we have seen earlier, are closely related to Leviathan and Rahab[126] and are sometimes described as being in confrontation with God. In view of this, it is noteworthy that Isa 27:1 creates a link between the serpent of Genesis 3 (nāḥāš) and these antagonistic forces: "On that day the LORD with his cruel and great and strong sword will punish Leviathan the fleeing serpent [nāḥāš], Leviathan the twisting serpent [nāḥāš], and he will kill the dragon [tannîn] that is in the sea." Accordingly, the serpent is not only described as "more crafty

---

125. Vanhoozer, *Pictures at a Theological Exhibition*, 252.

126. E.g., e.g., *tannîyn* is juxtaposed with Leviathan in Isa 27:1 and with Rahab in Isa 51:9; for a detailed intertextual analysis, see Giere, *New Glimpse of Day One*, 63–64.

than any other wild animal that the LORD God had made" (Gen 3:1), but it also belongs to a special class of creatures that was mentioned in the Bible to be in conflict with God.

Moreover, the serpent of Genesis 3 displays an unusual feature which is not characteristic of animals: it *talked*. There is only one other example in the whole Bible of an animal speaking in a human language, Balaam's donkey (Num 22:28–30), but it did so only after God "opened the mouth of the donkey" (v. 28). The Genesis narrative emphasizes twice that the serpent was an animal (Gen 3:1 and 14), and this would suggest that—similar to Balaam's donkey—the serpent needed some higher intelligence to enable it to talk. In Rev 20:2 (and also 12:9) we find a likely candidate for such a higher intelligence, as this verse links the serpent to Satan by using the same word, *ophis*, as the LXX translation of "serpent" in Genesis 3 and Isa 27:1: "... the dragon, that ancient serpent [*ophis*], who is the Devil and Satan ..." This scriptural association of the serpent with the devil has been accepted widely by commentators, but we need to be cautious about how to interpret the link, because, as we shall see in chapter 5, the "accuser" (*śāṭān*) of the Old Testament had not as yet evolved into the formidable arch-enemy of God's work that the Satan of the New Testament is portrayed as. However, Sydney Page is right when he argues, "Though it would be a mistake to read back into Genesis 3 the full-blown doctrine of Satan that later emerged, there is continuity between the way the serpent is represented in Genesis 3 and the later idea that Satan spoke through him."[127]

What we can safely conclude at this point is that the serpent is presented in the Genesis narrative as the mouthpiece of a power that was antagonistic to humankind,[128] and Page further adds that the fact that the serpent was cursed by God also indicates that he was treated as a responsible moral agent rather than just a brute beast.[129] The existence of a sophisticated spiritual agency behind the Fall is also supported by two further points: First, the shrewd scheme to beguile Adam and Eve was the work of someone who knew what the tree of the knowledge of good and evil represented and who was, therefore, in this respect similar to God (cf. Gen 3:22); second, the serpent clearly knew more than what he could have overheard when Adam told Eve about God's prohibition, as revealed by the fact that he was right

127. Page, *Powers of Evil*, 16. Blenkinsopp also points out a fact that may be more than a coincidence, namely that the Hebrew word for serpent is very similar to divination/occult. Blenkinsopp, *Creation*, 73.

128. There are several precedents in the Scriptures when Satan used someone as his mouthpiece or temporary agent, even renowned people such as King David (1 Chr 21:1), the Apostle Peter (Matt 16:23 and parallels) and Judas (Luke 22:3; John 13:27).

129. Page, *Powers of Evil*, 14; for a similar view, see Collins, *Genesis*, 171–72.

(a) when he said that Eve would not die (at least immediately), (b) when he predicted that the humans' eyes would be opened upon eating of the fruit, and (c) when he stated that by knowing good and evil Eve would become "like God," as this was later confirmed by the Creator himself (Gen 3:22).[130] Genesis 3 does not offer any further details about the nature and motives of this agency and therefore we shall come back to this matter when discussing the Book of Job in chapter 5, which adds a new dimension to the depiction of heavenly opposition to God.

Consequences of the Fall

We have seen earlier that, following Paul's summary in Romans, Christian theology has typically equated the primary consequence of the Fall with the unstoppable and universal spread of sin and death in the world, although without offering an unambiguous explanation of how Adam and Eve's transgression rendered humankind congenitally sinful. The Genesis narrative contains three featured elements related to the after-effects of the Fall that can be taken up in a canonical reading to explore the process whereby creation was derailed and set on a different trajectory: (a) the opening of the human eyes and its sexual impact; (b) a detailed address by God—usually referred to as the "Curse"—that describes a mixture of curses, punishments, and other consequences; and (c) Adam and Eve's banishment from the Garden of Eden. Let us finish this chapter by considering the role that these consequences played in the subsequent outworking of both human and nonhuman creation, concluded by a discussion of how "sin" and "death" can be understood from a progressive creational perspective.

"Then the eyes of both were opened"

After eating of the fruit, Adam and Eve's first reaction was to notice their own nudity, an awareness that was accompanied by a feeling of shame, as evidenced by their attempt to sew fig leaves to cover their nakedness (Gen 3:7). The text does not give an explanation of why the exposure to the knowledge of good and evil produced such a sense of uneasiness in Adam and Eve about their naked genitalia, apart from a brief exchange between Adam and God in which the man explained that he wanted to cover his nakedness because it made him feel "afraid" (v. 10). This suggests that the human couple's

130. See, e.g., Page, *Powers of Evil*, 18. Of course, De La Torre is right that "how humans defined 'godlike' was probably very different from how the serpent was defining it" (*Genesis*, 69).

newly formed carnal identity was characterized by considerable cognitive-emotional turmoil, and for the current discussion, it is the social aspect of this matter that is particularly pertinent: becoming aware of nakedness is an inherently social perception, involving a sensitivity to the "social gaze" of others,[131] which explains Adam and Eve's initial response of wishing to cover themselves and hide so as not to be seen. In other words, the opening of the human eyes inaugurated sexuality as a loaded social dimension, and several biblical passages in both Testaments confirm the lasting nature of this highly charged aspect of creatureliness, typically associating nakedness with shame.[132] Thus, eating of the fruit of the knowledge of good and evil brought an end to the "shame-free" innocence of nakedness, and as we shall see below, in the Curse we already find the first indications of interpersonal tension associated with sexuality.

The Curse

Genesis 3:14–19—usually referred to as the "Curse"—contains the Creator's pronouncement to each participant of the Fall, and the fact that God addressed each creature directly attests to the magnitude of what had happened. God's message includes a mixture of curses (on the serpent and the ground), punishments, and other consequences; in this section we shall consider what God said to the man and the woman, while the serpent will be further discussed in chapter 5, whose focus is on the spiritual opposition to humankind.

Significantly, the main thrust of God's message to Adam and Eve concerned their primary creational roles: It was declared that both the tilling of the ground (for the man) and the producing of future stewards (for the woman) would be painful, and the parallel nature of the two pronouncements was strengthened by the use of the same Hebrew word for pain//toil (*'iṣṣābôn*) in the verses addressed to both Adam and Eve: "I will greatly increase your pangs in childbearing; *in pain* you shall bring forth children . . .", "cursed is the ground because of you; *in toil* you shall eat of it all the days of your life . . ." (vv. 16, 17; emphases added).

Regarding the woman, not only was her maternity to be accompanied by pain, but her other creational role, being the man's helper and companion, was also to be fraught with difficulties. Understanding the exact nature of the predicted disruption depends on the interpretation

---

131. See e.g., Beier and Spelke, "Social Gaze."

132. E.g., Gen 9:20–24; Isa 20:4; 47:3; Hos 2:10; 1 Cor 12:23; Rev 16:15. For discussions, see Aune, *Revelation 6–16*, 897; Barr, *Garden of Eden*, 63.

of the key word translated as "desire" (*tĕšûqâ*) in Gen 3:16 ("your desire shall be for your husband, and he shall rule over you"). The close analogy with Gen 4:7 suggests that the semantic domain of the word goes beyond sexual yearning and also involves the wish to dominate.[133] Accordingly, God's pronouncement not only signaled the end of the initial "shame-free" harmony that had prevailed between man and woman before their eyes were opened, but it also forecast ongoing tension and struggle—or in some commentators' words, an outright "war of the sexes."[134] A common observation about the Curse is that it is difficult to separate the descriptive and prescriptive intent of God's words;[135] in this case, however, because the relationship between husband and wife already showed signs of cracks before the Fall, God's pronouncement appears to be not so much a sentence over the woman as a summary of the post-Fall upset of relations within marriage, which is the basic unit of human social organization. Thus, as Wenham succinctly sums up, "those who were created to be one flesh will find themselves tearing each other apart."[136]

Regarding the man, Gen 3:17 states that "cursed is the ground because of you." Most commentators interpret this causative link as reflecting the impact of the man's sinfulness, and in the light of the earlier discussion of the significance of stewardship, we can see how Adam and Eve's failure to fulfil their creational role to attend to the ground was a contributing factor in bringing about the sorry state of the land: "thorns and thistles it shall bring forth for you" (v. 18). In the Old Testament, thorns and thistles are signs of "nature untamed and encroaching"[137] (Kidner), with the same word pair occurring in Hos 10:8 to indicate destruction and in Isaiah 34:13 alongside *tōhû wābōhû* (formless void; 34:11) as a mark of the desolation in Edom after the Lord's day of vengeance. In the New Testament the phrase is used similarly to represent growth that is contrary to God's purpose, as for example in the Parable of the Sower.[138] Thus, God's pronouncement in the Curse makes

133. *Tĕšûqâ* is a rare word in the Bible, occurring only in two other places in the Old Testament: In the Song 7:10 it refers to a romantic desire between man and woman, but the other recurrence in Gen 4:7 is more important from our point of view, partly because of the vicinity of the two verses and partly because in addition to "desire" the latter verse also contains the other key verb of 3:16, "rule" (*mšl*): "sin is lurking at the door; its desire is for you, but you must master [*mšl*] it—in fact, Arnold (suggests that the twofold co-occurrence of the noun "desire" and the verb "rule" might indicate an idiomatic expression. B. T. Arnold, *Genesis*, 70.

134. Ferguson, *Genesis*, 45.

135. E.g., B. T. Arnold, *Genesis*, 70; Hamilton, *Genesis*, 201.

136. Wenham, *Genesis*, 89.

137. Kidner, *Genesis*, 76.

138. The Parable of the Sower (Matt 13:1–9 and parallels) talks about the thorns

it clear that once the couple have been expelled from Eden they can expect to find working the soil more of a struggle. The final sentence of the Curse foreshadows the sobering fact that without access to the tree of life, the stewards, who were created to subdue the earth, will *return* to the earth instead (Gen 3:19). However, von Rad may be right that God's pronouncement does not speak of death as a "primary issue, but rather of life";[139] that is, the emphasis is not so much on dying as on the added hardship of living.

Banishment from the Garden

Adam and Eve's story concludes with their banishment from the Garden of Eden: This is stated twice in the final two verses of Genesis 3, after which the first human couple, whom God had formed by his own hands, largely disappears from the Genesis narrative. Although Gen 3:22–23 connects Adam and Eve's expulsion to their previous disobedience, the specific reason that God gives for his decision is not a moral judgement; that is, the act is not justified as a punishment for sin but rather the text describes it as a *necessity* in order to prevent the couple from having access to the fruit of the tree of life (without explaining this necessity any further). It is important to note that humankind's primary creational role did not subsequently change with their expulsion, as they were still commissioned to steward the earth: "the LORD God sent him forth from the garden of Eden, to till the ground from which he was taken" (3:23).[140] However, the stewards' banishment and the Garden's subsequent disappearance from human history in the biblical narrative had a profound impact on the course of creation in three specific areas:

a. *The curtailment of Adam and Eve's maturation period.* According to the reading of the Genesis narrative presented above, the premature coming of age of the first human couple cut short the time they were to spend in the Garden of Eden, which was "a place of moral growth"[141] (Wilkin-

---

"choking" the good seeds and in Heb 6:8 the author compares people who fall away from God to the ground which "produces thorns and thistles," describing it as being "worthless and on the verge of being cursed; its end is to be burned over."

139. Von Rad, *Genesis*, 95.

140. As Heiser sums up, "The curse levied at Adam (Gen 3:17–19) did not supersede God's mandate to subdue the earth and take dominion. But it did make the task harder. The expulsion of humankind from Eden (Gen 3:22–25) turned a glorious dominion mission into mundane drudgery." Heiser, *Unseen Realm*, 88.

141. Wilkinson, *Creation*, 55. Goldingay summarizes the loss as follows: "It [Gen 1–2] does not describe them [Adam and Eve] as living lives of obedience and bliss, only as having the opportunity to learn obedience and grow to moral maturity. The tragedy

son). As we have seen above, this curtailment of Adam and Eve's maturation period impeded their social development in particular. The fact that Adam needed a companion to fulfil his creational role meant that he was to become a social being, which in turn required the formation of a social structure for humanity that would be conducive to the collective stewarding of the earth. The limitations of Adam and Eve as a married couple before the Fall demonstrated that the acquisition of interpersonal and social skills was not an automatic part of their creation, and the Genesis account of the complete failure of humankind to develop into an effective society of stewards before the Flood reveals the grave consequences of the insufficient learning period.

b. *Exposure to the harsh realities of corporeal existence.* After their expulsion, humans were forced to start eking out an existence outside the safe and sheltered environment of Eden. The end of abundance added a strong new incentive to the initial list of human motives that originally lured Adam and Eve away from God's purpose, namely the requirement to satisfy their physical needs, often in competition with other humans for limited resources. We shall see in chapter 7 the considerable power that such corporeal wants can exert.

c. *Insufficient tilling of the ground.* The expulsion from Eden further aggravated the problem of the insufficient tilling of the ground; thus, the world's ecosystem was launched not only without the direct nurturing and transformational influence of the Garden of Eden, but also without sufficient spiritual stewardship by the human representatives of the Creator.[142] This might explain the Apostle Paul's words that "the *whole* creation has been groaning in labor pains" (Rom 8:22; emphasis added); however, because the biblical canon is anthropocentric—that is, centered around human history—there are only scarce references to the plight of nonhuman creation. In Goldingay's words, "Humanity's vocation was to master the world so that it would not need to groan, but Adam and Eve's disobedience itself involved their failing to master nature. Henceforth outside Eden nature will resist their mastery."[143]

---

of Genesis 1–3 is not that human beings fell from a state of bliss but that they failed to realize a possibility" (*Old Testament Theology*, 146).

142. E.g., Wilkinson emphasizes that "Human sin has led to the land being cursed . . . This is because its chief steward is not in harmony with God and therefore does not care for it in the way it should be cared for" (*Creation*, 74).

143. Goldingay, *Old Testament Theology*, 148.

Understanding "Sin" and "Death" from
a Progressive Creational Perspective

McFarland defines sin as "an overarching term for human resistance to or turning away from God,"[144] and in progressive creational terms this can be understood as taking a developmental course that is different from God's plan, a point expressed by Stephens as follows: "If it is the case that God's creational activity provides the fundamental ground for all his actions, then . . . sin is understood as that which threatens to undo God's creation project."[145] The expulsion from Eden as a result of the Fall caused exactly such a "sinful" shift in humanity's trajectory and thereby justified Paul's statement in Romans 5 that "sin came into the world through one man" (v. 12), that is, as a direct consequence of Adam's disobedience. Furthermore, because the banishment from Eden resulted in humanity being denied access to the tree of life—indeed, this was the very purpose of the expulsion—"death came through sin" (ibid.) as an inevitable consequence for humanity. Finally, because the banishment from Eden affected *all* Adam and Eve's descendants—as humankind as a whole was confined to a course of life outside the Garden that was incongruent with God's original plan and was therefore "sinful" by definition—it is also true that "death spread to all because all have sinned" (ibid.).

Thus, from this canonical narrative perspective, the universal human mortality that was foretold in the Curse ("you are dust, and to dust you shall return" Gen 3:19) can be understood to correlate with sin through their common link to human existence outside the Garden, as humanity was set on a course divergent to the divine creative will and cut off from the source of eternal life. The creational trajectory of humankind was re-aligned with God's purpose only after the divine intervention of Jesus Christ coming to earth in bodily form: "for as all die in Adam, so all will be made alive in Christ" (1 Cor 15:22). This theme will be discussed in the next chapter.

3.4 Summary

Romans 8:22 states that "We know that the whole creation has been groaning in labor pains until now." This appraisal is consistent with the biblical characterization of the state of the world starting with Genesis 3 as well as with many people's subjective impression throughout the centuries as they have considered, in Moo's words, the "folly, degradation, and hatred that are

144. McFarland, "Fall and Sin," 140.
145. Stephens, *Annihilation or Renewal*, 268.

the chief characteristics of human history."[146] Indeed, as Wilkinson rightly points out, in the extract from Romans cited above Paul appealed to the "common knowledge of believers that the creation is in trouble."[147] Thus, whether we call it chaos, disorder, darkness, evil, or resistance to God's work, references to some kind of futility are an undeniable part of the biblical testimony about the initial created order of the material world. This chapter has inspected a range of scriptural motifs and images that might shed light on this canonical theme, with a special emphasis on the two dominant explanations of the futility of creation, the dark side of matter and human failing. Somewhat unexpectedly, the analyses of the various scriptural threads have converged on a statement of God in the middle of the second creation account, which marked the beginning of a series of subsequent events: The pronouncement declares Adam's situation to be "not good" (Gen 2:18), and it was argued—given that the "it is good" appraisals in Genesis 1 invariably concerned key aspects of creation—that when God declared the opposite about the pinnacle of material creation, it was nothing short of a dramatic announcement that signified a substantial issue.

The declaration that it was "not good" for Adam to be alone was immediately followed by God's statement of intention to make a partner for Adam to help him. Although it is not stated what tasks Adam required help with, the logic of the narrative suggests that it involved the duty that God had previously assigned to Adam: to till the ground and keep it. This was a fundamental matter, since the absence of tilling the ground was cited at the beginning of the second creation account as one of the main reasons for the inert, lifeless nature of the primeval land. It was argued that "tilling" and "keeping" the Garden were not so much agricultural as spiritual functions, related to stewarding the earth as God's representatives, and it was further suggested that the necessity for stewardship of the earth was related to the inherent dark side of matter and the *Chaoskampf* motif that the biblical canon bears witness to in several places.

The seriousness of the problem of Adam's insufficiency was confirmed by the chain of events that followed the Creator's pronouncement "it is not good." First, God sought a helper from among the animal world with no appropriate match found; then—through applying a new creational procedure—God made a fully compatible female companion for the man with whom Adam was finally pleased (Gen 2:23), thereby creating the rudiments of humankind as a species. However, rather than bringing a solution to the problem of Adam being alone, the introduction of a social aspect

146. Moo, *Romans*, 329.
147. Wilkinson, *Creation*, 240.

to human relations presented weaknesses in the short run that were duly capitalized on during the Fall. In this reading, the talking serpent is seen as acting on behalf of some larger spiritual force that was opposed to God's material creation and its stewards, but because the emphasis in Genesis 3 is on human disobedience, this was not pursued in any further depth in this chapter but will be revisited when discussing the question of spiritual opposition in chapter 5.

The serpent's cunning plot was successful and the resulting disobedience of the human couple had dramatic and far-reaching consequences. In Romans 5 the Apostle Paul relates these consequences to sin and death entering the world, and while this was indeed the ultimate outcome of the Fall, at the narrative level Genesis 3 culminates in the human couple's expulsion from the Garden of Eden. This banishment and the subsequent disappearance of the Garden from humanity's biblical history resulted in a course of development that fundamentally deviated from God's original creative purposes, thereby leading to universal sin and death. As we shall see in the next chapters, the central thrust of progressive creation after the expulsion of humans from Eden involves re-aligning humankind's trajectory with the original divine creative intent and transforming humanity into citizens of God's eschatological kingdom on earth.

4

Ongoing Creation and New Creation

> From this time forward I make you hear new things, hidden
> things that you have not known. They are created[1] now, not long
> ago; before today you have never heard of them ... (Isa 48:6–7)

AFTER THE EXPULSION OF Adam and Eve from Eden, the Genesis narrative
presents a bleak picture of the deteriorating state of human affairs: While at
the end of the sixth day of creation "God saw everything that he had made,
and indeed, it was very good" (Gen 1:31), now "God saw that the earth was
corrupt" (6:12). It is evident that the initial dissonance within the rudimen-
tary society of stewards (discussed in chapter 3) increased exponentially as
the human population grew, and what followed in response was a series of
divine interventions in the course of progressive creation that were aimed
at transforming humankind into citizens of God's eschatological kingdom.
This process comprises three broad phases: (a) the purging of the earth
through the Flood and the subsequent new beginning; (b) the raising of the
Israelites as a "a priestly kingdom and a holy nation" (Exod 19:6); and (c)
Jesus Christ's incarnation, life, death, and resurrection, which inaugurated
the new creation. The current chapter describes this progression as it unfolds in the Scriptures up to the point of Jesus' sacrificial death, while the
Atonement and its consequences will be covered in Chapter 6.

4.1 The Flood and Re-creation

The Flood is presented in the Genesis narrative as a response to the pervasive depravity of humanity, and the text suggests that this was more than
merely a dramatic punishment: Gen 7:11 states that "the fountains of the
great deep [*tĕhôm*; same word as in Gen 1:2] burst forth, and the windows

---

1. The same Hebrew verb, *br'*, is used for "create" as in Gen 1:1.

of the heavens were opened," indicating that God temporarily released the boundaries that separated the world of the living from the inert primordial matters of Gen 1:2. As McDonough succinctly puts it, "This is not simply a stretch of very bad weather: it is the collapsing back of the waters above and below which God had separated on day two."[2] The deluge was thus an act of "creation in reverse"[3] (Blocher) or "uncreation"[4] (Blenkinsopp), because, as Jackson expressively describes, "the power of sin was so great that God rebooted creation by bringing it back to its watery and chaotic beginnings."[5] God's communication to Noah in Gen 6:12–13 makes it clear that the purge targeted humankind for contaminating the created order— "I have determined to make an end of all flesh, for the earth is filled with violence because of them; now I am going to destroy them along with the earth" (Gen 6:12–13)—and accordingly, the subsequent re-creation of the world was also centered around humanity.

Significantly, Noah, the head of the only family saved from the Flood, was destined right from his birth to re-establish the harmony between steward and land: As his father, Lamech, said when he named him, "Out of the ground that the LORD has cursed this one shall bring us relief from our work and from the toil of our hands" (Gen 5:29). Noah's role in re-creation finds striking parallels with that of Adam. First, Noah is referred to as "a man of the soil" (9:20), which creates a direct link with Adam, who was originally made from soil (Gen 2:7) and whose main charge was to work the soil.[6] This link is strengthened by the emphasis that they have both been made in God's image (Gen 1:27; 9:6)—a motif that only occurs in Genesis in the Adam and Noah stories[7]—as well as by the facts that like Adam, Noah also "walked with God" (Gen 6:9) and Noah and his family received the same commission and blessing as the first couple did after they were created: "Be fruitful and multiply, and fill the earth" (Gen 9:1), reiterated a few verses later, "be fruitful and multiply, abound on the earth and multiply in it" (v. 7).

2. McDonough, *Creation and New Creation*, 2.

3. Blocher, *In the Beginning*, 206; he also notes that that the cosmic character of the Flood is further underlined by the fact that in the New Testament it is seen as the prefiguration of the end of the world, drawing a direct parallel with the *Parousia*: ". . . and they knew nothing until the flood came and swept them all away, so too will be the coming of the Son of Man" (Matt 24:39).

4. As Blenkinsopp summarizes, "The deluge is an undoing of what was done in creation, a return to chaos, an obliteration of the precarious space for ordered human life. It is therefore an act of un-creation" (*Creation*, 141).

5. Jackson, *Eden Project*, 46.

6. Gage and White, "John-Revelation Project," Part 7. They also highlight the wordplay in Gen 9:20 alluding to Adam's name: *'iš ha'adamah*.

7. Gage and White, "John-Revelation Project," Part 7.

There are some further similarities between the two figures that might be thought coincidental if considered independently but which, taken together, add to the overall pattern of correspondence:[8] their stories both involve a curse (from God and from Noah); both have three named sons, one of whom elicits a curse; both have a vital role to perform with reference to animals (naming and saving them, respectively); and finally, both get into the state of shameful nakedness after consuming some form of fruit. Interestingly, the parallels also extend to the worlds that Adam and Noah were part of, as both emerged from watery chaos initiated by the blowing of the 'wind'/Spirit of God (Gen 1:2 and 8:1; the word *rûaḥ* is used in both verses).[9] Because of this list of resemblances, many commentators perceive from the Scriptures that God had intended Noah to become like a new Adam whose commission to steward the earth remained the same as that of his ancestor.[10]

On the other hand, we also find some marked differences in the post-diluvian new beginning. First, although Noah himself "found favor in the sight of the LORD" (5:8) and was "a righteous man, blameless in his generation" (6:9), God launched re-creation in the full knowledge that "the inclination of the human heart is evil from youth" (8:21), and the original paradisiacal harmony between humankind and the living ecosystem was replaced by a new relationship: In the blessing pronounced over humans after the Flood (9:1–7), God omitted the element of subduing the earth and having dominion over every living thing on it, and instead, allowed humans to *kill* animals for food. Blenkinsopp rightly points out that this goes well beyond the initial mandate to rule over the animal world in the first creation,[11] and while animals were to multiply and abound on earth just like before (8:17), they would also live in "fear and dread" of humans (9:2). Thus, it may be concluded that "this new world order has a dark side. Fear becomes normative on the earth,"[12] an observation also supported by the subsequent discussion of the shedding of human blood (9:6), which fore-shadows the occurrence of humans killing humans.[13]

The Genesis narrative also includes two new elements in the role of humankind that reflect the altered nature of the postdiluvian phase

---

8. See ibid.; Waltke, *Genesis*, 127–28.

9. VanDrunen, *Divine Covenants and Moral Order*, 82.

10. E.g., Bartholomew and Goheen, *Drama of Scripture*, 32–34.

11. Blenkinsopp, *Creation*, 145.

12. De La Torre, *Genesis*, 122.

13. Alter submits that "Perhaps the ban on bloodshed at this point suggests that murder was the endemic vice of the antediluvians" (*Genesis*, 38).

of creation. First, God extends human authority to include punishment of murder by death: "Whoever sheds the blood of a human, by a human shall that person's blood be shed" (9:6). This implies a radical change in the world order: After administering justice through the Flood, God enlists social agency to enforce the principle of justice, signaling "the beginning of divinely mandated political authority."[14] We should note that this introduction of an authority structure at a societal level after the collapse of the social system closely parallels God's decree in the Curse concerning the authority structure within marriage (Gen 3:16) after the Fall. Second, Wenham highlights the fact that when Noah emerged from the ark, he built an altar "and offered burnt offerings on the altar" (Gen 8:20), thereby performing priestly ministry on behalf of humankind.[15] This is the first recorded act in the Bible of humans exercising spiritual stewardship, and we are told that the sacrifice was successful because "when the Lord smelled the pleasing odor" (v. 21), he declared: "I will never again curse the ground because of humankind, for the inclination of the human heart is evil from youth; nor will I ever again destroy every living creature as I have done. As long as the earth endures, seedtime and harvest, cold and heat, summer and winter, day and night, shall not cease" (Gen 8:20–22).

Thus, upon Noah's intervention, God promised to forego any future earthly retaliation for the evil deeds of humankind—by means of another flood or cursing of the ground—thereby re-establishing, in effect, the long-term and sustainable operational order of the world's ecosystem. This pledge was then affirmed in a formal covenant (9:9–17), accompanied by a blessing on humankind (9:1, 7). Nonetheless, the overall character of this new beginning was markedly different from the unspoiled and innocent state of humanity in the Garden of Eden, and any prospect of regaining a paradisiacal state is quickly dispelled by the subsequent narrative as it relates a bitter conflict in Noah's family (9:20–27), which leads to the first instance in the Bible of a human cursing a human (v. 25). Yet, there is also hope, because as Blocher's concludes, "When the whole sweep of the biblical panorama is considered, it is difficult not to discern in the story of Noah the prefiguration of the new creation announced by Isaiah and inaugurated by Jesus Christ."[16]

---

14. Reno, *Genesis*, 125.

15. Wenham, "Flood," 642; see also Alexander, *From Eden to New Jerusalem*, 28–29.

16. Blocher, *In the Beginning*, 209.

4.2 The Raising of the Nation of Israel

The discord within the first postdiluvian family, ending with Noah's cursing of Canaan, evidenced the fragility of the social fabric of the emerging new society of stewards, and the next episode chronicled in the Bible is the well-known story of the Tower of Babel (Gen 11:1–9), which describes how humanity as a collective unit turned against the will of God. The momentous nature of the following milestone in the Genesis narrative, the raising of the nation of Israel, becomes apparent against this sinister background, because it involved the election of a people "with a mission entrusted to them from God for the sake of God's wider purpose of blessing the nations"[17] (C. Wright). The emergence of the nation of Israel, whom Barth characterized as the "first, limited, and hidden form of the eschatological community,"[18] is complex and tortuous as God calls out his people and leads them ultimately to the holy land. Most narrations start the history of this process with God's initial calling of Abraham; however, as will be shown below, God's intervention to raise up Israel may also be connected to certain aspects of the story of Job, and especially the testing that both Job and Abraham underwent.

The Two "Godfearing" Patriarchs: Job and Abraham

The book of Job is an enigmatic book in many senses. The protagonist of the book, Job, is a Gentile, to whom we find only three references elsewhere in the whole biblical canon,[19] yet, God refers to him four times as "my servant," a title most frequently used in the OT for Moses and David.[20] Furthermore, the amount of Scripture devoted to Job's story is astounding: roughly three times as much is written about Job as, for example, about Abraham.[21] In terms of its content, the book of Job has several distinct layers, and it has been widely recognized to contain some of the most intense theological and intellectual discussions in the Old Testament;[22] Calvin, for example, is known to have preached over 150 sermons about Job over a period of two years.[23] In this

---

17. C. Wright, *Mission of God*, 65.

18. Barth, "Matthew 28:16–20," 66.

19. Ezek 14:14, 20; Jas 5:11.

20. Fyall, *Job*, 181.

21. The material in Genesis concerning Abraham from the first mention to his death (11:27—25:10) is roughly 14 chapters with 375 verses, whereas the Book of Job contains 42 chapters with 1070 verses.

22. See, e.g., Clines, *Job 1–20*, xii; Newsom, "Book of Job," 326.

23. For a selection of these sermons, see Calvin, *Sermons from Job*.

chapter we shall focus on one aspect of Job's story, his *testing*, while the next chapter will offer a more detailed overview of what the Book of Job reveals about the nature of the spiritual opposition to humankind.

Curiously, in spite of the length of the book, we learn very few details about Job himself as a person. The little information available about his life and his environment suggests that he was a patriarch not unlike Abraham; for example, Clines highlights the fact that like other patriarchs in Genesis, he lived a long life (140 years), his wealth was described in terms of his animals and servants, and perhaps even more importantly, as head of his family he offered sacrifices without the intervention of any priest (1:5).[24] However, Hartley correctly points out that while a patriarch is usually introduced in the Bible with a full genealogy (e.g., Abraham in Gen 11:26–29), no information is given about Job's tribe or clan, let alone his exact genealogy,[25] and as Whybray emphasizes, the absence of even the name of Job's father is an almost unique feature in Hebrew narrative.[26] We encounter a similar lack of specific details about the time when Job lived; the only indirect clues in this respect are the mention of the Sabeans and Chaldeans as nomadic raiders at the beginning of the book (1:15 and 17) as well as the conspicuous absence of any reference to the history of Israel throughout the text, which all point to the early, patriarchal era sometime in the second millennium BC.[27] This is further supported by the fact that in the poetic dialogue that makes up the bulk of the book, God is referred to by pre-Mosaic names such as El, Shaddai, and Eloah.[28]

Thus, although the sociohistorical details in the text place Job in the pre-Abrahamic era, there are good reasons to conclude that his story, as presented in the Bible, is not intended to be strongly associated with a specific historical period. This lack of specificity is also reflected in the fact that the Book of Job never acquired a fixed position within the canon, although in the Hebrew Bible it was grouped with the Psalms and Proverbs as part of the Writings, and the current English translations such as the NRSV and the NIV also place it before the Psalms and Proverbs.[29] This being the case, how does the Book of Job contribute to the canonical narrative of the transfor-

---

24. Clines, *Job 1–20*, lvii.

25. Hartley, *Job*, 66–67.

26. Whybray, *Job*, 14.

27. Ellison, "Book of Job," 589. A further link with the patriarchal era is the use of the word "*kesitah*" for a piece of coin in 42:11: This word occurs two more times in the Bible (Gen 33:19 and Josh 24:32), and in both occasions it refers to the money that the Patriarch Jacob paid to buy a field from the sons of Hamor.

28. Habel, *Job*, 39.

29. See e.g., Alden, *Job*, 31; Andersen, *Job*, 37.

mation of humankind? From the current chapter's perspective, its particular importance lies in the series of trials Job underwent to test his integrity:

a. his material possessions were destroyed, his children were killed and a horrible disease was inflicted on him;

b. his wife made an appeal to him to curse God and die;

c. his friends attempted to convince him that he was in the wrong and that his "theology" was flawed.

Curiously, most commentaries on Job's testing/suffering tend to focus on the first two sets of these challenges despite the fact that those are described only rather briefly in the prologue of the book, without any indication that they raised serious doubts in Job concerning his faith in God. Instead, Job's agonizing search for the truth and understanding of his condition began in earnest with the arrival of his three friends and their attempts to "comfort" him; this is the point when the scope of Job's trial extends beyond his immediate personal environment, and this transition is expressively marked in the text by a change from prose to poetry.

The length and prominence of the "poetic dispute" between Job and his friends—which, in filling over 30 chapters, constitutes the longest and most detailed discussion between people recorded in the whole biblical canon—particularly when compared to the brevity of Job's misfortunes described in the prologue, suggests that it is this socially orchestrated temptation to turn against God that the Book of Job foregrounds as the crucial test for Job. In contemporary terms, it can be understood as an extended "social trial" or "experiment" in which Job was nominated by God as "a blameless and upright man" (1:8) to serve as a "test case," as it were, for the integrity of humanity. In the light of the social vulnerability of humankind (described in chapter 3), this trial was of special significance as it assessed whether humanity at its best had the capacity to maintain their faith in God in the face of intense social pressure. The unique twist of Job's challenge was the fact that the temptation to turn away from the Creator came from his close friends, a scenario which is mentioned in Psalm 55 as a particularly difficult interpersonal trial.[30] Furthermore, these friends—in a similar mode to Satan' temptation of Jesus in the wilderness—drew on scriptural wisdom to support their arguments, which were nevertheless flawed as confirmed by God himself at the end of the book (see the next

30. Ps 55:12–14: "It is not enemies who taunt me—I could bear that; it is not adversaries who deal insolently with me—I could hide from them. But it is you, my equal, my companion, my familiar friend, with whom I kept pleasant company; we walked in the house of God with the throng."

chapter for a discussion). Interestingly, in reflecting on how difficult it may be to distinguish the true witness from the false, Barth fully acknowledges the negative role of these friends when he calls them "agents of Satan and the worst tempters of Job,"[31] although he adds that they were unaware of this and spoke "in all good faith."

The assumption underlying the discussion in this chapter is that Job's successful trial is described in much detail in the Bible because it provides compelling evidence for the potential integrity of humankind, and as such, it can be seen as a precursor to God's calling of Abraham, another "righteous" man (Gal 3:6). He was commissioned, in effect, to multiply his righteousness on a larger scale by modelling it to a new nation he was to become the father of, as confirmed by God's words in Gen 18:19: "for I have chosen him, that he may charge his children and his household after him to keep the way of the LORD by doing righteousness and justice." The select "task force" created in his way—the nation of Israel—was in turn charged with modelling social values and harmony among the nations and bringing God's blessing to them (see separate section below). Similar to Job, Abraham was also submitted to a severe trial when God instructed him to sacrifice his son as a test of obedience, and this was not the only parallel between the two patriarchs: Judy Klitsner highlights the fact that after Abraham passed the test, God called him "Godfearing" (*yārē' ĕlōhîm*; Gen 22:12*),* which is the very expression that is used of Job at the very beginning of his story (1:1),[32] and Harold Kushner adds that Abraham and Job were in fact the only men in the Bible to whom this phrase was applied.[33] Furthermore, when Job repented after God's second speech, he claimed that he was but "dust and ashes" (*'al-'āpār w·'ēper*; 42:6), and Klitsner points out that the only other biblical figure who employed this self-reference was Abraham (Gen. 18:27).[34]

To summarize, given the paramount importance of the role of the social dimension in humankind's deviation from God's creative purpose, it is unlikely to be a coincidence that the biblical canon presents a particularly detailed account of what could be viewed in contemporary psychology as a "social experiment" to test the integrity of a specially selected human specimen, the blameless and upright Job. Throughout his trial, Job successfully witnessed to his enduring faith, as did that other patriarch, Abraham, who subsequently became the centerpiece of a major divine intervention in the

---

31. Barth, *CD* IV/3.1, 454.

32. Klitsner, *Subversive Sequels*, xxi.

33. Kushner, *Job*, 20; the female midwives in Exod 1:17 are also described in this way.

34. Klitsner, *Subversive Sequels*, xxi.

history of humankind, the raising of the nation of Israel as a model and a vehicle for God's blessing for the nations. He was called to implement the human integrity that Job demonstrated on a larger, transformational scale, thereby becoming, in Bartholomew and Goheen's words, "the human channel through whom divine restoration will flow out over the whole world."[35] Thus, according to this reading, the successful trials of the two Godfearing patriarchs constitute a crucial turning point in the process of creation, whereby humanity started to show signs of maturation and began to reveal their God-given potential. We shall now turn to exploring some key elements of how God empowered the Israelites to become transformational agents in the world.

The Release of the Law

When the Israelites reached Mount Sinai after their exodus from Egypt, God instructed them to consecrate themselves and then appeared to them "in a dense cloud" (Exod 19:7) amidst "thunder and lightning . . . and a blast of a trumpet . . . while the whole mountain shook violently" (vv. 16, 18). These dramatic circumstances reflected the significance of the act that was to follow, the giving of the Ten Commandments and the Law. As the prophet Ezra later summarized it in his prayer, "You came down also upon Mount Sinai, and spoke with them from heaven, and gave them right ordinances and true laws, good statutes and commandments, and you made known your holy sabbath to them and gave them commandments and statutes and a law through your servant Moses" (Neh 9:13–14).

We saw earlier that humankind's initial social failure jeopardized the progress of creation, and this may explain why God's first direct interaction with the Israelites as a people group concerned giving them an elaborate set of guidelines for establishing social order among themselves. The Ten Commandments and the detailed instructions that followed in the Torah concerned every aspect of Israel's life, and the creational aspect of this comprehensive set of regulations is well summed up by Bernard Och as follows: "The Torah revelation is a new creation providing order and harmony within the social cosmos. At Sinai, a law is revealed whose purpose is to actualize creational order and harmony in historical time. At Sinai, the order of creation is given social and historical expression. Just as cosmic order was achieved through a series of separations that must be maintained if cosmic order is to continue, so also, human life and society

---

35. Bartholomew and Goheen, *Drama of Scripture*, 36

are established with boundaries and separations that must be maintained if human chaos is to be avoided."[36]

Och thus sees the Law as an elaborate "user manual" for the creation of social order, a point he reiterates in his conclusion: "The covenant law revealed at Sinai is the means by which the cosmic and human orders can be harmoniously integrated. It provides a blueprint whereby God's creational plan can be realized in all spheres of human life and existence."[37] Interestingly, there is a strong Jewish tradition that perceives a parallel between God's ten divine utterances of creation[38] and the Ten Commandments, whose Hebrew name (*aseret ha-devarim*) literally means "the ten words or utterances,"[39] and it is also of note that in Deuteronomy the Law was given a divine exhortation to ensure its profound and long-lasting transformational impact: "Keep these words that I am commanding you today in your heart. Recite them to your children and talk about them when you are at home and when you are away, when you lie down and when you rise. Bind them as a sign on your hand, fix them as an emblem on your forehead, and write them on the doorposts of your house and on your gates" (6:6–8).

Parallels between Material Creation and the Raising of Israel

The perceived link between the "ten divine utterances" and the Ten Commandments is but one of several parallels that we find between the biblical description of the raising of the nation of Israel and the Genesis accounts of creation; let us consider four further salient correspondences in this respect: (a) the creational term "separation" that is frequently used with regard to the Israelites; (b) the blessing of fruitfulness bestowed on the Israelites; (c) similarities in the biblical descriptions of Noah and Moses; and (d) several creational aspects of the tabernacle, the spiritual center of Israel.

36. Och, "Creation," 239.

37. Ibid.

38. Although in Genesis 1 there are only nine explicit "God said" utterances, the Jewish understanding is that "The world was created by ten utterances" (*Pirke Avot* 5:1), explained in the Talmud by the fact that Gen 1:1 is also a divine utterance referring to an act of creation: "The words 'in the beginning' are also an utterance, as it is written, By the word of the Lord the heavens were made . . . Hence the first verse of Genesis is equivalent to 'In the beginning God said, Let there be heaven and earth'" (Talmud, *Mas. Rosh HaShana* 4.6, 32a); see e.g., Patterson, *Open Wounds*, 112.

39. Greenberg et al., "Decalogue," 520.

The "Separation" of the Israelites

We saw in chapter 2 that one of the main processes involved in material creation was *separation:* First, light was separated from darkness (Gen 1:4–5), then "good waters" were separated from primordial waters (vv. 6–8) and finally terrestrial light was separated from terrestrial darkness (by means of created lights in the sky; vv. 14–18). The essence of these acts was to set apart and thus "ring-fence" key elements with a pronounced creational role so that by keeping them in a pure and concentrated form they could exert their beneficial transformational impact on the world. In view of this, it is noteworthy that the same Hebrew word is used repeatedly in the OT canon to describe the separation of the Israelites from among other nations. For example, in Leviticus we read that God declared: "I am the LORD your God; I have separated you from the peoples. . . . You shall be holy to me; for I the LORD am holy, and I have separated you from the other peoples to be mine" (20:26). Later, in the conclusion of his prayer of dedication of the First Temple, King Solomon substantiated his appeal to the Lord on behalf of the whole nation of Israel by referring to their separated status: "Let your eyes be open to the plea of your servant, and to the plea of your people Israel, listening to them whenever they call to you. For you have separated them from among all the peoples of the earth, to be your heritage, just as you promised through Moses, your servant, when you brought our ancestors out of Egypt, O Lord GOD" (1 Kgs 8:52–53).

The question of separation re-emerged several times as a critical issue in the Second Temple period,[40] and its significance is also manifested in what we may call the "fractal" nature of separation regarding three specific subgroups within the Israelite community that were "separated" from the rest (with the same verb used in the Scriptures to describe the process): the priests,[41] the Levites[42] and the Nazirites.[43] A particularly explicit affirmation of the creational aspect of separation occurs in Ezra 9:1–2 where it refers to the Israelites as "holy seed": "The people of Israel, the priests, and the Levites have not separated themselves from the peoples of the lands with their abominations . . . Thus the holy seed has mixed itself with the peoples of the lands."

These examples attest to the fact that the process of separation lay at the heart of the identity of the nation of Israel and their divine commission

---

40. See, e.g., Ezra 6:21; Neh 9:2; 10:30; 13:1–3, 23, 30–31.
41. 1 Chr 23:13
42. Deut 10:8; Num 8:14
43. Num 6:1:2, 17

to fulfil the role of being God's stewards, making them, in effect, a concentrated changing agent within progressive creation; in Och's words, the separation of Israel from the nations "has the same cosmic importance as the separations through which God first brought order out of chaos. . . . Sanctified by acts of distinction and separation, the people of Israel assumes the role which was originally assigned to humanity at creation."[44]

The Blessing of the Israelites

God promised to the Israelites that if they follow his statutes and observe his commandments faithfully, "I will look with favor upon you and *make you fruitful and multiply you*; and I will maintain my covenant with you. You shall eat old grain long stored, and *you shall have to clear out the old to make way for the new*. I will place my dwelling in your midst, and I shall not abhor you. And I will walk among you, and will be your God, and you shall be my people" (Lev 26:9–12; emphases added).

This remarkable passage reiterates the same blessing that God bestowed first on Adam and Eve (Gen 1:28) and then on Noah and his family (Gen 9:1, 7), and the creational parallel is reinforced by the explicit command in the passage "to clear out the old to make way for the new." Indeed, the "multiply and be fruitful" blessing goes back to the very beginnings of the nation of Israel: God pronounced it on Abraham when he called him (Gen 17:2–6; 22:17–18), and he then repeated the same blessing to Isaac (Gen 26:4, 24) and Jacob (Gen 35:11). As a result, we are told that "Thus Israel settled in the land of Egypt, in the region of Goshen; and they gained possessions in it, and were fruitful and multiplied exceedingly" (Gen 47:27).[45]

Similarities between Noah and Moses

A well-documented aspect of the raising of the nation of Israel that connects this process to the Genesis accounts is the existing parallels between Noah and Moses. These similarities involve the fact that both were saved by an "ark" (the same Hebrew word, *tēbâ*, is used; Gen 6:14; Exod 2:3); both oversaw an important building project following an explicit divine blueprint (Noah's ark and the tabernacle); both remained faithful in critical conditions when all

44. Och, "Creation," 237.

45. Then, in Ezek 37:26–27, the blessing of Israel is restated, along with the promise that God's dwelling place will be among the Israelites: "and I will bless them and multiply them, and will set my sanctuary among them forevermore. My dwelling place shall be with them; and I will be their God, and they shall be my people."

others sinned and, accordingly, both "found favor in the sight of the LORD" (Gen 6:8; Exod 33:12, 17); and finally, both performed priestly roles (Noah offered sacrifice, Moses intercession; Gen 8:20; Exod 33:12–18). Given that— as we saw earlier—Noah was portrayed in the Scriptures as a "new Adam," Moses's link with him creates a continuity that goes back to the beginnings of creation.[46] This link may be strengthened by what some authors see as an allusion in the description of the infant Moses as being "good" in Exod 2:2 to God's original commendation of the created order.[47]

Creational Aspects of the Tabernacle

The biblical description of the making of the tabernacle, which was to become the spiritual center of worship and identity for the Israelites, displays a number of strong creational allusions that, taken together, are unlikely to be the product of sheer coincidence:

- God initiated the construction of the tabernacle by appointing the master craftsman, Bezalel, and filling him with his "divine spirit" (*rûaḥ 'ĕlōhîm*; Exod 31:3), which is the same phrase as the one used in Gen 1:2.[48]

- There are striking similarities in the "conclusion formulae" associated with the creation of the world (Gen 1:31–2:3) and the construction of the Tabernacle (Exod 39:32–43); for example, "When Moses saw that they had done all the work just as the LORD had commanded, he blessed them" (Exod 39:43).[49]

- Both the accounts of creation and the building of the tabernacle are structured around a series of seven acts marked by the words "And God said" (Gen 1:3, 6, 9, 14, 20, 24, 26) and 'The Lord spoke to Moses' (Exod. 25:1; 30:11, 17, 22, 34; 31:1, 12).[50]

- Psalm 78 includes an explicit parallel between creation and the building of a "sanctuary" on earth: "He built his sanctuary like the high heavens, like the earth, which he has founded forever" (v. 69; here the same Hebrew word is used for "sanctuary" as the one used by God

46. See e.g., McKeown, *Genesis*, 64–65; Moberly, *Genesis*, 119–20.

47. E.g. Enns, *Exodus*, 61–62; McDonough, *Creation and New Creation*, 2.

48. Blenkinsopp, *Creation*, 282.

49. See Blenkinsopp, *Creation*, 280-282. In his evaluation of these linguistic parallels, Levenson concurs that "The verbal parallels . . . are too striking, for coincidence" (*Creation*, 85).

50. Beale, *Temple*, 61.

in Exod 25:8 referring to the tabernacle that he was instructing the Israelites to build).

There are also similarities between the tabernacle and the Garden of Eden. First, the most obvious parallel is that God appeared in both places and the Scriptures use the same Hebrew expression, "walk about" (*hithallek*) to refer to these appearances (Gen 3:8 and Lev 26:11; Deut 23:14; 2 Sam 7:6–7).[51] Second, we have already discussed that Adam's charge "to till it [the Garden] and keep it" (v. 15) includes the same pair of words used in Numb 3:7 and 3:8 to describe the duties of the Levites in tending and looking after the tabernacle. Third, after the expulsion from Eden, Adam's guardian role was taken over by the cherubim (Gen 3:24), and this creates a further link to the tabernacle, where two statues of cherubim were placed on either side of the ark (Exod 25:18–22). Other similarities include the fact that the entrance to both the Garden of Eden and the tabernacle was from the east, and the lampstand in the tabernacle with its "six branches," decorated with "three cups shaped like almond blossoms, each with calyx and petals" (v. 32) is perceived by many as representing the tree of life in Eden.[52]

The Creational Functions of the Raising of Israel

The allusions and connotations considered above imply that the raising of the nation of Israel had a marked creational function, and we can identify in the Scriptures three salient aspects of this function: (a) to become a "kingdom of priests" (Exod 19:6), (b) to conduct a mission among the nations, and (c) to prepare the ground for the next stage of creation, Jesus' ministry.

A Kingdom of Priests

Deuteronomy states that the selection of the Israelites to be God's chosen people was not because they were a mighty nation (indeed, they were "the fewest of all people" 7:7) or because they were righteous (as Moses affirmed, "Know, then, that the LORD your God is not giving you this good land to occupy because of your righteousness; for you are a stubborn people" 9:6), but because of God's love: "the LORD set his heart in love on your ancestors alone and chose you, their descendants after them, out of all the peoples, as

---

51. See e.g., Beale, *Temple*, 66; Beale, *New Testament Theology*, 617; Collins, *Genesis 1–4*, 185.

52. E.g., Alexander, *From Eden to New Jerusalem*, 34; Beale, *Temple*, 71; Beale, *New Testament Theology*, 619.

it is today" (10:16). Thus, the separation of Israel was motivated entirely by God's loving desire for the Israelites to become his "treasured possession among all peoples" (Exod 19:5). Significantly, this Exodus passage continues with God's declaration that "you will be for me *a kingdom of priests* and a holy nation" (vv. 5–6; NIV, emphasis added). Desmond Alexander argues that because the Hebrew phrase for "a kingdom of priests" denotes "a body of priests ruling as kings" or "a royal priesthood,"[53] this suggests that God destined them to fulfil the same role that he had originally assigned to Adam and Eve in the Garden of Eden. This message is also conveyed in Isaiah's eschatological prophecy about the Israelites—"but you shall be called priests of the LORD, you shall be named ministers of our God" (61:6)—affirming that the Israelites were raised to serve as spiritual representatives of the Lord, a function that was identified in chapter 3 as one of the core aspects of stewardship.

Mission among the Nations

As God's chosen task force, the Israelites were entrusted with a mission among the nations that was clearly stated at the initial call of Abraham in Genesis 12, and was summarized by Paul in his letter to the Galatians (citing Gen 12:3) as follows: "The Scripture foresaw that God would justify the Gentiles by faith, and announced the gospel in advance to Abraham: 'All nations will be blessed through you'" (3:8, NIV). This mission charge recurs in the Genesis narrative four more times (18:18; 22:18; 26:4–5; 28:14), which justifies C. Wright's conclusion that "Blessing for the nations is the bottom line, textually and theologically, of God's promise to Abraham."[54] There are numerous further biblical passages that echo and reinforce Israel's commission to be a light to the Gentiles (e.g., Josh 4:24; 2 Kgs 19:19; 1 Chr 16:8–10, 23–25; Pss 22:27; 86:9; Isa 25:6–8; 45:22), with one of the best-known examples being God's words to Isaiah, "I will give you as a light to the nations, that my salvation may reach to the end of the earth" (49:6), and Ps 67:1–2 reiterates this message:

> May God be gracious to us and bless us
>   and make his face to shine upon us,
> that your way may be known upon earth,
>   your saving power among all nations.

---

53. Alexander, *From Eden to New Jerusalem*, 84.
54. C. Wright, *Mission of God*, 194.

These verses of Scripture create a context for the declaration in John's Gospel that "salvation is from the Jews" (4:22), and the Israelites' creational function is summed up succinctly in Isaiah (60:21), where they are referred to as "the shoot that I [God] planted, the work of my hands." The same metaphor is used by Paul in Romans when he tells Christian believers that "you, a wild olive shoot, were grafted in their place [i.e., in the place of branches broken off] to share the rich root of the olive tree" (11:17). This image of the horticultural technique of stem grafting conveys expressively the commission of the Israelites: They were to be recognized as the root-stock that would sustain the new plant, and Paul warns his non-Jewish Christian readers to "remember that it is not you that support the root, but the root that supports you" (v. 18).

Preparing the Ground: The Jewish Canon of Scripture and the Role of John the Baptist

It was argued in chapter 2 that the process characterizing the creation of the material world involved a multi-phased progression that was incremental in the sense that every new phase built on, and thus added to, the state of the created order achieved in the previous stage. That is to say, each stage of the creational process *prepared the ground* for the next, and this progressive character also applies to the social transformation process that followed the primal creation. An example of this preparatory function within the current canonical reading was the way in which Job's successful trial paved the way for the raising of the nation of Israel (discussed earlier), and several aspects of the story of the Israelites can also be seen as preparing the ground for a radically new chapter within the creation process, the new creation heralded by Jesus Christ' incarnation and ministry. Let us consider what are arguably the two most salient manifestations of this preparatory function in Jewish history: the *composition of the Jewish canon of Scripture* and the *role of John the Baptist* in "preparing the way for the Lord" (Mark 1:3).

Jewish Scriptures: Sylvie Raquel offers a useful definition when she summarizes that "a text becomes recognized as Scripture when a community considers it imperative to conserve it because it exhibits a divine imprint and contains a transcendent message that will guide the practice of the community."[55] We have considered earlier the creational significance of the release of the Law, and the Jewish Scriptures performed a crucial part in conserving these regulations. The role modelling and missionary functions of the nation of Israel discussed above further underline the importance of

55. Raquel, "Canon."

the conservation of the Jewish canon; indeed, Psalm 22 declares that "future generations will be told about the Lord, and proclaim his deliverance to a people yet unborn, saying that he has done it" (vv. 30–31)—as C. Wright submits, the "whole history of Israel, we might say, is intended to be the shop window for the knowledge of God in all the earth."[56] In this sense, the written Jewish Scriptures serve as a solid foundation to build on, a role that was in fact already suggested at the beginning of the history of the Israelites when the tablets of the Ten Commandments were placed in the center of the tabernacle within the ark (Exod 25:19). In Romans, Paul also highlights the Israelites' link to the Scriptures when in his answer to the question "what advantage has the Jew?" (3:1) he states: "in the first place the Jews were entrusted with the oracles of God" (v. 2).

The preparatory function of the Jewish Scriptures is also prominent in the sense that in the New Testament the Jewish Bible is seen as the theological frame of reference for understanding and interpreting Jesus' ministry, death, and resurrection; this was demonstrated expressively, for example, in the story of the Road to Emmaus, where the two disciples could only recognize Jesus after he, "beginning with Moses and all the prophets . . . interpreted to them the things about himself in *all the scriptures*" (24:27; emphasis added). Likewise, in John 5:39 Jesus states, "You search the scriptures because you think that in them you have eternal life; and it is they that testify on my behalf," and talking about episodes in Israel's history, Paul sums up the foundational role of Scripture very clearly: "Now these things occurred as examples for us . . . These things happened to them to serve as an example, and they were written down to instruct us, on whom the ends of the ages have come" (1 Cor 10:6, 11). This instructional role is reiterated in Mark 12:24, where Jesus attributed the erroneous theology of the Sadducees partly to their insufficient knowledge of the Scriptures.

John the Baptist: Arguably the most explicit recognition of the preparatory function of the nation of Israel in the Bible can be found when John the Baptist is described in all the Gospels as one who was to fulfill Isaiah's (40:3) and Malachi's prophecies about "preparing the way of the Lord" (3:1).[57] He is not only presented in the Scriptures as exemplifying humankind's best—"among those born of women no one has arisen greater than John the Baptist" (Matt 11:11)—but also as someone who fully embodies the Jewish spiritual tradition, as indicated by the fact that Jesus referred to him as Elijah: "For all the prophets and the law prophesied until John came; and if you are willing to accept it, he is Elijah who is to come" (Matt

---

56. C. Wright, *Mission of God*, 127.
57. Mark 1:2–3; Matt 3:3; Luke 3:4; John 1:23.

11:13–14; see also 17:10–13). The same message was also communicated by an angel of the Lord to John's father, Zechariah, about the son who was to be born to him and Elizabeth: "He will turn many of the people of Israel to the Lord their God. With the *spirit and power of Elijah* he will go before him, to turn the hearts of parents to their children, and the disobedient to the wisdom of the righteous, to *make ready a people prepared for the Lord*" (Luke 1:16–17; emphases added).

The identification of John the Baptist with Elijah further affirms his pivotal role as "precursor"[58] (Green), as it alludes to Malachi's prophecy about Elijah's future ministry to prepare Israel for the day of the Lord (Mal 4:5–6). We are told about the scope of John's ministry that he reached "people from the *whole* Judean countryside and *all* the people of Jerusalem" (Mark 1:5; emphases added), as well as people from "*all* the region along the Jordan" (Matt 3:5; emphasis added)—as a result, even the chief priests acknowledged that "*all* regarded John as truly a prophet" (Mark 11:32; emphasis added). This was therefore outreach on a grand scale indeed, and yet John Nolland rightly underlines the fact that this "supreme figure in human history"[59] is immediately eclipsed in Luke's Gospel: After praising him, Jesus tells the crowds that "the least in the kingdom of God is greater than he" (7:28), thereby providing one of the clearest examples in the whole canon of the incremental nature of progressive creation.

4.3 Jesus Christ and the New Creation

Paul's letter to the Galatians states that God sent his Son "when the fullness of time had come" (4:4). The phrase "fullness of time" implies that the Incarnation happened in accordance with a greater plan, at a time when everything had fallen into place for the reception of Jesus Christ on earth.[60] Theology has traditionally held two contrasting views regarding the divine purpose behind the Incarnation, referred to as the "infralapsarian" and "supralapsarian" positions.[61] The former understands the Incarnation as contingent upon sin, that is, it perceives the primary purpose of God's sending his son as a redemptive act within salvation history to reconcile the sinful

58. Green, *Luke*, 294.

59. Nolland, *Luke 1–9:20*, 339.

60. De Boer explains that in Gal 4:1–2 Paul introduces the metaphor of a "will" or "testament"—as indicated by the use of the term "heir" (v. 1)—and therefore "the fullness of time" in v. 4 corresponds to "the date set by the father" in v. 2 on the analogy of a will/testament finally becoming effective. De Boer, *Galatians*, 261. See also Matera, *Galatians*, 150.

61. E.g., Berkhof, *Systematic Theology*, 118–25; van Driel, *Incarnation*, 4.

world to himself and thus to restore creation to its original goodness. The alternative supralapsarian view suggests that the central motive behind the Incarnation was something other than the need for reconciliation, without denying that Jesus' ministry did achieve this purpose.[62] The latter is admittedly the minority position in Western theology although it has been embraced by such influential modern scholars as Schleiermacher, Barth, and Rahner;[63] it also represents a continuous strand in Christology since the work of Duns Scotus in the thirteenth century, and indeed the origins of the argument for the absolute predestination of Christ can be traced back even earlier, to the writings of Rupert of Deutz (c. 1075—1129/30) and Robert Grosseteste (c. 1168—1253).[64] We must note here that neither approach is uniform: Infralapsarianism subsumes a variety of atonement and reconciliation models, while supralapsarianism shows variation regarding the actual reason why the Incarnation is seen as predestined (i.e., seen as part of the original creation plan regardless of Adam's sin).[65]

The key question of the infra/supralapsarian issue is whether the Incarnation would have taken place if humanity had not sinned. In this respect the approach followed in the current book falls under the supralapsarian rubric, viewing the Son of God's taking on of a human body as a necessary step toward the fulfilment of the progressive creational process in new creation. That is to say, the underlying assumption of the following discussion is that the "eternal purpose" of God mentioned in Eph 3:11—"This was in accordance with the eternal purpose that he has carried out in Christ Jesus our Lord"—refers to the fact that the Son of God was always intended to become incarnate, because he had, and continues to have, a decisive role to play in the creation process even beyond taking on the sin of humanity. In contrasting the *proton* (the beginning of creation) and the *eschaton* (the goal of creation), Van Driel takes the view that "the eschaton is not the restoration of the proton. In the eschaton there is an abundance, a richness in intimacy with God and in human transformation which the proton did not know";[66] he later summarizes this position succinctly by concluding that "In Christ we gain more than we lost in Adam,"[67] and using different language, Daly

62. Van Driel, *Incarnation*, 4.

63. Ibid., 175.

64. Horan, "Scotus on the Incarnation," 375.

65. Van Driel, *Incarnation*, 5.

66. Ibid., 6.

67. Ibid., 151. This belief is also shared by other theologians; for example, drawing on Moltmann, Childs states, "Moltmann has sounded a correct biblical note when he insists that the future envisioned as a new creation is not simply a return to an earlier, original condition. Paul's message of hope pulsates with his anticipation of a new

expresses the same conviction when he asserts, "I wish to contend that the scope of salvation includes, but far exceeds, the scope of sin."[68]

In agreement with this belief, the rest of this chapter examines the nature of the unique "abundance" and "richness in human transformation" that the Incarnation added to progressive creation by addressing five broad themes: (a) Jesus the last Adam, (b) "newness" and the new creation, (c) the kingdom of God and the commandment to love, (d) the making of disciples, and (e) the nature of human transformation. Of course, any discussion about the life, death, resurrection, and ascension of Jesus Christ is potentially infinite, so the treatment of these five points will be largely limited here to the creational aspects of the issues in question; further elaboration of some of the themes will be offered in the second part of the book when we consider the Atonement, the Eucharist, the Lord's Prayer, and the Great Commission.

Jesus the last Adam

Although the Incarnation is presented in the canon as embedded in the overall progression of the biblical narrative, it represents far more than merely a consecutive step in the story of creation, because it marks the beginning of a radically new phase in the transfiguration process of humanity. We saw earlier that Jesus is described in Rom 5:12–21 as a counterpart to Adam, representing a new trajectory for humankind that leads to righteousness and life, and accordingly, in 1 Cor 15:45 Paul calls Jesus "the last Adam" and a "life-giving spirit" from heaven. Identifying Jesus as an alternative to the first fallen man has strong creational implications, and Paul makes this juxtaposition more explicit in v. 49 when he states that "Just as we have borne the image of the man of dust, we will also bear the image of the man of heaven" (we shall consider in a separate section below what "bearing the image" might mean in a creational context).

Adam and the Incarnate Christ are also linked by the fact that both were created from matter that was then impregnated with divine substance: Adam was formed from dust and then God "breathed into his nostrils the

---

creation, hitherto unknown" (*Biblical Theology*, 394). Wilkinson similarly concludes, "The new creation is therefore not a return to Eden. The new creation is better than Eden, in terms of its security against evil and its freedom from sin" (*Creation*, 263). See also Fergusson, *Cosmos and the Creator*, 94.

68. Daly, *Creation and Redemption*, 4. It must be noted, however, that the "gaining-more-than-we-lost" principle is not necessarily supralapsarian in itself, because, for example, Augustine's doctrine of *Felix Culpa* also proposes that the redemption of sinners is a greater good than there being no sin at all.

breath of life" (Gen 2:7), while the Holy Spirit "came upon" Jesus' mother, Mary, and thus God "overshadowed her" (Luke 1:35). Indeed, Adam was created in God's image (Gen 1:26), while Jesus is the perfect image of God (2 Cor 2:4:4; Heb 1:3). Furthermore, and consistent with the progressive nature of the creational process, the Incarnation was itself incremental: Jesus was born as a human baby who had to grow into a mature adult before starting his ministry, and it was argued in the previous chapter that Adam, too, was expected to undergo a maturation process in the Garden of Eden so that at one point he could partake of the fruit of the tree of the knowledge of good and evil. The serpent's intervention at the Fall distorted Adam's mission and derailed the creational process; Jesus on the other hand did reach maturity and fulfilled his mission despite the fact that—as we shall see in chapter 5—Satan did his utmost to divert him from it.

According to the Synoptic Gospels, when Jesus formally assumed his public ministry at his baptism, a voice from heaven declared, "This is my Son, the Beloved, with whom I am well pleased." (Matt 3:16–17). When considered from the progressive creational perspective of this book, this divine statement might be seen to have special significance that is not usually highlighted in commentaries. The phrase "I am well pleased" is expressed by the same Greek word in all the three Synoptic Gospels, the first person singular derivative of the verb *eudokeō*. This compound word is made up of two parts, "good, well" and "to think, seem," thus having a literal translation of "think it good," "think well of" or "what seems good." This being the case, after Jesus' baptism and anointing by the Holy Spirit, God declared publicly that it was "good," which offers a striking parallel with God's appraisal of the creation of Adam and Eve as "very good" (Gen 1:31). Matthew's Gospel reports that God repeated this appraisal after Jesus' transfiguration (17:5), which is also affirmed in 2 Pet 1:17. Moreover and highly significantly, the divine endorsement of Jesus also offers an emphatic counterpoint to God's declaration about Adam in Gen 2:18 that "it is not good," thereby indicating that creation has finally been re-aligned with God's creative purpose.

"Newness" and New Creation

In his seminal paper on "The Concept of Newness in the New Testament," Roy Harrisville asserts that the "NT kerygma includes the idea that in Jesus something entirely new has occurred, that in him a new time phase, a 'new aeon' has begun by which the redemptive activity of God comes to its conclusion."[69] Indeed, in heralding a new era in creation, the Incarnation

---

69. Harrisville, "Newness in the New Testament," 73.

can be perceived as the commencement of the realization of several OT prophesies in this vein, most notably Isaiah talking about "new things" to come (42:9; 43:19; 48:6) and the "new heaven and new earth" that God will create (65:17; 66:22), Jeremiah foretelling the "new covenant" (31:31–34), and Ezekiel prophesying about the "new heart" (18:31, 36:26) and the "new spirit" that God will provide (11:19, 18:31, 36:26).[70] The books of the New Testament refer to the emerging "newness" in a variety of terms such as "new wine" (Mark 2:22; Luke 5:37–38), "new teaching" (Mark 1:27), "new commandment" of love (John 13:34; 1 John 2:8), "new covenant" (Luke 22:20; 1 Cor 11:25; 2 Cor 3:6; Heb 8:8, 13; 9:15; 12:24), "new creation" (2 Cor 5:17; Gal 6:15), "new man/humanity" (Eph 2:15; 4:24; Col 3:9–10), "new song" (Rev. 5:9; 14:3), and "new name" for believers (Rev 2:17; 3:12). Revelation also describes that in eschatological times—"at the renewal of all things" (Matt 19:28)—there will be "a new heaven and a new earth" (Rev 21:1; cf. 2 Pet 3:13), and a "new Jerusalem" (Rev 3:12; 21:2). All these concepts have been the subject of considerable theological reflection in the past, but what is particularly important for our current purpose is their cumulative presence and prominence, leading Murray Harris to submit that the theology of the New Testament "could be written around this theocentric concept of 'newness,' which is summed up in the statement . . . 'See! I make everything new!' [Rev 21:5]"[71]—indeed, the very name "New" Testament is itself testimony to the importance of this emerging "newness."[72]

Although not labelled explicitly as "new" in the Scriptures, the recurring mention of "mystery" also highlights an important aspect of newness in the New Testament. As T. J. Lang expounds, the term is consistently presented as something that had been kept hidden by God through the ages and was revealed to Christian believers only through the advent of Jesus.[73] The various uses of the term "mystery" in the New Testament cover a range of related issues, from the kingdom of God and Gentile salvation with its redemptive benefits to the "revelation of God's pretemporal plans for unity in the cosmos—whether that unity be the unity of the cosmos, the solidarity of Jews and Gentiles, or the oneness of the church and Christ."[74] What is important from the current discussion's perspective is that in all these cases a hidden/revealed binary is either implied or explicitly stated, with

70. In this respect, Stephens concludes that "the majority voice of the Hebrew Bible is one in which the eschatological future of Israel involves Yahweh remaining committed to the fulfilment of his creation project" (*Annihilation or Renewal*, 44).

71. Harris, *Second Corinthians*, 433.

72. Motyer, "New, Newness," 824.

73. Lang, *Mystery*, 32.

74. Ibid., 85.

the mystery being disclosed only in the new, post-Incarnation era. As Lang concludes, "Whether it be to divide time along the axis of Christ's advent and, in so doing, to bind the newness of Christianity to God's eternal plans (Ignatius and the Epistle to Diognetus), or to identify the once latent but now newly revealed christological meanings of prophetic scripture (Justin, Melito), and so to identify Christ with the God of Israel, as well (Tertullian), the logic of the 'once hidden, now revealed' mystery discourse supplies subsequent Christian thinkers with the essential conceptual apparatus for dealing with these pressing issues."[75]

The pervasive renewal themes in the New Testament have sometimes been referred to under the umbrella term "new creation." This usage is generally broader than Paul's use of the term in 2 Cor 5:17 and Gal 6:15—the only two places in the canon where the actual phrase occurs—since it is typically understood to refer to the whole ongoing process of transformation leading to the final eschatological consummation; as Mark Stephens summarizes, the phrase reflects "common scholarly parlance in which the term functions as a conceptual label to collate a range of cosmic eschatological images, not only within early Christian texts, but also in the Hebrew Bible and Second Temple Judaism."[76] A good illustration of this broader usage is offered by Moyer Hubbard in his monograph on *New Creation in Paul's Letters and Thought*:

> The motif of "new creation," however, is not confined to the opening and closing chapters of the Christian Scriptures. The prophets, the psalmists, the evangelists, and so on, all exhibit a robust faith in the creative activity of God, and this faith was not focused solely on the remote past or the distant future. The prayer of the penitent sinner that God would "create a pure heart, and grant a new spirit" (Ps 51:10), as well as the bold declaration of the prophet that Yahweh was, even now, "making something new" (Isa 43:18), reflect a deep-seated belief in

75. Lang, *Mystery*, 129. Although this goes beyond the canonical narrative perspective of the current book, it is interesting to note that, as Lang further explains about Justin's appropriation of the mystery concept, "by dividing Christians and Jews with the mystery of Christ and by substantiating the mystery of Christ by way of his totalizing rereading of scripture, Justin affixes Christianity to Israel's history but, in the same stroke, excludes Judaism from that heritage—not Judaism *in toto*, but Judaism insofar as it does not profess Christ" (ibid., 191). This parallel sense of continuity and discontinuity allowed Christians "to account for themselves as both genuinely new to world and yet also ancient according to God's designs" (ibid., 249).

76. Stephens, *Annihilation or Renewal*, 1.

the continuing new-creative work of God, and form part of the vibrant, if variegated, biblical witness to new creation.[77]

Let us turn now to examining how new creation was reflected in the two principal aspects of Jesus' teaching, the kingdom of God and the "new commandment" to love.

The Kingdom of God and the New Commandment of Love

One of the central themes in Jesus' public teaching was the "kingdom of God" (or its paraphrase in Matthew, the "kingdom of heaven").[78] The concept was already in circulation in first century Judaism referring both to God's everlasting rule over the world[79] and the eschatological kingly reign of God in the "Ages to Come,"[80] but Jesus extended the meaning of the phrase by describing the kingdom as something one can receive or inherit, as a blessing to experience, or even more broadly, as a hope for the fulfilment of God's purposes in human affairs.[81] Indeed, as Ladd summarizes, the kingdom of God in Jesus' teaching "stands as a comprehensive term for all that the messianic salvation included,"[82] and in this sense the term covers a semantic domain close to that of the eschatological renewal associated with new creation.

One aspect of Jesus' use of the term that has intrigued and divided scholars over the centuries is that although it has obvious eschatological connotations in many of Jesus' sayings, in some passages it appears to refer to the *immediacy* of God's presence in power, for example when Jesus sent out the Seventy and instructed them to tell the people that "The kingdom of God has come near to you" (Luke 10:9). This latter aspect of the concept, pointing to the present reality of the godly order on earth, has been famously

---

77. Hubbard, *New Creation*, 1.

78. Luke, for example, records Jesus saying, "I must proclaim the good news of the kingdom of God . . . because that is why I was sent" (4:43; see also Mark 1:14–15; Matt 4:17) and Matthew summarizes Jesus' mission in Galilee as "proclaiming the good news of the kingdom and curing every disease and every sickness among the people" (4:23; 9:35). See e.g., Chilton, "Introduction," 1; Farmer, "Kingdom of God," 126; Travis, *Second Coming of Jesus*, 49.

79. E.g., Ps 47:7–9; 145:13; 1 Chr 29:11.

80. E.g., Zech 14:9; see e.g., Jeremias, *New Testament Theology*, 96; Ladd, *Theology of the New Testament*, 45–46; Witherington, *Imminent Domain*, 2.

81. See e.g., Jeremias, *New Testament Theology*, 98; Patrick, "Kingdom of God," 68; Travis, *Second Coming of Jesus*, 51–52; 65.

82. Ladd, *Theology of the New Testament*, 72.

summarized by C. H. Dodd in his notion of "realized eschatology,"[83] and as a result of the difficulty of understanding the kingdom either as entirely future or entirely present, most modern interpreters have taken a halfway or mediating position, viewing the kingdom as somehow *both* present and future (the "now" and the "not yet"). Thus, "realized eschatology" was transformed into "eschatology in the process of realization,"[84] and those who advocated a futuristic view of the kingdom of God allowed for the emergence of some kind of inauguration or "foretaste"[85] of the heavenly rule of God in the ministry of Jesus.[86]

The notion of inaugurated eschatology is compatible with the concept of progressive creation, because an ongoing, gradual sense of the emergence of the kingdom of God was clearly implied when Jesus told the Pharisees, "The kingdom of God is not coming with things that can be observed; nor will they say, 'Look, here it is!' or 'There it is!' For, in fact, the kingdom of God is among you" (Luke 17:20–21). Jesus further underlined the progressive growth aspect of the kingdom in the two parables of the Mustard Seed and the Yeast (Luke 13:18–21), in the latter likening the concept to a kind of "changing agent" that transforms the created order from within.

This transformational aspect was also evident in the other major theme of Jesus's teaching, the "new commandment" to love one another (John 13:34; 1 John 2:8). We saw earlier that the release of the Decalogue and the Law constituted an important step in the process of creation, because it provided the Israelites with a template for social order to shape their community and to model it to other nations. Against this backdrop, Paul's statement in Romans that "the one who loves another has fulfilled the law" (13:8; reiterated in v. 10 for emphasis) is particularly momentous: It suggests that by introducing the new commandment, Jesus in effect placed the social transformational process of humanity on a renewed foundation, with the need to love one another as a guiding principle. Moo summarizes the creational aspect of this change as follows: "Paul proclaims the arrival of the 'new creation' in order to remind believers of the new set of values by which they are to live and look at all of reality. Central to these values, as the context of Galatians 5–6 makes clear, is love for others. Belonging to

83. For a review and discussion, see Ladd, *Theology of the New Testament*, rev. ed., 54–67.

84. This modification was also endorsed by Dodd; see Farmer, "Kingdom of God," 122.

85. Jeremias, *New Testament Theology*, 95.

86. See e.g., Caragounis, "Kingdom of God," 429–30; Marshall, *New Testament Theology*, 61, 78.

the new creation means fundamentally a reorientation of our focus from self to others."[87]

Accordingly, although the new commandment was already stated in Lev 9:18—"you shall love your neighbor as yourself"—it can be considered a novel element in the NT canon because it was intended to become, in Harrisville's words, the "the rule of the new eschatological community. . . . Its proclamation is the assurance that the new aeon has dawned."[88] Indeed, the replacement of the Law with love as the linchpin of social transformation constituted a radical shift as it represented a change from an externally imposed regulatory force to the internal, intrinsic power of love. In this way the prophecy of Jer 33:13 was fulfilled: "I will put my law within them, and I will write it on their hearts."

The Making of Disciples

One important aspect of Jesus' creational role was his selection of a group of disciples to become the kernel of the emerging Church and therefore the founding fathers of the new humanity. We find some unmistakable parallels between the making of disciples in the Gospels and certain creational themes in the Old Testament. First, at the climax of John's Gospel, Jesus is shown to "breathe" upon the Eleven in the same way as God breathed into Adam's nostrils the breath of life (Gen 2:7), declaring "Receive the Holy Spirit" (John 20:22).[89] Second, similar to how God established a succession of stewards by creating Eve and blessing the first human couple to be fruitful and multiply, Jesus established a succession of disciples during the Great Commission by declaring, "Go therefore and make disciples of all nations" (Matt 28:19) and "go and bear fruit, fruit that will last" (John 15:6). The Great Commission will be discussed in more detail in chapter 6, but it should be emphasized here that the aim of this commission was a comprehensive multiplication of the disciples; that is, in Turner's words, "The disciples' central responsibility is to reproduce themselves."[90] This creational interpretation of the making of disciples is corroborated by two additional considerations:

---

87. Moo, "Creation and New Creation," 59.

88. Harrisville, "Concept of Newness," 79.

89. For a similar conclusion, see Humphrey, "New Creation," 536.

90. Turner, *Matthew*, 689. In a similar vein, Barth also emphasizes that "the apostles are called to make apostolic Christians of all others" ("Matthew 28:16–20," 63).

- In 2 Corinthians, Paul, citing Isa 52:11, instructs the disciples to *separate* themselves from the unbelievers—"Do not be mismatched with unbelievers . . . Therefore come out from them, and be separate from them, says the Lord, and touch nothing unclean" (2 Cor 6:14, 17)—thereby emphasizing the creational need to keep God's stewards pure, similar to how the Israelites were to be separated from among other nations (discussed earlier).

- The "new song" in Rev 5:9 declares that Jesus has made the saints "to be a kingdom and priests serving our God, and they will reign on earth," a message echoed by 1 Peter when instructing Christian believers to "let yourselves be built into a spiritual house, to be a holy priesthood, to offer spiritual sacrifices acceptable to God through Jesus Christ" (2:5). Declaring the saints to be a holy priesthood is a direct extension of the message of Exod 19:5–6 discussed earlier, whereby the Israelites were commissioned to fulfil the stewardship role that God had originally assigned to Adam in the Garden of Eden.[91] A prophecy in Isa 66:21 already suggested that this role would be extended to incoming foreigners as well—"And I will also take some of them as priests and as Levites, says the LORD" (66:21)—and the NT passages above (see also Rev 1:6) indicate that Jesus' disciples were to assume this stewardship role.

In sum, Jesus' disciples were commissioned to become the new stewards of the earth—or as Paul put it, "ambassadors for Christ" (2 Cor 5:20)—and by making disciples Jesus performed a creational role, thereby manifesting the truth of the declaration in John 1:14 that in him the creative Word "became flesh."[92] We shall return to this matter in chapter 6 when we consider the Great Commission.

The Nature of Human Transformation

In an analysis of new creation, Moo argues that the new aeon inaugurated by the Incarnation is evidenced by ongoing human transformation: "'New creation' is manifested in the present through *transformed* Christians who live in *transformed* relationships with God, with one another, with all

91. For a similar argument, see also Alexander, *From Eden to New Jerusalem*, 125.

92. Osborn states in this respect, "Christ's significance for creation becomes explicit in the prologue to John's Gospel. It is none other than the Word by which God created that has become incarnate as Jesus Christ (John 1:14). He is the agent of creation and the source of life (John 1:4), and is thus not only involved in the original creative act but also intimately associated with God's continuing providential care for creation." Osborn, "Creation," 433.

people, and with the world of nature"[93] (emphasis added). Jesus' transformational role is made explicit in Phil 3:21—"He will transform the body of our humiliation that it may be conformed to the body of his glory, by the power that also enables him to make all things subject to himself"—and in Romans, Paul further explains that human transformation is not confined only to "the body of our humiliation" but also concerns the believers' mindset: "Do not be conformed to this world, but be transformed by the renewing of your minds, so that you may discern what is the will of God—what is good and acceptable and perfect" (12:2). As will be shown below, the NT canon includes a wide range of metaphors and images to describe the transformation of humans—from exposure to divine light to the infusion of the Holy Spirit—and this emphasis warrants a closer look at the specific processes involved.

We may gain a sense of how the diverse biblical accounts are related to the overall transfiguration of humanity by considering analogies offered by molecular biology concerning the alteration of the genetic makeup of living creatures. Broadly speaking, contemporary bioscience recognizes two ways of changing an organism's genetic endowment (i.e., the unique genetic codes that govern how creatures develop and what traits will be transferred to their offspring), either through *indirect* or *direct* means. The indirect approach involves traditional procedures such as "selective breeding" or "artificial selection" that have long been employed in agriculture to improve the crops and livestock, while direct methods concern various forms of biotechnological interventions, for example inserting a desired gene into a host genome or exposing genes to radiation or chemicals. Both types fall under the broad category of "genetic engineering," although in everyday parlance (and the popular press), this term—or its more common synonym, "genetic modification" (GM)—is applied primarily to the direct type.[94]

Several biblical descriptions of human transfiguration bear a distinct similarity with these biomolecular procedures. The selection of Noah and Abraham to be the fathers of new, improved human lines is consistent with the agricultural process of selective breeding, which is centered around a breeding stock of specimen with superior traits, and the separation of the Israelites—and then also of the Christian disciples—in order to preserve their purity (described earlier) follows similar principles. Moreover, the recurring exhortations in the NT canon to exercise self-regulation in order to resist temptation and avoid sin are also in harmony with the principles of artificial selection to promote certain desired phenotypic traits. Thus,

93. Moo, "Creation and New Creation," 59.
94. For an overview of genetic engineering, see Nicholl, *Genetic Engineering*.

there is ample biblical material focusing on human transformation through *indirect* means, but what is perhaps less obvious is that some other transformational images in the Bible appear to be more *direct* in nature, reminiscent of the second type of genetic engineering mentioned above, namely the procedures involving some form of gene manipulation. Let us look at three salient biblical processes of this latter type: human transfiguration through (a) becoming conformed to the divine image, (b) being exposed to divine light, and (c) receiving the Holy Spirit to dwell inside the believer.

Becoming Conformed to the Divine Image

Romans 8:29 states that Christian believers are "to be conformed to the image of his Son, in order that he might be the firstborn within a large family." The Greek term for "conformed to" (*symmorphos*) literally means "jointly formed" and it is used figuratively to express "similar" or "fashioned like/ onto." This makes sense within the context of becoming similar to Jesus, and Wright and Dunn, for example, follow this interpretation;[95] however, the actual text does not talk about being conformed to Jesus himself but rather to his "image," which makes the interpretation less straightforward: What does the phrase "the image of the Son" refer to and how can one become "jointly formed with" or "fashioned like/onto" this image? These questions become particularly important in view of the fact that in 2 Cor 4:4 Paul identifies Jesus as "the image of God," which is then reiterated in Col 1:15: "He is the image of the invisible God, the firstborn of all creation." Thus, it follows that Jesus' likeness, to which Christian believers are to become conformed, is the same kind of likeness as the one that the Son shares with the Father.[96] Furthermore, Rom 8:29 (cited above) also indicates that the believers' shared image with Jesus makes them become part of a "large family," and in 1 Cor 15:49 the term "image" is used to relate humanity to their ancestor Adam (in the first phase of creation) and then to Jesus (in new creation): "Just as we have borne the image of the man of dust, we will also bear the image of the man of heaven."

It is no straightforward task to define a common semantic denominator of the term "image" in these diverse passages, but a reading that makes sense when considering both family membership (Rom 8:29) and

---

95. Wright: "The emphasis of vv. 29–30 falls clearly on conformity to Christ. ("Romans," 602). Dunn: "suffering with him and sharing his death to the final dying of the mortal body in sure and certain hope of sharing his risen life to the full" (*Romans 1–8*, 495).

96. See e.g., Matera, *II Corinthians*, 102.

a hereditary sequence (in 1 Cor 15:49) is the perception of "image" as a shared core element, not unlike the genetic code in humans. That this understanding is possible even when it is applied to the Father–Son relationship (in 2 Cor 4:4) is evidenced by the Niceno-Constantinopolitan Creed, which states that Jesus is "of one substance with the Father" using the famous Greek term *"homoousios"* and its Latin translation "consubstantial."[97] Thus, reading Rom 8:29 in this way would suggest that to become "jointly formed with" or "fashioned onto" the image of Jesus refers to a process of being *transformed*—at least partially—into divine substance, an understanding that is not incompatible with Paul's description of human transfiguration in 2 Cor 3:18: "And all of us, with unveiled faces, seeing the glory of the Lord as though reflected in a mirror, are being transformed into the same image from one degree of glory to another; for this comes from the Lord, the Spirit."

In this last passage, Paul uses the same Greek word for "being transformed" (*metamorphoō*) as it appears in Mark (9:2) and Matthew (17:2) to describe the transfiguration of Jesus, and this is unlikely to be a coincidence since this verb is rare (besides these three examples there is only one other occurrence of it in the whole of the NT canon, in Rom 12:2). Therefore, its use here implies that the believer's transformation is comparable to the substantial metamorphosis that Jesus himself demonstrated on the Mount of Transfiguration. Such a profound change is also implied in the other *locus classicus* for human transformation, 2 Pet 1:4, which talks about escaping the corruption of the world and becoming "participants of the divine nature."[98] Again, it is unlikely to be a coincidence that a few verses later 2 Peter explicitly mentions Jesus' transfiguration (v. 16), making this the only direct reference to the Transfiguration in the canon outside the three primary accounts in the Synoptics, and thereby signaling an underlying belief in 2 Peter in the reality of divinity associating with matter.[99] Finally, Eph 4:23–24 also urges believers to put away their corrupt old self and "to be renewed in the spirit of your minds, and to clothe yourselves with the new self, created according to

97. The Son's *homoousion* with the Father has been subject to a large amount of theological reflection, because, as McGuckin summarizes, it was "the very hallmark of authenticity of Orthodox belief in antiquity, and it remains so to this day" (*Orthodox Church*, 146). However, for the present purpose it is enough to acknowledge that the reading of "image" as some kind of fundamental core is a legitimate one irrespective of the details of the various theological stances in this respect.

98. Starr argues that 2 Peter and Paul "work with the same constellation of ideas," a parallel which is further strengthened by 2 Peter's unique acknowledgement of Paul letters (3:15–16). Starr, "Deification," 89. For similar views, see Finlan and Kharlamov, "Introduction," 4; Finlan, "Divine Participation," 44.

99. Starr, "Deification," 84.

the likeness of God in true righteousness and holiness." This transformation of the self can again be perceived to go beyond purely a moral development; indeed, in Colossians the same metaphor "clothing oneself with the new self according to the image of its creator" (3:10) is linked to an ensuing renewal that results in the emergence of a new humanity: "In that renewal there is no longer Greek and Jew, circumcised and uncircumcised, barbarian, Scythian, slave and free; but Christ is all and in all!" (v. 11).

The notion of a communion with divine likeness is not alien to Christian theology, as attested to by the existence of a range of theological terms to refer to the acquisition of sanctity in some form, such as "progressive sanctification," "glorification," "divinization," "participation," "partaking," "union with God," "deification," "theosis," and "theopoiesis." These different terms occur extensively in theological works from the patristic era to modern times,[100] although they are admittedly not used consistently and their meaning does not always concur in the various usages.[101] The loose semantic domain is largely due to the fact that the biblical warrants for a transformation that goes beyond salvation tend to be brief and lack sufficient detail, rendering it therefore difficult to be more specific than concluding that "created in the image of God, [humankind] is called to achieve a 'divine similitude'"[102] (Meyendorff). Significantly, however, 2 Cor 3:18 suggests that the conformity to God's image is progressive in nature—"being transformed into the same image *from one degree* of glory *to another . . .*" (emphasis added)—and accordingly, deification is usually understood as "a process that begins in this life, certainly, but finds its fulfilment only in the next"[103] (Williams). Because the Scriptures do not offer any details of a timeline for the progression, from a canonical narrative perspective any

---

100. See e.g., Williams, *Deification*, 174. For other overviews, see, e.g., Christensen and Wittung, *History of Deification*; Finlan and Kharlamov, *Theosis*.

101. E.g., as Finlan and Kharlamov conclude with reference to patristic theology, "The popularity of the idea is matched by a lack of precise definition. The church fathers argue for, rather than spell out, deification" ("Introduction," 4). Also, in comparing how Gregory Palamas and Thomas Aquinas understood the doctrine of deification, Williams explains, "although Aquinas and Palamas share with the Fathers a common vocabulary of deification, individual terms within that vocabulary may not correspond exactly. . . . Thomas and Gregory are not always using the term participation in the same sense. For Thomas, anything's existence is a participation in divine nature of a sort; even the light of natural reason is a participation in divine light. Such usages differ from Gregory's, for in his lexicon participation seems equated solely with deification proper." Williams, *Deification*, 173.

102. Meyendorff, *Byzantine Theology*, 2.

103. Williams, *Deification*, 164; see also Cranfield, *Romans*, 432; Finlan and Kharlamov, "Introduction," 3; Finlan, *Atonement*, 123.

attempt to be more precise about concrete milestones of the human trans-figuration process is seen as inevitably somewhat speculative.

Being Exposed to Divine Light

Brilliant, radiant light associated with God's glory appears in several de-scriptions of theophanies in the Bible (e.g., Hab 3:3–4), and light is often associated in the Scriptures with the divine core of God, who "dwells in unapproachable light" (1 Tim 6:16). Hebrews also asserts about Jesus that "The Son is the radiance of God's glory," and this is affirmed in Jesus' famous declaration in John 8:12 that "I am the light of the world. Whoever follows me will never walk in darkness but will have the light of life" (reiterated in 9:5). The relevance of divine light to the current chapter is that several NT passages suggest that being exposed to it may bring about a profound change in humans,[104] with the best-known example being Paul's conversion on the road to Damascus, when he was enveloped in a "light from heaven, brighter than the sun" (Acts 26:13). As Paul expounds later, "all of us, with unveiled faces, seeing the glory of the Lord . . . are being transformed into the same image, from one degree of glory to another" (2 Cor 3:18). A few verses later, at the beginning of 2 Cor 4, Paul further expands on this point in two dif-ferent ways: First, he explains that the devil's strategy to keep unbelievers in bondage has been to veil the light of God's glory: "In their case the god of this world has blinded the minds of the unbelievers, to keep them from seeing the light of the gospel of the glory of Christ, who is the image of God" (4:4). Second, in 4:6, he explicitly connects human transformation with the creational light in Gen 1:3: "For it is the God who said, 'Let light shine out of darkness,' who has shone in our hearts to give the light of the knowledge of the glory of God in the face of Jesus Christ" (v. 6).

Thus, partly building on his own transfiguration experience, Paul came to associate the transformation of believers in general with exposure to divine light and glory, particularly as conveyed through the shining light of Jesus, an image that occurs in several places in the NT canon (e.g., Luke 2:32; Eph 5:14; Rev 1:16). In doing so, Paul viewed light and glory as manifestations of a transcendental reality rather than merely an expressive metaphor to refer to God's majesty, and Alan Segal summarizes the trans-figurational role of light and glory in Paul's overall approach to conversion as follows: "For Paul, as for the earliest Jewish mystics, to be privileged to see

---

104. An interesting analogy to this is that exposure to radiation in contemporary molecular biology—a process called "mutagenesis"—is a known technology to change the genetic makeup of a living organism.

the *Kavod* or Glory (*doxa*) of God is a prologue to transformation into his image (*eikōn*). Paul does not say that all Christians have made the journey literally but compares the experience of knowing Christ to being allowed into the intimate presence of the Lord. We do know that he himself has made that journey."[105]

Confirmation that this understanding of the transformational quality of exposure to divine light is not an arbitrary reading of the Scriptures can be found in Orthodox Christian theology, where beholding the "uncreated light" is perceived as a central motif.[106] The 1351 Eastern Church Council in Byzantium defined "uncreated light" as part of God's "energies," which "may be experienced by men in the form of light,"[107] a view supported by the Hesychast experiential tradition going back to the Desert fathers as well as the converging views of several church fathers and subsequent Orthodox theologians,[108] presented most influentially by Gregory Palamas (1296–1359). Regarding the transformational quality of uncreated light, Hireotheos Vlachos sums up that it is "not simply a symbolic vision, nor sensory and created, nor inferior to understanding, but it is deification,"[109] and in an analysis of Palamas's theology of deification, Williams concurs: "Deification is both the light encountered (inasmuch as it is a visible apparition) and something that attaches to the person, becoming one with her and changing her. It is both God as other and God transforming the human person from within."[110]

Orthodox theology maintains that the various biblical descriptions of divine light refer to the same manifestation of God's glory as the "uncreated" light that appeared on Moses' face on Mount Sinai, on Stephen's face before his martyrdom, in Paul's conversion on the road to Damascus and,

---

105. Segal, *Paul the Convert*, 60–61. In interpreting 2 Cor 4:1–6, Matera comes to a similar conclusion: "Having argued that God has qualified him to be the minister of a new covenant (2:14—3:6), and having compared the ministries of old and new covenant (3:7–18), Paul can finally explain how his ministry discloses God's glory: by the light that comes from the gospel of the glory of Christ that he preaches" (*II Corinthians*, 99).

106. As Lossky points out, all the Eastern liturgical texts are impregnated with references to uncreated light, and the spiritual richness of the Christian East cannot be separated from the mystic perception of light as the experience of God, because this provides "that inner warmth which rightly represents an intimate quality of Orthodox piety" (*In the Image*, 69).

107. Ware, "God Hidden and Revealed," 130.

108. E.g., Gregory Nazianzus, Cyril of Alexandria, Maximus the Confessor, John of Damascus, and Symeon the New Theologian.

109. Vlachos, *Orthodox Psychotherapy*, 348.

110. Williams, *Deification*, 105.

most importantly, on Jesus' face and clothes at the Transfiguration.[111] In the Parable of the Weeds, Jesus stated that "the righteous will shine like the sun in the kingdom of their Father" (Matt 13:43), and the unique aspect of Orthodox spirituality is the belief that as Christian believers earnestly seek God they may experience the shining light in their earthly lives as a tangible reality of their ongoing transformation. What is particularly relevant to our current theme is that Palamas understood the deifying vision of uncreated light also to have a social impact, and therefore the Orthodox theology of light is harmonious with the progressive creational view of the transformation of humanity: "The fire burns the beam that is in the eye and re-establishes the purity of the human spirit, so that, recovering the view that is ours by nature, *one will no longer see the splinter in the eye of one's brother*, but observe constantly the miracles of God"[112] (emphasis added).

Receiving the Holy Spirit

The Epistle to the Galatians states that Christian believers are "supplied with" the Holy Spirit (3:5) when God "sends the Spirit of his Son into their hearts" (4:6); as a result, the Spirit "dwells in them" (Rom 8:9), a point that Paul reiterates in Rom 8:9–11 as many as four (arguably five) times with variations: "But you are not in the flesh; you are in the Spirit, since the Spirit of God dwells in you. Anyone who does not have the Spirit of Christ does not belong to him. But if Christ is in you, though the body is dead because of sin, the Spirit is life because of righteousness. If the Spirit of him who raised Jesus from the dead dwells in you, he who raised Christ from the dead will give life to your mortal bodies also through his Spirit that dwells in you."

In 1 Corinthians the image of the indwelling Spirit is further reinforced by likening the believers' body to "God's temple" that accommodates "God's Holy Spirit" (3:16), and three chapters later Paul repeats the message that "our body is a temple of the Holy Spirit within you, which you have from God" (6:19). Accordingly, Paul tells believers to "glorify God in your body" (v. 20) and Timothy is instructed in a similar vein, "Guard the good treasure entrusted to you, with the help of the Holy Spirit living in us" (2 Tim 1:14).

God's sending of the Spirit into the believers' hearts is a powerful image, consistent with the discussion in the previous two sections in suggesting some form of communion between the corporeal and the divine. Although as with the other two images analyzed above—"becoming conformed to the divine image" and "being exposed to divine light"—the image of Christians

---

111. Lossky, *Mystical Theology*, 222; Ware, "God Hidden and Revealed," 130.

112. Palamas, *Triads*, III.1.40, cited by Williams, *Deification*, 113.

carrying the Holy Spirit in their hearts can be understood both metaphorically and in a more literal sense, the indwelling Spirit lends itself less readily
to a metaphorical interpretation because the Holy Spirit in the NT canon is
invariably referred to as a concrete rather than an abstract presence,[113] and
the Spirit's power is talked about as something that many have personally
experienced (e.g., 1 Cor 2:4; 1 Thess 1:5).[114] Thus, the infusion of the Spirit
suggests a powerful reality in the believers' lives, and it is highly noteworthy
that this infusion of the divine into the corporeal parallels the process underlying the Incarnation whereby the corporeal pregnancy of Mary was the
work of the Holy Spirit. Thus, in this sense, the release of the Spirit to the
believers "in Jesus' name" (John 14:26) can be seen as the expansion of the
new creation process that was set into motion by the Incarnation.

The Spirit's transformational role is highlighted in several biblical passages: Titus 3:5 specifically talks about the "renewal by the Holy Spirit" and
in 2 Cor 3:18 (cited earlier) after speaking about the human metamorphosis
into Jesus' image, Paul adds, "for this comes from the Lord, the Spirit." This
point is further developed in 2 Thess 2:13, where Paul refers to the "sanctification *by* the Spirit" (emphasis added) and then he makes this image more
specific in 1 Cor 6:11 when he states, "you were washed, you were sanctified,
you were justified in the name of the Lord Jesus Christ and in the Spirit of
our God."[115] Further evidence of the impact of the indwelling Spirit is offered
by Paul's discussion of the *fruit* of the Spirit (Gal 5:22–23) and the *gifts* of the

113. Persuasive evidence for the experiential reality of the Holy Spirit was provided
by the Council of Jerusalem (Acts 15:4–21), which discussed the critical question of
whether Gentile believers needed to be circumcised and whether they were to follow
the Law. The decisive argument in the debate was Peter's account of how "the Holy
Spirit fell upon" Cornelius's Gentile household when he preached the Gospel to them
(Acts 10:44–46), and thus, Peter concluded, "God, who knows the human heart, testi-
fied to them by giving them the Holy Spirit, just as he did to us" (15:8). His argument
carried the day, indicating that the Spirit's presence was an unambiguous and incontest-
able phenomenon, known to and accepted by those present in the Council.

114. Dunn summarized this clearly: "It is important to realize that for the first
Christians the Spirit was thought of in terms of divine power clearly manifest by its
effects on the life of the recipient; the impact of the Spirit did not leave individual or
onlooker in much doubt that a significant change had taken place in him by divine
agency. Paul refers his readers back to their initial experience of the Spirit again and
again. For some it had been an overwhelming experience of God's it had been an overwhelming experience of God's love (Rom 5:5); for others of joy (1 Thess 1:6); for others
of illumination (2 Cor 3:14–17), or of liberation (Rom 8:2; 2 Cor 3:17), or of moral
transformation (1 Cor 6:9–11), or of various spiritual gifts (1 Cor. 1:4–7; Gal. 3:5)."
Dunn, "Spirit, Holy Spirit," 1128.

115. Other related images concerning the Holy Spirit include being "marked with
the seal of the promised Holy Spirit" (Eph 1:13) and having "the first fruits of the Spirit"
(Rom 8:23).

Spirit (e.g., Rom 12:6–8; 1 Cor 12:1–11) as two concrete sets of outcomes of the transformation of human lives. In 1 Cor 12:7 Paul specifically calls the spiritual gifts "the manifestation of the Spirit,"[116] and it is particularly relevant from the social perspective of the human transformation process that Paul adds that the manifestation of the Spirit is "for the common good" (ibid). Indeed, although this is beyond the limits of a canonical narrative perspective, it is important to note that the missiological literature is explicit about the fact that during the period of early Christianity the radically transformed lives of the believers constituted one of the most potent factors in facilitating the unprecedented success of evangelization in the era.[117] Martyrdom, that is, the courage and willingness of transformed Christians to die for what they believed in, was particularly instrumental in the conversion of the nations of the world.[118]

Taken together, the above considerations substantiate Dunn's conclusion that "The Spirit is that power which transforms a man from the inside out, so that metaphors of cleansing and consecration become matters of actual experience in daily living."[119] Moltmann also believed that "the Spirit is the power of the new creation,"[120] and in a canonical narrative reading, this creational significance attached to the Holy Spirit in new creation may be seen as consistent with the part attributed to the Spirit before the Incarnation: God's spirit is mentioned in Gen 1:2 (as he "swept over the face of the waters"), the Spirit's creative power is stated in Ps 104:30 ("When you send forth your spirit, they [the creatures are created]"), and Zech 4:6 specifically declares, "Not by might, nor by power, but by my spirit, says the

116. Grudem points out in this respect that the Greek word translated "manifestation" (*phanerosis*) means "something that discloses" or "something that makes publicly evident or clear." Grudem, *Systematic Theology*, 639.

117. There are many ancient sources attesting to the missionary impact of a "radiant manifestation of the Christian faith and . . . a winsome lifestyle." Bosch, "Evangelism," 101. A particularly convincing case is the complaints of Julian the Apostate (331–63), the last non-Christian Roman Emperor, who tried to return the Empire to the traditional Greco-Roman religion. Hvalvik cites a letter Julian wrote to a pagan high-priest in Galatia in which he stated that the Christians' "benevolence to strangers, their care for the graves of the dead and the pretended holiness of their lives have done most to increase atheism [i.e., atheism from the pagan vantage point]" ("In Word and Deed," 285).

118. E.g., M. Green, *Evangelism in the Early Church*, xvi; see also Schnabel, *Early Christian Mission*, vol. 2, 1558–59.

119. Dunn, *Jesus and the Spirit*, 201. Hoch comes to a similar conclusion: "When a person becomes a Christian, the Holy Spirit begins a work of transformation and renewal so that the Christian's mind is enlightened concerning the truth of God, Christ, and the gospel" (*All Things New*, 219).

120. Moltmann, "Creation and Redemption," 128.

LORD of hosts." The Spirit's transformational capacity is further underlined by Isa 32:15—"a spirit from on high is poured out on us, and the wilderness becomes a fruitful field"—as part of a prophetic tradition in the Old Testament predicting the future outpouring of the Spirit (e.g., Isa 32:15; 44:3; Ezek 36:26; 37:14; 39:39; Joel 2:28), and Joel's prophecy in this vein was specifically appropriated (and cited) by Peter (Acts 2:17–21) in making sense of the dramatic events at Pentecost.[121]

A final point about the release of the Holy Spirit to humankind concerns the timing of this creational act. It did not happen during Jesus' earthly ministry, "because Jesus was not yet glorified" (John 7:37). For it to happen, Jesus first had to die on the Cross, be resurrected, and then ascend to heaven to be seated at God's right hand. In order to be able to integrate these conditions into a coherent understanding of progressive creation, chapter 5 will consider the nature of Jesus' atoning sacrifice and the victory he achieved on the Cross over opposition to God's plans.

4.4 Summary

We saw in the previous chapter that after the Fall and the subsequent expulsion of Adam and Eve from Eden the social and moral order of humanity collapsed, which led to the purging of the world by the Flood. After the waters had receded, a second phase of creation began, focusing on the transformation of the society of stewards into citizens of God's eschatological kingdom. The trials of Job and Abraham with their successful outcomes can be taken as evidence of the increasing maturation and God-given potential of humankind, and the OT canon then presents a series of divine creational interventions that include raising the nation of Israel, releasing the Law, and assembling the Jewish Scriptures into a written form. In Childs' summary, "God who 'always was' is not a static being, but is engaged in constant creative activity. . . . He entered into Israel's history and showed his continual presence through constant acts of mercy."[122] This phase of the history of humankind prepared the way for a radically new chapter in the progressive creational process, as foretold by the OT prophets on several occasions, that was inaugurated by the incarnation of Jesus Christ, the last Adam. The commencing new creation involved various indirect and more direct forms of transformational acts aimed at enabling humans to become conformed to God's image, culminating with the release of the Holy Spirit to dwell in the hearts of Christian believers. As Paul declared to the Philippians, the

121. See Hubbard, *New Creation*, 114.
122. Childs, *Biblical Theology*, 397.

unstoppable transfigurational influence of the Spirit from within will reach its conclusion at the *Parousia*: "I am confident of this very thing; that the Holy Spirit who has begun a good work in you, will bring it to completion at the day of Jesus Christ" (1:6).

A unique scene in all the three Synoptic Gospels, the Transfiguration, encapsulates the essence of the process described in this chapter in one powerful image; as Matthew (17:1–8) records,

> Jesus took with him Peter and James and his brother John and led them up a high mountain, by themselves. And he was transfigured before them, and his face shone like the sun, and his clothes became dazzling white. Suddenly there appeared to them Moses and Elijah, talking with him. Then Peter said to Jesus, "Lord, it is good for us to be here; if you wish, I will make three dwellings here, one for you, one for Moses, and one for Elijah." While he was still speaking, suddenly a bright cloud overshadowed them, and from the cloud a voice said, "This is my Son, the Beloved; with him I am well pleased; listen to him!" When the disciples heard this, they fell to the ground and were overcome by fear. But Jesus came and touched them, saying, "Get up and do not be afraid." And when they looked up, they saw no one except Jesus himself alone.

This dramatic event includes many of the key elements discussed in this chapter: Moses and Elijah represent the nation of Israel; God the Father speaking from a bright cloud repeats his declaration, first pronounced at Jesus' baptism, that it was "good"; Jesus reflects God's radiant glory as a foretaste of the deification of humanity; and the three disciples—Peter, John, and James—epitomize the emerging new society of stewards, the would-be Church. Although humankind at this point still faced a long process to cover, God's instruction concerning his incarnate Son—recorded in the Synoptic Gospels with identical words—could not have been any clearer: "Listen to him!" These words echoed unmistakably God's past promise to Moses: "I will raise up for them a prophet like you from among their own people; I will put my words in the mouth of the prophet, who shall speak to them everything that I command. Anyone who does not heed the words that the prophet shall speak in my name, I myself will hold accountable" (Deut 18:18–19).

We have seen that Jesus gave his disciples a new commandment—that they should "love one another" (John 15:12)—which was "the fulfilment of the law" (Rom 13:9), and this commandment aptly summarizes the fundamentally social nature of the new phase of creation that has been preparing the ground for the ultimate renewal of heaven and earth after Jesus' second coming.

5

Spiritual Opposition and
Jesus Christ's Victory

THE PAST THREE CHAPTERS have explored the progressive nature of material creation in relation to the imperfect state of the world, with only
brief mention made of the spiritual realm and that in connection with the
serpent's role during the Fall. However, throughout the Bible allusion is
made to spiritual forces whose purpose is not aligned with God's will and
who actively interfere with the lives of humans in pursuit of an alternative,
subversive agenda to derail God's creational purposes. If we understand sin
as the resistance to—or turning away from—God,[1] these opposing agents
represent an evil influence on humankind, and their sinister presence de-
velops into a central theme in the New Testament, where we encounter an
organized kingdom of darkness led by Satan (e.g., Matt 12:26), the "ruler
of this world" (John 14:30). In chapter 3, the serpent's role was given only
brief treatment because the main thrust of the Genesis 3 narrative focused
on the disobedience of the first human couple. However, because of the
direct bearing that spiritual adversaries have on humanity's struggles, the
current chapter revisits the theme of celestial opposition to God's creative
purpose by drawing on the Book of Job, which contains the most detailed
depiction of the subject not only in the Old Testament but arguably in the
whole biblical canon. Following this, the second half of the chapter examines how this celestial opposition was defeated by Jesus Christ through his
salvific work on the cross.

---

1. McFarland, "Fall and Sin," 140.

5.1 The Book of Job

As already described in chapter 4, the book of Job is enigmatic in terms of its contextual and temporal vagueness, and this elusiveness also applies to some of the content of the book. One of the primary experts on Job, David Clines, states for example that "no one can say, and certainly not this commentator, what the book of Job is all about,"[2] and there is an overall consensus among scholars on this view, well reflected in Ellison's conclusion in the *New Bible Dictionary*: "The poem is so rich in its thought, so wide in its sweep, that much in human experience and its mysteries has been found mirrored there."[3] This position is also shared by Jewish scholars, as attested to in the summary by Ginsberg et al. in the *Encyclopedia Judaica*: "Indeed, the Book of Job is a complex and profound literary work that may not be reduced to a single message."[4] Accordingly, commentators, Jewish and Christian alike, have been divided about the essence of the teaching of the book, highlighting disparate possible readings of the text and arriving at diverse and often conflicting conclusions. In traditional Jewish interpretation, for example, Job has been regarded by some as one of the few truly God-fearing men of the Bible and the most pious Gentile that has ever lived, while to others he was a blasphemer.[5] In commenting on why the book seems to defy definitive interpretation, Newsom contends that the way the text has been read throughout the ages has been colored by the intellectual and cultural biases of the interpretive communities because the book "lends itself well—perhaps too well—to being read in light of shifting philosophical and hermeneutical assumptions. Its complex and elusive nature allows interpreters to see mirrored in it perspectives congenial to the tenor of their own age."[6]

While a complex composition such as the Book of Job will always offer possible parallel meanings,[7] the starting point of the following discussion is the belief that one reason for the opaqueness of the book is the fact that a key passage, Eliphaz's nocturnal vision in chapter 4—which has a key role in shaping the friends' response to Job—has traditionally been misinterpreted by most commentators. The alternative reading presented below provides a

2. Clines, *Job 1–20*, xxix.

3. Ellison, "Book of Job," 590.

4. Ginsberg et al., "Book of Job," 346.

5. Ibid., 353.

6. Newsom, *Job*, 3.

7. E.g., the emphasis in most mainstream commentaries has been on the way the doctrine of retribution is handled in the text, which is a reading that the current discussion will not address in detail.

possible explanation of the age-old dilemma of why the seemingly righteous and Scripture-based arguments of Job's friends[8] were rejected by God, and it also offers more general insights into the underlying motivation of the celestial opposition to God's works.

Eliphaz's Vision (4:12–21)

In his first speech, after a short introduction, Eliphaz reveals the foundation of his spiritual stance, a message he has received in a nocturnal vision:

> Now a word came stealing to me,
>> my ear received the whisper of it.
> Amid thoughts from visions of the night,
>> when deep sleep falls on mortals,
> dread came upon me, and trembling,
>> which made all my bones shake.
> A spirit glided past my face;
>> the hair of my flesh bristled.
> It stood still,
>> but I could not discern its appearance.
> A form was before my eyes;
>> there was silence, then I heard a voice:
> "Can mortals be righteous before God?
>> Can human beings be pure before their Maker?
> Even in his servants he puts no trust,
>> and his angels he charges with error;
> how much more those who live in houses of clay,
>> whose foundation is in the dust,
>> who are crushed like a moth.
> Between morning and evening they are destroyed;
>> they perish forever without any regarding it.
> Their tent-cord is plucked up within them,
>> and they die devoid of wisdom." (Job 4:12–21)

The first part of the passage describes the vision in unique psychological detail, while the second part cites the spirit's actual communication to Eliphaz. According to the mainstream view, the passage depicts a divine

---

8. There is general agreement that on the surface Eliphaz and his companions seem to be saying all the right things, sometimes even quoting well-known wisdom statements; for example, Andersen states that "It is hard to find any proposition in the book which is not to some extent correct, taken in isolation" (*Job*, 98), and Barth contends that the friends "unquestionably speak good, earnest, and religious words" (*CD*, IV/3.1, 453).

visitation, and the content of the spirit's message is seen as legitimate wisdom teaching by most scholars; Robert Gordis's summary represents the conventional interpretation: "Eliphaz then describes a revelation from on high that has brought him new insight: all men are imperfect in the eyes of God; therefore, even the suffering of the righteous has its justification. In view of these two great truths it is foolish for Job to lose patience and surrender his faith in the divine government of the world."[9]

Expressed in this way, the spirit's words do sound sensible and are in line with the tenets of mainstream wisdom tradition in Scripture; this in turn can be taken to confirm that the source of the message is a *bona fide* divine voice. However, a closer reading of the passage raises doubts both about the divine origin of the messenger and the orthodoxy of the content of what is actually communicated.

The experience described in the text is undoubtedly a supernatural visitation, and by citing it to Job as a key element of his argument, Eliphaz implies (although never explicitly states) that the spirit he encountered was God's messenger. He does so even though he admits that he "could not discern its appearance" (4:16), an ambiguity of the source which is also reflected by the discourse itself, because the text deliberately leaves some uncertainty in this respect by not specifying a definite subject in v. 16. Habel thus sums up the scholarly consensus, "The identity of the apparition is never revealed; the message alone is recorded . . . The poet leaves Eliphaz—and us—floundering in wonder as to the source of the voice he hears."[10] This ambiguity is coupled with the fact that there are several sinister details in the scene which suggest that Eliphaz's nocturnal visitor may not have been a divine messenger but rather an evil spirit:

- It is unlike other prophetic accounts of visions described in the Bible that Eliphaz was unable to provide a clear identification, let alone a visual image, of the source of the message he had received.[11] Although he sensed a "form," which first moved and then stood still, the imagery remained obscure and deeply ambiguous. Therefore, Ash is right to conclude that "Eliphaz may imply that this is supernatural and

9. Gordis, *Job*, 41.

10. Habel, *Job*, 128; Newsom agrees: "Eliphaz' s choice of terms in the last part of the verse thus intimates but never explicitly claims that the apparition is a manifestation of God" ("Book of Job: Introduction," 378).

11. See Ash, *Job*, 106. Hartley also adds, "Though Eliphaz' s experience was primarily auditory, he did get a glimpse of something resembling a spirit. But no prophet ever mentions hearing a word from 'a spirit'" (*Job*, 111).

therefore authoritative, but the author of the book subverts that claim and makes us suspect that something less positive is going on here."[12]

- Several commentators have noticed the eclectic nature of the components of the scene; Whybray, for example, finds that the details "seem to have been collected from a variety of sources"[13] and according to Habel, the "bizarre collage of disparate allusions borders on a parody of traditional modes of revelation. Probable allusions to various revelatory traditions are deliberately brought into a clever juxtaposition of unlikely associations."[14] As he continues, "An anonymous word steals in, a vague sound is snatched, a nightmare intrudes on a deep sleep, a terror confronts the sleeper, a whirlwind makes him shiver, a veiled apparition is seen, something unknown stands before him, and finally a voice is heard after an ominous hush. The oracle received has no identified origin and is delivered by no known messenger. Eliphaz' message is a faint sound uttered by a fleeting specter."[15]

- This collage is thus rather *manufactured* in nature, almost as if it had been assembled to produce maximum impact on the receiver; as Ken Brown sums up in what has been the most detailed analysis of the vision to date, "Blending language and imagery from a vast array of distinct and often conflicting traditions, its every verse takes language that elsewhere reflects genuine revelatory activity, and twists it into something novel and unsettling."[16]

- There is a degree of eeriness in the way Eliphaz refers to the amorphous presence that visits him, describing its coming with the word "stealing" and not hiding the dread it evoked in him, causing him to tremble and his body hair to bristle.[17] While such paralyzing fear may not be indicative of anything unorthodox about the spirit—since the Bible records several occasions when humans feel terror in the

---

12. Ash, *Job*, 106.

13. Whybray, *Job*, 43.

14. Habel, *Job*, 121.

15. Ibid., 121–22.

16. K. Brown, *Vision in Job 4*, 98.

17. According to Pope, "This passage is one of the most uncanny in the OT. The poet toys in poetic fancy with the dread effect of contact with the divine" (*Job*, 36). Ash compares the scene to a "horror movie": "This is terrifying. We are in the presence of the numinous, of the supernatural world, of a world beyond our comprehension, of a scary dimension of the universe. And then, when our pulses are racing, 'it stood still.'" Ash, *Job*, 106.

presence of the numinous[18]—what is conspicuous here by its absence, is some form of reassurance or encouragement along the customary "Fear not!" pattern (e.g. Gen 15:1; Judg 6:23; Dan 10:12) or at least a reassuring self-identification of the messenger.[19]

Regarding the content of the spirit's message, Gordis's summary cited above illustrates well the standard interpretation of the revelation received by Eliphaz as being a paraphrase of conventional wisdom principles. Yet, commentators who hold this view also tend to remark on what they see as the *banality* of the spirit's first utterance—"Can mortals be righteous before God?" (4:17)—which comes at the climax of the scene built up previously. For example, Andersen sums up the general mood when he states, "After such a build-up, we expect to hear a revelation, not a truism. . . . The thing is so obviously impossible, that the banality makes Eliphaz sound pretentious."[20] One may indeed wonder what the need was for a supernatural visitation to reiterate to Eliphaz what scholars typically see as a variation of well-known wisdom truism? There is clearly something amiss with understanding the spirit's message as being a mere reiteration of stock wisdom teaching, and indeed, if we consider closely what the spirit actually says, we find that two aspects of the message are rather incompatible with established wisdom principles:

- First, while the primary concern of traditional wisdom teaching is with the nature of proper moral and religious conduct, this is not the tenor of the spirit's message in 4:17–21. Here he condemns the human race *en bloc*, without separating the righteous/wise from the wicked/ foolish and without offering any links between good conduct and well-being in an attempt to show ways to remedy human sinfulness.[21]

18. E.g., in Gen 15:12 we read, "As the sun was going down, a deep sleep fell upon Abram, and a deep and terrifying darkness descended upon him."

19. See Fyall, *Job*, 147; Paul, "Experience of Eliphaz," 115.

20. Andersen, *Job*, 114. This view has wide support; for example, Whybray concludes, "The reader is thereby led to expect some tremendous revelation; but when it comes it consists only of a truism: that no human being is pure in God's sight" (*Job*, 42). Agreeing with this view, Ash states, "This is a remarkable anticlimax. We might have expected some specific revelation about Job and his secret sins or a heavenly revelation of the reason for his sufferings (perhaps an insight into the heavenly scenes of chapters 1, 2). Instead we get a general statement of a kind that would be the staple diet of the wisdom of Eliphaz's tradition!" Ash, *Job*, 106.

21. Crenshaw defines the purpose of the wisdom literature as the "seasoned search for specific ways to ensure personal well-being in everyday life, to make sense of extreme adversity and vexing anomalies, and to transmit this hard-earned knowledge so that successive generations will embody it" (*Old Testament Wisdom*, 4). As he sums up,

That is, while biblical wisdom teaching does indeed condemn human sinfulness, Fyall correctly points out that it also "calls attention to the remedy and provides the strength to carry it out."[22] In contrast, in Eliphaz's terrifying vision there is no reassurance of any sort but only a sinister message that condemns the human race collectively and "slams shut the door of hope."[23] Thus, the usual characterization of Job's friends as members of the Wise who speak from within the mainstream wisdom tradition[24] does not apply to Eliphaz's recounting of the spirit's specific message; this message emphasizes one and only one point, the absolute worthlessness and insignificance of humans, which in turn explains why the first utterance is in an interrogative form: "Can mortals be righteous before God?" Clearly, the only expected answer to this rhetorical question is no, thereby affirming what the vision suggests: a doctrine of the depravity of mankind.

- Second, and even more importantly, the spirit provides a curious justification for human worthlessness. Rather than focusing on the sinfulness of human nature, the main reason being offered is an *a fortiori* argument in the rhetoric sense: By contrasting immortal heavenly beings and inferior humans "whose foundation is in the dust" (4:19), the spirit argues that when even angels fall short of the mark in God's eyes, how much more so must this be true of human mortals.[25] Given that this message actually comes from a spiritual being, that is, a member of the group reported to be wanting in God's eyes, it is possible to identify a sense of bitterness behind the spirit's words along the lines of "If even the likes of myself are not good enough for God, how dare you think that you, a mere mortal, stand a chance?"

In sum, while some aspects of Eliphaz's vision are reminiscent of theophanies described in the Bible (e.g., Ezek 1) and thereby suggest to some scholars that the visitation involves a messenger of God,[26] this conclusion is made arguably only with hindsight, in view of what these scholars perceive as a divine message delivering wisdom truisms.[27] Uneasy with

---

for the most part "success orientation . . . lay at the heart of the sapiential enterprise" (ibid.). The unconditionally negative appraisal of humans conveyed by the spirit's message is clearly at odds with this orientation.

22. Fyall, *Job*, 147.

23. Ibid.

24. E.g., Ellison *Job*, 590.

25. See Whybray *Job*, 43.

26. E.g., Andersen, *Job*, 82; Clines, *Job 1–20*, 130–31.

27. A good example of this is Ash's conclusion; as we saw earlier, although he

this traditional position, Gary Smith raised the question over 25 years ago as to whether Job 4 presented "a false vision inspired by 'the Satan' of the prologue,"[28] although he was quick to point out that "no one takes this position."[29] The mainstream interpretation has remained largely the same since the publication of Smith's paper; for example, in his recent detailed analysis, Ken Brown summarizes that treating the vision as unproblematic has been "by far the most common approach in early modern commentaries, still regularly affirmed up to the present."[30] Although he also maintains that "the claim that the friends are portrayed as mouthpieces for Satan is not plausible,"[31] we shall see below that some contemporary scholars have indeed raised this view, and it will be argued that an alternative position is not only plausible but is in fact more consistent with the actual text, particularly because it also offers an explanation of how the friends' righteous intentions have been "hijacked" so that they end up being denounced as wrong by God in the epilogue of the book.

An Alternative Interpretation of Eliphaz's Vision

At the beginning of his first speech (Job 4), Eliphaz strikes a conciliatory tone by emphasizing that Job has played an exemplary role in the past by supporting people and building up the weak, and urging him not to be impatient. His initial advice seems fittingly righteous: Fear God and trust him that "the integrity of your ways" (4:6) will bring you redemption. He even states one of the core principles of wisdom teaching, namely the traditional belief that God rewards the righteous and punishes the wicked:

> Think now, who that was innocent ever perished?
>   Or where were the upright cut off?
> As I have seen, those who plough iniquity
>   and sow trouble reap the same. (4:7–8)

The inconsistency between this reasonable start and the message of the subsequent vision that Eliphaz reports (4:12–21) has not escaped

---

perceives the sinister, unnatural nature of the scene clearly, he would not attribute the message to an evil spirit because of its wisdom content: "Incidentally, it is fascinating to see how Eliphaz combines the traditions of wisdom with the experience of mysticism, although his mysticism seems frighteningly close to the occult." Ash, *Job*, 106.

28. Smith, "Is It Eliphaz's Vision?" 453.

29. Ibid.

30. K. Brown, *Vision in Job 4*, 12.

31. Ibid., 21.

commentators, and several attempts have been made to "correct" or explain away the visionary passage, for example by detecting powerful irony in it,[32] by arguing that the text is written in such ambiguous Hebrew that it is impossible to deduce a single meaning,[33] by claiming that not all of the cited text is from God,[34] or—to take the most radical but widely accepted solution, usually referred to as the "Tur-Sinai and Ginsberg hypothesis"[35]—by suggesting that the vision was actually given to Job rather than to Eliphaz, and it was due to a redactional or copying error that it is now mistakenly attributed to Eliphaz. From a canonical narrative perspective, a more fitting solution to this puzzle involves the assumption that the message was indeed delivered to Eliphaz in the form in which it has been recorded, but accepting also that the communicator was not God's messenger but a spirit representing the same agenda as the *śāṭān* in the prologue. This view then suggests that the persuasive content of the spirit's words, accompanied by the sinister manner of their delivery, achieved its intended purpose of successfully distorting Eliphaz's initially righteous stance. This is confirmed by the fact that a few verses later we read a reiteration of the fundamental belief in human worthlessness, this time already paraphrased in Eliphaz's own words:

> For misery does not come from the earth,
> nor does trouble sprout from the ground;
> but human beings are born to trouble
> just as sparks fly upward. (Job 5:6–7)

Then, as a reflection of the extent to which Eliphaz adopted the stance of the nocturnal vision, in his second speech he delivers the same message again only in an even harsher manner, also reiterating the *a fortiori* argument:

> What are mortals, that they can be clean?
> Or those born of woman, that they can be righteous?
> God puts no trust even in his holy ones,
> and the heavens are not clean in his sight;
> how much less one who is abominable and corrupt,
> one who drinks iniquity like water! (15:14–16)

---

32. E.g., Clines, *Job 1–20*, 133; Habel, *Job*, 121–22; Janzen, *Job*, 73; Whybray, *Job*, 42.

33. Harding, "Spirit of Deception," 166.

34. E.g., Clines regards v. 17 alone as the divine word of revelation in Eliphaz' s vision. Clines, *Job 1–20*, 133–34.

35. For a description of this view, see Ginsberg et al., "Job," 352; Greenstein, "'On My Skin and in My Flesh,'" 66.

The language Eliphaz uses to dismiss humans with words such as "abominable" and "corrupt" is unusually strong and emotive,[36] suggesting, according to Newsom, an "almost visceral revulsion."[37] We may also ask: How does Eliphaz know that "God puts no trust even in his holy ones, and the heavens are not clean in his sight" (v. 15) with such certainty that he is ready to condemn humans in the most extreme terms? This conviction is undoubtedly rooted in the communication he received during the nocturnal visitation, indicating how the spirit's message infiltrated his whole mindset. Finally, given this by now fully internalized belief in human worthlessness—Harding aptly describes Eliphaz's position "entrenched"[38]—it comes as no surprise that in his third and final speech Eliphaz reiterates this position one more time:

> Can a mortal be of use to God?
>   Can even the wisest be of service to him?
> Is it any pleasure to the Almighty if you are righteous,
>   or is it gain to him if you make your ways blameless?
> Is it for your piety that he reproves you,
>   and enters into judgment with you?
> Is not your wickedness great?
>   There is no end to your iniquities. (22:2–5)

We should note at this point that Eliphaz is presented by the text as the highest status person among Job's friends: He speaks first to Job and later God addresses him on behalf of his two companions. Therefore, the tenor of this speech sets the overall tone of how the friends' discussion with Job progresses; this is evidenced by the fact that in the last recorded statement by any of Job's friends, Bildad repeats Eliphaz's central doctrine of human worthlessness:

> How then can a mortal be righteous before God?
>   How can one born of woman be pure?
> If even the moon is not bright
>   and the stars are not pure in his sight,
> how much less a mortal, who is a maggot,
>   and a human being, who is a worm!" (25:4–6)

---

36. The word translated by the NRSV as "abominable" (*tāʿab*) refers to something that is disgusting and repulsive, and "corrupt" (*ʿâlach*) in this case literally means filthy—as Hartley points out, in Arabic it is used for the souring of milk. Hartley, *Job*, 248.

37. Newsom, "Book of Job: Introduction," 450.

38. Harding, "Spirit of Deception," 157.

Besides its unequivocal blanket condemnation of humanity, the strik-ing feature of this passage—similar to Eliphaz's second speech—is the strongly reviling figures of speech Bildad uses to characterize mankind: "maggots" and "worms"; as Clines concludes, "Bildad is nothing if not brutal"[39] by comparing humans to unclean animals that are associated with decay and death. This passage also offers an illuminating comparison with Psalm 8, where the psalmist uses similar imagery but arrives at a very dif-ferent conclusion: Although here, too, we encounter a comparison between mortal human beings and heavenly entities such as the majestic moon and stars, humans are not described as maggots or worms but rather as stewards of the manifold works of God's hand, crowned with glory and honor:

> You have set your glory above the heavens.
>> Out of the mouths of babes and infants
> you have founded a bulwark because of your foes,
>> to silence the enemy and the avenger.
> When I look at your heavens, the work of your fingers,
>> the moon and the stars that you have established;
> what are human beings that you are mindful of them,
>> mortals that you care for them?
> Yet you have made them a little lower than God,
>> and crowned them with glory and honor.
> You have given them dominion over the works of your hands;
>> you have put all things under their feet. (Ps 8:1–6)

What is particularly significant from our point of view in this psalm is that we read—almost in direct response to Bildad's question, "How can one born of woman be pure?"—that "Out of the mouths of babes and in-fants you have founded a bulwark," attesting to the integral value attributed to humankind as even the weak and helpless children have power "not by virtue of their innate abilities but by virtue of God's ordaining it"[40] (Broyles). This is then affirmed by the honor and authority bestowed on human beings by God to steward the world despite being mere mortals. Incidentally, one cannot help wondering about the exact identity of the unspecified "enemy" and "avenger" who needs to be silenced at the end of the first stanza above. While this unnamed enemy can be understood to refer to the psalmist's earthly opponents[41] or the hostile forces discussed under the *Chaoskampf* rubric (in chapter 3),[42] the text does not explicitly say so and it is tempting

39. Clines, *Job 21–37*, 633.

40. Broyles, *Psalms*, 71.

41. E.g., Bratcher and Reyburn, *Psalms*, 79.

42. E.g., deClaissé-Walford et al., *Psalms*, 123.

to entertain the idea that the real enemy and avenger the psalmist is talking about might be spiritual opposition to God, especially the *śāṭān* whom we encounter in the Book of Job.

To summarize, we saw in chapter 4 that in the prologue of the Book of Job the conflict between God and his adversary, the *śāṭān*, surfaces when the *śāṭān* questions the integrity of humankind, even that of the most righteous man on earth, thereby expressing doubts about God's own testimony and, more generally, about the soundness of God's created order. The main argument of this chapter so far has been that Eliphaz, prompted by a supernatural encounter with an unidentified spirit, ends up in the same camp as the *śāṭān* when he represents the doctrine of human worthlessness instilled in him by his nocturnal vision.[43] This outcome—that is, the "fruit" of the message—as well as the eerie, fabricated nature of the visitation scene and the absence of any identified source or known messenger all point to the conclusion that the visitation that fundamentally shaped Eliphaz's world view did not originate from God but was part of a deception planted by God's spiritual opposition, most likely by the *śāṭān* himself.

Although the above understanding is admittedly a minority position, some scholars have pursued a similar train of argument. Most notably, Janzen contends in his commentary that "The 'inspiration' of Eliphaz derives, not from God, but from the Satan";[44] and Fyall goes one step further: "Eliphaz' s vision in 4:12–21 is not in fact God but the enemy masquerading as him"[45]—that is, as he concludes, the vision is "a brilliant deception of the enemy."[46] However, regarding the overall interpretation of this recognition, Fyall and Janzen's readings of the book differ from the one presented in the current work: Fyall believes that the enemy finds

---

43. A few modern commentators have also observed this link; Janzen for example states, "What Eliphaz, of course, does not know is that in imputing to humankind the qualities of inevitable untrustworthiness and inevitable error, he (or his 'revelation') is speaking on one side of the issue already joined in the heavenly meeting between Yahweh and the Satan. In that meeting, we recall, it was the Satan who called Job's moral and religious status question, and it was Yahweh who was willing to risk the test in hope of Job's vindication." Janzen, *Job*, 73. Ash holds a similar view: "The substance of the Satan's challenge in chapters 1, 2 is that no human being on earth is genuinely in the right with God. And so, quite unwittingly no doubt, and meaning well, Eliphaz becomes here the spokesman for the Satan. This strange visionary word emanates not from the God of the Bible but from the enemy and the accuser of the brethren." Ash then concludes that a "closer reading reveals some striking similarities between the portrayal of 'the satan' in the prologue and Job's friends." Ash, *Job*, 107.

44. Janzen, *Job*, 73.

45. Fyall, *Job*, 37.

46. Ibid., 147.

its culmination in the figures of Behemoth and Leviathan,[47] while Janzen considers Eliphaz's case a deliberate attempt by the author of the book to ironically subvert a speaker's intended meaning.[48] In a recent paper, Mart-Jan Paul has also proposed that "it seems likely that a negative or demonic spirit (related to Satan) tried to follow up the negative works of the first chapter,"[49] and he has made a further interesting point when he highlighted the fact that later in the book Job also complains about having terrifying visions and dreams himself (7:14). While Job, similar to Eliphaz, thinks that those visions were from God, their consequence—namely, that they made Job prefer death to living (v. 15)—suggests to Paul that Job, too, had "hair-raising encounters with very spooky apparitions,"[50] which in turn suggests ongoing spiritual interference.

The Celestial Forces Opposing God's Work

We have explored Eliphaz's vision in detail because it offers unprecedented insight into the mindset of the spiritual opposition to God's works. Taken together, the reading proposed above—along with other parts of the Book of Job that offer further details (most notably the prologue), as well as with related relevant passages in the rest of the canon—allows us to outline certain important themes concerning the nature and motivation of the celestial forces that consciously oppose God's creative purpose.

The Heavenly Assembly[51]

The prologue of Job describes two sessions of a divine assembly (in chapters 1 and 2) where "the heavenly beings came to present themselves before the Lord" (1:6), implying that such gatherings were not uncommon events. Although the canon never explains the nature of such assemblies in specific

---

47. Ibid.

48. Janzen, *Job*, 72.

49. Paul, "Experience of Eliphaz," 120.

50. Ibid., 118.

51. As pointed out in Chapter 1, there is a danger inherent to the canonical narrative of this book to discuss issues related to God's creative acts by means of excessive anthropomorphism. The conceptualization of the heavenly assembly is admittedly a case in point and it is better understood as an extended metaphor to express a collective sense which transpires from several verses of Scripture. In order to reconstruct the essence of this "sense," the discussion uses images that appear in the relevant biblical texts.

detail, there are numerous mentions of them in both Testaments that allow glimpses into the workings of God's celestial court.[52] These passages converge in depicting some kind of a collective body—or as Collins puts it, "an angelic council that surrounds God's throne"[53]—in which God is the undisputed ruler; however, what is significant for our current discussion is the fact that during these meetings God does appear to consider and weigh up the views of his celestial retinue. One prominent instance of such collective participation is presented in 1 Kgs 22:19–23, where we read that after God decided that King Ahab should die, he solicits a discussion about how this should be carried out, and when a spirit makes a constructive proposal, God sanctions it.[54] Similarly, in the prologue of the Book of Job, God agrees in the heavenly assembly to a request made by the śāṭān—submitting Job to harsh testing—almost against his better judgement. Page is right to underline that in both cases there is *two-way communication* between God and his entourage,[55] and it is noteworthy in both instances that the acts that are authorized in the end were initially put forward by a member of the divine assembly. Furthermore, in certain other passages in the canon, one can sense that God's decisions are associated with a degree of collective consensus; for example, Rev 16:5–7 concerning the seven bowls of the wrath of God—a passage that is usually taken as a doxology[56]—might also be read as an expressive example of collective endorsement of God's decision by the heavenly host: "And I heard the angel of the waters say, 'You are just, O Holy One, who are and were, for you have judged these things; because they shed the blood of saints and prophets, you have given them blood to drink. It is what they deserve!' And I heard the altar respond, 'Yes, O Lord God, the Almighty, your judgments are true and just!'"

Another possible indication of a collective consensus concerns the divine plural used in Gen 1:26: "Let us make humankind in our image, according to our likeness . . ." Although this plural referent is not emphasized or further illuminated in the canon and, therefore, past speculations about

---

52. E.g., 1 Kgs 22:19–23; Ps 82:1; 89:5, 7; Isa 6:1ff; 14:13; Jer 23:18, 22; Dan 7:9–10, 26; Zech 3:1–2; Rev 4–5. As Day summarizes the emerging scholarly consensus, "One subject on which there is now widespread, though not universal. agreement is the identity of the sons of God. It is now generally held that they denote God's heavenly court" (*From Creation to Babel*, 77). For detailed analyses, see Heiser, "Divine Council"; White, *Yahweh's Council*.

53. Collins, *Genesis 1–4*, 59–60.

54. See Heiser, *Divine Council*.

55. Page, *Powers of Evil*, 78–79.

56. Duvall characterizes this passage as "a spontaneous hymn of praise celebrating God's justice and bringing comfort to those who have suffered" (*Revelation*, 216).

who the pronoun "us" could refer to have been wide-ranging,[57] Barth—along with many other scholars—submits that the use of this plural is connected with the peculiar significance of the creation of man in relation to the activity of the divine assembly.[58] Moreover, as he continues,

> Gen. 1.26 does not speak of a mere entourage, of a divine court or council which later disappears behind the king who alone acts. Those addressed here are not merely consulted by the one who speaks but are summoned to an act (like the "going down" of Gen. 11.7), i.e., an act of creation, the creation of man, in concert with the One who speaks. There is no reason why we should assume . . . that they did not actually participate in the work in question but were merely present as interested spectators. The truth is rather that the saga wishes the creation of man to be understood in the true sense as a concerted act . . .[59]

57. As Samuelson sums up the various diverse suggestions in the rabbinic literature, "us" was thought to refer to the royal we, the earth and sky, the souls of the righteous, God's wind, the five prior days of creation, and the angels belonging to God's family. Samuelson, *Judaism and Creation*, 128–29. In the *Encyclopedia Judaica*, Paul and his colleagues also add the divine council as a likely referent, stating about Gen 1:26 that it is "a solemn declaration of purpose announced in the heavenly council" ("Creation and Cosmogony," 273).

The mainstream Christian understanding has been divided between two explanations: "Us" was seen either to refer to the threefold God, that is, the Trinity, or to the whole of the heavenly court (see Westermann, *Genesis*, 144). Regarding the former, although fully committed to the notion of Trinity himself, Barth warns that a Trinitarian rendering is "rather too explicit" (*CD* 3/1:192), and several other commentators present the same view, e.g., Collins, *Genesis*, 59–60; Heiser, *Unseen Realm*, 39. With respect to a third proposal, treating the "us" as a royal we, Westermann explains that the plural of majesty does not occur in Hebrew and has therefore been abandoned as an explanation by scholars; yet, he adds that there are some linguistic arguments to suggest that the grammatical construction may be a "plural of deliberation" (*Genesis*, 145), and Childs regards the plural referent as being a linguistic convention of "self-address" in Hebrew. Childs, *Biblical Theology*, 568.

However, in what is probably one of the most detailed treatments of the plural "us" pronoun, Carr explains that many of the attempts to try and explain away the collision between grammar and interpretation have been "interpretive sleight of hand" (*In His Own Image*, 18) and he presents detailed arguments why the referent should be seen as a "true plural" (ibid, 20); accordingly, he agrees with Wenham's conclusion that "'Let us create man' should therefore be regarded as a divine announcement to the heavenly court, drawing the angelic host's attention to the master stroke of creation, man" (*Genesis*, 28)—as Carr sums up, "Despite the theological turmoil that it entails, this latter opinion remains the consensus" (*In His Own Image*, 21). For a similar position, see Heiser, *Unseen Realm*, 39.

58. Barth, *CD* III/1, 191.

59. Ibid., 191–92.

It is important to note that the phrase "concerted act" that Barth uses at the end of the above quotation does not denote a joint process of creation, because Gen 1:27 presents the verb "create" in a singular form, assigning to it the singular pronoun that refers to God ("*he* created him"). Rather, the plural pronoun in Gen 1:26 is better understood as part of an address to a group of *concerned* members (or as Carr puts it, "God's attendant beings"[60]). The canon does not provide insights into the nature or implications of such a collective body,[61] but a collective understanding of God's pronouncements is further supported by Job 38:7, which states that during material creation "all the heavenly beings shouted for joy," and we find two further occurrences of the plural pronoun in the Genesis narrative where it is similarly associated with a collective sense, both times before highly important divine decisions: the expulsion of Adam and Eve from Eden ("See, the man has become like one of us, knowing good and evil," Gen 3:22) and the story of the Tower of Babel ("Come, let us go down, and confuse their language there," Gen 11:7).[62] The topic of the heavenly assembly will recur later in this chapter when we discuss the divine speeches at the end of the Book of Job and again when we explore the nature of Atonement.

Division among the Heavenly Host

The alternative interpretation of Eliphaz's dream proposed earlier, namely that it is a deception orchestrated by a spiritual being who was antagonistic to humanity, points to the existence of some kind of *disharmony* or *division* among the heavenly host. This inference is further corroborated by the description of the *śāṭān*'s desire to prove God's judgement wrong, as narrated in the prologue of Job, as well as by the text of Genesis 3 describing the conscious effort made by the serpent to go against God's explicit will. Although the canon does not provide any clarification about the background of this disparity, there are recurring references to dissent within the heavenly realm in several books of the Bible; Eph 6:10 for example mentions "spiritual forces of evil in the heavenly places" and Isa 24:21 declares that "On that day the LORD will punish the host of heaven in heaven . . ." We are not told about the

---

60. Carr, *In His Own Image*, 21.

61. Some rough analogies from our contemporary world could include a board of trustees, a senate, a cabinet, or some other kind of ruling/executive body.

62. One further example of the divine plural used in the same collective sense is Isaiah's (6:8) prophetic commission: "Then I heard the voice of the Lord saying, 'Whom shall I send, and who will go for us?'" This passage again implies that it is God who takes decisions but he does so on behalf of a collective group.

extent to which, or in what way, the heavenly faction of angels who harbored disobedience to God was represented in the divine assembly,[63] but Psalm 82 is revealing in this respect by indicating that issues concerning the standing of certain "children of the Most High" (v. 6) have been raised in God's court (vv. 1–2): "God has taken his place in the divine council; in the midst of the gods he holds judgment" over angels who are accused of showing partiality to the wicked among humankind. The psalm presents these angels to be responsible for displaying a similar kind of animosity toward the well-being of humankind as the *šāṭān* did, who was ready to destroy Job's family and inflict tremendous suffering onto Job in order to prove his point.

Psalm 82 also makes it clear that heavenly disobedience can have dramatic consequences for material creation: V. 5 states that as a result of it "all the foundations of the earth are shaken," and the gravity of this outcome is consistent with the *de facto* death sentence that God passed on the fallen angels involved: "You are gods, children of the Most High, all of you; nevertheless, you shall die like mortals, and fall like any prince" (vv. 6–7).[64]

Finally, an even more dramatic confrontation in heaven is presented in Luke 10:18 where the Evangelist reports Jesus telling his disciples, "I watched Satan fall from heaven like a flash of lightning," with more details of this ousting from heaven provided in Rev 12:7–9: "And war broke out in heaven; Michael and his angels fought against the dragon. The dragon and his angels fought back, but they were defeated, and there was no longer any place for them in heaven. The great dragon was thrown down, that ancient serpent, who is called the Devil and Satan, the deceiver of the whole world—he was thrown down to the earth, and his angels were thrown down with him."

The exact meaning and implications of Jesus' words in Luke and the related Revelation passage have understandably been the subject of a great deal of theological reflection,[65] but most scholars would agree with the point made in the current section, namely that these passages attest to the divided nature of the heavenly host. This is further corroborated by the hymnic passage in Revelation that immediately follows the news of Satan's expulsion

63. The fragmented biblical information does not allow for firm conclusions, particularly because there are hints in the canon that the heavenly realm had an intricate structure; White for example argues that there is more than one type of divine assembly presented within the Old Testament with several tiers of membership. White, *Yahweh's Council*, 173–74.

64. The punishment of sinning angels has also been recorded in two other passages in the New Testament, 2 Pet 2:4 and Jude 6.

65. For an insightful analysis, see Gathercole, "Jesus' Vision of the Fall of Satan," 143–63.

from heaven (12:10–11), in which Satan's role as an *accuser* is highlighted twice, implying that it was a primary reason for his expulsion;[66] therefore the hymn can be perceived as a celebration of the restoration of the *harmony* of the divine assembly.

The śāṭān and His Forces

The biblical canon presents several named or labelled spiritual authorities among God's adversaries, with some names being synonyms referring to the same being; for example, the three parallel versions of the Parable of the Sower in the Synoptic Gospels use three different expressions for Satan—"Satan" (Mark 4:15), "the evil one" (Matt 13:l9), and "the devil" (Luke 8:12)—without there being any obvious significance to this variation.[67] In other cases, however, it may be less straightforward to decide whether different names signify the same power or not; for example "Beelzebul" (Matt 12:24), "Beliar" (2 Cor 6:15), or phrases such as the "god of this world" (2 Cor 4:4), the "ruler of this world" (John 14:30), or the "ruler of the power of the air" (Eph 2:2) are likely to refer to Satan, whereas others, such as the "ravager/destroyer" (Isa 54:16; 1 Cor 10:10), the "lawless one" (2 Thess 2:3), or the "antichrist" (1 John 2:22) do not. This book is not concerned with the intricacies of these various referents (or with the different translations and forms of their names)[68] beyond suggesting that the canon portrays the forces that oppose God as being hierarchically ordered, led by a celestial being who is most often referred to as *the śāṭān* in the OT and Satan in the NT.[69]

66. See Aune, *Revelation 6–16*, 701.

67. Page, *Powers of Evil*, 115.

68. For overviews, see D. R. Brown, "The Devil," 200–227; Heiser, *Unseen Realm*, 323–30; Wink *Naming the Powers*. Reflecting on the variety of relevant terms found in the NT canon, M. Green makes an important point when he stresses that "the very number and variety of the names for these things shows us that the New Testament writers . . . had no interest in building up demonologies; they enumerated at random, only in order to show that these enemy forces were one and all disarmed by Jesus Christ" (*Satan's Downfall*, 82).

69. Page is right to caution that nowhere in the Old Testament are the celestial forces that are intent to harm humans explicitly described as being headed by the śāṭān; however, because the śāṭān is presented both in Job and Zechariah as the person whom God treats as the spokesman of the opposing views, this can be inferred. Page, *Powers of Evil*, 82. It is more straightforward to arrive at the same conclusion in the New Testament, because Beelzebul is characterized as "the ruler of the demons" (e.g., Luke 11:15), and Matt 25:41 uses the phrase "devil and his angels." Furthermore, phrases such as "the god of this world" (2 Cor 4:4) and the "ruler of this world" (John 14:30) suggest centralized leadership, also confirmed by 1 John 5:19, which states that "the whole world lies

The Hebrew noun *śāṭān* denotes the role of "adversary" or "accuser" in general and occurs several times in the Old Testament in this sense;[70] it is used to refer to God's adversary only in three books, in the prologue of Job (x14), in Zech 3:1–2 (x3), and in 1 Chr 21:1.[71] In Job and Zechariah, the word always appears with the definite article in the Hebrew text, which likely indicates that it was *not* used as a proper name but rather in reference to someone having a descriptive title.[72] In 1 Chr 21:1, as a single occurrence in the Old Testament, the absence of the definite article before *śāṭān* shows that the word here refers to a proper name, similar to how *Satanas*—a transliteration of the Hebrew word—is always used in the Greek text of the New Testament as a proper name in reference to God's archenemy.

It has been often pointed out by commentators that it may not be appropriate to read back into the OT portrayal of the *śāṭān* all the evil connotations that the NT Satan is associated with.[73] The arguments supporting this warning range from stating that the *śāṭān* was a legitimate member of the heavenly assembly who operated fully under God's mandate and within the confines set by God, to claiming that he was in fact a heavenly official of high standing, a kind of prosecuting attorney charged with the specific responsibility of exposing human sinfulness. In an extreme portrayal along the latter lines, Henry Kelly for example understands the *śāṭān* as a non-evil "functionary of the Divine Government" with a "tenure as Chief Tester and Accuser,"[74] and argues that even the Satan of the New Testament largely complies with this job description. Undeniably, Jesus' comment in Luke 22:31 that Satan demanded to "sift" the disciples "like wheat" does recall the Accuser in the prologue of Job asking for permission to uncover human failings, and it also signals that Satan was still subject to God's will. However, while a passage in Revelation also confirms Satan's role as an accuser, it describes at the same time his *expulsion* from heaven, with angels rejoicing that "the accuser of our comrades has been thrown down, who accuses

---

under the power of the evil one"—thereby implying the existence of a unified force of evil—as well as by Matt 12:26, which explicitly mentions Satan's "kingdom."

70. Num 22:22, 32; 1 Sam 29:4; 2 Sam. 19:22; 1 Kgs 5:4; 11:14, 23, 25; Ps 109:6.

71. Although the presence of the *śāṭān* is much smaller in the OT than Satan's in the NT, his three recorded appearances are highly important as they targeted King David, the High Priest Joshua, to whom God said, "I have taken away your sin, and I will put rich garments on you" (Zech 3:4), and Job, whom God described as "There is no one on earth like him; he is blameless and upright, a man who fears God and shuns evil" (1:8). Thus, the OT *śāṭān* intended to discredit some of the key OT figures.

72. Curiously, none of the major English translations reflect this linguistic point but translate the word as "Satan."

73. See Page, *Powers of Evil*, 25–26 for an overview.

74. Kelly, *Satan*, 7–8.

them day and night before our God" (12:10). It appears thus that this cosmic event concluded a process whereby the divinely mandated prosecutor of the Old Testament turned into an "evil, hostile prosecutor [who] . . . in his excessive zeal to find evidence . . . oversteps his bounds."[75] Indeed, as already mentioned, by New Testament times the initial heavenly dissent had grown into a systematic evil rebellion orchestrated by Satan, resulting in the kingdom of darkness prevailing on earth.

We must realize, however, that the Accuser of the prologue of Job was no benign prosecutor who was only carrying out an unenviable but necessary duty. Page rightly points out that the fact that in Job's first trial God had to set the condition that the *śāṭān* was not to touch Job's person, and in the second that he must not kill him, implies that God knew that the *śāṭān* might be prone to go too far,[76] and indeed the prologue of Job reveals a ruthless zeal in the *śāṭān*, a fervor to achieve his purpose with absolutely no concern for human life or suffering. In truth, neither the Job prologue nor Zechariah 3 present the *śāṭān* as a dutiful servant with a thankless task to perform, but rather as someone who had to be held back from unleashing his contempt and hatred against humanity. Furthermore, not only did the *śāṭān* fully represent in his own actions and intentions the same convictions about human worthlessness as those implanted into the minds of Job's friends in Eliphaz's vision, but he was also *willing to question* his Creator's judgement in this respect. And when his initial attempts to discredit humans failed, he was determined to "up his game," as it were, which may explain how he ended up locked into a struggle that turned the leader of the celestial opposition into a rebellious outlaw who is eventually expelled from heaven (Rev 12:9–10).[77]

There is thus some continuity between the *śāṭān* of the Old Testament and Satan in the New Testament, and indeed, in John's Gospel Jesus declares that Satan was "a murderer *from the beginning*" (8:44; emphasis mine), which is reiterated in 1 John 3:8: "the devil has been sinning from the beginning." The disloyalty to God and the desire to thwart God's creative work by inciting people against the Creator's purpose also points to a continuity between the serpent of Genesis 3 and the *śāṭān*—and consequently

75. Moses, "Satan," 26.

76. Page, *Powers of Evil*, 27.

77. It is significant in this respect that in three of his four appearances in the Old Testament the Accuser fails: After his two unsuccessful attempts to corrupt Job in Job, God concludes, "you incited me against him to ruin him without any reason" (2:3), and in Zechariah the Lord rebuked the *śāṭān* not once but twice (Zech 3:2). Interestingly, it is when describing his first *successful* effort to incite King David to commit sin in 1 Chr 21:1 that the canon first attributes to him the proper name "Satan."

also Satan. This is explicitly expressed in Rev 20:2, where, as we already saw in chapter 3, the Greek word for "serpent," *ophis*—the same word as the one used in the LXX translation of the serpent of the Fall in Gen 3:1, 2, and 14—is directly linked to Satan, and the reference to "that ancient serpent" in the same passage further strengthens the identification of Satan with the serpent of the Fall.[78]

The Power of the Celestial Opposition

One of the main—and rarely mentioned—lessons of the Book of Job is that the *śāṭān* was able to corrupt the beliefs of Job's friends, even though they were clearly seasoned sages (and were also in a close relationship with Job, who was repeatedly described as a blameless and upright person). It is sobering to realize that one nocturnal visitation was sufficient to sway the accomplished theologian Eliphaz, who then also turned his companions around to his corrupted views. This ability of the *śāṭān*/Satan to use people, even righteous ones, for his purpose is also displayed in several other passages of the canon (e.g., King David in 1 Chr 21:1 and Peter in Matt 16:23 and parallels), and with Judas—who was, we must not forget, Jesus' handpicked disciple for an extended period—we are told that Satan not only managed to manipulate him but actually "entered him" at one point (Luke 22:3; John 13:27), indicating an even more profound level of control. This manipulating/controlling capacity of Satan may explain Paul's cautioning in 1 Tim 3:7 that even church leaders might "fall into disgrace and the snare of the devil," and nothing illustrates the potency of the "snare of the devil" better than Peter's shift from being described in Matt 16:18 as a "rock" on which Jesus will build his church to becoming a "stumbling block" to Jesus only five verses later (v. 23). Finally, 2 Tim 2:24–26 makes an explicit reference to the grave fact that the "opponents" of the Lord's servants are "held captive by him [the devil] to do his will" (v. 26).

These examples attest to Satan's possession of a high level of controlling power over humans, which is further underlined in other NT passages: Heb 2:14 states that Satan has "the power of death" and 1 John 5:19 that "the whole world lies under the power of the evil one." Also, in his mission charge to Paul, Jesus specifically underlined that he was sending Paul to the Gentiles "to open their eyes so that they may turn from darkness to light and from *the power of Satan* to God" (Acts 26:18; emphasis added). Finally, the

---

78. As was already mentioned in chapter 3, the association of the serpent with the devil has been widely accepted by commentators; see e.g., Aune, *Revelation 6–16,* 696–97; Osborne, *Revelation,* 471.

fact that Satan could recruit for his cause a large number of angels (perhaps as many as one-third of the heavenly host if we consider Revelation 12:4 to be relevant here) also testifies to Satan's considerable sphere of influence.

The Motivation of the Celestial Opposition

Having established the significance of the role played by the śāṭān /Satan and his celestial followers, the logical question to ask is what motivated their actions. Eliphaz's vision is revealing in this respect, because the spirit's message suggests three underlying motives: (a) a disdain for humanity, (b) pride, and (c) bitterness against God.

Disdain for humanity. Job 38:7 states that the foundation of the earth was perceived with joy by all the heavenly beings, who therefore must have agreed with God's pronouncement in Gen 1:31 that material creation was "very good." However, as the emerging division among the heavenly host demonstrates, there was a change in the unanimous appreciation at one point, with a considerable faction of the heavenly host developing a dissident view. This opposing attitude was first reflected in the biblical narrative in the description of the serpent of the Fall; before that, the only negative aspect noted in Genesis was God's dramatic declaration of "not good" about Adam's position (2:18), and we saw in chapter 3 that this declaration constituted the starting point of a chain of events that included Adam and Eve's expulsion from Eden and then the Flood. Therefore, given the prominence of this ensuing setback, it may not be unreasonable to infer that the formation of the celestial opposition was somehow related to Adam's initial insufficiency. In fact, Adam's inadequacy to fulfil the role of God's steward—an indispensable condition for the progress of creation—is consistent with the spirit's contemptuous remarks in Eliphaz's vision about the futility of humanity, thereby lending support to the possibility that the negative predisposition of the celestial opposition stemmed from their loss of faith in the capability of corporeal humanity to see progressive creation to its successful completion.

In other words, the hostility of the celestial opposition may have originated, at least partly, from the extension of God's "not good" appraisal concerning Adam's specific situation to the evaluation of the viability of the whole of material creation; this would render them, to use a contemporary term, "ideologically motivated challengers," who became increasingly radicalized and went to further and further extremes in pursuit of their agenda. That such a broad underlying issue may have indeed been involved in their dissatisfaction is bolstered by the fact that, as seen above, until his defeat described in Revelation 12:7–9, Satan had a considerable sphere of influence among the heavenly host,[79] and further indirect evidence for assuming an ideological dissent is provided by the fact that until their final expulsion from heaven Satan and his followers remained a recognized part of the heavenly realm, unlike some other fallen angels who—as seen earlier—were punished harshly by the heavenly court.

Pride. It follows from the *a fortiori* argument in the spirit's communication to Eliphaz that the night visitor held himself and the angelic beings in general as being a class above humans: He argued that if even superior beings like himself and his ilk could be found fault with, what hope could there possibly be for the inferior species, humankind? Pride has traditionally been an explanation in theology for Satan's deviance, ever since Augustine identified it in his commentary on Genesis as the main reason why Satan rejected the blessed life open to all angels,[80] and two passages in the Old Testament have often been cited to provide (indirect) evidence for the reality of this claim: Isaiah 14:4–20 (and especially 12–15) and Ezekiel 28:12–19, each containing a song lamenting—or rather taunting—the death of a mighty ruler (of Babylon and Tyre, respectively).

Isaiah 14:12 concerns a powerful celestial being, referred to as "the morning star," who fell from heaven and was cast down to the earth because of his excessive pride as he wanted to become "like the Most High" (v. 14). Similarly, Ezekiel 28:12–19 describes a mighty figure who was originally "in Eden, the garden of God" (v. 13) but was then driven out by a "cherub" (v. 17) and was "cast . . . to the ground" (v. 17) because "Your heart was proud because of your beauty; you corrupted your wisdom for the sake of your splendor" (v. 17). Starting with Tertullian and Origen, these passages became associated with the fall of Satan in the patristic literature, and as a result, the term "Lucifer," which was the Latin rendering of the Hebrew word for "morning star" (*hêlēl*) in the Vulgate and was then adopted into the English translation of the King James Bible as such, was increasingly taken to mean the devil.[81] Although modern scholarship has been cautious about directly equating these mighty figures with Satan,[82] the passages do

79. Rev 12:7–9 describes a battle of Satan and "his angels" with the archangel Michael and his forces, and although Satan was defeated, the fact that this involved a full-scale battle reflects the size of the heavenly armies involved.

80. *De Gen. ad lit.* 11.14.18, cited in Mann, "Augustine on Evil and Original Sin," 46–47.

81. See e.g., Albani, "Downfall of Helel," 62; Patmore, *Adam, Satan, and the King of Tyre,* 212.

82. See e.g., Allen, *Ezekiel 20–48,* 95; Oswalt, *Isaiah,* 320; Page, *Powers of Evil,* 38–140.

offer a plausible biblical analogy to show how someone may forfeit his high celestial standing and close intimacy with God due to pride and the desire for more power. This analogy is strengthened by the fact that the texts associate both rulers directly with the heavenly assembly: The king of Babylon desired to "sit enthroned on the mount of assembly" (Isa 14:13) and the pride of the ruler of Tyre is related to the fact that he sits "in the seat of the gods, in the heart of the seas" (Ezek 28:2), with Heiser presenting philological evidence that both of the phrases used by Ezekiel denote the throne room of the divine council.[83]

Finally, the reality of pride as a general cause of heavenly dissent is further underscored by the fact that it also emerges in the case of the serpent of the Fall. Genesis 3:1 highlights that the serpent was "more crafty than any other wild animal that the Lord God had made,"[84] and the fact that pride—possibly related to this superior shrewdness—may have been involved in his action is indicated by the nature of God's punishment, expressed in the Curse: "upon your belly you shall go, and dust you shall eat all the days of your life" (Gen 3:14). Commentators are unanimous in that this symbolizes abject humiliation and subjugation in the Bible (as in Mic 7:17; Ps 44:25; 72:9), and moving on its belly also brands serpents as unclean and "detestable" (Lev 11:42);[85] accordingly, the "serpent, who had been characterized as the shrewdest of all the animals, will now become the most humble."[86]

Bitterness against God. The spirit's communication to Eliphaz conveyed tangible bitterness about the fact that some members of the group of beings that he belonged to had not been fully trusted by God and had been "charged with error" (Job 4:18).[87] We have seen earlier when discussing the division among the heavenly host that God has indeed called certain celestial beings to account (e.g., Ps 82; Isa 24:21) and has in some cases passed

83. Heiser, *Unseen Realm,* 76, n. 4. He goes even further by arguing that "an ancient tale of divine rebellion" accounts for the elements in both the Isa 14 and Ezek 28 passages, with particularly the former describing an "attempted coup in the divine council" (ibid., 85), an interpretation which would be consistent with the point made here.

84. The feeling of superiority may have given an opening for Satan to control the serpent, with an analogy offered by 1 Timothy, which cautions against appointing a recent convert as bishop or else "he may be puffed up with conceit and fall into the condemnation of the devil" (3:6).

85. Wenham, *Genesis,* 79.

86. B. T. Arnold, *Genesis,* 68; for a similar view, see e.g., Hamilton, *Genesis,* 196–97; Waltke, *Genesis,* 93; Wenham, *Genesis,* 89.

87. The exact meaning of the word translated as "error" (*tāhôlâ*) in v. 18 is not known; it occurs only here in the Bible and has been the subject of much guesswork; see Andersen, *Job,* 123; Hartley, *Job,* 114.

harsh sentences on them. Significantly, 2 Pet 2:4 mentions fallen angels cast into hell, committed to chains until final judgement, and referring to the same discredited spirits, Jude 6 adds that this happened because they "did not keep their own position, but left their proper dwelling." The direct dependence of Jude 6 on the pseudepigraphal book 1 Enoch (6–19)[88] leaves no doubt that the fallen angels in this epistle refer to the sons of God who illicitly intermarried with the daughters of men as described in a tantalizingly brief passage in Gen 6:1–4 just before the Flood.[89] This in turn points to the possible conclusion that the angelic fall—along with instances of impeachment of other angels as in Psalm 82—left a residue of resentment in some heavenly beings, including Eliphaz's night visitor.[90]

Jealousy. A final possible motive for the hostile stance of God's adversaries—not expressed explicitly in the Book of Job but closely related to the above three themes—is jealousy caused by the fact that, according to some passages in the Scriptures, God appeared to favor the material realm over the celestial one. The Old Testament contains repeated declarations that God intends to dwell among humans (Lev 26:11–12; Num 35:34), a point reiterated in Revelation 21:3, and as we saw in chapter 4, Revelation also asserts that the center of God's eschatological kingdom, New Jerusalem, will be erected on earth and be populated with resurrected humans.[91] Moreover, 1 Cor 6:2–3 states that the saints will judge not only the world but also the angels, and contrary to what the spirit intimated to Eliphaz about the limited wisdom of humankind, there is also a pronouncement in Ephesians that the mystery that had been hidden for ages was revealed to humans "so that through the church the wisdom of God in its rich variety might now be made known to the rulers and authorities in the heavenly places" (3:10). Finally, Heb 1:14 might also have relevance here, because it states that "all angels . . . are sent to serve for the sake of those who are to inherit salvation," underlining the importance of God's focus on salvation for humans,[92] who

88. This is not only observable from the intertextual links such as the quotation in Jude 14 from 1 En 1:9, but also from the fact that Jude 14 specifically cites Enoch by name; see e.g., G. Green, *Jude and 2 Peter*, 101–5; Bauckham, *Jude, 2 Peter*, 51–53.

89. See e.g., Page, *Powers of Evil*, 236 for a summary of this link.

90. Clines agrees that "the story of the union of the 'sons of God' with the daughters of men in Gen 6:1–4 is adequate traditional background for this assessment of angels' reliability" (*Job 1–20*, 134).

91. In this respect it is noteworthy that, as Evdokimov summarizes, Gregory Palamas saw the superiority of humans over the angels in their corporal condition, with their bodies being deified through salvation; Palamas even defined one of the goals of Incarnation as "to venerate the flesh, in order that the proud spirits may not dare to imagine that they are more venerable than man." Evdokimov, "Nature," 21–22.

92. Guthrie, *Hebrews*, 84.

are the "heirs of God" (Rom 8:17). The duty of heavenly beings is defined as assisting humankind along their journey to the kingdom of God, and as Donald Guthrie explains, in this passage—Heb 1:14—"the *all* (*pantes*) significantly includes all ranks of angels. Even the noblest are *sent forth to serve*" (emphases in the original).[93]

To summarize, the Bible offers no direct explanation of the roots of the celestial opposition to humankind, but a number of relevant details mentioned in the canon, and especially in the communication of Eliphaz's night visitor, suggest several likely factors that may have played a role in turning a significant faction of the heavenly host against God's works. It was argued that at the heart of this dissent was a growing skepticism about the viability of material creation and particularly of its stewards' capability to see it through to successful completion, and this seed of dissent found fertile soil in the combination of pride, jealousy, and bitterness. It is against this background that the significance of the extensive coverage of Job's story in the canon becomes clear, as it provides evidence of the *integrity* of humanity. The issue of mistrust toward material creation among the heavenly host is likely to be related to the reason why the Book of Job is concluded by two speeches from God specifically addressing the created order of the world and comprising some of the longest continuous divine communications recorded in the whole canon. Let us conclude the exploration of the Book of Job by examining these two speeches as well as the nature of Job's final victory as described in the prologue of the book.

The Divine Speeches and Job's Victory

The two divine speeches which conclude the poetic dispute section of the Book of Job have been the subject of much puzzled speculation among scholars, because the speeches do not directly address the issues that most commentators consider central to the previous discussion between Job and his friends.[94] That is, in his response to Job, God does not engage with the theological and philosophical arguments raised earlier about human suffering, justice, and retribution—in fact, apart from one short passage of five verses (40:10–14), God does not mention humans at all. These speeches therefore do not constitute a response in the strict sense, and yet God clearly intends them to be a reply to Job, and Job in turn accepts them as such. Therefore, without trying to be frivolous, we may ask: If the speeches

93. Ibid., 83.
94. E.g., Alden, *Job*, 368; Andersen, *Job*, 289.

are the answer, what is the question? That is, what is the main issue that God chose to respond to?

The essence of the divine speeches involves a crescendo of creation-related images in the first speech (chapters 38–39), culminating in the detailed description of two creatures of immense power in the second: Behemoth and Leviathan (chapters 40–41). The first speech offers glimpses into the immense and subtle complexity of the material world, as well as the intricacies of life in it. According to the reading of the current book, God's emphasis in the first speech is not so much on what commentators have often seen as the goal to "force Job in the end to recognize his utter insignificance and ignorance and so the enormity of his presumption in daring to summon God to trial"[95] (Whybray). Rather, the images are intended to accentuate the elaborate design and operation of the ecosystem, pointing to and illuminating the wisdom that holds the world and the cosmos together. It becomes clear after the first speech, however, that Job fails to understand God's message; therefore, in his second speech God changes his approach and replaces, in Newsom's words, the "sublime mode of repetitive excess" with "exorbitance"[96] by describing the terrible magnificence of the legendary beasts Behemoth and Leviathan. With these descriptions we arrive at the climax of the book: After these portrayals God will stop speaking and Job will repent. Therefore, we are left to ask: What is it about Behemoth and Leviathan that finally opens Job's eyes?

Behemoth and Leviathan

Behemoth and Leviathan are God's creatures,[97] representing "forces of the created world with which even God Himself is challenged to contend."[98] We are told that Behemoth was "the first of the great acts of God—only its Maker can approach it with the sword" (40:19), and as such it embodies the might of the material world: it is solid, confident, unshakable, and is beyond fear, full of placid strength. Its counterpart in the deep sea is Leviathan, the

95. Whybray, *Job*, 157.

96. Newsom, *Job*, 248.

97. As Gordis summarizes, the interpretation of Behemoth and Leviathan has oscillated through the centuries between two poles, mythical and real, with some scholars simply equating them with the hippopotamus and the crocodile. Gordis, *Job*, 569–70; see also Clines, "Job," 483. Although the description of the two creatures may well draw details from these specific animals, they are perceived in this chapter as primordial beasts of cosmic power.

98. Kushner, *Job*, 146.

sea monster,[99] who matches Behemoth's physical strength to the extent that "When it raises itself up the gods are afraid" (41:25). Its heart is "as hard as stone" (v. 24) and "terror dances before it" (v. 22)—thus, Leviathan is portrayed as an undaunted, untamed, and irresistible force at large, without any equals on earth (v. 33). At the same time, the description of Leviathan does not suggest any enmity between God and this beast. Instead, God seems to describe it—and also Behemoth—with evident admiration; as Newsom observes, "there is a curious level of identification between God and Leviathan. God represents himself as being in the image of Leviathan, only more so. Indeed, as has often been pointed out, the physical description of Leviathan is uncannily evocative of the theophanic descriptions of God."[100]

It is almost as if God is revealing to Job an aspect of his creation that goes beyond the orderliness of the regulated world—a "wild streak," as it were. The two beasts are not presented to Job with the purpose of underscoring the fact that only God has the ability to overcome them, because while this is true, Newsom rightly points out that this is taken as given.[101] Instead, God's message seems to make the point forcefully that Behemoth and Leviathan are an integral part of his created order, and a part that he is proud of. Thus, the divine speeches outline a portrayal of the cosmos as a place which accommodates both intricate order and untamed forces—as Fyall concludes about Leviathan, the "curbing of such a powerful monster is part of creation itself and this is a continuing task."[102]

From Job's perspective, the ultimate challenge he faced was to come to terms with the fact that, in Kushner's words, "bad things happened to good people,"[103] a perception of a seemingly twisted world order that is also voiced in Ecclesiastes (9:11–12): "Again I saw that under the sun the race is not to the swift, nor the battle to the strong, nor bread to the wise, nor riches to the intelligent, nor favor to the skillful; but time and chance happen to them all. For no one can anticipate the time of disaster. Like fish taken in a cruel net, and like birds caught in a snare, so mortals are snared at a time of calamity, when it suddenly falls upon them."

However, through a kaleidoscope of images illustrating the sheer complexity of material creation and the forces of cosmic intensity involved

---

99. Leviathan is mentioned earlier in Job (3:8) and also elsewhere in the Old Testament (Pss 74:14, 104:26; Isa 27:1), and it is likely to be linked to the sea monsters whose creation on the fifth day is recounted in Gen 1:21.

100. Newsom, *Job*, 251.

101. Ibid., 249.

102. Fyall, *Job*, 93.

103. Kushner, *Job*.

in it that need to be held together,[104] the divine speeches imply that if something does not appear consistent or right from a human point of view, this is because one's vision is not broad enough to behold such forces and creatures as Leviathan. As Ellison sums up, Job's concept of God initially collapsed because it was too small,[105] and by the end of the second speech he finally realizes this: "I have uttered what I did not understand, things too wonderful for me, which I did not know" (42:3). As a result, he repents of questioning God without knowledge: "therefore I despise myself, and repent in dust and ashes" (v. 6).

In sum, the picture painted by God in his response to Job is not a degrading depiction of material creation but just the opposite: It outlines the majesty of a powerful system of elemental forces and intricate components without the slightest hint that this part of the cosmos is in any way inferior to the celestial realm—after all, nobody but the Maker can approach Behemoth with a sword (40:19) and even the gods are afraid of Leviathan (41:25). Thus, in answer to the starting question of what exactly God responded to in the divine speeches, rather than focusing on suffering and retribution as many would have expected, he addressed the overall design of material creation, and by providing a series of fitting illustrations he reiterated his original appraisal that "it was very good" (Gen 1:31).[106] Wilson therefore is right in stating that God's response was "not rejecting the doctrine of retribution, but simply insisting that retributive justice is not the only principle on which God runs his world."[107]

Although God's response opened Job's eyes (Job 42:5), one cannot help sensing that the two speeches were aimed not only at Job but also at a larger heavenly audience who followed the progress and the outcome of Job's testing, and particularly at those celestial beings who harbored doubts. After all, God's question in 40:2—"Shall a fault-finder contend with the Almighty?"—is more pertinent to the śāṭān than to Job, as are God's concluding words targeting pride by declaring about Leviathan that it "surveys everything that is lofty; it is king over all that are *proud*" (41:34; emphasis added). Thus, similar to the way in which the trials of Job—as we learnt

104. Interestingly, our contemporary scientific understanding of the material world is compatible to some extent with a picture of the created order subsuming contradictory forces or antitheses: Physics presents the "positron" at the core of matter as being the antiparticle counterpart of the electron, which is why positrons are also referred to as the "antimatter."

105. Ellison, *Job*, 590.

106. Clines puts it this way: "Yahweh does not attempt a justification for anything that happens in the world . . . The world is as he designed it" (*Job 38–42*, 1090).

107. Wilson, "Job," 387.

from the prologue—were part of a broader scheme between God and the śā ṭān in which Job was selected merely as a test case, God's final communication has the air of a closing speech in a case that goes beyond an individual human being's life both in terms of the breadth of content and its universal relevance.

Job's Victory

The divine speeches present a testimony to the robustness of material creation, but they do not say anything about the integrity of God's stewards, even though the śā ṭān's initial challenge specifically concerned this aspect of creation. Furthermore, while Job did not turn against his Maker, he still had to repent of his previous words, which raises the question as to whether he did indeed pass the test successfully. Both issues are resolved in the epilogue of the book. The 11 verses of prose concluding the poetic part are often seen merely as a short bookend that confirms that in the poetic dispute between Job and his friends, the former was right and is then rewarded by God's restoring his fortunes. While such a reading is legitimate, there is a key element in the epilogue that is somewhat overshadowed by the divine verdict and the abundance of God's blessings on Job, and is thus mostly overlooked, namely the multiple acts of *forgiveness*. After Job repents and is justified, God is willing also to forgive Eliphaz and his two companions as long as his divine forgiveness is transmitted by means of Job praying for—and thus forgiving—his three friends, who had "tormented" and "wronged" him (19:2–3) earlier. It is only after this act of reconciliation that Job's full restoration took place: "the LORD restored the fortunes of Job *when he had prayed for his friends*" (42:10; emphasis added). We also learn in v. 11 that Job was reconciled with—and therefore forgave—his family and friends who had previously abandoned and ostracized him. As he earlier lamented,

> My breath is repulsive to my wife;
>   I am loathsome to my own family.
> Even young children despise me;
>   when I rise, they talk against me.
> All my intimate friends abhor me,
>   and those whom I loved have turned against me. (19:17–19)

Yet, in his newly found peace Job is ready to welcome in his house "all his brothers and sisters and all who had known him before, and they ate bread with him" (v. 11), indicating true reconciliation. We might see the real integrity of Job as a social being—and thus the evidence for his victory in the trials—just as much in these post-dispute actions as in his earlier perseverance in standing firm in his faith and not succumbing to the social pressure to turn away from God. Indeed, the combination of divine forgiveness consummated by human forgiveness—as presented in the epilogue—is precisely what is highlighted by Jesus in the Lord's Prayer: "And forgive us our sins, for we ourselves forgive everyone indebted to us" (Luke 11:4). Significantly, Jesus' prayer (which will be discussed in chapter 6) concludes with two further lines that are also relevant to the Book of Job: "And do not bring us to the time of trial, but rescue us from the evil one" (Mt 6:13). Finally, we shall see below in the concluding section of this chapter, that Jesus' victory on the cross—where he, too, was in physical torment, abandoned by his loved ones and seemingly forsaken even by his Father—was to a large extent prefigured by the righteous Job as he demonstrated the human capacity to persevere in one's faith in the face of suffering and to forgive those who had harmed him, as did Jesus on the cross.

5.2. Jesus Christ's Victory

Colossians 2:15 recounts a decisive divine victory over certain powers and authorities: "He disarmed the rulers and authorities and made a public example of them, triumphing over them in it." Although some details of this verse are ambiguous,[108] commentators are agreed on the overarching meaning: Jesus' crucifixion resulted in the exposure and defeat of formidable spiritual powers that sought to frustrate God's work, and within the New Testament context it is safe to identify these powers as Satan and his forces. From the point of view of the current discussion, it is the second half of the verse that is of particular importance. Here the text states that the victory was a public spectacle, which was—as the word "triumphing" (*thriambeuō*) suggests—comparable to the triumphal procession of a successful general in the Roman Empire after some glorious conquest.[109] However, and rather curiously, commentators rarely ask the question of *who* the intended audience of this metaphorical parade was.[110] This is a valid question, because

108. The two major points of dispute concern what the exact meaning of the verb translated as "disarmed" (*apekdyomai*) is within this context and who the subject of the sentence is, God or Christ; see e.g., Bratcher and Nida, *Colossians and Philemon*, 62–63; Dunn, *Colossians and Philemon*, 167; Moo, *Colossians and Philemon*, 212–14; Page, *Powers of Evil*, 251; Wright, *Colossians and Philemon*, 119–20.

109. The focus of the word is on the act of celebrating a military victory rather than on the victory itself; see e.g., O'Brien, *Colossians, Philemon*, 128.

110. E.g., none of the major commentaries of Colossians referenced in the previous two footnotes raise this issue in any way.

from a human perspective, the execution of Jesus on a cross at Golgotha was seen as anything but a resounding victory: The Scriptures are clear that the spectators at the scene became disheartened rather than inspired.[111] This would suggest that the audience to which the Colossians passage refers was more likely to be celestial rather than human, and therefore what the text declares is that the crucifixion offered the heavenly host an unmistakable and spectacular display of God's triumphant glory.[112] The powerful language describing the impact of this display further implies that the event was a momentous occasion in the heavenlies, one which—as will be argued later in this chapter—potentially constituted some kind of a cosmic shift or turning point. This, however, begs the question of *how* Jesus achieved this remarkable victory, an issue that is usually discussed in theology under the rubric of *atonement*.

Atonement

Atonement can broadly be defined as "reconciliation to God through the work of Christ" (Thiselton).[113] This is an area where the compositional character of the canon has led to several different, and sometimes contradictory, understandings of the exact nature of atonement throughout the centuries, affected by the commentator's background and theological orientation as well as the cultural setting and the target audience of the interpretation. While the essence of atonement—"in Christ God was reconciling the world to himself" (2 Cor 5:19)—is well-defined, many scholars point out that neither the classic creeds nor the earlier rule of faith provide any firm guidelines about how best to construe the specific mechanisms and soteriological ramifications of the salvific work of Christ.[114] That is, as Gerhard Forde con-

---

111. As evidenced for example by the obvious discouragement of two followers of Jesus on the road to Emmaus as reported by Luke, when they stated "with their faces downcast" (24:17) that "we had hoped that he was the one to redeem Israel" (v. 21). Their hopes were dashed and, as Howard Marshall summed up, there was a "mood of shattered expectations" (*Last Supper*, 80).

112. This striking imagery recurs in 1 Cor 4:9, where Paul talks about a "spectacle" in which "God has exhibited us apostles," and significantly, here the audience explicitly includes the whole universe, specifically mentioning "angels." The connection to the Passion has been highlighted by several commentators; e.g., Fee states, "The scandal of the cross is written large over Paul's vision of his own apostleship" (*First Corinthians*, 191) See also 1 Tim 3:16, where in what is usually considered a fragment of a christological hymn it is emphasized that Jesus was "seen by angels."

113. Thiselton, *Dictionary of Theology*, 60.

114. E.g., Brümmer, *Atonement*, 66; Kelly, *Early Christian Doctrines*, 375; Thiselton, *Dictionary of Theology*, 60.

cludes, "There is no official dogma of the work of Christ—not in the sense in which one could speak of the dogmas of the Trinity, of the person of Christ, or even of justification,"[115] and Robert Jenson rightly adds that "It is one of the more remarkable and remarked-upon aspects of theological history that no theory of atonement has ever been universally accepted. By now, this phenomenon is itself among the things that a proposed theory of atonement must explain."[116] The reason for the absence of a uniform interpretation of atonement has been not the paucity of any relevant material in the canon but rather the *diversity* of the existing material. The New Testament uses many different images to understand, explain, or apply the meaning of atonement, all centered around Jesus Christ the "savior," but without forming a cohesive message. Accordingly, most scholars would accept Maurice Wiles's conclusion made over forty years ago:

> The ancient church did not formulate its doctrine of the atonement with the same kind of precision that it brought to bear on the subject of christology. It was happy to give expression to its faith at this point with the aid of a rich mixture of pictorial images. But there was a firm central core of faith to which those images were giving expression . . . a belief that in the death and resurrection of Christ God had worked effectively in history to transform once for all man's status (or at the very least man's potential status) in relation to God.[117]

In a volume dedicated to bringing together different understandings of the nature of the Atonement,[118] Green presents what he calls a "Kaleidoscopic view," arguing that the wide array of models and images that the NT writers generated for communicating the notion of atonement congregate around five spheres of public life in antiquity: the court of law (e.g., justification), the world of commerce (e.g., redemption), personal relationships (e.g., reconciliation), worship (e.g., sacrifice), and the battleground (e.g., triumph over evil).[119] Similar taxonomies have also been proposed by other theologians[120] embracing theories ranging "from the mythological to the

---

115. Forde, "Work of Christ," 5.

116. Jenson, *Systematic Theology Vol 1*, 186.

117. Wiles, *Christian Doctrine*, 62–63.

118. Beilby and Eddy, *Atonement: Four Views*.

119. Green, "Kaleidoscopic View," 169.

120. A highly influential, classic categorizations of the various atonement theories and images into three broad paradigms—Christus Victor, objective, and subjective—has been provided by Aulén, *Christus Victor*. A tripartite model highlighting victory, justice, and sacrifice is presented by Gunton, *Atonement*. The variety of backgrounds of the images (forensic, economic, social, political, and apocalyptic) is emphasized by

metaphysical to the juridical to the psychological"[121] (Jenson). Green further notes that the variety of NT images is not simply due to the different authorship of the various books of the canon, because sometimes the same writer can be found to use different images depending on the specific context of his particular topic. Stephen Holmes highlights a good example of this practice in Rom 3:24–25, where Paul employs as many as three different pictures of atonement within a relatively short sequence: "justified by his grace as a gift, through the redemption that is in Christ Jesus, whom God put forward as a sacrifice."[122]

The above observations seem to confirm the belief held by many scholars that the levels of diversity within the soteriological landscape of the New Testament "cannot simply be 'synchronized'"[123] (van der Watt). That is, no single framework can exhaust all the teachings about atonement in the canon, and the various metaphors and conceptual frameworks concerning the saving work of Christ need to be seen in a non-reductionist manner as complementing each other.[124] Indeed, Trevor Hart underlines the benefits of the existence of multiple atonement metaphors by arguing that this many-colored plurality makes it easier for human communities to find aspects of Jesus' salvific act that will resonate with their own experiences: "the cornucopia of biblical imagery provides something for everyone, a gospel to fit all cultural shapes and sizes."[125] We should note, however, that some scholars, while acknowledging the reality of the multiple facets of the issue, still maintain the necessity of prioritizing certain themes as more fundamental than others, with penal substitution in particular having been seen as a central aspect of atonement since the Reformation.[126]

---

van der Watt, "Soteriology of the New Testament," 518–19. For a recent overview that distinguishes five NT atonement metaphors (ransom, sacrifice, reconciliation, victory, and Second Adam) see Brockway, "Atonement."

121. Jenson, *Systematic Theology Vol 1*, 185. For a similar view, see also Pfleiderer, "Atonement," 127.

122. See e.g., Holmes, *Wondrous Cross*, 7.

123. van der Watt, "Soteriology of the New Testament," 505.

124. See e.g. Adam Johnson's summary in his book-length overview of atonement: "Perhaps atonement theories, rather than being seen as competing to offer a comprehensive and sufficient account of the work of Christ, are best understood as mutually complementary accounts of different aspects of the work of Christ, which together work to fill out the substance of the doctrine" (*Atonement*, 5).

125. Hart, "Redemption and Fall," 189.

126. For a summary, see e.g., Tidball et al., *Atonement Debate*; Holmes, *Wondrous Cross*; Schreiner, "Penal Substitution." For a nuanced discussion of the retributive concepts in Paul's understanding of the death of Christ, see Travis, *Christ and the Judgement of God*, chs. 12–13. For a critical perspective, see Cahill, "Atonement Paradigm,"

A Canonical Narrative Approach to Atonement

Despite the wide array of atonement paradigms, there is one aspect that most of the images discussed above share in common: they tend to concern the *outcome* of atonement rather than the *process* whereby Jesus accomplished it; in other words, the emphasis in the New Testament, and especially in the Epistles, is on translating the significance of the saving work of Christ into images that people can comprehend and relate to. In a comment at the end of an essay on redemption, Howard Marshall has summarized this emphasis on product over process very clearly: "Paul's vocabulary expresses the result of Christ's death rather than its character, and this fits in with NT thought in general, which is more concerned with the nature of salvation than the precise way in which it has been achieved."[127]

In accordance with the overall approach of this book, the following discussion will seek to understand Christ's salvific action in relation to the process of progressive creation as presented in the biblical narrative. Similar to other paradigms, Christ's death on the cross is seen as a crucial moment in the progression, but the crucifixion will be examined not only in terms of the significance of Jesus's sacrificial death but also with regard to *what* was "finished" (John 19:30) when Jesus died on the cross.[128] This approach inevitably shifts the attention to the Gospels, where we find that the tenor of reflection on Jesus' death differs somewhat from the images of atonement discussed in the previous section.[129] There are two recurring biblical characterizations of Jesus' actions leading to Calvary which stand out by virtue of their frequency, "fulfilling the Scriptures"[130] and "'carrying out the Father's will."[131] They are related to each other in that they both concern *obedience* to God's divine purpose. Of course, this perception is not unique

---

418–32.

127. Marshall, "Doctrine of Redemption," 169.

128. Although Aulén's Christus Victor model is based on the understanding that "God in Christ overcomes the hostile powers which hold man in bondage" (*Christus Victor*, 59), McGrath is right in pointing out that the model offered "no rational justification for the manner in which the forces of evil are defeated through the cross of Christ. Why the cross? Why not in some other manner?" McGrath, *Christian Theology*, 337.

129. Baker remarks in this respect: "The NT provides rich and diverse atonement imagery. A weakness, however, of limiting thinking about and proclamation of the atonement to this imagery is that it too easily isolates the atonement from the life Jesus lived" ("Atonement," 83).

130. E.g., Matt 1:22; 2:15, 17, 23; 4:14; 8:17; 12:17; 13:35; 21:4; 26:54, 56; 27:9; Luke 4:21; 24:44; John 12:38; 13:18; 15:25; 17:12; 18:9; 19:24, 28, 36

131. E.g., Matt 26:39, 42; Mark 14:36; Luke 22:42; John 4:34; 5:30; 6:38; 14:31.

to the Gospels, as for example Phil 2:8 famously states that Jesus "became obedient to the point of death—even death on a cross." However, the Evangelists consistently point to Jesus' relationship of obedience and service to the Father as being not only one of the important aspects of his motivation but as his *primary* drive, and Jesus' determination to proceed with his God-ordained mission, come what may, is perhaps most clearly expressed in his response to the Pharisees who warned him to leave or risk being murdered by Herod: "Listen, I am casting out demons and performing cures today and tomorrow, and on the third day I finish my work" (Luke 13:32).

This verse is usually understood as a refusal by Jesus to listen to the warnings because he knew that God, rather than Herod, would determine when he was to die.[132] However, if we study the sentence more closely, it may also be understood as shorthand for Jesus' overall mission statement. Regarding the context, there can be no doubt that this was no ordinary exchange with the Pharisees but rather a life-and-death situation (especially in the light of what had happened to John the Baptist earlier) in which Jesus in effect declared under a death threat that he would disregard the warning and continue pursuing his agenda. It is remarkable *how* he described this agenda: The elements he highlighted, *deliverance* and *healing*, directly point to two earlier fundamental disclosures of his identity, first in the Capernaum synagogue when he cited Isaiah 61 (Luke 4:18–19)[133] and then in his message to John the Baptist when he was questioned about being the Messiah (Luke 7:22[134]). Thus, Green is right to point out that in this passage "exorcism and healing are metonymic for the whole of his divine mission."[135] Furthermore, the word that has been translated as "finish my work" (13:32) by the NRSV, *teleioumai*, is the passive form of the verb meaning "to complete," "to finish" or "to make perfect" (*teleō*), and a range of suggestions have been made regarding its actual meaning in the current context, from "I shall be perfected" (NKJV) to "I finish my course" (ESV) and "I will reach my goal" (NIV). John Nolland submits that the term was probably intentionally ambiguous in the original and therefore a generic translation such as "I am finished" is appropriate.[136] This sense of

132. E.g., Green, *Luke*, 535; Morris, *Luke*, 245; Nolland, *Luke 9:21—18:34*, 740.

133. "The Spirit of the Lord is upon me, because he has anointed me to bring good news to the poor. He has sent me to proclaim release to the captives and recovery of sight to the blind, to let the oppressed go free, to proclaim the year of the Lord's favor."

134. "Go and tell John what you have seen and heard: the blind receive their sight, the lame walk, the lepers are cleansed, the deaf hear, the dead are raised, the poor have good news brought to them."

135. Green, *Luke*, 535.

136. Nolland, *Luke 9:21—18:34*, 740.

the word, then, creates a link with Jesus' extended prayer recorded in John's Gospel (John 17:1–26)—the "High-Priestly Prayer," which can be seen as Jesus' farewell discourse[137]—where Jesus stated, "I glorified you on earth by finishing [*teleiōsas*] the work that you gave me to do" (v. 4), and there is a further significant direct link with the crucifixion where Jesus declared, "It is finished [*tetelestai*]" (John 19:30).

Thus, in light of the fact that the phrase "today, tomorrow . . . and on the third day" was a continuing idiom[138] expressing Jesus' will to "continue on his current course without interruption"[139] (Green), what Jesus in effect declared in Luke 12:32 was that he would succeed in his mission by staying the course that had been set for him by the Father and by resisting any attempts to deflect him from it, whether by Herod or any other authority. The Scriptures bear witness to the fact that Satan and his forces were aware of who Jesus was and what threat he posed to them,[140] and therefore they were likely to do their utmost to derail Jesus' progress. It is against this background that Jesus' temptations acquire special significance, as these constituted the very tool by which Satan intended to thwart God's purpose and deflect Jesus from his divinely given mission.[141] Accordingly, we may understand Jesus' victory in terms of his capacity to *persevere* in his obedience by *resisting* Satan's temptations, even in face of the ultimate trial on the cross.[142] It will be argued below that by doing so Jesus repeated Job's righteous steadfastness—this time, however, without any limits set to spare his life—thereby producing the ultimate evidence of the integrity of humankind. From this perspective, therefore, atonement can be seen as Jesus providing conclusive evidence for the obedience of God's stewards and for their capability of standing up against corrupting influences, whether internal or external, in overseeing the progress of new creation. As we shall see, the spiritual balance in the heavenlies swayed dramatically as a consequence of Jesus' victory, setting into motion a chain of events that led to the expulsion

137. Beasley-Murray, *John*, 293.

138. Marshall, *Luke*, 571.

139. Green, *Luke*, 536.

140. E.g., Matt 8:29 records an unclean spirit crying out to Jesus, "What have you to do with us, Son of God? Have you come here to torment us before the time?"

141. Ladd holds a similar view when he states, "The chief function of Satan in the Gospels is to oppose the redemptive purpose of God. In the temptation narrative he claims a power over the world that Jesus does not question. The temptation consists of the effort to turn him aside from his divinely given mission as the Suffering Servant and to gain power by yielding to Satan." Ladd, *Theology of the New Testament, Revised*, 47.

142. It is telling in this respect that in 2 Thess 3:5 Paul prays that the Lord will direct the readers' hearts to two virtues, "God's love and Christ's perseverance" (NIV), which implies the significance of Jesus' endurance, comparable only to divine love.

of Satan and his forces from heaven and ultimately to the establishment of the eschatological kingdom of God on earth.

The Temptations of Jesus

When talking about the temptations of Jesus, the emphasis is often only on the initial testing in the wilderness immediately after his baptism. This, however, constitutes merely the first phase of a series of trials, which, rather like Job's initial, personal-level testing, was covered relatively briefly in the Scriptures: Both Matthew and Luke devote only 13 verses each to describing Jesus' temptation in the wilderness, and Mark's coverage is even shorter, only two verses (30 words). However, Luke makes it clear that after the devil's initial failure to corrupt Jesus, he "departed from him until an opportune time" (4:13), and as we shall see below, after this initial face-to-face engagement, Satan used multiple means, spiritually and socially orchestrated, to try and divert Jesus from his path. Let us have a closer look at the sequence of these events in the continuing temptations of the Christ.

Temptation in the Wilderness

All three Synoptic Gospels describe Jesus' temptation by Satan in the wilderness that took place immediately after his baptism (Mark 1:12–13; Matt 4:1–11; Luke 4:1–13), and Matthew and Luke provide details of three concrete acts that the temptations involved: the call to turn stones into bread, the call to jump off the Temple roof, and the offer of power and splendor in return for worship. The puzzling question is why Satan believed in the first place that he might succeed with his scheme? There is no suggestion here or elsewhere in the canon that we should regard Satan as naïve, therefore he must have believed it possible to exploit Jesus' corporeal creatureliness. Indeed, he had some basis for this belief: After all, although John 1:14 declares that "the Word became flesh [*sarx*]," in Matt 26:41 Jesus himself states that "the flesh [*sarx*] is weak," and Heb 5:2 confirms that Jesus was "subject to weakness." Furthermore, Satan's scheme to tempt Jesus was more elaborate than Job's initial trials (described in the prologue of the book): While targeting areas of fundamental human vulnerability—physical needs (food), insufficient faith (leading to calls for testing God), and personal ambition/ desire for power—Satan adds here a further dimension to the temptations by attempting to justify his requests with extracts from Scripture and by calling on Jesus to perform acts which may appear to advance his messianic cause. By doing so, Satan applies a strategy similar to the one employed by the serpent to coax Adam and Eve to eat from the fruit *prematurely* during the Fall: By telling *half-truths*, he derailed the divine order of the first couple's development. Indeed, we find that variants of all the three acts that Satan called Jesus to perform in the wilderness did in fact take place later during Jesus' ministry, but not at Satan's initiative or timing, and certainly not under his authority:

- Regarding the first temptation, turning stones into bread, Jesus did demonstrate at the wedding of Cana (John 2:1–11) and also when he fed the multitudes (Matt 14:13–21; 15:32–39) that he possessed the transformational capacity that was needed, yet in the wilderness he rejects Satan by citing Scripture directed to the Israelites during the Exodus concerning their physical needs, namely that "one does not live by bread alone" (Deut 8:3).

- During the second temptation, Jesus refuses to jump off the highest point of the Temple, citing Deut 6:16 as his reason, "Do not put the Lord your God to the test." As Page points out, Luke's Gospel follows the temptation in the wilderness with the account of an enraged crowd that tries to hurl Jesus off a cliff in Nazareth (4:29),[143] but Jesus "passed through the midst of them and went on his way" (v. 30): This can be seen as a divine miracle that saved Jesus from falling to his death. Why did Satan think that Jesus might be tempted to jump? The answer is probably related to the Temple as the venue: A miraculous sign from God in saving Jesus here would have established Jesus' authority immediately, and the ensuing "star" status could have enhanced his effectiveness as the Messiah.[144] Of course, signs and wonders did indeed demonstrate Jesus' divine anointing on several later occasions, most notably in his healing and deliverance ministry.

- In the third temptation, Satan probably knew that wealth and status would not seduce the Son of God, but the secondary layer of this temptation directly concerned Jesus' messianic role, as the devil offered him no less than *all* the glory and authority of the material world. It is important to note that Jesus did not challenge Satan's claim that "the glory and all this authority [of all the kingdoms of the world] . . . has been given over to me, and I give it to anyone I please" (Luke 4:6); in fact, it was precisely the truth of Satan's claim that made this

---

143. Page, *Powers of Evil*, 97.

144. Grudem offers a similar interpretation: "the temptation to throw himself down from the pinnacle of the temple (Luke 4:9–11) was a temptation to 'force' God to perform a miracle and rescue him in a spectacular way, thus attracting a large following from the people without pursuing the hard path ahead" (*Systematic Theology*, 536–37).

offer so generous and thus tempting:[145] An affirmative answer would have given Jesus full control over the earth, allowing him to establish immediately an ideal kingdom of humankind under his rule, without having to go to Calvary. There was no subtlety in this proposed deal: everything material was on offer in return for the ultimate prize: turning Jesus away from God's path. Jesus rejected the deal by citing the words "Worship the Lord your God, and serve only him" (Matt 4:10) from a passage in Deuteronomy that contained a warning given by Moses to the Israelites against idolatry as they were to enter the promised land (Deut 6:10–15). Since the latter passage was in one of the best-known sections of the Torah, located after the "Shema Yisrael" (Deut 6:4–9), Jesus' message could not have been any clearer, and we must also note that in the end Jesus did received from the Father "all authority in heaven and on earth" (Matt 28:18).

In sum, Satan used a complex set of strategies in an attempt to unsettle Jesus's mission. Not only did each of his temptations concern some fundamental human vulnerability, they also invited Jesus to act in a way which may have appeared congruent with his fresh anointing to a messianic role (hence Satan's repeated appeal, *"If you are the Son of God . . ."* Matt 4:3, 6), an impression that was further enhanced by the citing of Scripture. Satan urged Jesus to act like a Messiah by taking things into his own hands and depending solely on his devices,[146] and he offered Jesus the prospect of achieving dominion over the whole earth without suffering (i.e., by avoiding the cross) and with immediate effect. One might speculate that the reason why Satan assumed that such a lure would be effective with the Son of God is that the same lure was a key motive for him (as discussed earlier). Finally, it is noteworthy that instead of simply saying "no," Jesus also cited from the Scriptures in his response to all the three temptations, which was consistent with the public nature of his testing: He did not merely persevere in trial but in justifying his refusals to submit to Satan he also produced a "counter case." This must have been at least partly aimed at the heavenly observers who were certainly present, as evidenced by Matthew's concluding remark in the temptation scene that after the devil left, "suddenly angels came and waited on him [Jesus]" (4:11).

---

145. See Theron, "Temptation Narrative," 212.

146. As Oates explains from a psychiatric perspective, the temptation "to be in God's place with no limits, to have all knowledge, and to be an exception to all other mortals" is a driving desire of the human psyche, closely associated with pride. Oates, *Temptation*, 19.

On the Road to Calvary

After the temptations in the wilderness, the Gospels describe several attempts of Satan to deflect Jesus from following his Father's will. Similar to Job's testing at the hands of his friends, Satan is not directly present during these attempts but rather orchestrates social situations that are aimed at "tripping Jesus up" in a variety of ways, under various guises, and through different agents; for example, the Pharisees ask "trick questions" about the legitimacy of divorce (Mark 10:1–12; Matt 19:1–12) and about paying taxes (Mark 12:13–17; Lk 20:20–26), or the crowds demand a sign, which Luke 11:16 explicitly relates to temptation: "Others, to test him, kept demanding from him a sign from heaven" (see also Matt 12:38–39; Luke 11:29–32; John 2:18; 6:30). The main emphasis of these trials is on the same two dimensions as the temptations in the wilderness, that is, the corporeal needs of the flesh and the lure of accomplishing the mission quickly and comprehensively. Because Jesus deeply cared for the well-being of his people (see for example his lament over Jerusalem in Matt 23:37–39), he must have felt many a time a powerful pull toward taking a more direct role in bringing relief to the hungry and the oppressed, and thereby becoming more like the liberating, militant Messiah whom the Israelites were longing for to set them free from Rome. Wright summarizes this ongoing pull clearly:

> We cannot doubt that Jesus was constantly tempted to share, and act in accordance with, the mindset of most Jews of his day. He cannot have been indifferent to the plight of his fellow Jews, as they were systematically crushed, economically, politically and militarily, by Rome. The temptation to be the sort of Messiah that many wanted must have been real and strong. But it was, from the point of his mindset, precisely a temptation. He had faced it, and defeated it in principle, and had thereby confirmed the direction for the mission that he should undertake.[147]

The issue of suffering and the lure toward side-stepping the cross resurfaces when Jesus must reprimand Peter ("Get behind me, Satan! You are a stumbling block to me . . ." Matt 16:23) for wanting to stop him when he told his disciples that he would "undergo great suffering at the hands of the elders and chief priests and scribes, and be killed" (Matt 16:21). Jesus' sharp and rather startling reaction against Peter's words—calling one of his most trusted disciples "Satan" and using the same verb in his reprimand (*hypagō* v. 23) as in his command to Satan in the wilderness ("Away with you, Satan!" Matt 4:10)—indicates that Peter's remark had hit a sore spot; as Garrett

147. Wright, *Jesus and the Victory of God*, 458.

sums up, "the rebuke is sharp because the temptation is profound."[148] The same issue comes to a head at Gethsemane, where Jesus experiences such "anguish" that "his sweat became like great drops of blood falling down on the ground" (Luke 22:44), and he tells his three accompanying disciples, "I am deeply grieved, even to death" (Matt 26:38). Significantly, Jesus warns his disciples at this point against the danger of "falling into temptation" (Matt 26:41), and the fact that he himself was strongly tempted to avoid his torturous death is shown by his prayer, "Father, for you all things are possible; remove this cup from me" (Mark 14:36). Three times he prays this prayer, asking for the elimination of the cross from the messiahship[149]—and desiring, in effect, a solution similar to what was offered in Satan's third temptation in the wilderness—but three times he also adds: "yet, not what I want, but what you want" (Mark 14:36). Thus, although Jesus was evidently dreading what was to come, his ultimate resolve to obey God did not falter. Hebrews offers an expressive summary of his agonizing experience: "In the days of his flesh, Jesus offered up prayers and supplications, with loud cries and tears, to the one who was able to save him from death, and he was heard because of his reverent submission. Although he was a Son, he learned obedience through what he suffered" (Heb 5:7–8).

The Passion

As discussed earlier, Col 2:15 describes the crucifixion as Jesus' resounding victory against Satan and his forces, and the description of the events on Calvary in the Gospels does indeed suggest that Jesus was involved in a fierce struggle that went far beyond merely withstanding the physical horrors of crucifixion. According to the Evangelists, between noon and 3 o'clock in the afternoon "darkness came over the whole land" (Matt 27:45), and when Jesus had breathed his last, "the curtain of the temple was torn in two from top to bottom. The earth shook and the rocks split. The tombs broke open and the bodies of many holy people who had died were raised to life" (Matt 27:51–52).

Although the crucifixion of Jesus was performed by human agents, the Gospels make Satan's involvement in the act unmistakable: The betrayal by Judas is attributed to Satan's influence (Luke 22:3; John 13:2, 27)—indeed, Judas is even referred to in one place as "a devil" (John 6:70)—and in John 14:30 Jesus declares, just before his arrest, that "the ruler of this world is coming," implying that Caiaphas's soldiers were also instruments

---

148. Garrett, *Temptations of Jesus*, 82.

149. See Gibson, *Temptation of Jesus*, 248.

of Satan.[150] The devil's role in Jesus' arrest is further reiterated in Luke 22:53, where the event is explicitly linked to "the power of darkness," which may also explain the subsequent physical darkness that enveloped the land in daytime during the crucifixion. Accordingly, most commentators agree with Raymond Brown's conclusion that Satan was one way or another behind the events related to the Passion,[151] and the canonical narrative reading presented in this chapter suggests that Satan used the cross in an ultimate attempt to corrupt Jesus through a concerted assault that he had been preparing ever since his failure in the wilderness. Thus, Calgary can be understood as the venue of the ultimate temptation and trial of Jesus, which is a view held by several scholars.[152]

At this point the question arises again: Why did Satan believe that he could succeed against the Son of God? It appears that in his disdain for humanity, Satan was convinced that no corporeal being, not even the sinless Jesus, was infallible and thus ready to defy his reign, and after Satan's initial failure in the wilderness he carefully prepared the final act of his scheme, and set into motion an incrementally unfolding scenario that culminated on the cross: From a physical point of view, the crucifixion was known to be among the most torturous methods of execution in the Roman Empire; from the point of view of Jesus' mission, at Calvary matters had seemingly unraveled to an extent of suggesting a complete failure on Jesus' part:

- Jesus was condemned by the scribes and teachers of his Father's law, and was arrested and sentenced to death on the instigation of the High Priest of his Father's church;

- he was mocked and rejected by his Father's chosen people, for whom he had done everything within his means and for whom he was about to sacrifice his life;

- he was betrayed by one of the twelve disciples whom he had hand-picked and then trained extensively, and indeed, after his arrest most of his disciples deserted him and fled;[153]

150. See Page, *Powers of Evil,* 129.

151. R. E. Brown, *Death of the Messiah,* 161. Similarly, Jenson concludes: "Jesus' mission had throughout his life set him against the demons, however we are to stipulate their ontological status; and that those who brought him to the cross did so in alliance with the same evil that had always cried out against him and fled before him." Jenson, *Systematic Theology, vol 1,* 193. See also Moses, *Practices of Power,* 118.

152. E.g., Calvin, *Harmony of the Evangelists,* 321; Garrett, *Temptations of Jesus,* 2, 91; Green, *Satan's Downfall,* 52; McKinley, *Tempted for Us,* 28; Theron, "Temptation Narrative," 209.

153. Matt 26:56 emphasizes the degree of abandonment of Jesus by talking about

- his three closest disciples—those who had witnessed his Transfiguration—could not even keep awake in the garden of Gethsemane, let alone support him in prayer, and the one whom he selected to be the foundation of his future church was about to deny him three times within a day.

The Scriptures do not offer any specific details about the spiritual confrontation that took place on the cross, although there are some strong intertextual echoes of spiritual confrontation in Jesus' "cry with a loud voice," a phrase that all three Synoptic Gospels use in describing Jesus' death-cry (Mark 15:34, 37; Matt 27:46, 50; Luke 23:46): Mark's Gospel describes the exorcism of demonized people as accompanied by such a cry (Mark 1:26; 5:7), and elsewhere in the canon, the phrase is often associated with intense, spirit-filled communication concerning "angels, spirits, or bearers of the Spirit"[154] (*TDNT*) and signaling deep spiritual engagement, such as a vision. In Acts 7:60 the phrase is used to describe the dying of Stephen in Acts 7:60—whose vision suggests a paranormal state—and the Septuagint also applies the expression in 1 Samuel 28:12 when the necromancer of Endor sees the spirit of Samuel.[155] In the light of these allusions, Rick Sterlan submits that "There is at least the suggestion that in his dying Jesus is in a state of prayer or even of possession,"[156] and Joel Marcus in his commentary of Mark's Gospel concurs with this conclusion: "Although Mark does not say so explicitly, therefore, the inference from his narrative may be that Jesus, on the cross, suffers such a sudden and intense Satanic assault that he becomes in some ways like a man possessed."[157]

In any case, Heb 12:2 pronounces that Jesus "endured the cross," and given that Jesus did *not* survive—that is, endure—the execution on Calvary, this pronouncement could not refer to his physical life but most likely to withstanding the temptation that he was exposed to. This temptation came partly from the people around him: Jesus was derided by the spectators and bystanders, mocked by the chief priests, the scribes and the elders, and taunted even by one of the criminals hanging alongside him (Matt 27:39–44), all

---

"all the disciples" deserting him, but this does not include some female followers or the "disciple whom Jesus loved" (John 19.26).

154. Betz, "Φῶς," 293.

155. Strelan, "Recognizing the Gods," 498–99.

156. Ibid., 500.

157. Marcus, *Mark 8–16*, 1063. Danker goes even further when he suggests that Jesus' loud cry on the cross was the sign of a successful act of self-exorcism: "Jesus as the victim of demonic possession struggled fiercely with the demon, but—and this is Mark's verdict on the struggle—he expels the demon with a final cry. This exorcism cost Jesus his life." Danker, "Demonic Secret in Mark," 67.

of them saying: "If you are the Son of God, come down from the cross" (v. 40). All were waiting to see whether Jesus would be able to liberate himself from the cross, just as he himself predicted at the very beginning of his ministry in Nazareth, "Doubtless you will quote to me this proverb, 'Doctor, cure yourself!'" (Luke 4:23). Matthew presents a summary of the ruling sentiment of these observers of the crucifixion as follows, "He saved others; he cannot save himself. He is the King of Israel; let him come down from the cross now, and we will believe in him. He trusts in God; let God deliver him now, if he wants to; for he said, 'I am God's Son'" (Matt 27:42–43).

Thus, these people echoed Satan's message in the wilderness, *"If you are the Son of God . . . ,"* telling Jesus that they would follow him if he could prove that he was the kind of Messiah they had been waiting for. The temptation to come down from the cross must have been particularly powerful because it was possible: Jesus knew he could have escaped the suffering, since on the eve of his arrest he himself told Peter, "Do you think that I cannot appeal to my Father, and he will at once send me more than twelve legions of angels?" (Matt 26:53). Bonhoeffer points out in this respect that while unavoidable suffering is indeed a severe trial, "much heavier is the suffering which, in the opinion of the world and of my flesh and even of my pious thoughts, is avoidable."[158] However, in the spiritual confrontation between Jesus and Satan, victory for Jesus meant resisting the temptation to fight back, that is, it involved remaining resolved in the face of Satan's attempts to deflect him from following the Father's will and being obedient at any cost, even at the cost of his own death.

The climax of Jesus' testing came after three hours on the cross. The Gospels do not describe exactly what he had to endure but offer three images of his last moments that highlight different aspects of his victorious struggle. Mark and Matthew state that Jesus cried out with a loud voice, "My God, my God, why have you forsaken me?" (Matt 27:46) and then uttered a final death-cry. From the canonical narrative perspective of this book, this would suggests that the *kenosis* that began at the Incarnation had been completed and the last leg of Jesus' journey had to be taken in spiritual (and literal) darkness, without any divine support, because this was the ultimate test of the human stewards of God's creation. John emphasizes that the process was "finished" (19:30), indicating that Jesus' trial had finally come to an end, and Luke focuses on the outcome of this trial when he cites Jesus' words: "Father, into *your* hands I commit my spirit" (Luke 23:46; emphasis added). In Calvin's interpretation of this statement, "he declared that, though he was fiercely attacked by violent temptations, still his faith was

---

158. Bonhoeffer, *Creation and Temptation*, 121.

unshaken, and always kept its ground unvanquished"[159]—Jesus remained faithful, resisted Satan's temptation, and chose obedience to God.

In sum, at Calvary Jesus re-enacted Job's testing at a cosmic level, and by enduring the cross, Jesus proved conclusively that a corporeal being who experienced all the constraints and temptations associated with his incomplete creatureliness was able to have the integrity to stand firm against corruption and had thus the potential to fulfil the role of God's steward on earth. In this way, Jesus did indeed make a public example of Satan the Accuser—who denounced humankind as worthless and depraved—demonstrating that God was right in declaring over material creation that "it was very good." At the heart of his triumph was his obedience to the Father; he did not waver, even in the face of suffering and death. Thus, as Calvin concluded, Christ abolished sin "by the whole course of his obedience,"[160] which is in accordance with Paul's testimony: "For just as by the one man's disobedience the many were made sinners, so by the one man's obedience the many will be made righteous" (Rom 5:19).

The Victory Unfolding

In attempting to deflect Jesus from his path, Satan did not hold back from having him killed—he evidently believed that his ultimate weapon against corporeal beings, death, would serve, if all else failed, as a last resource to eliminate the threat to his reign on earth that Jesus posed. Satan miscalculated: "God raised him [Jesus] up, having freed him from death, because it was impossible for him to be held in its power" (Acts 2:24). The fact that Satan had no knowledge that this might happen is consistent with the recurring mention in the canon of the fact that some mysteries are hidden even from celestial beings (e.g., Mark 13:32; Eph 3:10; 1 Pet 1:12; cf. Rom 16:25);[161] particularly relevant in this respect is 1 Cor 6–8: "But we speak God's wisdom, secret and hidden, which God decreed before the ages for

---

159. Calvin, *Harmony of the Evangelists*, 321.

160. Calvin, *Institutes*, 507.

161. Arnold states in this respect, "The intricacies of the plan of salvation were kept hidden, not only from humanity, but also from the angelic realm. The satanic opposition thus naively believed putting Jesus to death was the way to do away with the Son of God... The powers did not apprehend the full extent of God's wisdom—how the Father would use the death of Christ to atone for sin, raise him victoriously from the dead and create the church." C. E. Arnold, *Powers of Darkness*, 101, 104. See also Michaels, *1 Peter*, 48; Arichea and Nida, *First Peter*, 31. For a comprehensive overview of the mystery in the Pauline epistles, see Lang, *Mystery*.

our glory. None of the rulers of this age understood this; for if they had, they would not have crucified the Lord of glory."[162]

The canon contains virtually no details about what happened between the Crucifixion and "the first day of the week" (Matt 28:1) when the tomb was found empty. It is evident, however, that the heavenly host were involved in Jesus' resurrection: Matt 28:2 mentions a "great earthquake" and the Synoptics record angels rolling back the stone from the tomb and telling the women that Jesus was risen (Mark 16:5–6; Matt 28:3–6; Luke 24:4–5). Some intriguing insight is offered by a statement in 1 Pet 3:19 that Jesus "went and made a proclamation to the spirits in prison." Significantly, this account is placed in 1 Peter between the mention of Jesus' death (v. 18) and his resurrection (v. 21), which creates a possible link with the Christian tradition that Jesus "descended into hell" as recorded in the Apostles' Creed (placed in a similar position).[163] The comment in Eph 4:9 that Jesus "had also descended into the lower parts of the earth" may be seen as corroborating this understanding further, and commentators have also connected the statement in 1 Pet 3:18 to a later verse in the same epistle which states, "For this is the reason the gospel was proclaimed even to the dead, so that, though they had been judged in the flesh as everyone is judged, they might live in the spirit as God does" (4:6).[164]

While these textual fragments do not add up to a conclusive account, William Dalton's seminal work in this area, which has been accepted by most modern scholars as authoritative, provides a philological argument that the "spirits in prison" (1 Pet 3:19) refer to "hostile angelic powers in the heavens,"[165] leading him to paraphrase 1 Pet 3:19–20 thus: "Christ, as risen Kyrios, went and made proclamation to the angels who disobeyed . . . in the days of Noah."[166] Such an interpretation is consistent with the earlier discussion in this chapter of the existence of spiritual opposition and fallen angels, and it is also in accordance with the canonical narrative interpretation of Jesus' Christ's victory on the cross: Calvary demonstrated to the heavenly host the viability of material creation, and proclaiming this triumph to the imprisoned faction of the celestial opposition was a logical extension of this triumphant display "so that at the name of Jesus every knee should bend, in heaven and on earth and under the earth" (Phil. 2:10).

---

162. For a detailed analysis of this passage, see Lang, *Mystery*, 53–67.

163. See e.g., Jobes, *1 Peter*, 236.

164. For overviews, see e.g., Green, *1 Peter*, 119–25; Michaels, *1 Peter*, 196.

165. Dalton, *Christ's Proclamation*, 26.

166. Ibid., 176. Dalton also argues that the proclamation is probably a parallel to 1 Tim 3:16 ("He was seen by angels.")

To be sure, as 1 Peter continues, after Jesus ascended into heaven he took his place "at the right hand of God, with angels, authorities, and powers made subject to him" (1 Pet 3:22).

It is tempting to see Jesus' resurrection as an act of God to reinstate the new Adam as part of new creation, and it would be in line with our canonical narrative perspective to venture that the inability of death to hold Jesus in its power (Acts 2:24) was somehow connected to the fact that Jesus' victory on the cross enabled God's intervention. In any case, we learn from Scripture that this triumph led to the release of the Holy Spirit to the believers at Pentecost (John 14:16; Acts 2:33), and John 16:7 adds an important detail about this sequence by specifying an "if condition" regarding Jesus' ascension and the Spirit's arrival: "if I do not go away, the Advocate will not come to you." As Beasley-Murray summarizes, the condition that Jesus had to depart before the Spirit could come "has led to some questionable exegesis."[167] It has been proposed, for example, that it is mutually exclusive to have both Jesus and his Spirit on earth,[168] a point further refined by Brown in an argument that their joint presence would simply be a "contradiction" because the "Paraclete is the Spirit understood as the presence of the absent Jesus."[169] An alternative view is that Jesus had to complete his redemptive work *before* the Spirit could become effective because the Spirit's main task was to convey Jesus' saving power to the ends of the earth;[170] stated in another way, Christ's atoning work on the cross was necessary for people to be able to receive the Spirit in all its fullness.[171] Finally, many commentators have either left the question unaddressed and simply taken it for granted,[172] or chose to concentrate only on the positive side of the statement that immediately follows the negative condition in John's Gospel: "but if I go, I will send him to you" (16:7).[173]

Given the utmost significance of the sending of the Spirit to the believers with regard to the transfiguration of humanity (see previous chapter),

167. Beasley-Murray, *John*, 279.

168. E.g., Burge, *John*, 436.

169. R. E. Brown, *John XIII–XXI*, 211.

170. E.g., Beasley-Murray, *John*, 280; Lenski, *Matthew*, 1080.

171. Morris, *John*, 618.

172. In this respect Calvin's view is characteristic in that he simply forbids to ask the question "Could not Christ have drawn down the Holy Spirit while he dwelt on earth?" on the basis that "to dispute about what is possible would be foolish and pernicious." Calvin, *John*, 137.

173. E.g., Lindars argues, "On the other hand, if we do not press the negative aspect . . . but concentrate on the positive aspect, that *if I go, I will send him to you*, the argument is consistent with John's theology" (*John*, 500).

the timing of this act at this point and not earlier or later is potentially a crucial question for the canonical narrative of this book. The considerations presented above suggest an explanation whereby it was Jesus' final victory on the cross that confirmed to the heavenly assembly that the transformation of God's stewards could be taken to a "point of no return" by releasing the Spirit among them.[174] Although, as said before, it is difficult to establish how the biblical accounts of Satan's expulsion from heaven (Luke 10:18; Rev 12:7–9) relate to the milestones of Jesus' earthly ministry,[175] it is hard to imagine that Jesus' victory on the cross and Michael and his angels' triumph against Satan and his forces in heaven (described in Revelation 12) are unconnected.[176] Accordingly, this book adopts the understanding that Jesus' triumph resulted in a profound shift in the heavenly assembly, which was manifested in the expulsion of the forces opposing humanity and the conferring of "all authority in heaven and on earth" to Jesus (Matt 28:18). This allowed Jesus to fulfil the promise he made earlier about sending his Spirit to his disciples: "I will ask the Father, and he will give you another Advocate, to be with you forever" (John 14:16). Because God's Spirit, backed by a united divine assembly, is an unstoppable agent of change, it is only a matter of time before progressive creation reaches its culmination in the fully realized kingdom of God on earth.

5.3 Summary

It was shown in this chapter that the Scriptures contain unmistakable signs of the existence of an opposition to God's works within the heavenly

---

174. With regard to the timing of the sequence of the actual events, Acts 1:3 tells us that after his resurrection, Jesus appeared to the disciples for a period of forty days teaching them about the kingdom of God, concluded by the Ascension. Pentecost took place ten days later during the "festival of weeks" (also called "Shavuot"; see Deut 16:10), which was one of the three pilgrimage festivals in first century Judaism when all Israelite men had to gather in Jerusalem. Besides offering an opportunity for the release of the Holy Spirit to be experienced by representatives of the whole nation, a further significance of this feast was that according to Jewish tradition, Pentecost involved the commemoration of the day God gave the Torah to the Israelites assembled at Mount Sinai (which was, as we saw in chapter 4, a prominent step in the social transformation of humanity). This being the case, the release of the Spirit at Pentecost to dwell in the believers' hearts offered an obvious parallel in terms of the introduction of a "new covenant," which, according to Jeremiah's prophecy, was to "put my law within them, and I will write it on their hearts" (31:33).

175. See e.g., Gathercole, "Fall of Satan"; Page, Powers of Evil, 109–11.

176. E.g., Beale concludes, "It likely is Christ's resurrection that unleashes the effect of Michael's victory in heaven and defeat of the satanic powers" (New Testament Theology, 901).

assembly. Motivated by a combination of pride, jealousy, a disdain for humanity, and accumulated bitterness against God, these forces questioned the integrity of humans and their capability of fulfilling the role of God's earthly stewards. They are portrayed in both Testaments as wielding considerable power in their attempts to turn humans away from God, which is the backdrop against which the significance of the Book of Job within the canon becomes evident: It offers a demonstration of the human capacity to withstand the temptations of these subversive forces, to preserve one's faith even in the face of suffering, and to exercise forgiveness upon those who have done much harm. In this sense Job's successful testing prefigured Jesus Christ' ultimate trial and victory at Calvary.

The Scriptures present the *śāṭān* -turned-Satan as the leader of the celestial opposition, who is locked into an increasingly rebellious role that had evolved by New Testament times into his reigning position over a kingdom of darkness on earth. The NT canon is launched within this context with the description of the Incarnation of Jesus Christ, which heralded the new creation (as discussed in chapter 4). In Luke 12:32, Jesus declared his determination to succeed in his mission by staying the course that had been set for him by the Father, resisting any attempts to deflect him from it. Aware of the threat, Satan challenged Jesus through a series of trials, starting with the temptations in the wilderness immediately after Jesus' baptism. Jesus withstood all the attempts of Satan to unsettle his mission and remained "obedient to the point of death—even death on a cross" (Phil 2:18). During his ultimate trial at Calvary, he re-enacted Job's testing at a cosmic level, and by doing so he proved conclusively that a corporeal being who experienced all the constraints and temptations associated with his incomplete creatureliness could have sufficient integrity to stand firm against corruption, thereby evidencing the potential to fulfil the role of God's steward on earth. His endurance offered the heavenly host an unmistakable and spectacular display of God's triumphant glory, demonstrating that God was right in pronouncing over material creation that "it was very good."

Jesus' victory and subsequent resurrection led to a cosmic shift in the celestial realm: All authority on heaven and earth was conferred to him and the opponents to God's work were eventually expelled. The heavenly host finally committed themselves fully to humanity and the Holy Spirit was poured out on the earth to act as the ultimate changing agent who transfigures believers by dwelling within them. In this way progressive creation reached a "point of no return," and it is only a matter of time before it reaches its culmination in the fully realized kingdom of God on earth.

6

Three Assignments from Jesus

The Eucharist, the Lord's Prayer, and the Great Commission

A DISTINCTIVE FEATURE OF the biblical canon is that its readers are themselves part of the unfolding process of creation as they have lived, or will be living, during the transitional period leading to the eschatological conclusion of new creation. The Scriptures acknowledge this special audience perspective by including specific assignments for believers to carry out, as well as by providing instructions and teaching on how to conduct themselves in the face of the difficulties that are bound to occur. In this way, the canon in effect positions Christian believers as agents within the ongoing transformation process and calls them to play a proactive role in the advancement of creation. The focus of the current chapter is on three specific assignments that Jesus gave his followers to continue with after his ascension—to celebrate the Eucharist, to pray the Lord's Prayer, and to fulfil the Great Commission—while the next chapter will conclude the book by considering a range of practical advice and exhortations offered in the NT canon for the purpose of helping Christian believers to "fight the good fight of the faith" (1 Tim 6:12) and thus to benefit fully from the ongoing transformation process (as discussed in chapter 4).

The three topics explored in this chapter—the Eucharist, the Lord's Prayer, and the Great Commission—have understandably been the subject of a large amount of theological reflection by church leaders and academic scholars alike, often leading to diverse interpretations and dissimilar liturgical/ecclesiastical practices.[1] The following discussion will consider a

---

1. For example, O'Loughlin points out, that the Eucharist has attracted "not only enormous devotion and great energy, but also unparalleled levels of sustained argument and in-fighting" (*Eucharist*, xv), and Spinks's historical overview also illustrates that the eucharistic rites and liturgies pursued by the Church over the past two millennia have

relatively narrow segment of the multiple layers of meaning attached to the three divine assignments by focusing primarily on their contribution to the process of creation.

6.1 The Eucharist

The canonical sources of the Eucharist involve the Synoptic accounts of the Last Supper that Jesus shared with his disciples on the evening before his crucifixion (Mark 14:12–25; Matt 26:17–29; Luke 22:7–23) as well as a passage in Paul's first letter to the Corinthians (11:17–34), which focuses on the "words of institution" of celebrating the Eucharist, and constitutes, according to Marshall, a stereotyped form of instructions handed down in order to provide the Church with a template to follow.[2] John's Gospel also has a description of Jesus' farewell meal with his disciples that includes teaching on a range of topics (in chapters 13–17), but this lacks any Eucharist institution narrative (i.e., there is no mention of the bread being identified as the body of Christ), although the theme of "feeding on Jesus" does appear earlier in John's Gospel when Jesus declares in chapter 6, "I am the bread of life" (v. 35).[3] This eucharistic motif becomes even more explicit a few verses later:[4] "Very truly, I tell you, unless you eat the flesh of the Son of Man and drink his blood, you have no life in you. Those who eat my flesh and drink my blood have eternal life, and I will raise them up on the last day; for my flesh is true food and my blood is true drink. Those who eat my flesh and drink my blood abide in me, and I in them" (6:53–56).

The words of institution, particularly with Paul's emphasis that he had received them from the Lord (1 Cor 11:23), are an unmistakable indication that future Christians are to repeat the procedures in some way;[5] that is,

---

displayed a diversity that defies any attempt to identify a coherent underlying theme or an evolutionary trend. Spinks, *Eucharist*. The Lord's Prayer has also provided a springboard for a particularly wide variety of theological elucidation, ranging from seeing it by Cyprian as "a compendium of the heavenly doctrine" (*Lord's Prayer*, 9) to regarding it by Wright as "a distillation of Jesus' own sense of vocation, his own understanding of his Father's purposes" (*The Lord and His Prayer*, 2). With respect to the Great Commission, Church history has born witness to the fact that the "commission" aspect has been understood disparately throughout the ages in terms of its nature and mandatory force; for example, as Hvalvik explains, even early Christians were divided on how relevant or binding they saw the duty to take active part in evangelism and thus to fulfil Jesus' mission charge. Hvalvik, "In Word and Deed," 279.

2. See Marshall, *Last Supper,* 34.

3. See Spinks, *Eucharist,* 21.

4. See also Jeremias, *Eucharistic Words of Jesus,* 108.

5. See Spinks, *Eucharist,* 20.

as Jenson concludes, the texts present "a quite deliberate institution: Jesus' disciples are told 'Do this' in a narrative context where only the church's post-Resurrection actions can obey the command."[6] On the other hand, the actual wording of the relevant biblical passages leaves the way by which the Eucharist is to be celebrated relatively open, with no particular mandate provided in the canon on how or by whom the bread and the wine should be distributed, nor what words should be spoken.[7] Two key aspects of the act, however, are clearly stated: believers need to (a) identify the bread and the wine with Jesus' body and blood, and (b) remember Jesus' sacrificial death. These points have a marked relevance to the discussion of progressive creation in this book.

The Bread and the Wine

Irrespective of how one understands the Eucharist's theological meaning and liturgical implications, the core of the eucharistic activities both in the Scriptures and in Church practice is related to the essential human function of eating and drinking, that is, to nourishing the corporeal body: During a communal meal at Passover,[8] Jesus identified his body with the bread that he shared with his disciples and his blood with the cup of wine they were to drink. In doing so, Jesus linked his eucharistic message to one of the most profound processes underlying material existence whereby a living organism ingests some external substance, and the quality of the resulting fusion

6. Jenson, *Systematic Theology*, vol. 2, 186.

7. For a discussion, see e.g., Blomberg, *1 Corinthians*, 232. The adaptable nature of the eucharistic mandate is related to how Leonhard more generally characterizes the canonical description of the Last Supper: "The narratives of the last supper are, indeed, undetermined enough to allow one to add the rituals of Exodus 12, the Pesah Haggada, as well as elements of fourth century Christian celebrations of Easter in order to replenish the event with any detail that one should want to have been present in that situation." Leonhard, *Jewish Pesach*, 34.

8. The exact timing of the Last Supper is problematic—it is, in D. Wenham's words, a "particularly knotty question of gospel harmony" ("Last Supper," 13)—because while the Synoptic Gospels suggest that it was a Passover meal, John's Gospel gives the impression that the Jewish Passover meal was to take place *after* Jesus' crucifixion (for summaries of different explanations, see e.g., Jeremias, *Eucharistic Words of Jesus*, 15–88; Marshall, *Last Supper*, 57–75; McKnight, *Jesus and His Death*, 259–73). However, from our current perspective the details of this debate are of secondary importance, because even if the Last Supper took place a day earlier—that is, on the Day or Preparation—the Passover connotations of the meal in the canon are clearly not accidental; as Spinks concludes, "What can be said is that the cumulative witness of the New Testament associates the last meal with the time of Passover, even if it was not actually celebrated on the Passover" (*Eucharist*, 6).

between nourishment and body determines how the organism will develop and function. In a discussion of the theology of eating, Méndez Montoya sums up this point as follows: "There is nothing more vital and intimate than eating . . . To eat—in its many forms and fashions, including drinking, absorbing a substance, and the like—is a way of being incorporated into the micro and macro organic cycle of life. . . . Eating transforms food so that it becomes a vital part of our bodies, and, simultaneously, the embodied individual is also transformed by the act of eating."[9]

Thus, Jesus related the basic fabric of material creation to himself, and—in accordance with the declaration in John 6:54 that "Those who eat my flesh and drink my blood have eternal life"—he called his disciples to form a lasting union with him. The question of union with Christ was already discussed in chapter 4, where we saw that the NT canon uses a variety of metaphors and images to characterize the process of ongoing human transformation in order to become conformed to the image of Jesus. With its close relationship to the notion of ingestion—and thus to growth and change—as well as by foregrounding the fusion with some aspect of Jesus' body and blood, the Eucharist is consistent with these images. Viewing the Eucharist as a potent vehicle of human metamorphosis into Christlikeness is in keeping with Jesus' proclamation in John 6:55–56: "for my flesh is true food and my blood is true drink. Those who eat my flesh and drink my blood abide in me, and I in them."

Remembering Jesus' Death

A central aspect of the Eucharist is the exhortation to remember Jesus: Luke's Gospel records the explicit command, "Do this in remembrance of me" (Luke 22:19), which is then repeated twice by Paul (with regard to both the bread and the wine; 1 Cor 11:24 and 25). Given that the words of institution of the Last Supper were aimed at Christians, an obvious question to ask is why remembrance needed to be thus emphasized—was there any real danger that believers would forget about Jesus? That forgetting is no minor issue in the Bible is evidenced by the fact that there are several places in the canon besides the discussion of the Eucharist where remembrance receives a special emphasis. Indeed, the very context of the Last Supper, the festival of Passover, was itself a feast of remembrance when the Israelites commemorated the exodus and their liberation from slavery.[10] Within the

9. Méndez Montoya, *Theology of Food*, 1.

10. See e.g., Jacobs et al., "Passover," 678. We should note that while this is a widely accepted view, the association between the Pesah and Exodus 12 has not always been

New Testament we find several passages that are intended as reinforcement of teaching that the Christian audience will have previously received,[11] with an example that is highly relevant to the current discussion being clearly articulated in 2 Pet 1:3–15.

The central theme of this passage is the urging of believers to remember "the knowledge of him who called us by his own glory and goodness" (v. 3), because "being ineffective and unfruitful in the knowledge of our Lord Jesus Christ" (v. 8) is a function of being "forgetful of the cleansing of past sins" (v. 9). To emphasize this point, 2 Peter not only offers a further reminder—"I intend to keep on reminding you of these things" (v. 12)—but in the following three verses the importance of remembering is reiterated two more times: "I think it right, as long as I am in this body, to *refresh your memory* . . . And I will make every effort so that after my departure you may be able at any time to *recall* these things" (vv. 13–15; emphases added).[12] Therefore, Kelly rightly comments that 2 Peter was intent to leave behind a permanent testimony to help people remember Jesus,[13] and such a lasting reminder is precisely what is intended in the Eucharist. What makes the 2 Peter passage particularly pertinent to the current chapter is its unmistakable reference to progressive human renewal. It starts out by pronouncing that the knowledge of Jesus leads to receiving "very great promises" through which believers "may escape from the corruption that is in the world because of lust, and may become *participants of the divine nature*" (1:4; emphasis added). This last clause was cited in chapter 4 as a *locus classicus* for human transformation, and it is also of note that the rare Greek term used

---

straightforward throughout Jewish history; see e.g., Leonhard, *Jewish Pesach*, 118. Nevertheless, O'Loughlin's conclusion about the relevant perceptions in NT times is still likely to hold: "For the Jews of the second temple period, all meals were ritualized as proper by the act of blessing, but meals of the past were also re-remembered as their celebration of identity, and none more so than Passover" (*Eucharist*, 143).

11. Moo, for example, highlights Paul's practice in this area (e.g., 1 Cor 4:17; 15:1; 2 Cor 10:7; 2 Tim 2:14), underscoring in particular Rom 15:14–15): "I myself am convinced, my brothers, that you yourselves are full of goodness, complete in knowledge and competent to instruct one another. I have written you quite boldly on some points, as if to remind you of them again . . ." Moo. *2 Peter and Jude*, 66. See also Jude 5.

12. In commenting on this text, M. Green states that "Peter can hardly overemphasize the importance of reminders" (*2 Peter and Jude*, 98), and Kelly similarly asserts, "Again we have the stress on reminder (*hypomnēsis*), a fundamental and constant feature of the early Christian paraenetic style" (*Peter and Jude*, 313).

13. Kelly, *Peter and Jude*, 314. Such an interpretation also supported by Moo's (*2 Peter and* Jude, 61) linguistic analysis of the unexpected future tense in 1:12 ("So I will always remind you . . ." NIV), which suggests that the reminding will take place in the future, leading Moo to the conclusion that "as he does again at the end of the paragraph, Peter probably refers to the permanent effect he hopes his words in this letter will have."

for "promise" (*epangelma*) in this verse occurs only one more time in the New Testament, later in the same epistle (2 Pet 3:13), where it concerns "new heavens and a new earth." Therefore, the exhortation to remember Jesus and the warning about the danger of forgetfulness in 2 Peter are ultimately related to the success of partaking in the process of renewal within progressive creation.

The Nature of Eucharistic Remembrance

Jesus' assignment to celebrate the Eucharist "in remembrance of me" (Luke 22:19; 1 Cor 11:24–25) is in full accordance with the above considerations as it offers a continuing way to combat the detrimental effect of the believers' fading memory of what Jesus has done for them.[14] This raises the question of what exactly the act of "remembering" involves in a eucharistic sense? The semantic domain of the Greek word used in Luke 22:19 and 1 Cor 11:24 for "remembrance" (*anamnesis*) is broader than purely cognitive recollection as it carries with it a sense of the participatory act of "making the past present,"[15] a point confirmed by the *TDNT*, which describes the meaning as the "reliving of vanished impressions by a definite act of will."[16] O'Loughlin offers an expressive description of this sense of awareness: "By 'memory' we do not mean simply 'tales from long ago' or even 'our Story' but that profound awareness of reality which appreciates its origins and its ends. This awareness is the realization, in this moment as we eat, that we have an actual connection to a much larger reality."[17]

Many scholars maintain that the act of remembrance of Jesus in the Eucharist has echoes of the Passover rituals commemorating the Exodus.[18]

---

14. Marshall summarizes this issue as follows: "For the problem at issue is how the disciples may continue to remain attached to Jesus during his physical absence. The answer to the problem is that by celebrating the Lord's Supper they remember him, and they remember him in the same kind of way as the Jews remembered the Passover and thought of themselves as partakers in the act of redemption. . . . The proclamation of the gospel in the breaking of bread and the sharing of the cup makes the saving event real for all generations." Marshall, *Last Supper,* 90–91.

15. E.g., Kelly, *Early Christian Doctrines,* 197; Spinks, *Eucharist,* 20; Thiselton, *Dictionary of Theology,* 551.

16. Behm, "Ανάμνησις," 348.

17. O'Loughlin, *Eucharist,* 119.

18. E.g., Marshall, *Last Supper,* 90–91; Thiselton, *Systematic Theology,* 331. Moo states in this regard: "What the Israelites were to do was not just, in an intellectual sense, recall what had happened in the past. They were to 'bring it to mind' in a way that informed their entire being: intellect, will, emotions, and behavior. Remembering God's work on their behalf would make it present for them; and so the Jewish family,

Indeed, the words of institution of the Last Supper invite believers to engage with Jesus' sacrificial death in a manner that is deeper and more intensive than merely refreshing their memories, similar to the instructions given in Exodus concerning the commemoration of the Passover:

> This day shall be a day of remembrance for you. . . . Remember this day on which you came out of Egypt, out of the house of slavery, because the Lord brought you out from there by strength of hand. . . .You shall tell your child on that day, "It is because of what the LORD did for me when I came out of Egypt." It shall serve for you as a sign on your hand and as a reminder on your forehead, so that the teaching of the LORD may be on your lips; for with a strong hand the LORD brought you out of Egypt. You shall keep this ordinance at its proper time from year to year. (12:14; 13:3; 8–10)

Further elucidation of the nature of a remembered/relived relationship with the living Christ will be given in the final part of the current chapter when considering the notion of "discipleship" in the Great Commission, because as O'Loughlin explains, "there is that level of memory and awareness when in the midst of gathering bonded by discipleship we are conscious of the kinship that gathers us, we recall the memory that constitutes our identity, and give thanks for all of the Father's goodness in union with the Christ. . . . This level of remembering is bound up with knowing that our meal takes place in the presence of the risen One and that, through him, we are present to the Father in our meal sharing."[19]

Eucharistic Remembrance and Love

The final question to ask in this section is how the eucharistic remembrance impacts on believers' lives. In chapter 4 we saw that by offering the "new commandment" Jesus placed the process of human transformation on a renewed social order based on *love*, which could thus be seen as a general guiding principle for the emerging Church. Significantly, in John

---

celebrating Passover, was to identify with that desert generation, sharing in their salvation and making the Exodus events and their corollaries part of themselves." Moo, *2 Peter and Jude*, 65–66. We must, however, also note Leonhard's caution that the present form of the Passover recital of the Exodus (i.e., the *Haggadah*) was most likely developed *after* NT times and therefore there may not be any direct historical parallel between aspects of the eucharistic rites and the current Jewish practice of reliving the dramatic narrative of the Passover. Leonhard, *Jewish Pesach*, 118.

19. O'Loughlin, *Eucharist*, 120.

15, after Jesus reiterated the commandment to love (v. 12), he explained that the epitome of love is "to lay down one's life for one's friends" (v. 13), a point restated in 1 John 3:16: "We know love by this, that he laid down his life for us." Thus, Jesus' sacrificial death expressed the essence of love, and the divine origin of this love is summarized clearly in John 3:16: "For God so loved the world that he gave his only Son . . ." Therefore, by calling believers to remember Jesus' sacrificial death, the Eucharist in effect invites them to recall and relive Jesus' love for them. The impact of this remembering on the believers' life is mediated by the fact that, according to Scripture, divine love is the *antecedent* of human love: "not that we loved God but that he loved us and sent his Son to be the atoning sacrifice for our sins" (1 John 4:10), that is, "We love because he first loved us" (4:19). Therefore, when believers remember Jesus' sacrificial death, this act helps to evoke a sense of divine love in them, which in turn gives rise to their own capacity to love others. In this way the eucharistic communion with Jesus may become a potent vehicle to foster the new commandment to love one another, thus placing the Eucharist at the heart of the social transformation process of the new creation.

6.2 The Lord's Prayer

In the canon, Jesus is recorded as teaching only one prayer to his disciples, traditionally called the Lord's Prayer or Pater Noster. It is included in two short passages in Matt 6:9–13 and Luke 11:2–4, and contains six or seven petitions depending on whether the final two petitions on temptation and evil (or the evil one; see later) are regarded as one extended or two separate petitions—for the sake of clarity, the current discussion will take the latter view. In commentaries these petitions are often divided into two broad sets, the "Thou-petitions" (1–3) and the "we-petitions" (4–7), on the basis of the common perception that the first half of the prayer speaks of "God in heaven" and the second half "purely of the needs and dangers of the supplicants on earth"[20] (Lohmeyer).

Despite the existence of the extensive literature on the content of the petitions, the task of identifying an overarching leitmotif that unites them into one coherent prayer has been challenging, and this has been reflected, for example, in the very general and abstract nature of the descriptors used to characterize the essence of the prayer, ranging from "a key to the whole

20. Lohmeyer, *Lord's Prayer,* 272.

business of living"[21] to "a summary of basic religious education."[22] The elusiveness of an overarching theme has been partly due to the fact that the Lord's Prayer does not fit neatly into any obvious prayer genre or category: It is not a prayer of thanksgiving, praise, or worship,[23] and neither is it a prayer for salvation, which is implicit in the fact that Jesus taught it to his closest disciples; in fact, the early Church restricted the use of the Lord's Prayer to Christian believers only and even surrounded it with firm secrecy ("*disciplina arcani*") in the third and the fourth centuries;[24] in Joachim Jeremias's words, as "one of the most holy treasures of the church, the Lord's Prayer, together with the Lord's Supper, was reserved for full members, and it was not disclosed to those who stood outside."[25] Furthermore, although technically the Lord's Prayer is a petitionary prayer, it has a strong collectivist sense that seems to transcend the petitioning of an individual,[26] not only because of the use of first person plural but also because the Thou-petitions request for, in Eleonore Stump's words, "a certain state of affairs involving all or most men, the state of affairs at the end of the world."[27] Moreover, according to Christian beliefs, the future arrival of this state of affairs has already been predetermined by the Creator,[28] and therefore Jesus' instruction to pray this prayer has often been perceived to encompass some more fundamental function or meaning than individual petitioning, well reflected

21. Packer, *Lord's Prayer*, 11.

22. Ayo, Lord's Prayer, 2. Other examples include "the compendium of the whole gospel" (Tertullian, *On Prayer*, 1), "a synthesis of the faith" (Hardon, *Catholic Dictionary*, 366), "the map of the consciousness of God and of one's relationship to him" (Chilton, *Jesus' Prayer*, 50–51), "the heart of the new covenant charter" (Wright, "Lord's Prayer," 147), or "the one and all-embracing, all-demanding, all-giving mark of the disciples" (Lohmeyer, *Lord's Prayer*, 297).

23. "Hallowed be your name" does not so much express praise as a plea for the sanctification of God' name in the face of it being profaned; see Kendall, *Lord's Prayer*, 67–68; O'Collins, *Lord's Prayer*, 60.

24. Hammerling, "Lord's Prayer," 167.

25. Jeremias, *Lord's Prayer*, 4.

26. As Dunn explains, "The pray-er prays as part of and on behalf of the whole community of those dependent on God. The one is benefitted only by that which benefits all" ("Prayer," 622).

27. Stump, "Petitionary Prayer," 82.

28. As Stump argues about the Though-petitions, "All three seem to be requests for the millennium or for God's full reign on earth. But it appears from New Testament prophecies that God has already determined to bring about such a state of affairs in the future. And if God has predetermined that there will be such a time, then what is asked for in those three requests is already sure to come." Stump, "Petitionary Prayer," 82–83.

by the fact that it was often taken as a compendium of Christian doctrine, despite the fact that it is not one.[29]

So, what is the Lord's Prayer? Given that in Matthew's Gospel Jesus tells the disciples to "Pray then in this way . . ." (6:9), and in Luke's Gospel the instruction is even more direct: "When you pray, say . . ." (11:2), it has been seen by many as a model prayer that offers a specific pattern to follow.[30] This, however, raises the question of *how closely* one should adhere to the formula Jesus gave the disciples. It appears that Jesus' instruction does not exclude praying other sorts of prayers as there are several examples in the New Testament of prayers addressing points not directly included in the Lord's Prayer.[31] This suggests that when Jesus told the disciples to pray the Lord's Prayer he did not do this to restrict but to *enrich* their prayer practice in some way. This enriching role can be understood by considering the Lord's Prayer in terms of the "short prayer" form in Judaism.

The "Short Prayer" Form in Judaism

In a personal reflection on Jewish prayer, Baruch Graubard recalled a period in 1944 when he was hiding from the Nazis in a Franciscan monastery in Slovakia. By that time the traumatic experiences of avoiding arrest had caused him to largely forget his Jewish identity until he encountered the Lord's Prayer and, quite unexpectedly, found relief in it: "I discovered a

29. Although Matthew's Gospel presents the prayer as a center piece of the Sermon on the Mount, it is not formulated as a doctrinal text to offer a distillation of the key issues, and neither does it address the same basic themes as, for example, the Ten Commandments or the Creeds, which are often seen as ethical and doctrinal summaries; see e.g., Lochman, *Lord's Prayer*, 1. Accordingly, Luz concludes that attempts to elicit principles of Christian dogmatics from the prayer have often "made the Lord's Prayer a stranger to itself" (*Matthew 1–7*, 387).

30. E.g., Kendall's summary expresses this view well: "All good praying should, in some way, be consistent with the pattern, order, content and intent of the Lord's Prayer. It is a prayer to be prayed, but the words of the Lord's Prayer serve as an outline of appropriate praying. We should see each line of the Lord's Prayer—that is, each petition—as the solid foundation for truly worshipful and selfless praying. Thus everything we say should be an extension, or filling out, to some degree, of every line in the Lord's Prayer. Our praying should build on the Lord's Prayer." Kendall, *Lord's Prayer*, 19–20.

31. For example, Paul often prays for other Christians and their communities, and an extensive example of this, which is considerably longer than the Lord's Prayer, has been recorded in Eph 3:14–21. While this prayer does share aspects with the Lord's Prayer, it clearly was not intended to follow the latter as a template; in fact, in Matt 9:37–38, even Jesus himself is recorded to instruct the disciples to pray to the Father in a way that is different from it: "The harvest is plentiful, but the laborers are few; therefore ask the Lord of the harvest to send out laborers into his harvest."

token of this identity in the Lord's Prayer. That was like a Jewish prayer, like an abbreviation of the Prayer of the Eighteen Benedictions."[32] Graubard's impression about the abridged nature of the prayer may not have been an accident, since Matthew's Gospel specifically records that Jesus emphasized the virtue of *brevity* in prayer immediately before he presented the Lord's Prayer to the disciples: He warned them not to be like the Gentile pagans, who "think that they will be heard because of their many words" (6:7). Brief prayer summaries were a known genre in the Judaism of Jesus' time, and the condensed version of the Eighteen Benedictions—referred to as the "*short Tefillah*" or "*Habinenu*"—was designed to be used when time or circumstances prevented the reciting of all the benedictions in full.[33] Even more importantly, rabbis also taught their disciples short prayers that were characteristic of their spiritual priorities and preferences, and the Talmud presents a collection of the signature prayers of several famous rabbis, some of them from NT times.[34]

Could it be the case that the Lord's Prayer was also such a rabbinic "shorthand" for a more comprehensive whole? To be sure, several of the petitions bear a close resemblance to central parts of well-known Jewish prayers[35] as well as to other rabbinic short prayers recorded in the Talmud,[36] and we find further endorsement for this suggestion in Luke's introduction to the Lord's Prayer, where we read that "one of his [Jesus'] disciples said to him, 'Lord, teach us to pray, as John taught his disciples'" (11:1). This

32. Graubard, "*Kaddish* Prayer," 61.

33. See e.g., Abrahams, *Studies in Pharisaism*, 99.

34. E.g., *Babylonian Talmud, Berakoth* 16b–17a, 29a–30a (see Note 36 for examples); Abrahams, *Studies in Pharisaism*, 103–4; Bivin, *Difficult Words of Jesus*, 60.

35. E.g., the third, the sixth, and the ninth benedictions of the Eighteen Benedictions state: "We will sanctify [or hallow] your name in this world just as it is sanctified in the highest heavens"; "Forgive us, O our Father, for we have sinned; pardon us, O our King, for we have transgressed; for you pardon and forgive"; and "Bless this year for us, O Lord our God, together with all the varieties of its produce, for our welfare" (translations are taken from Bivin, *New Lights*, 62–66). Also, the beginning part of the Qaddish displays an unmistakable parallel to the first two petitions of the Lord's Prayer: "Exalted and hallowed be his great name in the world, which he created according to his will"; "May he establish his kingdom in your lifetime and in your days, and in the lifetime of the whole household of Israel, speedily and at a near time." See Petuchowski, "Jewish Prayer Texts," 37.

36. E.g., "Do Thy will in heaven above and grant relief to them that fear Thee below and do that which is good in Thine eyes" (*Babylonian Talmud, Berakoth* 29b); "May It be Thy will, O Lord our God, to give to each one his sustenance and to each body what it lacks" (*Babylonian Talmud, Berakoth* 29b); and "Forgive us so that we may be redeemed, and keep us far from our sufferings, and fatten us in the pastures of Thy land" (*Babylonian Talmud, Berakoth* 29a).

was not an invitation to offer instruction on prayer in general but rather a specific appeal to be provided with a *unique* prayer, similar to the ones that marked the various Jewish religious groupings including, as the passage suggests, the followers of John the Baptist. Accordingly, Jeremias explains that this appeal can be seen as the reflection of Jesus' followers beginning to form a distinct group identity,[37] which is further confirmed by the fact that only a few generations later the *Didache* (8:2–3) insisted that Christians should be distinguished from the "hypocrites"[38] by the fact that they regularly pray the Lord's Prayer. Thus, the Lord's Prayer fits the genre of the rabbinic short prayer as an identity marker for disciples, which would explain why commentators have consistently referred to it over the centuries as a kind of Christian "précis" or compendium even though, strictly speaking, it was not intended as such.

The Petitions

How does the Lord's Prayer facilitate the believers' transformation into citizens of the kingdom of God? With this question in mind, let us consider some of the key aspects of the individual petitions, starting with the unique salutation.

Our Father in Heaven

It is generally believed that Jesus originally used the word 'Abba' in addressing his Father—similar to Mark 14:36, where the Aramaic word is preserved—and this practice is regarded as a unique feature of the Lord's Prayer that became established in the early Christian community, as attested to by Rom 8:15 and Gal 4:6.[39] The remarkable feature of this salutation is that through it Jesus, in effect, authorizes his disciples to share in his divine sonship,[40] which is fully in line with Paul's explanation in Galatians 4:6 that

37. Jeremias, *Lord's Prayer,* 16.

38. That is, pious Jews; Stevenson, *Lord's Prayer,* 24.

39. E.g., Jeremias, *Lord's Prayer,* 19; Wright, "Lord's Prayer," 134. Jeremias has also championed the influential view that *Abba* was a tender address of a child to its father, signifying a special, intimate relationship, but recent scholarship does not support this view—see e.g., Marshall, "Jesus: Teacher of Prayer," 128—furthermore, the addition of "in heaven" to *Abba* in Matthew's Gospel also contradicts an overly cozy tenor; see Turner, *Matthew,* 186. However, most scholars would agree with Jeremias in that the use of the term emphasized the personal *sonship* aspect. Jeremias, *Lord's Prayer,* 20.

40. The sonship aspect is such an important facet of being a Christian believer that it is reiterated in several other places in the canon, e.g., Matt 23:9; John 1:12; 1 John

God has sent the Spirit of Jesus into Christian disciples' hearts making them cry "Abba! Father!" Thus, besides being an affectionate address and a profession of faith,[41] the salutation is also a claim of membership in God's family, with all the empowering assets associated with being *heirs* of God. This is consistent with Paul's further explanation in Romans: "For all who are led by the Spirit of God are children of God. For you did not receive a spirit of slavery to fall back into fear, but you have received a spirit of adoption. When we cry, 'Abba! Father!' it is that very Spirit bearing witness with our spirit that we are children of God, and if children, then heirs, heirs of God and joint heirs with Christ" (Rom 8:14–17).

Hallowed Be Your Name

To "hallow" means to honor as holy, to sanctify, or to glorify. Luz explains that to "hallow God's name" was an established phrase in NT times to express obedience toward God's commands, especially the speaking of prayers and the keeping of the second commandment of the Decalogue.[42] Several commentators submit that the specific act of sanctifying God's name highlighted in the Lord's Prayer receives its full meaning when contrasted to the profaning of God's name; in other words, "to sanctify/hallow" in this context is best understood semantically as the antonym of "to profane," and therefore the petition's main concern is to end the profaning of God's name in the world so that God's holiness is recognized by all.[43] Further contextualization of the meaning of "hallowing God's name" is offered by two biblical passages that contain particularly detailed pertinent material:

- Ezekiel 36:16–38 presents a long proclamation by God that is entirely centered around the sanctification of his name [with the LXX using the same Greek verb, *hagiazō*, as the Lord's Prayer] "which the house of Israel had profaned among the nations to which they came" (v. 21). In this prophetic passage God promises a thorough cleansing of Israel

---

5:1; Gal 3:26.

41. Wright claims, for example, that "Saying 'Our Father' means signing on for the kingdom of God" (*The Lord and His Prayer*, 19–20).

42. Luz, *Matthew 1–7*, 379–80.

43. Because the passive verb construction does not specify the subject behind achieving this purpose, there have been arguments advocating the referent agency of both God (in which case the construction is an example of a divine passive)—e.g., Crump, *Petitionary Prayer*, 116; Meier, *A Marginal Jew*, 297; Soulen, *Divine Name(s)*, 196–97—and humans through their deeds (e.g., several rabbinic examples cited by Keener, *Matthew*, 219). However, the formulation of the petition—along with the subsequent two petitions—allows for reference to both human and divine action.

(v. 25) and a complete renewal of their hearts (v. 26), a process that also involves putting God's Spirit in the people (vv. 26–27) so that they will renounce their past sinful behavior. The whole passage is framed by a repeated declaration that the renewal process is not for the sake of Israel (vv. 22, 32) but for a broader purpose, so that "the nations shall know that I am the Lord" (v. 23; see also v. 36). Significantly, the language that is used to characterize the renewal of Israel includes explicit creation imagery, promising in v. 34 that the "land that was desolate shall be tilled [the same Hebrew word as in Gen 2:15]" and then likening the new Israel to the "garden of Eden" (v. 35). In sum, Ezekiel associates the sanctification of God's name with a process of profound rejuvenation.

- John 12 narrates that toward the end of his public ministry Jesus felt and expressed strong personal turmoil regarding the approaching hour of his death (v. 27) and cried out, "Father, glorify your name" (v. 28), which is a close variant of "hallowed be your name."[44] The response to this cry is one of the rare instances in the canon when God's audible voice is heard in public: "I have glorified it, and I will glorify it again" (v. 28). What makes this occasion particularly instructive from our current discussion is that following God's response Jesus offers the bewildered crowd an explanation: "This voice has come for your sake, not for mine. Now is the judgment of this world; now the ruler of this world will be driven out . . ." (vv. 30–31). Therefore, this passage shows a link between the desire for God's name to be hallowed with the promise of the forthcoming defeat of the devil.

Taking the two passages together with the first petition of the Lord's prayer in a canonical narrative reading, it may be concluded that the plea for God's name to be hallowed has strong biblical connotations of infusing new life into a world where God's name has been profaned (Ezekiel), and of delivering the world from the evil one (John).

Your Kingdom Come

We saw in chapter 4 that the NT usage of the term "kingdom of God" (or its paraphrase by Matthew, the "kingdom of heaven") is characterized by a dual

---

44. According to Schnackenburg, "The short prayer can be regarded as a Christological rephrasing of the petition in Our Father, 'Hallowed be thy name" (*John*, 397). For similar views, see e.g., Borchert, *John 12–21*, 55; and Michaels, *John*, 693; and Carson, *John*, 440–41, who also notes the link with Ezek 36.

temporality: It has both present and future aspects ("already" and "not yet"), which is sometimes referred to by the phrase "inaugurated eschatology." It was also argued there that the "coming of the kingdom" expresses a progressive sense of transformation (see e.g., in Luke 17:20–21 or the Parables of the Mustard Seed and the Yeast in Luke 13:18–21) that has already started among the disciples. This point has been summed up by Ben Witherington as follows: "The new creation began during Jesus' ministry, reached its first climactic point with the resurrection of Jesus, and will not be completed until Christ comes again."[45] Therefore, the second petition of the Lord's Prayer can be perceived to call for this progressive transformation to come to pass. The plea, however, also has a secondary meaning if we put the emphasis on "your" in "*your* kingdom come": It suggests a contrast between God's kingdom and an alternative reign, which is highly relevant in the light of the discussion in the previous chapter, where we saw that several biblical passages identify a dominion on earth reigned over by the "ruler of this world" (John 14:30) or the "god of this world" (2 Cor 4:4)—indeed, 1 John 5:19 explicitly states that "the whole world lies under the power of the evil one." Taking together the two readings, the second petition can be understood as a specific plea for the final realization of God's kingdom and for the end of the devil's reign over the material world.

Your Will Be Done

The inclusion of this petition in Matthew's version of the Lord's Prayer (it is absent from Luke's Gospel) holds the implication that God's providence on earth is somehow incomplete,[46] and the essence of the plea is that God's will—rather than someone else's will—should prevail. Regardless of whether the alternative will originates in human nature or the deliberate subversive attempts of hostile spiritual powers, the very fact that we *need to* pray for God's will to be done shows the potency of the opposition to it. Indeed, we saw in chapter 5 how Jesus' agony at Gethsemane illustrated that even the Son of Man experienced a conflict between human and the divine trajectories, and Jesus' response—"not my will but yours be done" (Luke 22:42)—is essentially identical to the third petition. Accordingly, "Your will be done" has often been interpreted as a declaration of the renunciation of

45. Witherington, *Imminent Domain*, 51.

46. This has caused considerable unease among some commentators; e.g., Lohmeyer asks, "But is not this will in fact always done, is it not done every morning, when he makes the sun rise again, and will it not be done as long as the earth endures and the heaven is spread out over it?" Lohmeyer, *Lord's Prayer*, 129.

all personal human will and the acceptance of God's will in all things.[47] This self-denial and deference to the will of God is consistent with Jesus' teaching about discipleship: "If any want to become my followers, let them deny themselves and take up their cross and follow me" (Matt 16:24).

We must note, however, that the passive construction in the petition leaves the agency associated with this petition unspecified—be done *by whom?*—which allows for the broadening of the potential reference of the plea. In contrast to the typical reading whereby the passive voice points to the creatures of the world, Raymond Brown raises a possible alternative meaning: "we may ask if in this petition, as in the previous petitions, it is not primarily a question of God's action, of God bringing about His own will on earth and in heaven."[48] This interpretation is centered around God's overall plan for the universe, and would mean, according to Brown, that the plea of the third petition is that "God's will bring about the eschatological completion of His salvific plan."[49] As we shall see below when we consider the ending of this petition—". . . on earth as it is in heaven"—the plea for the realization of God's will in this broader sense can be understood as the general desire for material creation to become amenable to the divine principles that already govern the heavenly realm.

On Earth as It Is in Heaven

The concluding section of the "Thou-petitions"—"on earth as it is in heaven"—is unclear in its reference: Does it belong only to the third petition related to God's will, or also to the first two that address God's name and his kingdom?[50] The question cannot be answered unambiguously on linguistics grounds, but the brevity and the fully parallel structure of the three petitions—in Greek they contain the same number of words, the same parts of speech, the same word order, and the same rhythm[51]—renders it unlikely that the conclusion of this sequence would apply only to the last constituent. Accordingly, France concludes, "in view of the careful balance of the three

---

47. Lohmeyer, *Lord's Prayer*, 123.

48. R. E. Brown, *New Testament Essays*, 298.

49. Ibid., 300.

50. The predominant historical understanding linked the ending with the third petition, although there was also a strong "minority view" represented by scholars such as Origen, John Chrysostom, and Meister Eckhart, who believed that "on earth as it is in heaven" concerned the "Thou-petitions" as a block; see Stevenson, *Lord's Prayer*, 223.

51. Ayo, *Lord's Prayer*, 51.

preceding clauses, [*on earth as it is in heaven*] is probably to be taken with all of them rather than as an extension of the last."[52]

A second question we need to ask is why the addition of this concluding section was necessary at all? In such a condensed prayer as the Lord's Prayer, to add an ending to the "Thou-petitions" that is longer than any of the petitions individually cannot be a mere stylistic issue. If the phrase simply meant "in heaven and on earth" (as is often found in other parts of the canon, e.g., Ps 135:6; Matt 28:18), it would be somewhat redundant and would not be missed by its omission—after all, where else could the petitions apply? However, the phrase—literally translated as "as in heaven (so) also on earth"—can also be understood to express the plea that God's will be established on earth *in the same way* as it is already done in heaven. In this light, it gains additional significance that the Lord's Prayer starts with the characterization of our Father as being "in heaven": This positive connotation of "heaven" supports the interpretation that the heavenly sphere represents divine standards that are to be reached "also on earth."[53] In this sense, the addition of the ending "as in heaven (so) also on earth" takes the "Thou-petitions" beyond general prayers for the increase of God's providence on earth: The call becomes directional, aiming at the unification of the material and the spiritual worlds under the principles that are already established in heaven. The fact that Jesus instructed his disciples to pray about this process evidences the fact that although it was ongoing, its successful completion had not yet come about on earth.

Give Us This Day Our Daily Bread

On the surface, the fourth petition is textually straightforward: It asks for God's provision. However, the text hides a semantic ambiguity—the exact meaning of the Greek word translated as "daily" (*epiousion*)—which is central to this plea, because the way we interpret it affects the perceived meaning of the whole petition. As a result, this petition has arguably been the subject of more scholarly effort (and debate) than any other part of the Lord's Prayer. The philological ambiguity stems from the fact that, as already noted by Origen in the first half of the third century, the word

---

52. France, *Matthew*, 139.

53. In supporting this reading, Davies and Allison point out that heaven is consistently described as an untarnished place in Matthew's Gospel and thus they conclude, "All we can say is this: heaven is the sphere in which God's will is now done. But one fact is plain: the eventual unity of creation is presupposed" (*Matthew*, 606). For a similar conclusion, see also e.g., Deissler, "Lord's Prayer," 10.

epiousion does not appear to exist in Greek outside the Gospels.[54] As Origen was one of the most educated and renowned exegetes of his time as well as a native speaker of Greek, his comment suggests that the term was specifically coined when Jesus' original words (spoken either in Aramaic or Hebrew) were translated into Greek. The fact that a neologism was created indicates that the original word carried some unique meaning that could not be rendered into Greek using a more straightforward term. Unfortunately, there is insufficient linguistic or etymological evidence to identify unambiguously the originally intended meaning,[55] but modern commentators increasingly incline toward understanding the petition as "Give us this day the bread that we need."[56]

With regard to the overall meaning of the petition, a common interpretation is that it is a plea for divine provision and thus a "powerful expression of trust and dependence."[57] However, this meaning appears to be at odds with Jesus' explicit instruction in the Sermon on the Mount—that is, in the very section of teaching in Matthew's Gospel that contains the Lord's Prayer—that believers should *not* worry about their daily subsistence (Matt 6:25, 31–33). A solution to this dilemma is offered when we consider an OT passage that the "daily bread" probably alludes to, a part of the oracle of Agur (Prov 30:8b–9), which scholars have often linked to the Lord's Prayer:

> give me neither poverty nor riches;
> feed me with the food that I need,
> or I shall be full, and deny you,
> and say, "Who is the LORD?"
> or I shall be poor, and steal,
> and profane the name of my God.

Here, Agur's plea is for just the right amount of provision from the Lord[58] and he spells out what "right" means in this respect: neither too

---

54. "Let us now consider what the word *epiousion*, needful, means. First of all it should be known that the word epiousion is not found in any Greek writer whether in philosophy or in common usage, but seems to have been formed by the evangelists." Origen, *On Prayer*, 17. One more occurrence of the term is in the *Didache* 8:2, where the Lord's Prayer is reproduced, and there has been an incorrect report of the word appearing in a papyrus document that has since been found to be a mere transcribing error; see Nijman and Worp "Documentary Papyrus," 233.

55. See e.g., Dunn, "Prayer," 622; Stevenson, *Lord's Prayer*, 44; Young, *Lord's Prayer*.

56. See e.g., Dunn, "Prayer," 622; Lochman, *Lord's Prayer*, 92; Stevenson, *Lord's Prayer*, 225.

57. Dunn, "Prayer," 622.

58. This meaning is expressed particularly clearly in the Septuagint, which offers an interpretive translation of Prov 30:8: ". . . and give me neither riches nor poverty, but

much, because it makes one sin and neither too little, because that, too, makes one sin. It is also noteworthy that the Hebrew word translated as "food" (*lechem*) in v. 8 also means "bread," which strengthens the link between the relevant part of the oracle and the fourth petition—so much so that the NIV, for example, translates Proverbs 30:8c as "but give me only my daily bread."[59] This suggests that the full meaning of the fourth petition is more complex than the mere request for sustenance; in Dunn's words, the plea is, "Give us what we need, not what we want, or even what we think we need, but what God sees our need actually to be."[60] In the light of Proverbs 30:8–9, the petition can also be said to concern the right amount of provision in order to set boundaries to one's inclination to sin, thereby keeping the praying person safe.[61]

Finally, while the discussion has centered so far around the belief that the fourth petition is concerned with receiving sustenance for our material existence, an alternative understanding of "bread" has also been in circulation ever since Tertullian's commentary on the Lord's Prayer at the turn of the third century;[62] he and many theologians since then have related the fourth petition to a passage in John's Gospel regarding Jesus being the "bread of life":

> Then Jesus said to them, "Very truly, I tell you, it was not Moses who gave you the bread from heaven, but it is my Father who gives you the true bread from heaven. For the bread of God is that which comes down from heaven and gives life to the world." They said to him, "Sir, *give us this bread always*." Jesus said to them, "I am the bread of life. Whoever comes to me will never be hungry, and whoever believes in me will never be thirsty. (John 6:32–35; emphasis added)

---

order what is necessary and sufficient for me."

59. It may not be a coincide that the Hebrew word used to express "daily" in Agur's petition is *ḥuqqi*, whose meaning according to the BDB is "something prescribed," with the root of the term also meaning "prescribed limit" or "boundary"; indeed, in Job 38:10 God uses exactly the same form of the word when he states that he has set "boundaries" for the sea (an act that, as we saw in chapter 2, formed a central part of God's creative act).

60. Dunn, "Prayer," 622.

61. Related to this point, 1 Tim 6:9–10, expounds on how wealth, for example, can lead people into temptation and then into sin, declaring that "the love of money is a root of all kinds of evil" (v. 10).

62. Tertullian: ". . .we may rather understand, 'Give us this day our daily bread,' spiritually. For Christ is our Bread; because Christ is Life, and bread is life. 'I am,' says He, 'the Bread of Life'. . . And so, in petitioning for daily bread, we ask for perpetuity in Christ, and indivisibility from His body" (*On Prayer,* 6).

Quite remarkably, the people's request in the passage—"give us this bread always"—is very close to the text of the fourth petition, and the relevance of the text becomes even stronger if we also consider an instruction Jesus gave to the crowd prior to this teaching: "Do not work for the food that perishes, but for the food that endures for eternal life, which the Son of Man will give you" (v. 27). The spiritual understanding of bread is, of course, further reinforced by the Eucharist as discussed earlier, and although Jesus taught the disciples the Lord's Prayer before the Last Supper had taken place, the clear spiritual resonance might not be a coincidence. Indeed, breaking bread for Jesus was both a physical and a deeply spiritual act (e.g., when he shared life-changing meals with sinners as in Matt 9:10–13), and in this sense the word "bread" has a meaning that encompasses both our daily physical and spiritual needs.[63]

Forgive Us Our Debts as We also Have Forgiven Our Debtors

The meaning of the first part of this petition appears to be straightforward: It asks for God's mercy and forgiveness, but we must note that the two Gospel versions of the fifth petition differ in that Matthew uses the Greek term "debts" (*opheilémata*) while Luke uses "sins" (*hamartias*).[64] Dunn submits that this variation is of no great importance so far as the overall meaning of the petition is concerned, because there can be little doubt that the petition concerns primarily moral rather than financial matters.[65] However, the text does allow for an alternative reading, and given the importance of financial matters in the material world and the salience of economic imagery in several parts of the NT canon (particularly in Matthew's Gospel[66]), the use of a monetary metaphor may not be merely a

63. This was famously expressed by Augustine in his *Commentary on the Lord's Sermon on the Mount* (7:27): "... at one and the same time we are praying for the needful daily bread for the body, and the consecrated visible Bread and the invisible bread of the Word of God." For modern commentaries in this vein see e.g., O'Collins, *Lord's Prayer*, 88–89; Subramanian, "Lord's Prayer," 119.

64. A generally accepted explanation for this discrepancy is that the original Aramaic or Hebrew word that Jesus used when he taught the disciples expressed both meanings, and Matthew opted for a rendering with a more Semitic flavor, while Luke translated the term into a Greek word that was more easily comprehensible for a Gentile audience; see e.g., R. E. Brown, *New Testament Essays,* 308–9; Geldenhuys and Bruce, "Lord's Prayer," 696; Young, *Lord's Prayer,* 30.

65. Dunn, "Prayer," 622.

66. As Eubank summarizes, Matthew's Gospel contains a "striking preponderance of economic imagery, especially in passages dealing with sin, righteousness, and divine recompense" (*Wages of Cross-Bearing,* 1).

stylistic issue. Indeed, Nathan Eubank explains that for Matthew, sin and debt are closely interrelated; in passages such as Matt 25:29 and 6:19–24 the Evangelist presents a picture whereby

> God repays righteous deeds generously and cancels the debts of those who ask him. But those who refuse to earn wages or refuse to cancel the debts of others will be punished. To store up treasure in heaven is to be generous to the poor, rather than clinging to ephemeral earthly possessions.[67]

Thomas Neufeld further argues that "cancelling the debts" in the Lord's Prayer alludes to the Old Testament law of cancelling debts and freeing slaves "in the year of jubilee" (Lev 25:10).[68] This is consistent with the statement in Jesus' first sermon in Nazareth, where, citing Isaiah, he declares that he has come to "proclaim the year of the Lord's favor" (Isa 61:2; Luke 4:19), which several commentators take as a reference to the Year of Jubilee.[69] Accordingly, Neufeld concludes that in Matthew's portrayal

> Forgiveness of debts is a way of giving people, families, and nations a chance to start afresh. Such forgiveness is an integral part of the fabric of a society being renewed; it is part of the socially concrete way in which the kingdom of God is making its presence felt.[70]

The second half of the fifth petition has been the source of considerable theological bewilderment in that it makes human forgiveness appear as a condition for divine forgiveness, even though in 1 John 1:9 there is no mention of humans having to forgive others ("If we confess our sins, he who is faithful and just will forgive us our sins and cleanse us from all unrighteousness") and neither is there any reference to confession in the Lord's Prayer. Scholars have also been puzzled by the fact that within a series of petitions to God, one of them is linked to a human act. There is no other such occurrence in the prayer, which raises the question of what it is about this specific act which warranted its featured inclusion, particularly as it is not one of the human behaviors highlighted in the Ten Commandments or in Jesus' Greatest Commandment. As if anticipating the difficulty of taking this human condition on board, Matthew's Gospel adds a postscript to the Lord's Prayer that not only refers back to this, and only this, issue—"For if you forgive others their trespasses, your heavenly Father will also forgive

---

67. Ibid., 200.
68. Neufeld, *Recovering Jesus*, 223.
69. See Watts, *Isaiah 34–66*, 873.
70. Neufeld, *Recovering Jesus*, 24.

you" (v. 14)—but in the subsequent verse reiterates it from the opposite perspective to avoid any misinterpretation: "but if you do not forgive others, neither will your Father forgive your trespasses" (v. 15). This is thus undoubtedly a point of utmost significance.

The requirement to forgive others is also highlighted in several other places in the canon, thereby underlining the importance of this act,[71] and it is also noteworthy in this respect that the verse from Leviticus whose second half Jesus cited in the Greatest Commandment begins with "You shall not take vengeance or bear a grudge against any of your people" (19:18). In an explanation of why so much significance is attached to forgiveness in the Bible, Anthony Bash proposes that the real danger of bearing a grudge against another person lies in the fact that "unforgiving people cut themselves off from God's forgiveness" because they will not be "in a frame of mind to seek or receive God's forgiveness."[72] Furthermore, not only can an unforgiving state obstruct a person's relationship with God, but as Paul further indicates in 2 Cor 2:10–11, this state can also be utilized by the devil to gain advantage over humans:

> Anyone whom you forgive, I also forgive. What I have forgiven, if I have forgiven anything, has been for your sake in the presence of Christ. And we do this *so that we may not be outwitted by Satan*; for we are not ignorant of his designs. (emphasis added)[73]

The validity of the link between unforgiveness and human vulnerability to hostile spiritual interference has been born out in practice during actual healing and deliverance ministry; as Peter Horrobin, the founder of one of the most influential contemporary ministries in this area ("Ellel Ministries"[74]), summarizes, "We have probably seen more healing and deliverance take place through applying the principles of forgiveness

---

71. E.g., as we also saw in the last chapter, God's forgiveness and blessing of Job *followed* Job's forgiveness of his friends and family. In the New Testament the Beatitudes state that "Blessed are the merciful, for they will receive mercy" (Matt 5:7), and Mark 11:25 overtly sets human forgiveness as a *precondition* for God's mercy: "Whenever you stand praying, forgive, if you have anything against anyone; so that your Father in heaven may also forgive you your trespasses."

72. Bash, *Forgiveness*, 19.

73. A related principle concerning an opposite of forgiveness, hating someone, is established in 1 John 2:9–11: "Whoever says, 'I am in the light,' while hating a brother or sister, is still in the darkness. Whoever loves a brother or sister lives in the light, and in such a person there is no cause for stumbling. But whoever hates another believer is in the darkness, walks in the darkness, and does not know the way to go, because the darkness has brought on blindness."

74. http://ellel.org

than through any other spiritual discipline."[75] This would suggest that the inclusion of this act in the fifth petition is aimed at the protection of the petitioner: Even if one repents and has his/her sins forgiven, this cleansed state needs to be safeguarded against the corrupting consequences of unforgiveness toward others.

Lead Us not into Temptation

The sixth petition of the Lord's Prayer has been the source of a great deal of theological speculation because the surface meaning of the plea suggests that God is the originator of temptation. This is not only conceptually puzzling but seems also to contradict the prominent verse in James 1:13, which declares, "No one, when tempted, should say, 'I am being tempted by God.'" Accordingly, much theological effort has been devoted to developing interpretations that would avoid an understanding of this petition as God's direct agency causing human temptation. The typical argument is that the Greek word for "temptation"—*peirasmos*—should be interpreted differently, as either referring to "testing"[76] or to the eschatological Great Tribulation.[77] According to a third proposal, the original Aramaic or Hebrew version of the petition contained a causative/desiderative verb construction with a permissive sense that the Greek translation misrepresented because of a lack of a similar grammatical construct expressing a permissive nuance in Greek.[78] A wide variety of alternative translations have been suggested

75. Horrobin, *Healing Though Deliverance*, 37. Elsewhere, Horrobin argues further that unforgiveness builds up bitterness, resentment, and anger in a person, acting like "cancers on our emotions" (*Most Powerful Prayer*, 32).

76. The Greek word for "temptation" (*peirasmos*) can indeed mean "testing" and the canon does contain examples when God exposed people to trials in order to test them (see chapter 7 for further discussion). However, it is not clear why believers should pray to stop this divine practice; therefore, this interpretation has usually been further qualified, resulting in some version of "lead us not into more testing than we can handle"; see e.g., Carl, *Lord's Prayer*, 72. Of the mainstream English Bible translations, the Good News Bible follows this practice and translates the petition as "Do not bring us to hard testing."

77. Jeremias and Brown, among others, have equated the meaning of *peirasmos* not with trials in general but with *the* ultimate eschatological trial, the Great Tribulation, which includes the revelation of the Antichrist, the persecution of the saints, the final onslaught of Satan, and the ultimate battle between God and Satan. Jeremias, *Lord's Prayer*, 30; R. E. Brown, *New Testament Essays*, 316. Indeed, in Rev 3:10 the message to the church of Philadelphia contains the promise that "Because you have kept my word of patient endurance, I will keep you from the hour of trial that is coming on the whole world to test the inhabitants of the earth."

78. E.g., Jeremias, *Lord's Prayer*, 29–30; Lochman, *Lord's Prayer*, 145–46; Meier, *A

along this latter line, for example "do not let us enter into temptation,"[79] "do not allow us to be led into temptation by him (of course) who tempts,"[80] "suffer us not to be led into temptation,"[81] "let us not fall into temptation,"[82] "do not abandon us in temptation which we cannot bear,"[83] "let us not be caught in the sphere of temptation,"[84] "let us not succumb to temptation,"[85] "let us not come into the attack, into the danger of falling,"[86] "grant that we may not fail in the test,"[87] "do not allow us to come to the test,"[88] and "do not let us yield to temptation."[89]

However, in light of all these efforts to make sense of the petition, it is surprising that the original Greek translators of Jesus' words did not appear to be exercised about the content of this petition and neither did the Evangelists citing it (if it was not one of them who himself provided the translation): Luke's version of the Lord's Prayer, which deviates from Matthew's slightly in some places to offer a different shade of interpretation, presents an identical text for this petition. There are two factors in combination which might offer an explanation for this lack of concern about the meaning of the text. First, John Meier submits that the issue simply may not have appeared to be significant for early Christians:

> many writers in the OT and the NT were not bothered by problems of primary and secondary causality. In keeping with their strong monotheism, usually expressed by mythic stories rather than by philosophical theology, they frequently attributed all events directly to God, with no great concern about whether these events were good or bad. The important point was to exclude any second power, good or evil, that might seem equal to God. This simple and direct faith in the one God who controls all things corresponds perfectly to the simple and direct petitions that make up the Our Father. Worrying about whether

---

Marginal Jew, 301–2.

79. Lamsa's Bible translation of the Peshitta.

80. Tertullian, *On Prayer*, 8.

81. Cyprian, *Lord's Prayer*, 7.

82. Dionysius of Alexandria, cited by Lohmeyer, *Lord's Prayer*, 102.

83. Hilary of Poitiers, cited by Stevenson, *Lord's Prayer*, 93.

84. Johannes Heller, cited by Lochman, *Lord's Prayer*, 145.

85. Jeremias, *Lord's Prayer*, 30.

86. Kuhn, "New Light on Temptation," 109.

87. Geldenhuys and Bruce, "Lord's Prayer," 696.

88. Meier, *A Marginal Jew*, 301.

89. *Catholic Catechism*, No. 2846.

God directly causes or merely permits evil may lie beyond the horizon of this utterly simple prayer.[90]

Second, the assumption that first century Christian believers prayed the Lord's Prayer without being overly concerned about any possible theological contradiction in the sixth petition would gain considerable support if it could also be shown that the original Aramaic or Hebrew version of the "lead us not into . . ." construct was a formulaic, conventionalized phrase that was used in everyday language in a sense which did not point to the agency of God. There is considerable evidence that this was indeed the case,[91] suggesting that the "do not lead/bring us into . . ." phrase was an established idiomatic construction that did *not* imply that God was causing any of the sin, iniquity, trespass, temptation, or disgrace that the phrase referred to. It was a highly conventionalized formula that had evidently become an integral part of the Jewish prayer lexicon, and therefore when Jesus included the same construction in the Lord's Prayer, it will have sounded natural to the disciples, without raising any concerns about God's role in human temptation. Interestingly, the frequent use of the Lord's Prayer over the past two millennia has resulted in a similar process of conventionalization among Christians, as most believers who say the Lord's Prayer are unlikely to be worried about the fact that something might be amiss with the agency of the sixth petition in this respect.

Thus, the most satisfactory interpretation of the sixth petition is that it expresses the believers' plea to God to keep them safe from falling into temptation. We saw in chapter 5 that Satan used temptation as the primary tool in his attempt to deflect Jesus from his divinely ordained course, and

90. Meier, *A Marginal Jew*, 302.

91. The Talmud, for example, prescribes an evening prayer that contains a similar construction that could not be understood as caused by God: ". . . accustom me to the performance of religious duties, but do not accustom me to transgression; and *bring me not into sin, or into iniquity, or into temptation, or into contempt*" (*Babylonian Talmud, Berakoth* 60b; emphasis added). Then, the subsequent morning prayer in the Talmud reiterates the italicized part almost identically, and Young also reports a prayer of Rabbi Judah the Prince, which again reiterates the relevant part: "Do not bring us into the grasp of sin, and not into the grasp of trespass and iniquity, and not into the grasp of temptation or disgrace." Young, *Lord's Prayer*, 33. The fact that these were common prayers is indicated by the fact that the relevant section is still part of the contemporary authorized Jewish Daily Prayer Book: "Lead us not into error, transgression, iniquity, temptation or disgrace" (Singer, *Prayer Book*, 21). A further example of the "lead somebody not into . . ." construction used in the same sense occurs in an ancient Jewish thanksgiving psalm that has been found both in a Syriac manuscript and the Dead Sea Scrolls (usually marked as Psalm 155): "Remember me and forget me not, and lead me not into situations too hard for me" (v. 11). W. Wright, "Apocryphal Psalms in Syriac," 70–72.

the next chapter will show that temptation is one of the major battlefields for believers in the turbulence of the current transitional age. The fact that Jesus included a plea about temptation in the Lord's Prayer confirms that Christians cannot stand firm in the face of temptation without divine support; in Dunn's words, "It [the sixth petition] is a prayer of conscious and confessed human weakness; it makes no pretense of confidence in its own strength and commitment; rather it expresses an unconditional abandonment to the will and grace of God."[92]

But Deliver Us from the Evil One

The seventh petition has often been regarded as an extension of the sixth because of the linguistically connected nature of the two clauses, and James Packer rightly remarks that both clauses express a single thought: "Life is a spiritual minefield; amid such dangers we dare not trust ourselves; Father, keep us safe."[93] In this sense, the first half of the extended petition can be seen as focusing on internal or situational challenges that the tempted person faces, whereas the second half shifts the emphasis to an external corrupting force from which the petitioner needs to be rescued.

The exact characterization of this "external corrupting force" in the seventh petition has divided scholars, because the final Greek word of the Lord's Prayer (*ponērou*) can refer to "evil" in general or to "the evil one" (i.e., the devil) in particular.[94] Given the controversial nature of the subject—as it touches upon the question of how real one considers Satan and his involvement in the world to be—the literature has shown a sharp division among commentators concerning this matter since ancient times.[95]

---

92. Dunn, "Prayer," 623.

93. Packer, *Lord's Prayer*, 85.

94. Usually, this issue should be relatively easy to resolve based on whether the word is a neuter (meaning "evil") or a masculine (meaning "evil one"); in this case, however, the grammatical position of the word within the sentence is such that the two genders cannot be distinguished, and therefore, from a linguistic point of view both meanings are possible.

95. Initially, the Greek fathers tended to understand the word as the "devil", while the Latin west, starting with Augustine and followed by the Reformers on the whole, favored the more general, non-personalized interpretation of "evil"; see e.g., Lochman, *Lord's Prayer*, 152; Stevenson, *Lord's Prayer*, 79–80. In contemporary theology, the reading of the petition is influenced partly by the interpreter's disposition toward charismatic styles of spirituality and partly by church traditions; e.g., the Catholic Church supports "evil one": According to *Catechism of the Catholic Church*, No. 2851, "In this petition, evil is not an abstraction, but refers to a person, Satan, the Evil One, the angel who opposes God." Regarding mainstream Bible translations, both the NRSV and the

Although there are several scholarly analyses examining a wide range of potential factors and considerations that might proffer a resolution to this dilemma,[96] one cannot help thinking that given the centrality of the prayer and the concise, tightly formed nature of the text, the open-endedness of the discourse was not merely a coincidence or an awkward formulation of language but rather it was actually intended to allow for multiple readings. One may even argue that the exact conceptualization of *ponērou* does not make a major difference in the understanding of the overall thrust of the petition, so long as we recognize that the plea concerns a powerful force of evil that can gain a hold on the individual and, therefore, from which one needs to be rescued by divine help. After all, as we saw in the previous chapter, the canon describes the devil as being able to perform his subversive role not only directly but also indirectly, through the corruption of social systems or the manipulation of people and circumstances that then activate the targeted person's own sinful inclinations.[97]

If the seventh petition was considered to be merely an extension of the sixth with an analogous meaning, one might ask why such an extension was added to the Lord's Prayer, particularly in such a significant, final position. Indeed, a strong indication that this petition does contribute unique meaning to the prayer is its close parallel to an essential component of Jesus' Priestly Prayer (John 17:1–26): Here, after stating that while he was with the disciples he protected them (v. 12), Jesus then asks his Father "to protect them from the evil one" (v. 15) as he is about to leave this world. The text of this plea, which is virtually identical to the seventh petition, suggests that during the turbulent transitional times leading up to the *Parousia*, the sixth petition by itself may not provide believers with sufficient protection against temptation without being complemented by an explicit reference to deliverance from external hostile powers[98]—in Raymond Brown's words, "A titanic

---

NIV renders *ponērou* into "evil one" as their first choice, with also mentioning "evil" as a possible alternative in the footnotes, while the ESV does exactly the opposite.

96. For overviews of the two sides, see e.g., R. E. Brown, *New Testament Essays,* 317–18 and Page, *Powers of Evil,* 112–14 representing "evil one," and Luz, *Matthew 1-7,* 385 and Davies and Allison, *Matthew,* 615, which on balance favor "evil."

97. Calvin held a similar view: "Whether by the term evil we understand the devil or sin, is not of the least consequence. Satan is indeed the very enemy who lays snares for our life, but it is by sin that he is armed for our destruction. Our petition, therefore, is, that we may not be overcome or overwhelmed with temptation, but in the strength of the Lord may stand firm against all the powers by which we are assailed; in other words, may not fall under temptation: that being thus taken under his charge and protection, we may remain invincible by sin, death, the gates of hell, and the whole power of the devil; in other words, be delivered from evil." Calvin, *Institutes,* 3.20.46.

98. It is noteworthy that, as Stevenson explains, this confession was also reflected

struggle with Satan stands between the community and the realization of its prayer, and from this it asks to be delivered."[99]

Overall Theme

Even the brief exegesis of the Lord's Prayer presented above reveals a characteristic of the text that is rarely mentioned in commentaries, namely that in several places the carefully crafted petitions appear to have been formulated in such an open-ended manner as to allow for, rather than restrict, multiple shades of meaning in the prayer. This characteristic might be related to the fact that the prayer was intended to be prayed regularly and universally, and thus the subtlety of its layered meaning could emerge gradually over time in dynamic interaction with the petitioner's personal circumstances. However, despite the perceived ambiguities, a common theme does emerge in the petitions regarding their concern for the cleansing and protection of the believer: Christians make themselves vulnerable if they do not hallow God's name (but profane it); if they do not commit themselves to God's kingdom (but to the kingdom of darkness); if they do not follow God's will (but rather their own or the enemy's); if they have materially too much or too little (which may lead them to sin); if they do not repent of their sins; if they bear resentment toward others; if they succumb to temptation; and if they fall into bondage to forces of evil.

The function of purification in the prayer has been highlighted in an intriguing textual variant of Luke's version of the Lord's Prayer: In the fourth century, Gregory of Nyssa reported a version in which the second petition ("Your kingdom come") had been replaced with "May your Holy Spirit come upon us and cleanse us,"[100] and the fact that at least two medieval manuscripts containing the alternative petition are extant[101] indicate that this alternative wording was still being copied several hundreds of years later. Houlden argues that the variation may have originated in the use of the Lord's Prayer in prebaptismal teaching,[102] and indeed, the prayer's links

---

by a pre-Reformation practice whereby a short prayer (an "embolism") was appended to the end of the Lord's Prayer reiterating the theme of deliverance: "deliver us, Lord." Stevenson, *Lord's Prayer*, 6.

99. R. E. Brown, *New Testament Essays*, 320.

100. See Parker, *Living Text of the Gospels*, 66. Ayo mentions Tertullian and Maximus Confessor as further witnesses to this alternative wording. Ayo, *Lord's Prayer*, 42.

101. Miniscule 700, 11th c., British Library; Miniscule 162 (or Codex Barberinianus 11), 1153, Vatican Library.

102. Houlden, "Lord's Prayer," 357.

with baptism can be traced back to the first century,[103] evidencing that it was regarded as a potent tool for spiritual cleansing and for socializing converts into the Christian community.[104]

In the light of all the above considerations, how can we best describe an overarching function of the Lord's Prayer which binds together the petitions into a coherent whole? One term that might be effective in expressing the commonality in the pleas is "alignment," as used by N. T. Wright: "To pray 'your kingdom come' at Jesus' bidding, therefore, meant to align oneself with his kingdom movement and to seek God's power in furthering its ultimate fulfilment."[105] That is, the central role of the Lord's Prayer in Christianity can be seen as (re)aligning the petitioners with God's redemptive-creative purposes and acting as a spiritual "firewall" so that believers can stand firm in the face of various inevitable difficulties. This is in accordance with Revelation's "call for the endurance and faith of the saints" (Rev 13:10), a theme that will be further discussed in the next chapter. According to the sayings of the desert fathers, Abba Arsenius once pronounced, "Strive with all your might to bring your interior activity into accord with God."[106] This is exactly what the Lord's Prayer helps believers to achieve, and it is probably in this sense that Jean Carmignac has concluded, "The Lord's Prayer aligns us immediately with the purest and most absolute theocentrism."[107] In keeping the believers attuned and pure, the prayer helps them to perform their stewardship role of being transformational agents of the world.

6.3. The Great Commission

In his sermon in Cornelius's house in Caesarea, the Apostle Peter told the assembled believers that "[Jesus] *commanded* us to preach to the people and to testify that he is the one ordained by God as judge of the living and the dead" (Acts 10:42; emphasis added). In accordance with this reference, the Gospels do indeed record a prominent mission charge that Jesus gave his disciples immediately before his ascension. Different versions of this message—usually referred to as the Great Commission—are presented in three places—Matt 28:18–20, Luke 24:46–49, and Acts 1:8[108]—among which

103. Jeremias, *Lord's Prayer*, 3.

104. For an informative summary, see Stewart-Sykes, "Catechumenate and Contra-Culture," 289–306.

105. Wright, "Lord's Prayer," 135.

106. Chryssavgis, *Desert Fathers and Mothers*, 22.

107. Carmignac, "Lord's Prayer," 140.

108. The ending of Mark's Gospel also contains relevant material, but I will not

Matthew's account is the best-known and most often discussed. A passage in John (20:21–23) is also frequently referred to in the literature as a variant of the Great Commission, although its context makes it clear that it was not part of the same discourse as the others; it is, however, relevant to the discussion because it contains an explicit sending message by the resurrected Christ shortly before his ascension. All the four extracts are brief and recount different yet complementary aspects of Jesus' missionary directive. A good starting point in examining the creational aspects of this directive is to reiterate the link between the commission to make disciples and the creation of a succession of stewards discussed in chapter 4.

The Succession of Stewards

According to Matt 28:19–20, Jesus told the Eleven, "Go therefore and make disciples of all nations, baptizing them in the name of the Father and of the Son and of the Holy Spirit, and teaching them to obey everything that I have commanded you." It has been observed by many that in these verses Jesus in effect commissions his disciples to *reproduce themselves* so that a continuous chain of disciples can be witnesses "in Jerusalem, in all Judea and Samaria, and to the ends of the earth" (Acts 1:8).[109] It was noted in chapter 4 that this commissioning in order to generate a succession of stewards is analogous in creational terms with the creation and blessing of the human species, "Be fruitful and multiply, and fill the earth and subdue it" (Gen 1:28). This parallel is further strengthened by John's account that after Jesus said to his disciples "As the Father has sent me, so I send you" (20:21), he "breathed on them and said to them, "Receive the Holy Spirit" (v. 21), which is an unmistakable allusion to Gen 2:7, when God "breathed into his [Adam's] nostrils the breath of life." In this sense, the Great Commission formed a central part of Jesus' assuming a divine creational role, and indeed, at the beginning of Matthew's account of the Great Commission, Jesus declared in no uncertain terms that all authority in heaven and on earth had been given to him (Matt 28:18).

The Great Commission signaled a momentous milestone in the course of progressive creation: We saw in chapter 3 that the crisis signaled by God's

---

include it in the following analysis, because of the serious doubts about the authenticity of the "longer ending" of this gospel; see e.g., Collins, *Mark*, 799.

109. E.g., Nolland points out, "The idea of replication is fundamental to Matthew's thought here" (*Matthew*, 1271), and Barth sums up the essence of this approach as "Make them what you yourselves are!" Barth, "Matthew 28:16–20," 63. See also e.g., Blomberg, *Matthew*, 431; Turner, *Matthew*, 689.

"It is not good" declaration in Gen 2:18—followed by the Fall and the expulsion of Adam and Eve from Eden—was to a large extent a *stewardship crisis,* first with Adam being unable to perform his duties alone and then the extension of stewardship to the human species failing to produce a harmonious and productive society. Against this backdrop, Jesus' sending out of the disciples to reach out to the whole world—and thereby making them agents of the divine strategy to advance the kingdom of God—indicated that the postdiluvian process of transforming humanity had arrived at a point when a section of the human population had reached sufficient maturity to fulfil their stewardship role, so long as they became Jesus' disciples and, subsequently, disciplers of others. Blomberg underlines, however, that becoming a disciple in the sense of the Great Commission does not merely entail making a profession of faith[110] but also requires meeting two further conditions: (a) being baptized in the name of the Father and of the Son and of the Holy Spirit, and (b) being taught to obey everything Jesus had commanded his followers. Let us examine these conditions more closely.

"Baptizing them in the name of the Father and of the Son and of the Holy Spirit"

The Great Commission is not the first occasion presented in the Scriptures when Jesus sends out his disciples on a mission. Matthew 9:36—11:1 tells how he commissioned the Twelve to "proclaim the good news, 'The kingdom of heaven has come near.' Cure the sick, raise the dead, cleanse the lepers, cast out demons" (vv. 10:7–8), and this mission charge is accompanied by detailed guidelines that are often referred to as the "Missionary Discourse."[111] Mark and Luke's Gospels also record this missionary tour (Mark 6:6–13; Luke 9:1–6), and Luke describes a further commissioning of the Seventy(-two[112]) disciples (10:1–12; 17–20).[113] The mandate of these missions, however, differs from the Great Commission in two key

110. Blomberg, *Matthew,* 431.

111. For a comprehensive analysis, see Weaver, *Missionary Discourse.*

112. Early manuscripts contain two variants of the number of disciples in Luke 10—seventy or seventy-two—and in a detailed analysis of a wide range of relevant external and internal evidence, Bruce Metzger submits that the evidence is evenly divided and concludes that "on the basis of our present knowledge the number of Jesus' disciples referred to in Luke X cannot be determined with confidence." Metzger, "Seventy or Seventy-Two," 306.

113. The relationship between these two mission trips is debated because of the overlap in the content of the accounts; therefore, Jesus' instructions contained in them are often discussed together; see e.g., Harvey, "Mission," 42–43.

respects: First, the disciples' earlier outreach was restricted to ministering only to "the lost sheep of the house of Israel" as they were forbidden to go among the Gentiles or the Samaritans (Matt 10:5–6); and second, the Great Commission involves the act of *baptizing* people as a central component, whereas this was not part of the Missionary Discourse. First Peter 3:20–21 offers some relevant insight to this: "when God waited patiently in the days of Noah, during the building of the ark, in which a few, that is, eight persons, were saved through water. And baptism, which this prefigured, now saves you—not as a removal of dirt from the body, but as an appeal to God for a good conscience, through the resurrection of Jesus Christ . . ."

Although the Greek text of this passage is difficult to translate,[114] the central theme of the message has a clear creational dimension: We saw in chapter 4 that the Flood functioned as a kind of "un-creation" with Noah's family representing the subsequent "re-creation" in the form of the new humanity, and 1 Peter draws a direct parallel between this new humanity and the baptized believer, while also explaining that the new beginning was made possible by the resurrection of Jesus. In other words, the passage in 1 Peter affirms that, as a result of Christ's atoning work, people can be saved through baptism in the same way as Noah's family was saved from perishing in the Flood. In Rom 6:4 Paul uses similar resurrection imagery to describe the "newness of life" that baptism brings about: "Therefore we have been buried with him by baptism into death, so that, just as Christ was raised from the dead by the glory of the Father, so we too might walk in newness of life." When Jesus sent out the Twelve and the Seventy, they were to minister only to the lost sheep of Israel, and even though John 4:1–2 shows that they also performed baptisms and made disciples on other occasions, these, too, were restricted to Jews. After Calvary, however, Jesus' victory on the cross appears to have afforded to baptism the potency to "save," thereby rendering it fit to be used also with Gentiles to bring them into membership of God's family.[115]

The fact that the Great Commission authorized the disciples not only to recover the lost sheep but also to add new sheep to the fold is in accordance with the incremental nature of progressive creation: Before Christ's

---

114. Largely caused by the unclear meaning within this context of the Greek words translated as "appeal" (*eperōtēma*) and "conscience" (*syneidēsis*); see e.g., Achtemeier, *First Peter*, 268–72; Dalton, *Christ's Proclamation*, 89–214; Jobes, *1 Peter*, 251–56.

115. It may well be the case that the specification in the Great Commission that the disciples should baptize people "in the name of the Father and of the Son and of the Holy Spirit" (Matt 28:19) was also related to the increased salvific potency of the post-Easter baptism, in contrast to other occasions when some believers "had *only* been baptized in the name of the Lord Jesus" (Acts 1:8; emphasis added).

atonement, the Bible presents the Israelites as the primary changing agents of humanity, and therefore Jesus' sending out the Twelve and then the Seventy aimed at increasing their transformational potency. After Calvary and Pentecost, however, the task force of stewardship has been extended to all Jesus' future disciples, regardless of their ethnic background.

"Teaching them to obey everything that I have commanded you"

The second key element of the Great Commission concerns the *instruction* of the new disciples, with the short participle clause "Teaching them to obey everything that I have commanded you" (Matt 28:20) containing two significant details: first, that the ultimate goal of the instruction should be *obedience*, and secondly, that this obedience should be comprehensive, that is, it should involve observing *everything* Jesus has commanded. A remarkable aspect of these specifications is what is missing from them: The focus of teaching highlighted here is not what most contemporary readers would probably consider to be the obvious target of instruction, namely knowledge, but rather the disciples' *behavior*; what is emphasized is that the conduct of the new converts should reflect obedience to all the directives that Jesus' own disciples have received. As Turner points out, this implies that the "goal of Jesus's commission is disciples who obey his teaching, not just casual hangers-on who listen to his teaching but do not practice it,"[116] which is consistent with Jesus' Parable About the Two Builders (Matt 7:24–27; Luke 6:47–49)[117] at the conclusion of the Sermon on the Mount, which declares that "everyone who hears these words of mine and does not act on them will be like a foolish man who built his house on sand" (v. 26). We shall consider the significance of "doing" versus merely "hearing" as a central theme in the next chapter.

The second implication is even more relevant to the current chapter and concerns the requirement that *all* the principles and instructions that Jesus enjoined on his own disciples were to be transmitted to successive generations. This was clearly intended to ensure that the essence of discipling would remain constant over time and thus future believers would carry on bearing the hallmarks of Jesus' disciples "by proxy."[118] Jewish dis-

---

116. Turner, *Matthew*, 691.

117. There is also a parallel with the Parable of the Two Sons (Matt 21:28–32), which praises the son who obeys his father in action rather than in words only.

118. According to the *TDNT*, the term "disciple" had a broad meaning in ancient Greek that also subsumed an intellectual link between people who were considerably

ciples in NT times were expected to follow their master in every respect, often literally imitating him,[119] and indeed, Jesus himself also asserted that "A disciple is not above the teacher, it is enough for the disciple to be like the teacher" (Matt 10:24–25).[120] Thus, by training the first generation of the succession of disciples, Jesus provided a paradigm that was to be replicated, thereby rendering all his future followers "sent ones" and "senders" at the same time. This process is reminiscent of Abraham being commissioned to multiply his righteousness on a larger scale to a new "task force"—the nation of Israel he was to become the father of—but what adds further significance to this process in Jesus' case is the fact that, as he explained at the Last Supper, the teaching he conveyed to the first generation of disciples originally came from the Father: "I have called you friends, because I have made known to you *everything* that I have heard from my Father" (John 15:15; emphasis added).

In sum, when Jesus pronounced to his disciples as part of his act of commissioning that "As the Father has sent me, so I send you" (John 20:21), he identified their missionary mandate with his own, and by emphasizing *obedience* as one of the central aspects of being a disciple, he highlighted the same quality that—as we saw in chapter 5—led him to be victorious over both human temptations and Satan's deliberate attempts to deflect him from his course. By presenting the Great Commission, Jesus conveyed his trust in the fact that the succession of Christian disciples would have the necessary integrity to fulfil the role of being obedient stewards of the earth, thereby enabling progressive creation to run its full course. Commissioning a section of humanity to act as "ambassadors for Christ" (2 Cor 5:20) was thus a declaration of hope; it was an indication of the possibility that the social crisis that had plagued humanity ever since the Fall could in time be resolved. In order to support these standard bearers, Jesus promised them that they would "receive power when the Holy Spirit has come upon you" (Acts 1:8), and he also reassured them that "I am with you always, to the end of the age" (Matt 28:20).

---

removed in time; for example, there was a widespread view that Socrates was "the true μαθητής of Homer," because of the shared inner fellowship. Rengstorf, "Μαθητής," 416–17.

119. See Wilkins, "Disciples," 206.

120. Davies and Allison explain the motif of *"Imitation Christi"* as follows, "The Christian Lord is, for Matthew, the incarnation of proper Christian behavior and therefore its model. His words and deeds supply an example that demands and fortifies at the same time." Davies and Allison, *Matthew*, vol. 2, 197. For similar views, see e.g., Harvey "Mission," 43; Luz, *Matthew 1–7*, 63.

6.4 Summary

The three assignments that Jesus gave his followers had important bearings on the ongoing transformation process of humankind. Linked to the essence of corporeal existence, the Eucharist offers a recurring reminder of Jesus' sacrificial death, which fosters the believers' union with the living God and activates love in them. The Lord's Prayer helps to align petitioners with God's creative purposes and offers cleansing and protection so that they can stand firm in the face of the inevitable difficulties that they are confronted with. Finally, the Great Commission stands as evidence for the fact that a section of the human population was ready to fulfil the role of stewardship over material creation; accordingly, by training a group of handpicked disciples and then providing a paradigm of replication, Jesus raised up a lasting succession of stewards. In this way, the progression of material creation that was derailed during the Fall got back on track: Jesus reset the trajectory of the first Adam that deviated from God's creative purpose—and thus led to sin and death—onto a gradually *converging* course leading to righteousness and life in new creation. The work of the new society of stewards was to be empowered—as the Great Commission confirms—by the indwelling Holy Spirit and Jesus' never-ceasing presence, with the Eucharist and the Lord's Prayer helping to keep believers aware of, and attuned to, this divine source of power. In this way they can be aligned to God's creative purpose and fulfil their role as stewards of the earth. Chapter 7 will consider further teaching in the NT canon on the nature of the optimal human conduct that can maximize the effectiveness of human stewardship.

7

Humanity's Plight and "Fighting the Good Fight of the Faith . . ."

IT WAS ARGUED AT the beginning of the previous chapter that the Scriptures provide extensive teaching and advice on how believers should conduct themselves in the face of the difficulties they are bound to encounter, and that through adherence to these teachings, the readers are in effect positioning themselves within the ongoing transformation process as active agents who are called to deal with various emerging internal and external challenges. The focus of the current chapter is this dimension of the biblical material: The first two sections survey these challenges by offering an overview of the biblical description of humanity's plight in relation to various underlying human weaknesses and related temptations. Following this, the second half of the chapter considers a range of practical advice and exhortations present in the canon for the purpose of helping Christian believers to "fight the good fight of the faith" (1 Tim 6:12) and thus to fully participate in, and benefit from, the ongoing transformation process within progressive creation.

7.1 The Threefold Nature of Human Struggle

The previous chapters have outlined three fundamental areas of vulnerability that can divert people from following God's will (i.e., cause them to sin): the imperfection of their corporeal creatureliness; the deficient social system that emerged when humans became social beings; and human susceptibility to the interference of hostile spiritual forces. In his overview of temptation in Markan soteriology, Ernest Best summarizes this trio of potential urges to sin as follows:

> Looking back now over the path which we have traversed from the Old Testament through late Judaism to the New Testament period we see that there are three ways in which a man may be incited to do evil: temptation may start within himself, it may start in the world around him and it may start supernaturally through an assault by the powers of evil.[1]

Christian theology has traditionally referred to the threefold source of human vulnerability as "the world, the flesh, and the devil,"[2] and a prominent example of this wording that spread the phrase in the English language occurs in the Litany of the Anglican Book of Common Prayer, which asks for deliverance "from all the deceits of the world, the flesh, and the devil." The canon refers to this triad in several places, but a closer look at the usage of the first two concepts—the "world" and the "flesh"—reveals that they occur with a range of different senses[3] and, as we shall see below, they are also used as shorthand for notions that go beyond the simple semantic referents of the terms. For this reason, the three facets of human vulnerability would be better described in more specific terms such as *corporeality, sociality,* and *spiritual corruptibility;* however, even these categories do not denote sharp divisions, because the three areas are often closely connected. The joint working of their concerted power will be apparent in the following overview.

---

1. Best, *Temptation*, 54–55. For a similar conclusion, see C. E. Arnold, *Three Crucial Questions*, 32.

2. E.g., Thomas Aquinas in *Summa Theologica* (III.41.1; see also I.114.1) and Luther in *Sermons on the Catechism* (1528) in Dillenberger, *Martin Luther*, 226. The Sixth Decree of the Council of Trent (on Justification, 1547) also highlighted "the combat which yet remains with the flesh, with the world, with the devil."

3. E.g., Hultgren explains that while Paul often uses "flesh" to refer to the arena in which sinful inclinations reside, in some Pauline passages the term appears in a neutral sense meaning earthly existence (e.g., Gal 2:20; 2 Cor 10:3; Phil 1:22, 24) or even human standards (e.g., 1 Cor 1:26; 2 Cor 1:17). Hultgren, *Romans*, 300–301. Keener also emphasizes that in NT times "flesh" was not understood as inherently evil but "some Jews employed the term for human weakness in its susceptibility to sin" (*Romans*, 96). The Eerdmans Bible Dictionary offers a good illustration of the varied portrayal of the notion of "world" in the NT canon by contrasting the usage of John 3:16 which states that "God so loved the world that he gave his only Son" with the warning in 1 John 2:15 that one should "not love the world" because "The love of the Father is not in those who love the world." Myers, ed., 1066. For an overviews of the biblical use of the two terms, see e.g., Sasse, "Κοσμέω," 868–98; Schweizer et al., "Σάρξ," 98–151.

The "Triple Alliance" of
Corporeality, Sociality, and Spiritual Corruptibility

As we saw in Chapter 5, the spirit in Eliphaz's dream in the Book of Job had a disparaging view of humans,

> who live in houses of clay,
>> whose foundation is in the dust,
>> who are crushed like a moth.
> Between morning and evening they are destroyed;
>> they perish forever without any regarding it.
> Their tent-cord is plucked up within them,
>> and they die devoid of wisdom. (4:19–21)

While the motivation behind instilling this view into Job's friends was evidently wrong, the picture itself is not entirely inaccurate because the corporeal reality of human existence is fragile—or as Matt 26:41 puts it, "the flesh is weak." For example, in discussing the ascetic life of the desert fathers, Benedicta Ward emphasizes the power of humanity's physiological needs when she concludes that even for these spiritual warriors the "control of the appetite was never over; it is instructive that it is gluttony as much as sexuality which was their continuous field of battle."[4] Consistent with this observation, the biblical canon highlights several areas of corporeal existence that can render people self-centered and can thus turn them away from God, ranging from metabolic needs[5] and yearnings for material possessions[6] to sexual desires[7] and the fear of pain and death.[8]

---

4. Ward, "Introduction," 37.

5. E.g., Num 11:4–6 narrates that the Israelites had such an overwhelming desire for meat and other produce which they used to have before the exodus that they wept and regretted leaving Egypt; in fact, according to Phil 3:19, human beings can be so vulnerable in this respect that for some "their god is the belly."

6. According to Jas 4:1–4, this can lead to serious interpersonal conflicts and even to murder, and indeed, guidelines on ownership issues and disputes make up a large part of the ordinances in the Book of Exodus. Also, the love of wealth is described in several places as a major source of temptation that, according to the warning of 1 Tim 6:9–10, can plunge people "into ruin and destruction" and is "a root of all kinds of evil."

7. These are frequently presented as exerting corrupting power, associated with sinful behaviors such as fornication, adultery, and rape (e.g., King David's adultery with Bathsheba in 2 Samuel 11). In the Sermon on the Mount, Jesus specifically warned not only against committing adultery but also against engaging in lustful fantasizing (Matt 5:27–30), and Eph 5:3 characterizes fornication as being so perilous that it "must not even be mentioned among you, as is proper among saints."

8. Exodus 14 expressively describes that the Israelites' fear of death was so strong when Pharaoh was closing on them in pursuit that it overrode all their previous experiences of the might of the Lord and led them to wish to return to slavery in Egypt (Exod 14:11–12). Even Jesus experienced in Gethsemane—as we saw in chapter 5—the concentrated fear of the flesh, that is, the dread of pain, torture, and death.

Regarding the second facet of human vulnerabilities, *sociality*, chapter 3 described how the co-existence and interdependence of human beings aggregated the deficiencies of the flesh, and there is ample evidence throughout the canon that the social structures developed by humankind are often flawed or unjust, oppress the weak and the righteous, and can promote sinful behavior. For example, we read in Amos in reference to the society of the Israelites that "you trample on the poor and take from them levies of grain . . . you who afflict the righteous, who take a bribe, and push aside the needy in the gate" (5:11–12), and Numbers 11–14 offer a sobering account of a process whereby a new leadership structure—the appointment of seventy elders—set up by God himself to alleviate Moses's burdens was undermined by a series of human failings and thus became ineffective in preventing a rebellion against Moses. The subsequent books of the Old Testament bear witness to the fact that leadership issues remained a continuing problem among the Israelites,[9] and Matthew's Gospel records that Jesus also expressed compassion for the crowds "because they were harassed and helpless, like sheep without a shepherd" (Matt 9:36).

The New Testament also presents fundamental problems with the world order that include but also go beyond inadequate social systems when it describes the overall nature of the world as being estranged from God; for example, the term "world" sometimes takes on a meaning that places it in opposition to new creation (e.g., Rom 12:2) and it also represents a spirit that is contrary to the Holy Spirit (e.g., 1 Cor 2:12), is alienated from Jesus (e.g., John 8:23), and functions as an active source of diversion from faithfulness (e.g., Matt 13:22; 1 John 2:15–16). The association of the world with an inherently sinful state is expressed particularly starkly in Jas 4:4, where it is stated that any "friendship with the world is enmity with God." Translating the scriptural language into modern social categories, theologians have equated the evil influence of the world order with various immoral aspects of the prevailing society and culture, including depraved social values and traditions, oppressive political regimes, and corrupt economic structures; they have also introduced some expressive new terminology—such as "structural sin," "social sin," and "systematic social evil"[10]—to convey the

---

9. E.g., in Jer 50:6 God declares, "My people have been lost sheep; their shepherds have led them astray," and Ezekiel was instructed to "prophesy against the shepherds of Israel" (34:2), so he announced, "You have not strengthened the weak, you have not healed the sick, you have not bound up the injured, you have not brought back the strayed, you have not sought the lost, but with force and harshness you have ruled them" (v. 4). See also Mic 3 for an extended criticism of the "heads of Jacob and rulers of the house of Israel" (v. 1).

10. E.g., Ayo, *Lord's Prayer*, 97; Eddy and Beilby, "Spiritual Warfare," 33; González Faus, "Sin," 537.

recognition that individual-level sinfulness can be elevated onto a higher, societal level where it can be locked into pervasive and entrenched social realities with far-reaching negative consequences. Such social evil, as Nicholas Ayo states succinctly, "traps good people in a web of bad deeds,"[11] resulting in oppressive bondage instilled by human society through its sociopolitical institutions, as manifested for example by a variety of "isms" such as racism, sexism, nationalism, fascism, or materialism.

In some NT passages the inadequacy of the world order is characterized in an even more sinister manner, describing the social realm of humanity as a sphere that belongs to Satan, the "ruler/god of this world" (John 12:31; 2 Cor 4:4; see also 1 John 5:19). This creates a link to the third component of the triad of human vulnerabilities, the susceptibility to the corrupting influences of the *devil*. Some have argued that the devil only brings to the fore existing flaws in humanity, not unlike an *agent provocateur*, punishing sinners so that this may lead to their rehabilitation,[12] and Jesus' assertion in Mark 7:21 that evil resides within humans is consistent with such a claim: "For it is from within, from the human heart, that evil intentions come." To be sure, one might contend that during the Fall creation was derailed because it *could* be derailed. However, as will be shown below in the discussion on temptation, the canon provides many examples where Satan is described as going well *beyond* merely enhancing the sinful leanings and propensities of humanity by also capitalizing on other vulnerabilities of the flesh—such as its susceptibility to pain, disease, injury, and death—in an effort to bring out the worst in God's creatures, thereby turning them away from hearing God's word and leading them into bondage.[13] In this sense, Satan is not merely amplifying a pre-existing problem but is part of the problem itself; in Ladd's passionate words, "He is the tempter who seeks through affliction to turn believers away from the gospel (1 Thess 3:5), to hinder God's servants in their ministry (1 Thess 2:18), who raises up false apostles to pervert the truth of the gospel (2 Cor 11:14), who is ever seeking to overwhelm God's people

---

11. Ayo, *Lord's Prayer*, 97.

12. E.g., Kelly, *Satan*, 58, 171.

13. This view is also implied by the metaphor "the flaming arrows of the evil one" (that are launched at the believers) in Eph 6:16, which is seen by many commentators as referring to more than merely the intensification of the recipients' inner cravings; e.g., O'Brien submits that "the burning arrows depict, in highly metaphorical language, every kind of attack launched by the devil and his hosts against the people of God . . . and include not only every kind of temptation to ungodly behavior, doubt, and despair, but also external assaults, such as persecution or false teaching" (*Ephesians*, 480). For similar views, see e.g., C. E. Arnold, *Ephesians*, 118; Lincoln, *Ephesians*, 450.

(Eph 6:11, 12, 16), and who is even able to bring his attacks in the form of bodily afflictions to God's choicest servants (2 Cor 12:7)."[14]

Despite the validity of these observations, Marshall is right to emphasize that although the "present world has become the realm of Satan, where people are under his control (Mark 3:24–25) . . . to some extent the captives are *willing captives*, who need to shake themselves free of what binds them" (emphasis added).[15] As already addressed briefly in chapter 5, the Scriptures describe Satan in several places as acting through *human agents* without himself or his demonic forces being directly involved in the events. These human agents must have therefore responded in one way or another to Satan's solicitation to sin, and Jesus' statement to the unbelieving Jews in John 8:44—"You are from your father the devil, and you choose to do your father's desires"—not only highlights the fact that such responses may involve a degree of choice, but also underlines the prevalence of such behind-the-scene manipulation. Indeed, beginning with the Fall, the Scriptures present evil spiritual interferences and the imperfections of humankind at the individual and social levels as being inextricably intertwined, a confluence which has aptly been called the "triple alliance"[16] (Cantalamessa) to express the interrelated nature of the three sources of sin.[17]

The predominant portrayal in the canon of how the triple alliance of corporeality, sociality, and spiritual corruptibility impacts the lives of humans concerns various forms of *temptation* that people are exposed to. Indeed, the Bible specifically refers to Satan as the "tempter" (Matt 4:3; 1 Thess 3:5), thereby highlighting that his effort to expose people to sinful enticements and urges is one of his main undertakings. Let us examine more closely the nature of the process of temptation before we discuss, in the second part of the chapter, how it can be resisted.

---

14. Ladd, *Theology of the New Testament, Revised,* 440.

15. Marshall, *Concise New Testament Theology*, 21.

16. E.g., Cantalamessa, *Come Creator Spirit*, 287.

17. The dynamic interplay of these three strands has been articulated clearly by Arnold in the conclusion of his analysis of the principalities and powers in Paul's letters: "Paul's teaching suggests that the explanation for our behavior is not to be found exclusively in human nature or in terms of the world's influence. Similarly, an exclusively demonic explanation for deviant behavior is unduly myopic. Rather, we should explain behavior on the basis of human nature, environment and the demonic—all three simultaneously. One part may play a leading role, but all three parts need to be considered." C. E. Arnold, *Powers of Darkness*, 125–26.

7.2 Temptation

In both Hebrew and Greek, the semantic domain of the word "temptation" (*nāsâ* and *peirasmos*, respectively) has a broader range than their English equivalent as it denotes as well as "temptation," also "testing" and "trial" at the same time, and the term is used in the Scriptures to refer not only to the actions of Satan but also to those of God (e.g., Deut 8:2), Jesus (John 6:6), and humans (e.g., Mark 10:2). All these different usages, however, share in common the experience in humans of an internal conflict between one's better judgement and an urge to do something that promises to *satisfy* some personal or social need or *avoid* some hardship or affliction. Curiously, although the phenomenon of temptation/testing is a salient human experience and it also appears many times in the Bible—the terms *nāsâ* and *peirasmos* occur in the sense of temptation/testing over 60 times in the canon—the notion of temptation has received little attention in psychological research[18] and is considered somewhat marginal even in theology.[19]

The experience of temptation is closely related to the human vulnerabilities discussed above in the sense that humans are tempted because they *can* be tempted. In biblical usage the term is associated with three main purposes in this respect: to *test* what a person is really like (i.e., evaluating human vulnerabilities), to *strengthen* a person's faith (i.e., decreasing human vulnerabilities), and to *corrupt* a person and thus turn him/her away from God (i.e., increasing and capitalizing on human vulnerabilities).[20]

---

18. The American Psychological Association's official database, "PsycINFO," lists fewer than 500 entries related to the term, which is a very low number relative to the 68,000+ entries related to "motivation" for example. For similar conclusions, see Godin, "Psychology of Temptation," 74–75; Oates, *Temptation*. Moreover, the use of "temptation," in psychological research is largely restricted to the examination of human desires that are linked to forbidden or obviously harmful acts such as illegal drug use, smoking, or over-eating, which suggests that the rarity of the term in psychology is related to the fact that it is perceived to carry too much moral loading for general use, and therefore André Godin is right to conclude that "temptation is a situation exclusively hemmed in by religious expectations or reflections" ("Psychology of Temptation," 75).

19. E.g., in one of the rare book-length discussions of the topic of temptation in theology, Wayne Oates poses the question, "When was the last time you heard a sermon, read an article or a book, or had a serious conversation with a friend about temptation? The word is still in our dictionaries, but it is not used very much" (*Temptation*, 11). And as Oates continues, "As I began gathering materials for writing this book, I was immediately struck by the scarcity of contemporary books and serious articles on temptation" (ibid.). This situation has hardly changed over the past twenty-five years (i.e., since the publication of Oates's book).

20. Sometimes, however, a specific act can serve multiple purposes: God for example may allow Satan to tempt a person to sin in order to test the person's faithfulness and integrity, and if the experience is processed successfully (i.e., without sinning), it can

These three functions make particular sense from a progressive creational perspective:

- *Testing* can be understood as a way for the Lord to assess how humanity's transformation is progressing and whether key characters (e.g., Job or Abraham) or people groups (e.g., the Israelites as a nation) are mature enough to move on to a higher level.

- *Strengthening* is linked to the process of personal maturation of humans, so much so that James 1:2–4 actually advises believers that they should rejoice about undergoing temptation: "brothers and sisters, whenever you face trials of any kind, consider it nothing but joy, because you know that the testing of your faith produces endurance; and let endurance have its full effect, so that you may be mature and complete, lacking in nothing." The same maturation process is also highlighted in Romans when Paul declares that "we also boast in our sufferings, knowing that suffering produces endurance, and endurance produces character, and character produces hope" (5:3–4), and several other biblical passages compare this maturation process to a "refining fire" in analogy with the smelting of mineral ore.[21]

- Finally, the *corrupting* function—which is the main semantic domain of the English word "temptation"—directly targets the imperfect, transitional character of human creatureliness: Although the temptation to do wrong is often connected to the works of Satan and his forces in the canon, James 1:14 emphasizes that "one is tempted by one's own desire, being lured and enticed by it," which indicates that the roots of temptation lie in human incompleteness. The pivotal role of this function in defining the plight of humankind warrants a closer look at this process.

The Temptation to Do Wrong

The essence of the corrupting function of temptation is to incite a person to do something that he/she knows is wrong (i.e., induce to sin). Therefore,

---

contribute to the maturation and strengthening of the person as a kind of refining fire.

21. One of the most striking examples of how the "refining fire" is applied for the sake of purifying and maturing God's people is Zech 13:8–9, and it is of note that Zechariah's prophecy points to the same conclusion as James' declaration: "Blessed is anyone who endures temptation. Such a one has stood the test and will receive the crown of life that the Lord has promised to those who love him" (1:12). See also Prov 17:3, 1 Pet 1:6–7.

the prerequisite for successful temptation is to make the "wrong" aspect of the act appear either more desirable or less negative somehow. The biblical narratives present three main ways of achieving this objective: through *seduction, affliction,* or *deception.*

Seduction involves attaching some coveted element to the "wrong" aspect, such as money, pleasure, power, or some other benefit. The added attraction can sometimes be of considerable magnitude, such as Satan's offer in the wilderness to give Jesus control over the whole earth; however, it may also involve more mundane enticement, for example the lure of alleviating hunger (as in Jesus' first temptation) or satisfying a sexual urge. Sexual desire is presented in the Bible as a particularly potent weapon of temptation; for example, in the concluding part of a series of paternal instructions Proverbs 7 specifically highlights the dangers of sinful sexual behavior by describing how "seductive speech" (v. 21) can lead someone onto "the way to Sheol, going down to the chambers of death" (v. 27). The overpowering strength of sexual temptation is attested to by 2 Samuel 11, which offers a vivid description of how the sight of Bathsheba naked led King David first to adultery and then to murder; as M. Green concludes, "It is a story that has been repeated countless times. Indeed, lust has become one of the major weapons, perhaps the most important of all, in Satan's armory."[22]

Affliction operates on a different principle from seduction: Instead of attaching additional value to the "wrong" element, it increases the *relative* attraction value of "wrong" by inflicting suffering on the individual and thus creating a situation where doing wrong will offer relief or where resisting wrong will no longer make sense; in other words, with the worsening of someone's overall circumstances, the "wrong" aspect becomes more attractive or less marked by contrast. The most obvious form of affliction in NT times—frequently mentioned in the canon—involved coercion by means of the *persecution* of believers, a process that leaves all subtlety behind and expresses the bare bones of temptation: direct pressure is exerted on people in order to turn them away from God. In 1 Thessalonians, for example, Paul warned the church in Thessaloniki that they "were to suffer persecution" (3:4), and he specifically linked this to the devil's work in his statement that he was "afraid that somehow the tempter had tempted you and that our labor had been in vain" (v. 5).[23]

---

22. M. Green, *Satan's Downfall,* 68.

23. The theme is reiterated with regard to the church in Smyrna in Revelation, where the devil's specific involvement in the acts of persecution is explicitly stated: "Do not fear what you are about to suffer. Beware, the devil is about to throw some of you into prison so that you may be tested, and for ten days you will have affliction. Be faithful until death, and I will give you the crown of life" (2:10).

Deception follows a third approach to corruption whereby the deterrent value of "wrong" is *reduced* through the creation of confusion in the targeted subject about what is wrong and what is right. Temptation of this type can be seen as frustrated or befuddled motivation: When humans submit to it, they believe they are doing the right thing, or at least that they are not doing anything overtly sinful. The strategy can take many forms, such as false teaching, raising doubts about the truth, blinding the person's faculties to see the truth, and even outright lying—after all, the devil is not called "the father of lies" in John 8:44 for no reason, and Revelation 12:9 simply describes him as "the deceiver of the whole world." For maximum effect, deception is often accompanied by seduction and affliction; for example, Satan offered Eve a highly attractive fruit—"it was a delight to the eyes, and was to be desired to make one wise" (Gen 3:6)—while accompanying this source of seduction with the raising of doubts about God's instructions through subtle but effective deception (in 3:1 and 4: "Did God say . . . ?" "You will not die . . .").

Deception is by definition as inconspicuous and subtle as possible, and John Stott rightly points out that Satan is "at his wiliest when he succeeds in persuading people that he does not exist."[24] Page adds that, as a master of subterfuge, Satan can even turn an act of religious devotion into the launchpad for an attack upon the believer, which is illustrated by the fact that in Matt 4:6 (during Jesus' temptation in the wilderness) the devil cites Scripture to Jesus in his attempt to win him over. This point is developed more fully by Paul in 2 Corinthians, where he underlines the fact that the servants of Satan can masquerade as Christians and that Satan can disguise himself as God's angel (as seen for example in Eliphaz's vision discussed in chapter 5).

Finally, it is important to emphasize that temptation is far from being a rare or unique phenomenon that happens to few people only. The Scriptures confirm that to experience some form or degree of temptation is an inevitable corollary of being human; for example, 1 Cor 10:13 states, "No testing has overtaken you that is not common to *everyone*" (emphasis added; cf. also Heb 4:15), and in Matt 18:7 Jesus declared, "Woe to the world because of stumbling blocks! Occasions for stumbling *are bound to* come" (emphasis added). On the other hand, 1 Cor 10 also offers believers a word of hope: "God is faithful, and he will not let you be tested beyond your strength, but with the testing he will also provide the way out so that you may be able to endure it" (v. 13).

24. Stott, *Ephesians*, 265. This point is particularly relevant in our contemporary times when a significant proportion of believers regard the devil merely as a myth or a symbol.

7.3 Fighting the Good Fight of the Faith

Having reviewed the main areas of human vulnerability and the ensuing temptations that form the primary battleground of the human plight, let us consider how Christian believers are encouraged in the Bible to withstand these temptations and, more broadly, what criteria are presented in Scripture for successful human conduct during the transitional age of inaugurated eschatology. A key passage in this respect is 1 Tim 6:11–12, which—after describing the depravity of the world in some detail—offers a concise summary of "fighting the good fight of the faith": "But as for you, man of God, shun all this; pursue righteousness, godliness, faith, love, endurance, gentleness. Fight the good fight of the faith; take hold of the eternal life, to which you were called . . ."

This passage suggests that it may be possible for believers to take hold of eternal life, but in order to do so they must "fight," a point which is affirmed in the solemn farewell note in 2 Tim 4:7, "I have fought the good fight, I have finished the race, I have kept the faith." Although the specific strategies of the "good fight" are not described in these passages, the use of the military metaphor is clearly intended to evoke the image of an effortful struggle in one's pursuit of one's faith. That the martial tenor of this portrayal was deliberate is corroborated by the fact that the image of the "Christian warrior" is pervasive in the NT canon (see e.g., Matt 10:34; Rom 13:12; 2 Cor 6:7; Eph 6:10–17; Phil 2:25; 1 Thess 5:8; 1 Tim 6:12; 2 Tim 2:3–4; Phlm 2; 1 Pet 4:1), and in several places there is also mention of Christians being involved in a "war" (1 Pet 2:11; Jas 4:1; Rom 7:23; 2 Cor 10:3). The sense of militancy is further augmented by the use of the verb "conquer/overcome" (*nikaō*) in the New Testament in describing the success for believers; in Revelation, for example, the verb is part of the concluding statement of all the letters to the seven churches in chapters 2–3, and it is associated each time with an eschatological promise (2:7, 11, 17, 26–28; 3:5, 12, 21). Although the specific letters contain markedly different messages, Bauckham stresses that their common conclusion presents the act of conquering as "the only way for Christians to reach their eschatological destiny."[25] Furthermore, at the end of revelation "conquering/overcoming" is directly linked to receiving eternal life, and the act is then contrasted with sinfulness and eternal death:

> To the thirsty I will give water as a gift from the spring of the water of life. Those who conquer will inherit these things, and I will be their God and they will be my children. But as for the cowardly, the faithless, the polluted, the murderers, the fornicators,

---

25. Bauckham, *Theology of Revelation*, 92.

the sorcerers, the idolaters, and all liars, their place will be in the
lake that burns with fire and sulphur, which is the second death.
(Rev 21:6–8)

Thus, the language of warfare is firmly rooted in the Bible, portraying the struggle facing believers as comparable to the intensity of a military
fight. The other side of the coin, however, is that a central aspect of Jesus'
teaching was the rejection of any form of militancy; for example in the Sermon on the Mount he preached that believers should love their enemies
and pray for those who prosecute them (Matt 5:44), and that rather than
resisting evildoers, one should turn the other cheek when being struck (v.
39), which is rather different to what one would normally associate with a
disposition to warfare.[26] And although Luke's account of the Last Supper
does include a statement by Jesus that can be read as extending his initial
mission directive by also including weaponry—"And the one who has no
sword must sell his cloak and buy one" (Luke 22:36)—the interpretation
that Christians should respond to hostility literally with a sword is explicitly
invalidated a few verses later in Luke's Gospel when Jesus rebuked Peter
who drew a sword at Jesus' arrest (vv. 49–51),[27]

Moreover, a closer look at the linguistic context of the specific military
metaphors in the canon also reveals a peculiar feature, namely that they
tend not to be related to any overt enemy; for example, even though the use
of the verb "conquer/overcome" is clearly associated with warfare—because
failure carries the possibility of death[28]—in none of the instances cited
above is it accompanied by a direct object, leaving it largely unspecified who
or what needs to be conquered. Similarly, all mentions of "waging war" cited
earlier refer to *internal* battles rather than facing an actual enemy, a point
explicitly underlined by Paul when he states in 2 Cor 10:3 that "we do not
wage war according to human standards." That is, although the Scriptures
strongly imply that following Jesus will mean that believers will enter some

26. And so is Jesus' further teaching that believers should "do good to those who
hate you, bless those who curse you" (Luke 6:27–28). Indeed, instead of fighting back,
Jesus declared that "if anyone forces you to go one mile, go also the second mile" (Matt
5:41), and when Peter talked to the household of Cornelius, he stated clearly that the
message God sent to the people of Israel involved "preaching peace by Jesus Christ"
(Acts 10:36).

27. See Green, *Luke,* 774–75; he also points out that Jesus' exasperated response to
his disciples in v. 38 ("It is enough") when they misunderstood Jesus' teaching to be an
encouragement to literally possess weaponry further confirms the symbolic use of the
military language.

28. God's pronouncement in Revelation 21:7–8 offers only two options for humanity: either people conquer and become God's children or they will suffer the second
death in the lake of fire; see also Aune, *Revelation 6–16,* 151.

kind of "warzone," the battle they join is a curious one in that it does not involve any combat in the traditional military sense.

These curious nonmilitant connotations of the biblical references of "fighting the good fight of the faith fight" are fully consistent with the conclusion of the previous section, namely that the primary battleground for believers is their inner struggle against temptation. Indeed, in Jesus' "Apocalyptic Discourse" (Matt 24:1—25:46) the verb "endure" is used in a similar function to how "conquer" was used at the end of Revelation cited earlier ("To the thirsty I will give water as a gift from the spring of the water of life. Those who conquer will inherit these things" Rev 21:6): "But the one who endures to the end will be saved" (Matt 24:13). We may gain further insights into the nature of this internal Christian fight by considering Paul's discussion of the existence of a bitter conflict between two warring "mindsets" in Romans 7–8.

Paul's Conception of Two Warring Mindsets

The New Testament contains several expressions of the antithesis between what Dunn calls two "opposing patterns of mind-set and lifestyle . . . two basic levels on which individuals can operate,"[29] with the most elaborate description to be found in Romans 7–8 (and especially in 7:14–23 and 8:5–8). The essence of this conflict is summarized in 8:5–6 as follows:

> For those who live according to the flesh set their minds on the things of the flesh, but those who live according to the Spirit set their minds on the things of the Spirit. To set the mind on the flesh is death, but to set the mind on the Spirit is life and peace.

Galatians 5 reiterates the contrast between the two directions associated with the flesh and the Spirit, and by doing so it affirms the more general existence of a "'two regime' framework that is fundamental to all of Paul's teaching (and, indeed, to all of the New Testament)" (Moo)[30]:

> Live by the Spirit, I say, and do not gratify the desires of the flesh. For what the flesh desires is opposed to the Spirit, and what the Spirit desires is opposed to the flesh; for these are opposed to each other, to prevent you from doing what you want. (Gal 5:16–17)

29. Dunn, *Romans 1–8*, 442.
30. Moo, *Romans*, 240.

In an effort to find a label that captures the essence of the two opposing human orientations, scholars have used a wide range of phrases such as
"spheres of the Spirit/flesh,"[31] "basic orientations,"[32] "possibilities of human
existence,"[33] and "mind-sets or attitudes,"[34] but attempts to find a fitting term
have been hampered by the complexity of the human concepts involved in
defining the issue, such as "body," "mind," and "soul," and within the latter
domain, "cognition," "motivation," and "affect." Although all of these notions have been in circulation since the time of ancient Greek philosophers,
they have not been used in any consistent way either in philosophy[35] or
in modern psychology,[36] and neither does the biblical canon include any
precise anthropological definition for them.[37] Arguably, the most clear-cut
treatment of the matter in the Bible occurs in Rom 8:5–6 (cited above),
and on the basis of this passage, commentators have increasingly adopted
the contemporary term "mindset" to refer to the sphere where the conflict
described by Paul takes place.[38] While this is by and large a satisfying rendering of the semantic domain of the original Greek word *phronēma* (Rom
8:6, 7, 27), we need to emphasize that the term "mindset" is used here in a
modern psychological sense rather than within the philosophical context
of the "mind-body" dualism, where the "mind" is primarily associated with
cognitive faculties. Indeed, exegetes have stressed that *phronēma*—as with
the psychological understanding of "mindset"—subsumes emotional, mo-
tivational, and spiritual capacities besides the cognitive facet.[39] A further

31. E.g., Keener, *Romans*, 101.

32. E.g., Bertram, "Φρήν," 232.

33. E.g., Byrne, *Romans*, 238.

34. E.g., Jewett, *Romans*, 486.

35. See, e.g., Betz, "Inner Human Being," 315–41; Lorenz, "Theories of the Soul."

36. See, e.g., Scherer, "Plato's Legacy"; Matthews and Zeidner, "Trilogy of the
Mind"; Mayer et al., "Conation, Affect, and Cognition."

37. E.g., D. Wenham underlines the "notorious difficulty of Paul's anthropological
terminology" ("Christian Life," 85), and Hultgren also concludes that in Romans 7 the
"anthropological aspects appear rather imprecise" (*Romans*, 290). For an overview, see
Betz, "Inner Human Being."

38. E.g., Byrne states, "The modern term "mind-set" usefully captures the sense
in a general kind of way" (*Romans*, 244), and Dunn concurs: "The modern composite
'mind-set' probably comes closest to the sense, including both a fixed and resolute way
of thinking" (*Romans*, 426).

39. E.g., Bertram explains in the *TNDT* that "*phrēn*," which is the root of the word
(usually used in the plural form "*phrenes*"), was understood to determine the nature
and strength of the human spirit and its emotions, as well as the intellect. Bertram,
"Φρήν," 220. Moo also maintains that in Greek the root "connotes not a purely mental
process but, more broadly, the general direction of the will, encompassing 'all the faculties of the soul—reason, understanding, and affections'" (*Romans*, 487), a view which is

analogy between the Greek and English terms (i.e., *phronēma* and mind-set) is that they both express a sense of *intentionality* as they refer to the outcome of "setting one's mind on something."[40] This active sense is well illustrated, for example, by Jesus' reproval of Peter: "Get behind me, Satan! For you are setting your mind [*phroneis*] not on divine things but on hu-man things" (Mark 8:33).

Thus, the fundamental internal tension in human beings that Paul re-fers to in his epistles may be portrayed as a conflict of two mindsets—one that is flesh-centered, and the other that is Spirit-centered—and what is particularly important from the perspective of the current chapter is that these opposing mindsets are associated with two distinct *life trajectories*, one leading to death, the other to life. This is directly stated in Rom 8:6 (cited above) and is then reiterated a few verses later: "if you live according to the flesh, you will die; but if by the Spirit you put to death the deeds of the body, you will live" (8:13). This duality echoes Paul's earlier teaching in Rom 5:12–21—discussed in chapter 3—concerning the two contrasting trajecto-ries associated with the first and the last Adam, one leading to sin and death, the other to righteousness and life;[41] in fact, N. T. Wright suggests that the clue to understanding the whole passage of Rom 8:1–11 is to see it as "the unfolding of the Adam/Christ contrast of 5:12–21."[42] The fact that these two trajectories are associated with two internal mindsets in Romans 8 points to the conclusion that after Pentecost these mindsets came to *co-exist* in parallel and thus offer humankind a choice: By believing in Jesus Christ and receiving his Spirit one can leave Adam's fleshly trajectory and align with the Spirit-filled trajectory of Jesus Christ. This understanding is endorsed by Dunn in his explanation that in Rom 7:14–23 the conflict between the two "I"s (e.g., in v. 15: "I do not do what I want, but I do the very thing I hate") is testimony to the fact that "the Adam of the old epoch is still alive,"[43] a point he expands on as follows:

---

consistent with Plato's tripartite understanding of the "soul"—see e.g., Scherer, "Plato's Legacy."

40. *Phronēma* is a cognate of the verb *phroneō*, with the *(-ma)* suffix indicating the result or the consequence of the process; see e.g., Byrne, *Romans*, 244; Dunn, *Romans*, 426.

41. Interestingly, in Phil 2:5 believers are encouraged to "have the same mindset as Christ Jesus."

42. Wright, "Romans," 574.

43. Dunn, *Romans*, 405.

> The trouble is, the old epoch itself has not yet run its full course. So long as the resurrection is not yet, the "I" of the old epoch is still alive, still a factor in the believer's experience in this body.[44]

In summary, the curious nature of Christian warfare described above is related to the fact that the primary battleground for the Christian warrior is the frontline between two mindsets, one that is Spirit-centered and one that is flesh-centered and thus susceptible to temptation. This conceptualization is consistent with the "fight" metaphor found in other parts of the NT canon in that it conveys the existence of underlying intentionality, since if it were not possible to exercise at least some degree of volitional control over how one sets one's mind, the repeated calls to do so (e.g., Col 3:2; cf. Matt 6:23) would make no sense.[45] Accordingly, "conquering/overcoming" within the context of the Christian fight can be perceived as *winning the battle of the mindsets*. While Romans 7–8 does not include any concrete suggestions on how this battle can be fought to good effect, but merely specifies the nature and the locus of the conflict, elsewhere in the Scriptures we find extensive advice on how to fight the "good fight of the faith." Two books in the New Testament in particular—Ephesians and James—stand out in terms of the richness of the relevant guidance they contain, and therefore the final part of this chapter will take these texts as the starting point for discussing the practical implications for the plight of the Christian believer.

7.4 The Battle of the Mindsets in Ephesians and James

With the prominence of their pastoral concern, Ephesians and James have traditionally been seen as two of the most "applied/applicable" books of the Bible, containing ample advice both for the Church and for its members on how to conduct themselves in the transitional period leading up to the *Parousia*.[46] This is reflected, for example, by the fact that James contains the

44. Ibid.

45. Indeed, the call to be self-controlled is a recurring message in the NT canon, well illustrated by the fact that "self-control" is one of the key points in Titus 2 (recurring as many as four times: vv. 1, 5, 6, 12) within the summary of what believers should be taught "consistent with sound doctrine" (2:1).

46. E.g., Laws states that James is "the most consistently ethical document in the New Testament" (*James,* 27), and according to Snodgrass, few books have shaped the life and spirituality of Christians more than Ephesians (including the impact on Christian liturgical prayers and short readings). Snodgrass, *Ephesians,* 17. Likewise, Brown ranks only Romans ahead of Ephesians in this respect. R. E. Brown, *New Testament,* 620. For a similar view, see Turner, "Book of Ephesians," 186.

highest frequency of imperative verbs aimed at chastising, exhorting, and encouraging among all the NT books,[47] and the density of verbs in the imperative form (a total of 36) is also a noteworthy feature of the "paraenetic section" of Ephesian (4:1—6:20).[48] In addition, as McCartney rightly emphasizes, the Letter of James contains a "large supply of memorable phrases and aphorisms that encapsulate many aspects of the practical Christian life,"[49] something that could equally be said about Ephesians—after all, who has not heard about the need to "put on the full armor of God" (6:11)? The two books also have some unique relevance to the current work. A passage at the beginning of Ephesians sets the scene for discussing humanity's plight by addressing the temptations of the world, the flesh, and the devil in an integrated manner, offering the clearest example in the whole NT canon of the three components of this triad occurring together:

> You were dead through the trespasses and sins in which you once lived, following the course of this *world*, following the ruler of the *power of the air* [i.e., the devil], the spirit that is now at work among those who are disobedient. All of us once lived among them in the passions of our *flesh*, following the desires of flesh and senses . . . (2:1–3; emphasis added)

Regarding the Letter of James, although at first glance it may appear like a loose collection of pastoral teachings,[50] we can identify some broad, overarching themes that link the distinct episodes together, and foremost of these is the issue of testing/temptation and endurance.[51]

Furthermore, both letters highlight the battle of the mindsets as a framework for the discussion. In Ephesians, non-believers are notably characterized by "the futility of their minds darkened in their understanding alienated from the life of God because of their ignorance and hardness of heart" (4:17–18), and in order to get rid of this "old self" (v. 22) one should be "renewed in the spirit of your minds" (v. 23). In James, one central passage (3:13–18) is fittingly entitled both in the NRSV and the NIV as "*Two Kinds of Wisdom*" as it presents two opposing mindsets described

---

47. Moo, *James*, 1.

48. R. E. Brown, *New Testament*, 623.

49. McCartney, *James*, 1.

50. Dibelius, for example, described it as a rather loose text that "strings together admonitions of general ethical content" (*James*, 3).

51. Reflected e.g., by the fact that the letter starts out with a discussion of this subject in 1:2–4 and then elaborates on it a few verses later in vv. 12–16; accordingly, Marshall concludes that "James is essentially concerned with living the Christian life amid temptation" (*New Testament Theology*, 257).

in a manner that closely parallels the Spirit-centered versus flesh-centered contrast: One wisdom is "from above" and is "pure, then peaceable, gentle, willing to yield, full of mercy and good fruits" (3:17), whereas the other "does not come down from above, but is earthly, unspiritual, devilish" (v. 15). God-centered wisdom is also mentioned at the beginning of the same epistle (Jas 1:5–8), where, significantly, doubters are portrayed as "double-minded" (v. 8), and it is of note that the Letter to the Ephesians also instructs believers to be "careful then how you live, not as *unwise* people but as *wise*" (5:15; emphasis added), a warning that could have come from the passage in James concerning the two kinds of wisdom.[52]

Finally, at the beginning of James 4, an analogy is made between the "cravings that are at war within [the believer]" (v. 1) and "friendship with the world" (v. 4), the latter being declared to be in "enmity with God" (ibid); therefore, as the text reiterates for emphasis, "whoever wishes to be a friend of the world becomes an enemy of God" (ibid). Following this, James makes a momentous declaration: "Submit yourselves therefore to God. Resist the devil, and he will flee from you. Draw near to God, and he will draw near to you" (4:7–8). These three short sentences come to life in the light of our earlier discussion: They offer the reassurance that as long as believers submit themselves to God and draw near to him (i.e., adopt a Spirit-centered mindset), and resist the devil (which, in practical terms, is closely related to resisting the devil-enhanced lure of the flesh-centered mindset), God will draw near to them and the devil will have no choice but to flee. This is surely the epitome of the success of the Christian warrior's "conquering/overcoming." Thus, James situates "drawing near to God" at the heart of victorious Christian warfare, and in 4:8 he reiterates the importance of the battle of the mindsets by referring to sinners as "double-minded" (a rare word which only occurs in the Bible here and in 1:8), which identifies the root of a sinful state in one's double allegiance both to the world and to God.

The following picture of how to "draw near God" and how to fight the "good fight of the faith" will be made with broad brush strokes, in the form of presenting a template consisting of three facets: (a) *adopting* the Spirit-centered mindset, (b) *resisting* any influence that would divert from it, and (c) *consolidating* the Spirit-centered mindset through living it out in one's

---

52. Indeed, Baugh rightly draws a parallel between this latter exhortation and Paul's description of the two mindsets (discussed earlier): "As has marked Paul's exhortations many times previously, there is a behavior to put off from the old, Adamic existence (cf. 4:22) and one to put on in the Last Adam (cf. 4:24), which is marked by truth and righteousness (e.g., 4:25). Here in 5:15 the language is compressed and in effect summarizes what has gone before as rejecting a walk in folly and the need to substitute wisdom instead." Baugh, *Ephesians*, 448.

everyday life. These elements were also present in the three assignments that Jesus gave his followers (discussed in the previous chapter):

- Through fostering the believers' communion with the living God and activating love in them, the Eucharist helps to align them with God's creative purpose, and the "Thou-petitions" of the Lord's prayer further facilitate attuning oneself to God's empowering wavelength (*adopting the Spirit-centered mindset*).

- The "we petitions" of the Lord's Prayer offer cleansing and protection so that believers can stand firm in the face of the various inevitable difficulties they are confronted with (*resisting diverting influences*).

- The Great Commission requires believers to "go," that is, to step out and proactively establish effective and lasting stewardship on earth (*consolidating the mindset through action*).

Adopting a Spirit-centered Mindset:
Singing, Thanksgiving, Humility, and Prayer

Ephesians warns believers to "Be careful then how you live, not as unwise people but as wise" (5:15), and then the text goes on to state that the key to accomplishing this goal is

> [to] be filled with the Spirit, as you sing psalms and hymns and spiritual songs among yourselves, singing and making melody to the Lord in your hearts, giving thanks to God the Father at all times and for everything in the name of our Lord Jesus Christ. (vv. 18–20)

The present imperative form of the verb translated as "be filled" (*plērousthe*) suggests that believers should continuously seek the Spirit's infilling, leading some commentators to interpret the passage in a way that fits the pattern of the progressive creational perspective of this book; for example, O'Brien concludes that "readers are urged to let the Spirit change them more and more into the image of God and Christ,"[53] and Snodgrass states, "Surely the intent is that the persons chosen should be characterized by wisdom and live in tune with God's Spirit."[54] The imperative form "*be filled* with the Spirit" may seem curious in that it indicates that believers have some personal responsibility and volitional control in this matter—af-

---

53. O'Brien, *Ephesians*, 391.
54. Snodgrass, *Ephesians*, 290.

ter all, how can people be commanded to be filled with the sovereign Holy Spirit?[55]—but we should recognize that being instructed thus is entirely consistent with the battle-of-mindsets metaphor: Being filled with the Spirit can be understood as believers successfully attuning themselves to the power of the indwelling Spirit, not unlike having to tune into a radio station before one can receive its broadcast or putting a plug into a socket to receive electricity. Indeed, and in full accord with this proactive view, Eph 5:19–21 lists a series of modifying participles attached to the "be filled" imperative that outline three broad strategies that can help believers to fulfil the admonition:

- *Musical praise and worship:* Singing "psalms and hymns and spiritual songs" (v. 19) can establish a state of mind that resonates with the Spirit, expressively voiced in the text as "making melody to the Lord in your hearts" (v. 19). Similarly, James 5:13 also encourages believers to "sing songs of praise."

- *Thanksgiving:* Musical worship should be accompanied by "giving thanks to God the Father at all times and for everything in the name of our Lord Jesus Christ" (Eph 5:20), a combination that is perhaps most clearly modelled in Rev 11:16–17, where we read that the twenty-four elders "worshiped God, singing, 'We give you thanks, Lord God Almighty . . .'"[56] Giving thanks to God is a regular theme of the NT canon,[57] and in Rom 1:21, for example, Paul directly links the absence of this thankful state of dependence on God to "senseless minds" that are "darkened."

- *Humility:* The final participle in Eph 5:18–20 is usually translated as a separate command, but in fact it is still related grammatically to the primary imperative in v. 18 ("be filled with the Spirit").[58] This participle concerns the instruction to "submit to one another out of reverence for Christ" (v. 21; NIV) and has a salient parallel in the Letter of

55. See e.g., Snodgrass *Ephesians*, 289. Commentators also point out that the wording of the "be filled with the Spirit" command is unusual and unparalleled elsewhere in the Bible; e.g., O'Brien, *Ephesians*, 390; Fee, *God's Empowering Presence*, 721–22.

56. See also 1 Cor 14:15–16: "I will pray with the spirit, but I will pray with the mind also; I will sing praise with the spirit, but I will sing praise with the mind also. Otherwise, if you say a blessing with the spirit, how can anyone in the position of an outsider say the 'Amen' to your thanksgiving, since the outsider does not know what you are saying?"

57. E.g., most of Paul's letters begin with a note of thanksgiving to God (Rom 1:8; 1 Cor 1:4; Phil 1:3; Col 1:3; 1 Thess 1:2; 2:13; 2 Thess 1:3; 2:13; Phlm 1:4); see C. E. Arnold, *Ephesians*, 355; Dunn, *Paul*, 59.

58. See e.g., Fee, *God's Empowering Presence*, 719.

James, where immediately before the passage discussed earlier about resisting the devil, Jas 4:6 cites Prov 3:34—"God opposes the proud, but gives grace to the humble"—and then summarizes the importance of humility in a final admonition: "Humble yourselves before the Lord, and he will exalt you" (Jas 4:10). Linking humility to being exalted is again a recurring motif in the canon,[59] and we have also seen in earlier chapters that the opposite of humility, pride, was a key aspect of both Eve's disobedience and the assumed reason for Satan's deviation from God's purpose.

Prayer

Praise, worship, and thanksgiving are in a broad sense all different aspects of prayer,[60] and submitting oneself in humility is also an essential component of prayer, as evidenced in the Parable of the Pharisee and the Tax Collector (Luke 18:9–14), where Jesus declares that it is the prayer of the person who humbled himself (i.e., the tax collector) that would be answered because "all who humble themselves will be exalted" (v. 14). Prayer is undoubtedly a potent way of attuning to a Spirit-centered mindset, because it involves, by definition, personal communication and some form of an encounter with God.[61] Indeed, both Ephesians and James conclude by highlighting the significance of prayer (Eph 6:18 and Jas 5:13–18):

- The emphasis in Eph 6:18 is on linking every aspect of prayer to the Spirit-filled mindset—"Pray in the Spirit at all times in every prayer and supplication"—and although this exhortation is placed immediately after the passage concerning the armor of God (6:13–17; to be discussed below), Arnold correctly points out that it is not presented as an additional weapon but rather as a more foundational act;[62] as

59. E.g., Job 5:11; 22:29; Ps 149:4; Prov 3:34; Ezek 17:24; Matt 23:12; Luke 14:11; 18:14; 2 Cor 11:7; 1 Pet 5:6.

60. E.g., 1 Cor 14:15–16; 2 Chr 5:13–14; 20:21; 1 Thess 5:16–18; Phil 4:6; Col 4:2; Heb 13:15; see e.g., Liefeld, "Prayer," 937–38; Moo, *James*, 181.

61. Discussing the Lord's Prayer, Chilton expresses a more general principle about how prayer can activate in the praying person an awareness/consciousness of God, which is closely related to how the Spirit-centered mindset is conceptualized in this chapter: "The distinctiveness of the prayer is nothing other than that consciousness of God and of one's relationship to him which is implied, and which is recapitulated whenever one prays in this way. Such an awareness of God and of oneself is what Christians kindle when they pray the Lord's Prayer." Chilton, *Jesus' Prayer*, 50.

62. Arnold explains that "Paul utilizes a number of stylistic means to highlight prayer and to set it off from the six pieces of armor. (1) He mentions prayer without

he concludes, this imperative "epitomizes what Paul has said in Eph 6:10 ('be strong in the Lord') because it represents calling on God to empower his people to fulfil what he has called them to be and to do."[63]

- The final section of James 5—which is labelled by both the NRSV and the NIV as *"The Prayer of Faith"*—provides first general encouragement to pray in every circumstance (v. 13) and then focuses on the issue of illness and how it relates to intercession, forgiveness, and confession (vv. 14–16). The main theme of the passage is the same as the commendation in Ephesians 6, namely that prayer is a substantial source of strength that can be appropriated at all times.

The canon offers several striking examples of when the potent combination of prayer, worship, thanksgiving, and praise is associated with the release of power[64]—akin to the act of accessing an electric circuit—and Jesus' response to the Samaritan woman in John's Gospel also underlines the significance of Spirit-filled worship: "the true worshipers will worship the Father in spirit and truth, for the Father seeks such as these to worship him. God is spirit, and those who worship him must worship in spirit and truth" (4:23–24). In Rom 8:26, Paul offers a glimpse into the workings of the Spirit's empowering presence—"the Spirit helps us in our weakness; for we do not know how to pray as we ought, but that very Spirit intercedes with sighs too deep for words"—and in 1 Thess 5:16–19 Paul cites prayer and thanksgiving as a kind of antidote to losing touch with to the Spirit-centered mindset: "Rejoice always, pray without ceasing, give thanks in all circumstances; for this is the will of God in Christ Jesus for you. Do not quench the Spirit." Finally, the exhortations that conclude the Letter of Jude not only reiterate the call of Eph 6:18 to engage in Spirit-filled prayer but also relate this prayer to a state—or mindset—characterized by an experience of God's love: "build yourselves up on your most holy faith; pray in the Holy Spirit; keep yourselves in the love of God" (v. 20–21).

---

attaching to it a corresponding metaphor of weaponry or armor (such as a spear or greaves). (2) He changes the tense to the present. All of the previous verbal elements were aorist. (3) He uses the word "all" ($\pi\acute{\alpha}\varsigma$) four times in connection with it. (4) He makes use of alliteration by the recurring "p" (π) sound that occurs eight times in the verse." C. E. Arnold, *Ephesians*, 463.

63. Ibid., 464.

64. Ranging from the dedication of Salomon's Temple (2 Chr 5:13–14) and King Jehoshaphat's defeating a seemingly overwhelming army of the Moabites and Ammonites (2 Chr 20:21–23) to the New Testament episode that describes how an earthquake freed Paul and Silas of their chains when they were imprisoned in Philippi (Acts 16:25–26).

Resisting Diverting Influences

Once a Spirit-centered mindset has been successfully adopted, the second broad strategy to be employed in the battle of the mindsets is to resist any influence that would divert one from this Spirit-filled state. Both Ephesians and James contain multiple warnings about diverting influences that may weaken the believers' relationship with the indwelling Spirit and thereby shift them toward a flesh-centered state of mind. It is useful to discuss the relevant biblical teaching according to the three dimensions of human vulnerability discussed earlier, namely the resisting of temptation to sin at the individual, social, and spiritual levels.

Resisting Individual Temptation

After encouraging believers to draw near to God so that he can draw near to them (Jas 4:7–8), James highlights sinful living as a barrier to being receptive to attuning to the Holy Spirit by urging the readers to "Cleanse your hands, you sinners, and purify your hearts, you double-minded" (v. 8). Warnings to avoid sinful behavior are a recurring theme in the canon, with the obstructive impact of sin expressively summed up, for example, in Isaiah 59:2: "your iniquities have been barriers between you and your God, and your sins have hidden his face from you so that he does not hear." Sinfulness can thus obscure the Spirit-centered mindset and lock people into the flesh-centered mindset, as underlined for example in John 8:34, where Jesus declares, "Very truly, I tell you, everyone who commits sin is a slave to sin."

We find a corresponding message about sinful human conduct in Ephesians, where a long passage contrasts the believers' old and new lives (4:17—5:20). As already mentioned briefly, the passage first emphasizes the "futility of the mind" (v. 17) that is attached to the former corrupt way of living, and then continues with a series of specific exhortations concerning various immoral acts. Inserted among these is the extraordinary admonishment, "And do not grieve the Holy Spirit of God, with which you were marked with a seal for the day of redemption" (4:30).[65] This strongly implies

---

65. The only other verse in the Bible that specifically concerns "grieving" the Spirit is Isa 63:10, where the grief is caused by the people's rebellion and it results in turning God into their enemy. Fee argues on linguistic grounds that Eph 4:30 is actually a citation of the LXX translation of Isaiah, even though the text uses the Greek word *lypeō* rather than *paroxynō* to translate the Hebrew word for "grieve" (ʿāṣab). The latter change, according to Fee, is due to the fact that, *lypeō* better expresses the original Hebrew term's meaning, and thus the Ephesians version in effect "corrects" the LXX translation (and indeed, as Fee points out, this is the only instance in the LXX where ʿāṣab is rendered into *paroxynō*). Fee, *God's Empowering Presence*, 713.

that sinful behavior works against, and thus hinders, the empowering presence of the indwelling Spirit.[66] Furthermore, commentators often highlight
the close parallels between this Ephesians passage and Rom 1:21–32, which
also speaks about non-believers' "futile thinking" (v. 21) and where Paul
also emphasizes the close link between the disorientation of the "debased
mind" (v. 28) and "every kind of wickedness" (v. 29).

Resisting Social Temptation

Having warned of the bondage that can be caused by sinful behavior, Ephesians 5 shifts attention to social relationships that can prevent believers from
"submitting to one another" (5:21). What follows in the epistle is a long
section that elaborates on household codes (5:22—6:9; also discussed in Col
3:18—4:1; 1 Pet 2:18—3:7), typically referred to in the literature by the Ger-
man term "*Haustafel*." The purpose of these is to regulate the relationships
within the Christian household—between family members and between
masters and slaves[67]—and their main substance involves advocating mu-
tual respect and love by taking Christ as the model.[68] We saw in chapter 3
how the social extension of human stewardship—through creating Eve as
Adam's companion—led to relational weaknesses in the first human couple,
which were duly capitalized upon by the serpent of the Fall. The disharmony
between the first husband and wife was followed by their failure to bring
up their firstborn child, Cain, in such a way that he could resist the pull of
sin "lurking at the door" (Gen 4:7), which in turn led to murder and, subsequently, to the collapse of the social order of humanity before the Flood.
The significance of the *Haustafel* in Ephesians becomes evident against this
backdrop: By providing a pattern for harmonious social coexistence in the
Christian household—the cornerstone of the society of stewards—it offers
a distinctive set of social guidelines and role expectations, which help to

66. This might also underlie the very harsh verdict of eternal condemnation
pronounced on those who "blaspheme against the Holy Spirit" (Mark 3:29; Luke 12:10;
Matt 12:31–32).

67. These relationships were generally regarded by ancient political theorists as the
basic paradigm of the broader social order; e.g., in his work on *Politics* (1.1235b) Ar-
istotle argued that understanding the working of a state needs to start with discussing
household management, and he then distinguished exactly the same three key relational patterns in the household as Ephesians did: husband and wife, parent and child,
and master and slave; see Gombis, "*Haustafel* in Ephesians," 320.

68. As stated elsewhere in Ephesians, believers are to become "citizens with the
saints and also members of the household of God, built upon the foundation of the
apostles and prophets, with Christ Jesus himself as the cornerstone" (2:19–20).

establish a relational system that is resilient to social temptations and interpersonal conflicts which could potentially stand in the way of humans accessing the Spirit-centered mindset.

Timothy Gombis's conclusion is that the *Haustafel* laid out "a manifesto for the New Humanity, painting in broad strokes a vision for how believers ought to conduct themselves in new creation communities, thus epitomizing the triumph of God in Christ."[69] Consistent with this vision, the message to avoid interpersonal conflicts is reiterated in another passage in Ephesians concerning social harmony within the Church, which encourages believers to make "every effort to maintain the unity of the Spirit in the bond of peace" (4:3). The harmful impact of conflicts, disputes, and jealousy are further underlined in the Letter of James (4:1–2), and this epistle also highlights the social dimension of the Christian fight in its reiteration of the Great Commandment: "You shall love your neighbor as yourself" (2:8).

Resisting Spiritual Temptation

Directly following the *Haustafel*, Ephesians presents the well-known and often cited passage concerning the donning of the full armor of God (6:10–20). This can be seen in many ways as the culmination of the epistle: Snodgrass, for example, provides a detailed list of cross-references demonstrating that virtually every important term used in 6:10–20 has already been addressed in earlier parts of the letter,[70] and Lincoln argues that from a rhetorical perspective the section functions as a *peroratio* that recapitulates the main themes and brings the author's address to an appropriate conclusion while also arousing emotions.[71] Ephesians 6:10–20 has often been treated as the *locus classicus* for discussions of the theme of "spiritual warfare"—that is, taking a stand against, and engaging in some form of struggle with, spiritual forces that oppose God's works and interfere with human affairs (see chapter 1)—because the source of the believers' struggle, and thus the target of their fight, is explicitly named here as "the wiles of the devil" (v. 11), which is then elaborated on as follows: "our struggle is not against enemies of blood and flesh, but against the rulers, against the authorities, against the cosmic powers of this present darkness, against the spiritual forces of evil in the heavenly places" (Eph 6:12).

However, the actual nature of the warfare described in Eph 6:10–20 has surprisingly little to do with the popular understanding of "spiritual

---

69. Gombis, "*Haustafel* in Ephesians," 319.

70. Snodgrass *Ephesians*, 335.

71. Lincoln, *Ephesians*, 432.

warfare" in terms of engaging in some form of healing or deliverance ministry. What is presented here is fully consistent with the curious nature of the Christian fight as observed throughout this chapter: Instead of advocating practices to proactively take on and defeat demonic powers, Christians are encouraged to "proclaim the gospel of peace" (v. 15) and "stand firm" (v. 13), a disposition which is emphatically underlined by the fact that the Greek word for "stand" appears four times in the passage.[72]

Thus, the main message of Eph 6:10–20 is encouraging Christian warriors to *resist* the devil, and this message also appears in Jas 4:7 ("Resist the devil, and he will flee from you") as well as in 1 Pet 5:9 ("Resist him steadfast in your faith"). Victory is ascribed to being dependent on the believers' reliance on God, as is emphasized at the beginning of the Ephesians passage: "be strong in the Lord and in the strength of his power" (6:10). Indeed, we must recall that the Ephesians passage is about getting equipped with *God's* armor, the heart of the matter being that the battle ultimately belongs to the Lord. This is further emphasized by the particular nature of the armor in question: The first five pieces mentioned—belt, breastplate, shoes, shield, and helmet—all serve defensive/non-combative purposes; only the last piece listed, the sword, is a weapon that can be used to attack, but it is prominently marked out as belonging to God—it is described as the "sword *of the Spirit*, which is the word *of God*" (v. 17; emphases added). Moreover, although commentators rarely remark on this, it is conspicuous that there is no mention in the passage of any of the other standard offensive weapons of the Roman infantryman such as the dagger or the javelin.[73]

Thielman makes a further important point regarding the linguistic context of the listing of God's armor, namely that only the first four pieces—associated with truth, righteousness, the gospel of peace, and faith—require *active* behavior from the believer, as the verbs expressing the act of putting them on are grammatically linked to the initial imperative "stand," while the last two pieces—associated with salvation and the sword of the Spirit—are connected to a new verb in the imperative form, "receive" (v.17), thereby emphasizing their status as *divine gifts*. In sum, and consistent with the curious fight of the Christian warrior described earlier, the military imagery in Eph 6:10–20 highlights the fact that believers need to be battle-ready by equipping themselves with specific protective armor that symbolizes

---

72. *"Histēmi"* (or cognate) is used in vv. 11, 13 (twice), and 14. For a discussion, see C. E. Arnold, *Three Crucial Questions*, 41–42; C. E. Arnold, *Ephesians*, 472. Lincoln also points out that standing firm is a recurring theme in the Pauline epistles; see e.g., 1 Thess 3:8; 2 Thess 2:15; 1 Cor 10:12; 15:1; 16:13; 2 Cor 1:24; Rom 5:2; 11:20; Phil 1:27; 4:1; Col 4:12. Lincoln, *Ephesians*, 447.

73. See also Thielman, *Ephesians*, 415–16.

faithful and righteous human conduct, and this equipment, accompanied by salvation and the Spirit's power that they receive, will allow them to stand firm in the face of the enemy's attacks.[74]

Consolidating the Mindset through Being "Doers of the Word"

We have seen so far that the plight of Christian believers involves fighting a battle of the mind, so that they can align themselves with a Spirit-centered mindset in the face of multiple temptations that push them toward a flesh-centered frame of mind. However, in what is arguably the best-known verse in the Letter of James,[75] believers are also told to be "doers of the word, and not merely hearers who deceive themselves" (1:22). On the face of it, this emphasis on "doing" might be seen as going against our earlier characterization of the curious nature of Christian warfare, because "doing" concerns outward action rather than internal struggle. Therefore the importance attached to "doing" may suggest that "conquering/overcoming" may not be limited in the canon in a figurative sense to mental combat only, but should also be extended to the world of action.[76] So, what does "doer of the word" mean in this context and how does it relate to being attuned to the indwelling Spirit?

Martin explains that the "word" in James 1:22 is synonymous with "word of truth" as used in 1:18, both referring to "God's message of new life and salvation,"[77] and commentators agree that James applies the Greek word translated as "doer" (*poiētēs*) here and elsewhere (e.g., in 1:25; 4:11) in the

---

74. It is interesting to note the continuity with the OT in this respect: In 2 Chr 20:17, God's communication to King Jehoshaphat and the assembly of Judah and Jerusalem is as follows: "This battle is not for you to fight; take your position, stand still, and see the victory of the LORD on your behalf."

75. So Moo, *Letter of James*, 89.

76. In fact, James goes even further later when he asks, "Can faith save you?" (2:14), and the obvious expectation of a negative answer to his rhetorical question goes against the declared prominence of grace over works elsewhere in the New Testament (e.g., Rom 3:28; 4:3–5; Gal 3:6–9; 5:6; Heb 11:1–40). Ever since Luther's rejection of the notion that works is meritorious for salvation and his insistence that justification is by faith alone (*sola fides*), the question of how to interpret the emphasis on works in the Letter of James in relation to faith has been an issue subject to much debate. Because the presumed conflict between Paul and James is not directly relevant to the canonical narrative pursued in the current book, it will not be considered further here; for a recent discussion that represents multiple views, see Wilkin et al., *Four Views on the Role of Works*.

77. Martin, *James*, 49.

sense of "practitioner" or "observer."[78] Accordingly, the implication of James's message is that merely being aware of, or even believing in, God's truth is *insufficient* without also taking appropriate action, consistent with the saying "practice what you preach." This is clearly a significant theme in the epistle, because it is reiterated later (2:14–26), and we must also note that the emphasis on action is not specific to this book only: The same (or a very similar) injunction occurs in several other places in the canon from Ezekiel to Romans (Ezek 33:31–32; Matt 7:24–27; Matt 25:31–46; Luke 6:47–49; Luke 11:28; 1 John 3:18; Rom 2:13), all suggesting that faith without action is of little value. Moreover, the same principle also surfaces in the biblical expression that the quality of a tree is shown by its fruit (e.g., Matt 7:15–20; 12:33–37; Luke 3:7–9; 6:43–45), and Paul uses in Galatians a further image, that of sowing and reaping, to link a person's action to the corresponding mindset: "If you sow to your own flesh, you will reap corruption from the flesh; but if you sow to the Spirit, you will reap eternal life from the Spirit. So let us not grow weary in doing what is right, for we will reap at harvest time, if we do not give up. So then, whenever we have an opportunity, let us work for the good of all, and especially for those of the family of faith" (6:8–10).

Is there thus a possible tension between mindset and behavior—that is, between internal and external action—in the Christian fight? Immediately after James calls believers to be "doers of the word" (1:22), he offers a way of resolving this question by suggesting that the significance of "doing" is that it makes one's faith *enduring*: Without becoming a "doer," a person's faithful mindset will be as transient as a forgettable image of oneself in the mirror:

> For if any are hearers of the word and not doers, they are like those who look at themselves in a mirror; for they look at themselves and, on going away, immediately forget what they were like. (1:23–24)

In other words, James emphasizes that "doing" is necessary to make the faithful mindset a *lasting* part of one's identity; the mindset needs to be backed up by action so as not to fade away like a dim reflection in the mirror. This point is consistent with the grave dangers for believers of forgetting, as discussed in the last chapter concerning the Eucharist, and this emphasis is also reflected in the linguistic analysis of the changing verb tenses of "look," "go away" and "forget" in the passage (aorist tense, perfect tense, and back to aorist tense, respectively): As Varner explains, the perfect tense "frontgrounds" the action in the narrative, and therefore, "what James wants the reader to focus on is the forgetful looker's state of having departed

---

78. E.g., Dibelius, *James*, 114; Martin, *James*, 49; McCartney, *James*, 119.

from looking in the mirror."[79] The same point, namely that only action creates sufficiently solid foundations for enduring faith, is also made by Jesus in the Parable About the Two Builders (Matt 7:24–27; Luke 6:47–49), the parable concluding the Sermon on the Mount:

> Everyone then who hears these words of mine and acts on them will be like a wise man who built his house on rock. The rain fell, the floods came, and the winds blew and beat on that house, but it did not fall, because it had been founded on rock. And everyone who hears these words of mine and does not act on them will be like a foolish man who built his house on sand. The rain fell, and the floods came, and the winds blew and beat against that house, and it fell—and great was its fall![80]

Taking these verses together, the implication is that even if a person does have faith and can tune into the Spirit-centered mindset, this state can only prevail in the person's life if it is internalized to such an extent that it is also manifested in his/her actions. That is, James describes "works" not as a prerequisite for achieving salvation but rather as a necessary condition for *sealing* this state—as he pronounces, "faith was brought to *completion* by the works" (2:22; emphasis added).[81] Indeed, as James reiterates a few verses later from the reverse perspective, "just as the body without the spirit is dead, so faith without works is also dead" (2:26). Thus, real and enduring faith for James equals "faith in action," and if the actional component is missing, faith is doomed to fail. We should also note that the understanding that good works will seal one's faithful mindset is in full accordance with the earlier observation concerning the contrasting, flesh-centered mindset, namely that sinful behavior solidifies this into a sinful disposition and locks people into a "debased mind" (Rom 1:28). Biblical teaching therefore points to the conclusion that corresponding action consolidates a mindset, which raises the question of what kind of action is presented in the canon as corresponding to the Spirit-centered mindset.

---

79. Varner, *James*, 78.

80. It is unlikely to be a coincidence that a few verses earlier Matthew also cites Jesus' teaching about the tree and its fruit, emphasizing that "every good tree bears good fruit" (7:17).

81. This interpretation is consistent with Eph 2, which first states that "by grace you have been saved through faith, and this is not your own doing; it is the gift of God—not the result of works" (vv. 8–9) but then also adds: "we are . . . created in Jesus Christ for good works" (v.10). Also, in Titus 3 it is explicitly stated that believers are saved "not because of any works of righteousness that we had done" (v. 5), but three verses later "those who have come to believe in God" are to be urged "to devote themselves to good works" (v. 8).

What Does "Doing" Involve in the Canon?

Appeals to believers to actively help people in need are common in the Bible (e.g., Isa 58:7; Ezek 18:7; Matt 25:35–40; Luke 3:11; Acts 20:35; Rom 12:13; 2 Cor 8:2–3; Tit 3:14), and James, too, calls believers to care for orphans and widows (1:27), as well as to provide for people who are hungry or who lack clothes (2:15–16). In the latter case, James also explicitly declares the futility of kind but empty words: "If a brother or sister is naked and lacks daily food, and one of you says to them, 'Go in peace; keep warm and eat your fill,' and yet you do not supply their bodily needs, what is the good of that? So faith by itself, if it has no works, is dead" (vv. 15–17).

In Eph 4:28, an exhortation against stealing offers a good example of how righteousness and charitable efforts are interlinked: The command does not merely tell thieves to stop sinning (as we find for example in the Ten Commandments) but also instructs them to engage in labor that is beneficial to others in need: "Thieves must give up stealing; rather let them labor and work honestly with their own hands, so as to have something to share with the needy." These verses are consistent with Jesus' teaching that people cannot inherit the kingdom without manifesting one's faith in terms of good deeds:

> You that are accursed, depart from me into the eternal fire pre
> pared for the devil and his angels; for I was hungry and you gave
> me no food, I was thirsty and you gave me nothing to drink, I
> was a stranger and you did not welcome me, naked and you did
> not give me clothing, sick and in prison and you did not visit
> me. (25:41–43)

Thus, we find unambiguous canonical support for what is often re-ferred to in contemporary Church circles as "social action." However, from the perspective of the current book the concluding two verses of the Letter of James also deserve special attention as they highlight a type of "doing" that is different from charitable deeds: Unlike most NT epistles,[82] James does not end with a conventional benediction or salutation, but concludes with a final summons to action to help fellow Christians who are in *spiritual trouble*:

> My brothers and sisters, if anyone among you wanders from
> the truth and is brought back by another, you should know
> that whoever brings back a sinner from wandering will save
> the sinner's soul from death and will cover a multitude of sins.
> (5:19–20)

82. 1 John is similar to James in this respect.

The target of this action is very general—"anyone" who has strayed away from the truth—and the verb used for "wandering from the truth" in v. 19 (*planaō*; also repeated in v. 20 in a noun form) is the same as the word used by Jesus, for example, in Matthew 24:4–5 when he warned his disciples not to be "led astray" by false Messiahs. James' directive clearly concerns grave sin, possibly apostasy, which would, if left unattended, result in the death of the sinner's soul (v. 20), and the fact that James charges believers to bring back their fallen brothers and sisters implies that the latter would not be able to avoid their tragic destiny if left to their own devices. Significantly, the concluding exhortation in the Letter of Jude is a similar appeal to "save others by snatching them out of the fire" (v. 23), and these calls to redeem people who are in danger of suffering eternal damnation echo Jesus' teaching in the Parable of the Lost Sheep (Luke 15:3–7), where he highlights the importance of going after the sheep that is lost in the wilderness, as "there will be more joy in heaven over one sinner who repents than over ninety-nine righteous persons who need no repentance" (Luke 15:7).

Similar to Jude, by placing this appeal in an emphatic position at the very end of his letter, James underlines the significance of the act he is calling for, and further emphasis is added by stressing that it will "save the sinner's soul from death and will cover a multitude of sins" (5:20). Commentators have been divided on whose sins are "covered," the saver's or the wanderer's;[83] while the obvious referent would be the sinner who is to be redeemed, in the light of the earlier discussion, it might well be the case that the text has intentionally left the referent open, because the saving person's righteous act can also help to stabilize—or seal—his/her own Spirit-centered mindset and can thus cover the multitude of sins that are associated with its flesh-centered counterpart in the battle of the mind. This open interpretation would be consistent with 1 Tim 4:16, which states, "Pay close attention to yourself and to your teaching; continue in these things, for in doing this you will save both yourself and your hearers."[84]

In sum, the Epistle of James underlines the importance of "doing" as an integral part of the process of aligning one's whole life to one's faith, and after underlining the significance of social action in this respect, the concluding exhortation highlights a further aspect of "doing": helping to

83. For different views, see e.g., Davids, *James*, 200; Dibelius, *James*, 258–59; Martin, *James*, 220; Michaels, *1 Peter*, 247.

84. McCartney cites Ezek 3:19–21 as a further possible parallel: "But if you warn the wicked, and they do not turn from their wickedness, or from their wicked way, they shall die for their iniquity; but you will have saved your life. . . . If, however, you warn the righteous not to sin, and they do not sin, they shall surely live, because they took warning; and you will have saved your life." McCartney, *James*, 263.

bring others in spiritual need back into the fold. Yet, despite its prominent position, this latter outreach imperative has been largely overshadowed by the content of the rest of the letter, which is partly due to the fact that it is mentioned only briefly, and no specific guidelines are offered. The same issue, however, is addressed elsewhere in the New Testament in considerable detail, most notably in Jesus' "Missionary Discourse" (Matt 10:5–42) that he delivered when he sent out the Twelve to reclaim "the lost sheep of the house of Israel" (Matt 10:6). The correspondence between James' message and Jesus' discourse gains even more salience by the fact that Jesus specifically refers here to the disciples as "laborers"—"The harvest is plentiful, but the laborers are few; therefore ask the Lord of the harvest to send out laborers into his harvest" (Matt 9:37–38) —using the derivative of the same Greek word (*ergon*) that we find in several key verses in James, for example, in 2:17: "So faith by itself, if it has no works (*erga*), is dead." In view of the close link between this matter and the requirement of ongoing Christian commitment set out by Jesus in the Great Commission (discussed in the previous chapter), the final part of this section explores the implications of such outreach for the plight of the believer.

Christian Outreach: Going on the Offensive

James' instruction to assist strayed believers to return to the fold goes beyond the previously mentioned core strategy of the Christian warrior— namely, putting on the full armor of God and standing firm in the face of temptation—as it urges believers to go on the *offensive*. The importance of such outreach is corroborated by the detailed description in the New Testament of a mission journey (Matt 10:5–42; Luke 9:1–6; see also 10:1–20) that involved Jesus sending out his twelve disciples to minister to "the lost sheep of the house of Israel" (Matt 10:6). While the target of this particular mission was restricted to Jews, we saw when discussing the Great Commission in the previous chapter that Jesus' victory on the cross prepared the ground for extending Christian mission to also adding *new* sheep to the fold, that is, making disciples among the Gentiles. The close link between "recovering old sheep" and "finding new sheep" is further illustrated in the Parable of the Sower (Matt 13:1–18; Mark 4:1–20; Luke 8:4–15), where the three failed scenarios (i.e., when the seed does not bring forth grain) fall somewhere in between (fruitless) evangelization and sheep straying away, as they concern a combination of failure to develop sufficient spiritual roots and the detrimental effects of various temptations.[85] Furthermore, in a related parable

85. First, "the evil one comes and snatches away what is sown in the heart" (Matt

in Matthew's Gospel, the Parable of Weeds Among the Wheat (13:24–30), a similarly "complicated" mission field is presented in which "while everybody was asleep, an enemy came and sowed weeds" (v. 25), thereby resulting in spiritual contamination.

The closely intertwined nature of recovering straying sheep and finding new sheep is fully reflected in the Missionary Discourse of Matthew's Gospel: The text presents material that is relevant to the specific Galilean mission of the Twelve (e.g., "Go nowhere among the Gentiles, and enter no town of the Samaritans" (10:5), and material which hints at evangelism in a broader sense and in a wider setting (e.g., "you will be dragged before governors and kings because of me, as a testimony to them and the Gentiles" v. 18). As Dorothy Weaver summarizes, this inconsistency "has long proved problematic to scholars [because] a closer look at the actual contents of the discourse reveals that certain elements within it do not appear congruent with the setting designated by the narrative framework."[86] This incongruity concerns not only the geographical/ethnic target of the mission but also the temporal dimension: Weaver is right in pointing out that when Jesus submits that "you will be hated by all because of my name. But the one who *endures to the end* will be saved" (v. 22; emphasis added), he is referring to the end of the age, thereby "bursting the time boundaries of the mission previously described."[87]

What may appear as an incongruity in the text, however, can also be seen as an affirmation that Jesus' instructions are intended to apply more widely than the specific Galilean setting, indeed to the whole spectrum of Christian mission. The most salient element of the Missionary Discourse that transcends the geographical and temporal boundaries is the warning that the disciples' mission would take them on a collision course with hostile forces. The initial caution that they will not be welcome by everybody (v. 14) gains gravity when Jesus declares, "I am sending you out like sheep into the midst of wolves . . ." (v. 16), and further substance is added by the mention of the likelihood that they might be flogged (v. 17). A few verses later, Jesus foresees family feuds (v. 21), and this is reiterated in vv. 35–36, followed by the stark warning that the disciples will be hated (v. 23) and persecuted (v. 24).

13:19) of a person who "hears the word of the kingdom and does not understand it" (v. 19); second, someone "hears the word and immediately receives it with joy. . . but endures only for a while" (vv. 20–21) because of inadequate roots and subsequent persecution; third, it is "the cares of the world and the lure of wealth choke the word"(v. 22).

86. Weaver, *Missionary Discourse*, 13.

87. Ibid., 15–16.

Jesus' message could hardly be clearer: Christian outreach will inevitably add hardship to the Christian plight, and because it involves incurring into "enemy territory" it will also lead to spiritual confrontation. This confrontation is different from the need to resist the devil's assaults by putting on God's protective armor as discussed earlier. For the purpose of reaching out to people who have been afflicted by some kind of spiritual deception or bondage, Jesus equipped his disciples by giving them "authority over unclean spirits, to cast them out, and to cure every disease and every sickness" (10:1). Indeed, when Luke's Gospel narrates the return of a larger group of disciples (the Seventy) from a subsequent mission journey, they report joyfully, "Lord, in your name even the demons submit to us!" (10:17), to which Jesus answers, "See, I have given you authority to tread on snakes and scorpions, and over all the power of the enemy; and nothing will hurt you" (v. 19). Thus, the Apostle Paul was right to conclude that "we do not wage war according to human standards; for the weapons of our warfare are not merely human, but they have divine power to *destroy strongholds*" (2 Cor 10:3–4; emphasis added), and as we saw in the previous chapter in relation to the Great Commission, this empowerment was extended to all future disciples when Jesus promised that they would "receive power when the Holy Spirit has come upon you" (Acts 1:8).

It is important to reiterate that the kind of spiritual warfare necessitated by the mandate for Christian outreach to the "lost sheep" is different from that of standing firm in the face of spiritual assaults. Biblically grounded analyses of spiritual warfare in the past have too often focused exclusively on the latter type, typically using Ephesians as the canonical basis and justification.[88] The concern with this exclusivity is its imbalanced emphasis on holding ground only rather than also *taking* ground; if this moral stance is adopted without any consideration of the calls in the canon for Christian outreach, one may easily end up with a principle that is restricted to the tenet that "To win spiritual warfare is simply to live as light in a dark world"[89] (Powlison). In

---

88. E.g., Powlison accurately points out in the respect that the "church has always looked to Eph 6:10–20 as the centerpiece for understanding how to engage complex evil" ("Classical Model," 92).

89. Powlison, "Classical Model," 98. An examples of such an exclusive approach occurs in a recent analysis of Ephesians by Timothy Gombis, which generalizes the interpretation of 6:1–10 as follows: "Spiritual warfare against Satan and the power of darkness, therefore, does not involve wild behavior or direct engagement with demonic entities. We do not rebuke Satan, nor do we command demons. Our warfare against the powers takes place on a mundane level . . . we wage our warfare . . . when we resist idolatrous and destructive patterns of life. We battle the powers when we refuse to participate in their corruptions of creation." Gombis, *Ephesians*, 183. A similar view is expressed by Bolt and West: "it is clear that when Ephesians talks about a 'spiritual

contrast, the above considerations imply that *as well as* winning the battle of the mindsets—and thus living and being guided by the Spirit (Gal 5:25)—the Christian fight ought to also include proactive confrontation with spiritual forces in order to set spiritual captives free, similar to what Jesus modelled in his earthly ministry in accordance with the Isaiah passage he cited at the beginning of his mission: "He has sent me to proclaim release to the captives and recovery of sight to the blind, to let the oppressed go free" (Luke 4:18).[90] That is, with respect to the different models of spiritual warfare reviewed in chapter 1, the current canonical narrative re-reading of the Scriptures suggests an approach that includes strategies from both the indirect and the more direct positions—the Book of Acts (e.g., 5:16; 8:6–7; 19:11–12) bears witness to the fact that Jesus' disciples appropriated this broader approach to fighting the good fight of the faith.

7.5 Summary

This chapter started out with reiterating that the canonical narrative of progressive creation is peculiar in the sense that the readers of the Bible are themselves participants in the process, and therefore the narrative has a pronounced practical dimension that includes specific teaching on how believers should conduct their lives in order to be fully aligned with the advancement of God's inaugurated kingdom. Chapter 6 discussed three assignments set by Jesus that can be seen to belong to this practical dimension, and the current chapter continued to explore the relevant implications in the NT canon, focusing particularly on the books of Ephesians and James, both of which are generally noted for their pastoral concerns. In order to establish some broad organizing principles, section 7.1 discussed the main sources of human struggle in terms of three facets of human vulnerability—corporeality, sociality, and spiritual corruptibility—and it was argued in section 7.2 that these weaknesses are reflected throughout the canon in connection with various forms of temptation/testing.

    Section 7.3 examined the "Christian fight" metaphor that is widely used in the Bible to characterize the intense efforts required to overcome

---

warfare', it is referring to the Spirit-given ability to 'stand'; that is, to continue to live in Christ's new way, in the midst of the ordinary relationships of life." Bolt and West, "Christ's Victory," 219. For a critique of the exclusive emphasis on the "standing-firm" stance, see Boyd, "Response to Powlison," 117–22.

90. See e.g., Ladd, who argues that "At the very heart of our Lord's mission is the need of rescuing people from bondage to the satanic kingdom and of bringing them into the sphere of God's Kingdom. Anything less than this involves an essential reinterpretation of some of the basic facts of the gospel" (*Theology of the New Testament,* 50).

human vulnerability, and this section also highlighted the curious nature of the language of Christian warfare: The frequent military images are clearly intended to imply that believers enter some kind of warzone, but the battle they are joining does not appear to involve engagement in literal combat with an actual enemy in the traditional military sense. Rather, the mention of waging war in the NT canon tends to refer to battlegrounds internal to the believer, and the discussion has foregrounded two conflicting mindsets—one centered around the indwelling Spirit, the other around the constraints of the flesh—that Paul referred to repeatedly when describing the believers' internal struggle.

Building on these foundations, section 7.4 identified three broad strategies mentioned in the canon that can be seen as potential ways of achieving success in the Christian warfare: adopting a Spirit-centered mindset, resisting influences that would divert one away from this mindset, and consolidating the mindset through conducive action, thereby making it an integral part of one's life. The third strategy draws attention to the fact that although the reading presented in this chapter emphasized the internal nature of the primary battlefront in the Christian struggle, the call to be also "doers of the word" is an important aspect of fighting the "good fight of the faith": It requires Jesus' disciples to live out the implications of their faith through ministering to people who are in physical or spiritual danger or destitution, that is, to engage in social action and Christian outreach. The latter aspect involves the mission to "save the sinner's soul from death" (Jas 5:20), characterized by a twofold process of reaching out to both straying disciples and people who are as yet undiscipled, thereby building up the new society of the citizens of the kingdom of God.

There are repeated warnings in the Bible that obedience to Jesus' outreach mandate may take believers onto a collision course with hostile principalities and powers, and the combination of such confrontations with the multitude of human temptations that a believer is exposed to by living in the "world" accounts for the often highly challenging nature of the "good fight of the faith." Yet, the canon also makes it clear that this fight is not at all a losing battle: Jesus reassured his disciples that all authority in heaven and on earth had been given to him and that he will be with them always, "to the end of the age" (Matt 26:20). He also promised them that they would be "clothed with power from on high" (Luke 24:49), a promise he reiterated just before his ascension: "you will receive power when the Holy Spirit has come upon you; and you will be my witnesses in Jerusalem, in all Judea and Samaria, and to the ends of the earth" (Acts 1:8). Thus, the reassurance Jesus gave to the Twelve before their first mission journey, namely that they should not be afraid because the Father was looking after them (Matt 10:29–31), was extended to all of Jesus' disciples—past, present, and future—thereby giving them confidence that they will prevail and will be able to "run with perseverance the race marked out for us, fixing our eyes on Jesus, the pioneer and perfecter of faith" (12:1–2, NIV).

Conclusion

THE TITLE OF THIS book has been made up of two parts, with the main title denoting the subject matter (progressive creation and humanity's struggles) and the subtitle the hermeneutical method applied (a canonical narrative interpretation). How do these two parts relate to each other? This question could be likened metaphorically to considering a guidebook describing a new hiking path through the Yorkshire Dales that walkers could take to get a real sense of the Dales as a whole and see some of the best bits[1]—the question in this case would be whether the primary subject matter of this guide is the new trail or the Dales themselves. Of course, the difference between the two options is mostly in emphasis, since even if we were to focus primarily on the novelty aspect of the new route, this would still involve presenting a range of views and understandings that have been opened up by the trail, and would therefore include extensive discussion of various aspects of the Dales itself. Yet, this matter is of some importance, because it was argued in chapter 1 that the novelty aspect of the content of this book lies partly in its unique rootedness in Scripture, that is, in the way the various details are woven together into a coherent and overarching reading of the whole of the canon. This in turn foregrounds the method whereby this rootedness and coherence was achieved, and it highlights the specific nature of the canonical narrative pathway that was followed to produce the interlinked tapestry.

To use the Yorkshire Dales metaphor one more time, the final form of the book is more about the Dales than about the canonical narrative trail: During the preparation of this work the discussion shifted toward the exposition of the new understanding that has emerged, rather than toward the analysis of the nature of the pathway that was necessary to gain this

---

1. I am grateful to Karen Kilby for suggesting the Yorkshire Dale imagery as a metaphor to illustrate the two levels of the book.

understanding. This does not mean that the canonical narrative approach was not essential in determining the direction of the inquiry, because in several places, particularly in the second half of the book, it served as the primary driving force in taking the discussion forward and producing intertextual links. Indeed, following the scriptural leads resulted several times in an experience similar to the one described by John Peckham concerning his pursuit of a canonical theological investigation: "the answers I would have posited at the outset of the study markedly differ from the conclusions that I arrived at . . . This was . . .in retrospect, quite encouraging in that it appears that I was at least partially successful in allowing the canonical data to reform my own preconceptions."[2]

Yet, underlying the current work as a whole was the motivation to explore why the Christian walk appears to be riddled with many and varied challenges, and the final presentation of the material focused on the main outcome of this exploration, the positioning of human struggles in the Bible within an unfolding process of creation. Accordingly, the antecedents of these struggles were identified as the incompleteness of the primal created order and the accompanying spiritual opposition to material creation, whereas the "plot" of the process was provided by the biblical accounts of the tortuous progression of human transformation that spans the entire canon.

Somewhat unexpectedly, the initial analysis homed in on one particular verse in the Genesis accounts of the making of the world—"It is not good that the man should be alone" (2:18)—that appeared to signal a turning point in the creation process, marking the beginning of a chain of events that eventually led to the "de-creation" by the Flood. The subsequent new beginning—or "re-creation" of the world—was followed by a series of divine interventions aimed at advancing human transformation, which can be roughly divided into two major phases, the raising of the Israelites to become God's "elite task force," as narrated in the Old Testament, and the new creation inaugurated by the incarnation of Jesus Christ, as described in the NT canon. The canonical narrative perspective adopted for the portrayal of these developments contextualized humanity's ongoing struggles at three levels—corporeal, social, and spiritual—and the analysis of the biblical material that addressed the ensuing human temptations and the ways by which they could be overcome outlined a broad framework of human conduct that may be instrumental to "fighting the good fight of the faith" in the face of multiple challenges.

As a result, the canonical narrative presented in this book has attempted to delineate a comprehensive biblical theology of humanity's struggles

---

2. Peckham, *Canonical Theology*, 249.

that subsumes a number of themes that are rarely discussed together in an integrated manner such as the often seemingly irresistible power of tempta-tion, the recurrent deficiency of social structures in the world, and the much debated notion of spiritual warfare. By adopting a "low-inference" approach to biblical interpretation, the investigation has addressed these topics with ongoing reference to Scripture, thereby attempting to ensure the validity of the findings. Yet, as was stated in the introductory chapter, not even a close alignment of any biblical interpretation with an overarching canoni-cal narrative will guarantee a fully unified, comprehensive reading of the canon; indeed, there are several biblical topics that are given significance in Scripture but are not served particularly well by the current canonical narrative. It is therefore appropriate to finish this Conclusion by listing the most important omissions of this kind.

One prominent theme that exemplifies the inevitable partiality of the current reading concerns the question of *continuity* versus *discontinuity* in the Bible. The canonical narrative presented in this book paints a picture of a more or less continuous, incremental development that will one day reach its inevitable completion. However, another interpretation of the Scriptures may convey a sense of discontinuity based on passages that suggest that this world is heading for decay and death, but then to be followed by some radi-cal newness predicted for the future. Put this way, the Christian story may be seen as centered around overcoming death, and the current book has little to say about death and resurrection, or indeed the related debates in Pauline theology between the so-called apocalyptic and salvation-historical readings of the Bible.

Alternatively, in other places in the canon we find *more steady* and *less dramatic* standards of human existence than the ongoing struggle and the requirement to "fight the good fight of faith" foregrounded in this book. For example, 1 Thess 4:11 urges believers "to aspire to live quietly, to mind your own affairs, and to work with your hands, as we directed you, so that you may behave properly toward outsiders and be dependent on no one."[3] This issue is related to, but at the same time goes beyond, the appeal to steer clear of interpersonal conflict and to seek social harmony—as discussed in chapter 7—in order to avoid obstacles that would stand in the way of ac-cessing the Spirit-centered mindset. There are also several passages in the wisdom literature which promote living a secure life "at ease, without dread of disaster" (Prov 1:33),[4] and in Ecclesiastes not only do we find an endorse-

3. 1 Tim 2:2–3 also expresses this sense: ". . . so that we may lead a quiet and peace-able life in all godliness and dignity. This is right and is acceptable in the sight of God our Savior"; see also 2 Thess 3:11–12.

4. See also Prov 8:35–36; 17:1.

ment of the "quiet words of the wise" (9:17) over the "weapons of war" (v. 18), but there is also an emphasis on portraying the unbroken, cyclical, and regular order of the world, in which "For everything there is a season, and a time for every matter under heaven" (3:1), and where "there is nothing new under the sun" (1:9).

A further biblical theme that the present canonical narrative could not accommodate is the complex notion of *predestination*, even though it has undeniable bearings on human transfiguration ("those whom he predestined he also called; and those whom he called he also justified; and those whom he justified he also glorified" Rom 8:30). More could have also been said about the *new covenant* and the way Hebrews 9 describes Jesus Christ as the "high priest" (v. 11) and the "mediator" (v. 15) of this covenant "so that those who are called may receive the promised eternal inheritance" (ibid). Even more relevant to creation is a striking passage in Proverbs 8:22–31, which describes the connection between a personalized Woman Wisdom and God's creative works: It is stated that Wisdom was formed at the beginning of his work, even before establishing the heavens (v. 27), and she was present during the creation of the material world (vv. 27–29). The interpretation of this passage poses several difficulties at the textual level,[5] and it also raises a keenly debated question that has been put by Derek Kidner as follows: "Is wisdom here conceived as a hypostasis (i.e., an actual heavenly being) or as a personification (i.e., an abstraction, made personal for the sake of poetic vividness)?"[6] The current book did not explore this question, and the role of Wisdom was not integrated into the canonical narrative.

Finally, a recurring issue throughout the discussion that has never been fully resolved concerns the puzzling question of why the Scriptures sometimes offer tantalizing hints and glimpses regarding certain apparently important matters but fail to fill in the blanks, which is a feature that becomes particularly apparent when trying to construct a coherent canonical narrative. Indeed, why do readers of the Bible so often have the sense that they are pointed in a certain direction without receiving a full explanation, and why do certain parts of the biblical canon appear as if they have been left intentionally ambiguous? Unfortunately, a canonical narrative approach is not well suited to contemplating on what is not included or explicated in the canon.

---

5. See e.g., Murphy, *Proverbs*, 52–53.

6. Kidner, *Proverbs*, 74.

Bibliography

Abrahams, Israel. *Studies in Pharisaism and the Gospels.* Vol. 2. Cambridge: Cambridge University Press, 1924.

Achtemeier, Paul J. *1 Peter: A Commentary on First Peter.* Hermeneia. Minneapolis: Fortress, 1996.

Albani, Matthias. "The Downfall of Helel, the Son of Dawn: Aspects of Royal Ideology in Isa 14:12–13." In *Fall of the Angels,* edited by Christoph Auffarth and Loren Stuckenbruck, 62–86. Themes in Biblical Narrative 6. Leiden: Brill, 2004.

Alden, Robert L. *Job.* New American Commentary 11. Nashville: Broadman & Holman, 1993.

Alexander, T. Desmond. *From Eden to New Jerusalem: Exploring God's Plan for Life on Earth.* Nottingham, UK: Inter-Varsity Press, 2008.

Allen, Leslie C. *Ezekiel 20–48.* WBC 29. Dallas: Word Books, 1998.

Alter, Robert. *The Art of Biblical Narrative.* New York: Basic Books, 1981.

————. *Genesis: Translation and Commentary.* New York: Norton, 1996.

Andersen, Francis I. *Job: An Introduction and Commentary.* Tyndale Old Testament Commentaries 14. Leicester, UK: Inter-Varsity, 1976.

Angel, Andrew R. *Chaos and the Son of Man: The Hebrew Chaoskampf Tradition in the Period 515 BCE to 200 CE.* Library of Second Temple Judaism 60. London: T. & T. Clark, 2006.

Arichea, Daniel C., and Eugene Albert Nida. *A Translator's Handbook on the First Letter from Peter.* Helps for Translators. New York: United Bible Societies, 1980.

Arnold, Bill T. *Genesis.* New Cambridge Bible Commentary. Cambridge: Cambridge University Press, 2009.

Arnold, Clinton E. *Ephesians: Power and Magic: The Concept of Power in Ephesians in Light of Its Historical Setting.* Society of New Testament Studies Monograph Series 63. Cambridge: Cambridge University Press, 1989.

————. *Powers of Darkness: Principalities and Powers in Paul's Letters.* Downers Grove, IL: IVP Academic, 1992.

————. *Three Crucial Questions about Spiritual Warfare.* Grand Rapids: Baker Academic, 1997.

Ash, Christopher. *Job: The Wisdom of the Cross.* Preaching the Word. Wheaton, IL: Crossway, 2014.

Augustine. *City of God: Concerning the City of God against the Pagans.* Translated by Henry Bettenson. Harmondsworth, UK: Penguin, 1984.

———. *The Literal Meaning of Genesis (De Genesi ad Litteram)*. Translated by John Hammond Taylor. New ed. New York: Paulist, 2004.

Aulén, Gustaf. *Christus Victor: An Historical Study of the Three Main Types of the Idea of the Atonement*. 1951. Reprinted, Eugene, OR: Wipf & Stock, 2003.

Aune, David. *Revelation 6–16*. WBC 52B. Nashville: Nelson, 1998.

Ayo, Nicholas. *The Lord's Prayer: A Survey Theological and Literary*. Notre Dame: University of Notre Dame Press, 1992.

Baker, Mark D. "Atonement." In *Dictionary of Scripture and Ethics*, edited by Joel B. Green, 81–84. Grand Rapids: Baker Academic, 2011.

Barbour, Ian G. *Issues in Science and Religion*. London: SCM, 1966.

———. *When Science Meets Religion: Enemies, Strangers, or Partners?* New York: HarperOne, 2000.

Barr, James. *The Garden of Eden and the Hope of Immortality*. London: SCM, 1992.

———. *Holy Scripture: Canon, Authority, Criticism*. Oxford: Clarendon, 1983.

Barrett, C. K. *A Commentary on the Epistle to the Romans*. 2nd ed. Black's New Testament Commentary. London: A & C Black, 1991.

Barth, Karl. *Church Dogmatics III/1: The Doctrine of Creation*. Edinburgh: T. & T. Clark, 1958.

———. *Church Dogmatics III/3: The Doctrine of Creation*. Edinburgh: T. & T. Clark, 1960.

———. *Church Dogmatics IV/3.1: Jesus Christ, the True Witness*. Edinburgh: T. & T. Clark, 1961.

———. "An Exegetical Study of Matthew 28:16–20." Translated by Thomas Wieser. In *The Theology of the Christian Mission*, edited by Gerald H. Anderson, 55–71. London: SCM, 1961.

Bartholomew, Craig, and Michael Goheen. *The Drama of Scripture*. 2nd ed. London: SPCK, 2006.

Bash, Anthony. *Forgiveness: A Theology*. Cascade Companions 19. Eugene, OR: Cascade Books, 2015.

Bauckham, Richard J. *Bible and Mission: Christian Witness in a Postmodern World*. Milton Keynes, UK: Paternoster, 2003.

———. *Jude, 2 Peter*. WBC 50. Waco, TX: Word, 1983.

———. "Reading Scripture as a Coherent Story." In *The Art of Reading Scripture*, edited by Ellen F. Davis and Richard B. Hays, 38–53. Grand Rapids: Eerdmans, 2003.

———. *The Theology of the Book of Revelation*. New Testament Theology. Cambridge: Cambridge University Press, 1993.

Baugh, S. M. *Ephesians*. Evangelical Exegetical Commentary. Bellingham, WA: Lexham, 2015.

Beale, G. K. *A New Testament Biblical Theology: The Unfolding of the Old Testament in the New*. Grand Rapids: Baker Academic, 2011.

———. *The Temple and the Church's Mission: A Biblical Theology of the Dwelling Place of God*. Leicester, UK: Apollos, 2004.

Beasley-Murray, George R. *John*. WBC 36. Nashville: Nelson, 2002.

Behm, Johannes. "Ἀνάμνησις, Ὑπόμνησις." In *TDNT* 1:348–49. Grand Rapids: Eerdmans, 1964.

Beier, Jonathan S., and Elizabeth S. Spelke. "Infants' Developing Understanding of Social Gaze." *Child Development* 83 (2012) 486–96.

Beilby, James K., and Paul Rhodes Eddy, eds. *The Nature of the Atonement: Four Views.* Downers Grove, IL: IVP Academic, 2006.

———. *Understanding Spiritual Warfare: Four Views.* Grand Rapids: Baker Academic, 2012.

Berkhof, Louis. *Systematic Theology.* Grand Rapids: Eerdmans, 1938.

Bertram, Georg. "Φρήν, Ἄφρων, Ἀφροσύνη, Φρονέω, Φρόνημα, Φρόνησις, Φρόνιμος." In *TDNT* 9:220–35. Grand Rapids: Eerdmans, 1974.

Best, Ernest. *The Temptation and the Passion: The Markan Soteriology.* 2nd ed. Cambridge: Cambridge University Press, 1990.

Betz, Hans Dieter. "The Concept of the 'Inner Human Being' in the Anthropology of Paul." *NTS* 46 (2000) 315–41.

Betz, Otto. "Φῶς, Φωτίζω, Φωτισμός, Φωτεινός, Φωσφόρος, Φωστήρ, Ἐπιφαύσκω, Ἐπιφώσκω." In *TDNT* 9:279–309. Grand Rapids: Eerdmans, 1974.

Bivin, David. *New Lights on the Difficult Words of Jesus: Insights from His Jewish Context.* Holland, MI: En-Gedi Resource Center, 2007.

Blenkinsopp, Joseph. *Creation, Un-Creation, Re-Creation: A Discursive Commentary on Genesis 1–11.* London: T. & T. Clark, 2011.

Blocher, Henri. *In the Beginning: The Opening Chapters of Genesis.* Translated by David G. Preston. Leicester, UK: Inter-Varsity, 1984.

———. *Original Sin: Illuminating the Riddle.* Grand Rapids: Eerdmans, 1997.

Blomberg, Craig L. *1 Corinthians.* NIVAC. Grand Rapids: Zondervan, 1994.

———. *Matthew.* New American Commentary. Nashville: Broadman, 1992.

Boer, Martinus C. de. *Galatians: A Commentary.* New Testament Library. Louisville: Westminster John Knox, 2011.

Bolt, Peter G., and Donald S. West. "Christ's Victory over the Powers and Pastoral Practice." In *Christ's Victory over Evil: Biblical Theology and Pastoral Ministry,* edited by Peter G. Bolt, 211–32. Nottingham, UK: Apollos, 2009.

Bonhoeffer, Dietrich. *Creation and Temptation.* London: SCM, 1966.

Bonner, Gerald. *The Warfare of Christ.* London: Faith Press, 1962.

Borchert, Gerald, L. *John 12–21.* New American Commentary 25B. Nashville: Broadman & Holman, 2002.

Bosch, David J. "Evangelism: Theological Currents and Cross-Currents Today." *International Bulletin of Missionary Research* 11 (1987) 98–103.

Boyd, Gregory A. "Evolution as Cosmic Warfare: A Biblical Perspective on Satan and "Natural" Evil." In *Creation Made Free: Open Theology Engaging Science,* edited by Thomas Jay Oord, 125–45. Eugene, OR: Pickwick Publications, 2009.

———. *God at War: The Bible and Spiritual Conflict.* Downers Grove, IL: IVP Academic, 1997.

———. "The Ground-Level Deliverance Model." In *Understanding Spiritual Warfare: Four Views,* edited by James K. Beilby and Paul Rhodes Eddy, 129–57. Grand Rapids: Baker Academic, 2012.

———. "Response to David Powlison." In *Understanding Spiritual Warfare: Four Views,* edited by James K. Beilby and Paul Rhodes Eddy, 117–22. Grand Rapids: Baker Academic, 2012.

———. *Satan and the Problem of Evil: Constructing a Trinitarian Warfare Theodicy.* Downers Grove, IL: InterVarsity, 2001.

Bratcher, Robert G., and Eugene Albert Nida. *A Handbook on Paul's Letters to the Colossians and to Philemon*. Helps for Translators 20. New York: United Bible Societies, 1993.

Bratcher, Robert G., and William David Reyburn. *A Handbook on the Book of Psalms*. Helps for Translators. New York: United Bible Societies, 1991.

Brockway, Dan. "Atonement." In *The Lexham Bible Dictionary*, edited by John D. Barry et al. Bellingham, WA: Lexham, 2015.

Brodrick, Robert. "From Divine Action to Divine Presence: The Next Step in an Integrated Cosmology of Science and Theology." *Lumen et Vita* 2 (2012) 1–15.

Bromiley, Geoffrey W. "Anthropomorphism." In *The International Standard Bible Encyclopedia, Revised*, edited by Geoffrey W. Bromiley, 1:386. Grand Rapids: Eerdmans, 1988.

Brown, Derek R. "The Devil in the Details: A Survey of Research on Satan in Biblical Studies." *Currents in Biblical Research* 9 (2011) 200–27.

Brown, Ken. *The Vision in Job 4 and Its Role in the Book: Reframing the Development of the Joban Dialogues*. Forschungen zum Alten Testament 2/75. Tübingen: Mohr/Stebeck, 2015.

Brown, Raymond E. *The Death of the Messiah: From Gethsemane to the Grave: A Commentary on the Passion Narratives in the Four Gospels*. ABRL. Vol. 1. New York: Doubleday, 1994.

———. *The Gospel according to John (XIII–XXI)*. AB 29A. Garden City, NY: Doubleday, 1970.

———. *An Introduction to the New Testament*. ABRL. New York: Doubleday, 1997.

———. *New Testament Essays*. Garden City, NY: Doubleday, 1968.

Broyles, Craig C. *Psalms*. Understanding the Bible. Grand Rapids: Baker, 1999.

Brueggemann, Walter. *Genesis*. Interpretation. Atlanta: John Knox, 1982.

Brümmer, Vincent. *Atonement, Christology and the Trinity: Making Sense of Christian Doctrine*. Aldershot, UK: Ashgate, 2005.

Bruner, Jerome. "Life as Narrative." *Social Research* 54 (1987) 11–32.

Brunner, Emil. *The Christian Doctrine of Creation and Redemption*. Translated by Olive Wyon. Vol. 2, London: Lutterworth, 1952.

Burge, Gary M. *John*. NIVAC. Grand Rapids: Zondervan, 2000.

Byrne, Brendan. *Romans*. Sacra Pagina. Collegeville, MN: Liturgical, 1996.

Cahill, Lisa Sowle. "Quaestio Disputata the Atonement Paradigm: Does It Still Have Explanatory Value?" *Theological Studies* 68 (2007) 418–32.

Calvin, Jean. *Commentary on a Harmony of the Evangelists, Matthew, Mark, and Luke*. Translated by William Pringle. Vol. 3. Edinburgh: Calvin Translation Society, 1555/1846.

———. *Institutes of the Christian Religion 1 & 2*. Edited by John T. McNeill. Translated by Ford Lewis Battles. Vol. 1. Louisville: Westminster John Knox, 1536/2011.

———. *Sermons from Job*. Translated by Leroy Nixon. Grand Rapids: Baker, 1979.

———. *Commentary on the Gospel according to John*. Translated by William Pringle. Vol. 2, Bellingham, WA: Logos, 2010.

Cantalamessa, Raniero. *Come Creator Spirit: Meditations on the Veni Creator*. Translated by Denis Barrett and Marlene Barrett. Collegeville, MN: Liturgical Press, 2003.

Caragounis, C. C. "Kingdom of God/Kingdom of Heaven." In *Dictionary of Jesus and the Gospels*, edited by Joel B. Green and Scot McKnight, 417–30. Downers Grove, IL: InterVarsity Press, 1992.

Carl, William J. III. *The Lord's Prayer for Today*. Louisville: Westminster John Knox, 2006.

Carmignac, Jean. "The Spiritual Wealth of the Lord's Prayer [English Translation of Chapter 21 of *Recherches Sur Le "Notre Père"*]." Translated by Elizabeth R. Petuchowski. In *The Lord's Prayer and Jewish Liturgy*, edited by Jakob J. Petuchowski and Michael Brocke, 137–46. New York: Seabury, 1978.

Carr, W. Randall. *In His Own Image and Likeness: Humanity, Divinity, and Monotheism*. Culture and History of the Ancient Near East 15. Leiden: Brill, 2003.

Carson, D. A. *The Gospel according to John*. PNTC. Grand Rapids: Eerdmans, 1991.

Childs, Brevard S. *Biblical Theology of the Old and New Testaments: Theological Reflection on the Christian Bible*. London: SCM, 1992.

———. *Isaiah*. Louisville: Westminster John Knox, 2001.

Chilton, Bruce. "Introduction." In *The Kingdom of God*, edited by Bruce Chilton, 1–26. London: SPCK, 1984.

———. *Jesus' Prayer and Jesus' Eucharist*. Valley Forge, PA: Trinity, 1997.

Christensen, Michael J., and Jeffery A. Wittung, eds. *Partakers of the Divine Nature: The History and Development of Deification in the Christian Traditions*. Grand Rapids: Baker Academic, 2007.

Chryssavgis, John. *In the Heart of the Desert: The Spirituality of the Desert Fathers and Mothers*. Bloomington, IN: World Wisdom, 2008.

Clines, David J. A. "The Image of God in Man." *Tyndale Bulletin* 19 (1968) 53–103.

———. "Job." In *New Bible Commentary*, edited by D. A. Carson et al., 459–84. Nottingham, UK: Inter-Varsity, 1994.

———. *Job 1–20*. WBC 18. Dallas: Word, 1989.

———. *Job 21–37*. WBC 18A. Dallas: Word, 2006.

———. *Job 38–42*. WBC 18B. Nashville: Nelson, 2011.

Cogliati, Carlo. "Introduction." In *Creation and the God of Abraham*, edited by David B. Burrell et al., 1–10. Cambridge: Cambridge University Press, 2010.

Collins, Adela Yarbro. *Mark: A Commentary*. Hermeneia. Minneapolis: Fortress, 2007.

Collins, C. John. *Genesis 1–4: A Linguistic, Literary, and Theological Commentary*. Phillipsburg, NJ: P & R Publishing, 2006.

Cranfield, C. E. B. *A Critical and Exegetical Commentary on the Epistle to the Romans*. Vol. 1. International Critical Commentary. Edinburgh: T. & T. Clark, 1975.

Crenshaw, James L. *Old Testament Wisdom: An Introduction*. 3rd ed. Louisville: Westminster John Knox, 2010.

Crites, Stephen. "The Narrative Quality of Experience." *Journal of the American Academy of Religion* 39 (1971) 291–311.

Crump, David. *Knocking on Heaven's Door: A New Testament Theology of Petitionary Prayer*. Grand Rapids: Baker Academic, 2006.

Culver, Robert D. "Anthropomorphism." In *Baker Encyclopedia of the Bible*, edited by Walter A. Elwell and Barry J. Beitzel, 117–18. Grand Rapids: Baker, 1988.

Dalton, William Joseph. *Christ's Proclamation to the Spirits: A Study of 1 Peter 3:18–4:6*. 2nd ed. Analecta Biblica 23. Rome: Editrice Pontifico Istituto Biblico, 1989.

Daly, Gabriel. *Creation and Redemption*. Theology and Life Series 25. Wilmington, DE: Glazier, 1989.

Danker, Frederick W. "The Demonic Secret in Mark: A Reexamination of the Cry of Dereliction (15 34)." *Zeitschrift für die neutestamentliche Wissenschaft* 61 (1970) 48–69.

Davids, Peter H. *The Epistle of James: A Commentary on the Greek Text*. NIGTC. Grand Rapids: Eerdmans, 1982.

Davies, William David and Dale C. Jr. Allison. *A Critical and Exegetical Commentary on the Gospel according to Saint Matthew*. Vol. 2. International Critical Commentary. Edinburgh: T. & T. Clark, 1991.

———. *Matthew: A Shorter Commentary*. London: Continuum, 2004.

Davis, Ellen F. "Critical Traditioning: Seeking an Inner Biblical Hermeneutic." In *The Art of Reading Scripture*, edited by Ellen F. Davis and Richard B. Hays, 163–80. Grand Rapids: Eerdmans, 2003.

Day, John. *From Creation to Babel: Studies in Genesis 1–11*. London: Bloomsbury, 2013.

De La Torre, Miguel A. *Genesis*. Belief. Louisville: Westminster John Knox, 2011.

deClaissé-Walford, Nancy et al. *The Book of Psalms*. NICOT. Grand Rapids: Eerdmans, 2014.

Deissler, Alfons. "The Spirit of the Lord's Prayer in the Faith and Worship of the Old Testament." In *The Lord's Prayer and Jewish Liturgy*, edited by Jakob J. Petuchowski, 3–17. New York: Seabury, 1978.

DeLamater, John, and William N. Friedrich. "Human Sexual Development." *Journal of Social Issues* 39 (2002) 10–14.

Dibelius, Martin, and Heinrich Greeven. *James: A Commentary on the Epistle of James*. Translated by Michael A. Williams. Hermeneia. Philadelphia: Fortress, 1975.

Dillenberger, John, ed. *Martin Luther: Selections from His Writings*. Garden City, NY: Doubleday, 1961.

Dunn, James D. G. *The Epistles to the Colossians and to Philemon: A Commentary on the Greek Text*. NIGTC. Grand Rapids: Eerdmans, 1996.

———. *Jesus and the Spirit: A Study of the Religious and Charismatic Experience of Jesus and the First Christians as Reflected in the New Testament*. London: SCM, 1975.

———. "Prayer." In *Dictionary of Jesus and the Gospels*, edited by Joel B. Green and Scot McKnight, 617–25. Downers Grove, IL: InterVarsity, 1992.

———. *Romans 1–8*. WBC 38A. Dallas: Word, 1988.

———. "Spirit, Holy Spirit." In *New Bible Dictionary*, edited by I. Howard Marshall et al., 1125–29. Downers Grove, IL: InterVarsity, 1996.

———. *The Theology of Paul the Apostle*. Grand Rapids: Eerdmans, 1998.

Duvall, J. Scott. *Revelation*. Teach the Text Commentary Series. Grand Rapids: Baker, 2014.

Eddy, Paul Rhodes, and James K. Beilby. "Introducing Spiritual Warfare: A Survey of Key Issues and Debates." In *Understanding Spiritual Warfare: Four Views*, edited by James K. Beilby and Paul Rhodes Eddy, 1–45. Grand Rapids: Baker Academic, 2012.

Ellison, H. L. "Book of Job." In *New Bible Dictionary*, edited by I. Howard Marshall et al., 589–90. Downers Grove, IL: IVP Academic, 1996.

Emerson, Matthew Y. *Christ and the New Creation: A Canonical Approach to the Theology of the New Testament*. Eugene, OR: Wipf & Stock, 2013.

Enns, Peter. *Exodus*. NIVAC. Grand Rapids: Zondervan, 2000.

Eubank, Nathan. *Wages of Cross-Bearing and Debt of Sin: The Economy of Heaven in Matthew's Gospel*. BZNW 196. Berlin: de Gruyter, 2013.

Evdokimov, Paul. "Nature." *Scottish Journal of Theology* 18 (1965) 1–22.

Farmer, Ron. "The Kingdom of God in the Gospel of Matthew." In *The Kingdom of God in 20th-Century Interpretation*, edited by Wendell Willis, 119–30. Peabody, MA: Hendrickson, 1987.

Fee, Gordon D. *The First Epistle to the Corinthians*. Rev. ed. NICNT. Grand Rapids: Eerdmans, 2014.

———. *God's Empowering Presence: The Holy Spirit in the Letters of Paul*. Peabody, MA: Hendrickson, 1994.

Ferguson, J. Wesley *What the Bible Teaches: Genesis*. Kilmarnock, Scotland: John Ritchie, 2010.

Fergusson, David A. S. *Creation*. Grand Rapids: Eerdmans, 2014.

———. "Creation." In *The Oxford Handbook of Systematic Theology*, edited by John Webster et al., 72–90. New York: Oxford University Press, 2007.

———. *The Cosmos and the Creator: An Introduction to the Theology of Creation*. London: SPCK, 1998.

Finlan, Stephen. *Problems with Atonement: The Origins of, and Controversy about, the Atonement Doctrine*. Collegeville, MN: Liturgical, 2005.

———. "Second Peter's Notion of Divine Participation." In *Theosis: Deification in Christian Theology*, edited by Stephen Finlan and Vladimir Kharlamov, 32–50. Eugene, OR: Pickwick Publications, 2006.

Finlan, Stephen, and Vladimir Kharlamov. "Introduction." In *Theosis: Deification in Christian Theology*, edited by Stephen Finlan and Vladimir Kharlamov, 1–15. Eugene, OR: Pickwick Publications, 2006.

———. *Theosis: Deification in Christian Theology*. Princeton Theological Monograph Series 156. Eugene, OR: Pickwick Publications, 2006.

Fischer, Rainer. "Revelation as Gestalt." Translated by John Barton. In *Revelation and Story: Narrative Theology and the Centrality of Story*, edited by Gerhard Sauter and John Barton, 79–97. Aldershot, UK: Ashgate, 2000.

Forde, Gerhard O. "The Work of Christ." In *Christian Dogmatics*, Vol. 2, edited by Carl E. Braaten and Robert W. Jenson, 1–99. Philadelphia: Fortress, 1984.

France, R. T. *Matthew: An Introduction and Commentary*. Tyndale New Testament Commentaries 1. Nottingham, UK: Inter-Varsity, 1985.

Frei, Hans W. *The Eclipse of Biblical Narrative: A Study of Eighteenth and Nineteenth Century Hermeneutics*. New Haven: Yale University Press, 1974.

———. "Response to 'Narrative Theology: An Evangelical Appraisal.'" *Trinity Journal* 8 (Spring 1987) 21–24.

Fyall, Robert S. *Now My Eyes Have Seen You: Images of Creation and Evil in the Book of Job*. Leicester, UK: Apollos, 2002.

Gage, Warren Austin, and R. Fowler White. "The John-Revelation Project." http://web.archive.org/web/20041121164345/http://www.knoxseminary.org/prospective/Faculty/FacultyForum/JohnRevelationProject/part7.html.

Garrett, Susan R. *The Temptations of Jesus in Mark's Gospel*. Grand Rapids: Eerdmans, 1998.

Gathercole, Simon. "Jesus' Eschatological Vision of the Fall of Satan: Luke 10,18 Reconsidered." *Zeitschrift für die Neutestamentliche Wissenschaft* 94 (2003) 143–63.

Geldenhuys, J. N., and F. F. Bruce. "The Lord's Prayer." In *New Bible Dictionary*, edited by I. Howard Marshall et al., 695–96. Downers Grove, IL: InterVarsity, 1996.

Gibson, Jeffrey B. *The Temptation of Jesus in Early Christianity*. Sheffield: Sheffield Academic, 1995.

Giere, Samuel D. *A New Glimpse of Day One: Intertextuality, History of Interpretation, and Genesis 1.1–5*. BZNW 172. Berlin: de Gruyter, 2009.

Ginsberg, Harold Louis et al., "Book of Job." In *Encyclopedia Judaica*, edited by Michael Berenbaum and Fred Skolnik, 341–59. Detroit: Macmillan Reference, 2007.

Godin, André. "The Psychology of Temptation." *Journal of Empirical Theology* 5 (1992) 74–85.

Goldingay, John. "Biblical Narrative and Systematic Theology." In *Between Two Horizons: Spanning New Testament Studies and Systematic Theology*, edited by Joel B. Green and Max Turner, 123–42. Grand Rapids: Eerdmans, 2000.

———. *Old Testament Theology 1: Israel's Gospel*. Downers Grove, IL: InterVarsity, 2003.

———. "The 'Salvation History' Perspective and the 'Wisdom' Perspective within the Context of Biblical Theology." *Evangelical Quarterly* 51 (1979) 194–207.

Gombis, Timothy G. *The Drama of Ephesians: Participating in the Triumph of God*. Downers Grove, IL: IVP Academic, 2010.

———. "A Radically New Humanity: The Function of the Haustafel in Ephesians." *Journal of the Evangelical Theological Society* 48 (2005) 317–30.

González Faus, José Ignacio. "Sin." In *Mysterium Liberationis*, edited by Ignacio Ellacuría and Jon Sobrino, 532–42. Maryknoll, NY: Orbis, 1993.

Gordis, Robert. *The Book of Job: Commentary, New Translation and Special Studies*. New York: Jewish Theological Seminary of America, 1978.

Graaf, Hanneke de, and Jany Rademakers. "The Psychological Measurement of Childhood Sexual Development in Western Societies: Methodological Challenges." *Journal of Sex Research* 48 (2011) 118–29.

Graubard, Baruch. "The *Kaddish* Prayer." In *The Lord's Prayer and Jewish Liturgy*, edited by Jakob J. Petuchowski, 59–72. New York: Seabury, 1978.

Green, Gene L. *Jude and 2 Peter*. BECNT. Grand Rapids: Baker Academic, 2008.

Green, Joel B. *1 Peter*. Two Horizons New Testament Commentary. Grand Rapids: Eerdmans, 2007.

———. *The Gospel of Luke*. NICNT. Grand Rapids: Eerdmans, 1997.

———. "Kaleidoscopic View." In *The Nature of the Atonement: Four Views*, edited by James Beilby and Paul Rhodes Eddy, 157–85. Downers Grove, IL: IVP Academic, 2006.

———. "Narrative Theology." In *Dictionary for Theological Interpretation of the Bible*, edited by Kevin J. Vanhoozer, 531–33. London: SPCK, 2005.

Green, Michael. *2 Peter and Jude: An Introduction and Commentary*. Tyndale New Testament Commentaries 18. Downers Grove, IL: InterVarsity, 1987.

———. *Evangelism in the Early Church*. updated ed. Guildford, UK: Eagle, 1970.

———. *I Believe in Satan's Downfall*. 3rd ed. London: Hodder & Stoughton, 1995.

Greenberg, Moshe et al. "Decalogue." In *Encyclopedia Judaica*, edited by Michael Berenbaum and Fred Skolnik, 520–26. Detroit: Macmillan Reference, 2007.

Greenstein, Edward L. "'On My Skin and in My Flesh': Personal Experience as a Source of Knowledge in the Book of Job." In *Bringing the Hidden to Light: The Process of Interpretation: Studies in Honor of Stephen A. Geller*, edited by Kathryn F. Kravitz and Diane M. Sharon, 63–77. Winona Lake, IN: Eisenbrauns, 2007.

Greer, Rowan A. "The Christian Bible and Its Interpretation." In *Early Biblical Interpretation*, edited by James L. Kugel and Rowan A. Greer, 109–208. Philadelphia: Westminster, 1986.

Gregersen, Niels Henrik. "From Anthropic Design to Self-Organized Complexity." In *From Complexity to Life: On the Emergence of Life and Meaning*, edited by Niels Henrik Gregersen, 206–34. New York: Oxford University Press, 2003.

Griffin, David Ray. "Creation out of Nothing, Creation out of Chaos, and the Problem of Evil." In *Encountering Evil: Live Options in Theodicy*, edited by Stephen D. Davis, 108–44. Louisville: Westminster John Knox, 2001.

Griffiths, Paul. "The Limits of Narrative Theology." In *Faith and Narrative*, edited by Keith E. Yandell, 217–36. New York: Oxford University Press, 2001.

Grudem, Wayne. *Systematic Theology: An Introduction to Biblical Doctrine*. Nottingham, UK: Inter-Varsity, 1994.

Gunton, Colin E. *The Actuality of Atonement: A Study of Metaphor, Rationality and the Christian Tradition*. Edinburgh: T. & T. Clark, 1988.

Guthrie, Donald. *Hebrews: An Introduction and Commentary*. Tyndale New Testament Commentaries 15. Downers Grove, IL: IVP Academic, 1983.

Habel, Norman C. *The Book of Job: A Commentary*. Cambridge Bible Commentary. London: SCM, 1985.

Hamilton, Victor P. *The Book of Genesis: Chapters 1–17*. NICOT. Grand Rapids: Eerdmans, 1990.

Hammerling, Roy. "The Lord's Prayer: A Cornerstone of Early Baptismal Dedication." In *A History of Prayer: The First to the Fifteenth Century*, edited by Roy Hammerling, 167–82. Brill's Companions to the Christian Tradition 13. Leiden: Brill, 2008.

Harding, James E. "A Spirit of Deception in Job 4:15? Interpretive Indeterminacy and Eliphaz's Vision." *Biblical Interpretation* 13 (2005) 137–66.

Hardon, John A. *Catholic Dictionary: An Abridged and Updated Edition of the Modern Catholic Dictionary*. New York: Image, 2013.

Harris, Murray J. *The Second Epistle to the Corinthians*. NIGTC. Grand Rapids: Eerdmans, 2005.

Harrisville, Roy A. "The Concept of Newness in the New Testament." *Journal of Biblical Literature* 74 (1955) 69–79.

Hart, Trevor. "Redemption and Fall." In *The Cambridge Companion to Christian Doctrine*, edited by Colin E. Gunton, 189–206. Cambridge: Cambridge University Press, 1997.

Hartley, John E. *The Book of Job*. NICOT. Grand Rapids: Eerdmans, 1988.

Harvey, John D. "Mission in Jesus' Teaching." In *Mission in the New Testament: An Evangelical Approach*, edited by William J. Jr. Larkin and Joel F. Williams, 30–49. Maryknoll, NY: Orbis, 1998.

Hauerwas, Stanley, and L. Gregory Jones. "Introduction: Why Narrative?" In *Why Narrative? Readings in Narrative Theology*, edited by Stanley Hauerwas and L. Gregory Jones, 1–18. Grand Rapids: Eerdmans, 1989.

Haught, John F. *God after Darwin: A Theology of Evolution*. 2nd ed. Boulder, CO: Westview, 2008.

———. "In Praise of Imperfection." *Theology and Science* 6 (2008) 173–77.

———. *Resting on the Future: Catholic Theology for an Unfinished Universe*. New York: Bloomsbury Academic, 2015.

Hays, Richard B. "Reading the Bible with Eyes of Faith: The Practice of Theological Exegesis." *Journal of Theological Interpretation* 1 (2007) 5–22.

Heiser, Michael S. "Divine Council." In *The Lexham Bible Dictionary*, edited by John D. Barry et al. Bellingham, WA: Lexham, 2015.

———. *The Unseen Realm: Recovering the Supernatural Worldview of the Bible.* Bellingham, WA: Lexham, 2015.

Hick, John. *Evil and the God of Love.* 2nd ed. Basingstoke: Macmillan, 1985.

Hoch, Carl B. Jr. *All Things New: The Significance of Newness for Biblical Theology.* Grand Rapids: Baker, 1995.

Holmes, Stephen R. *The Wondrous Cross: Atonement and Penal Substitution in the Bible and History.* Milton Keynes, UK: Paternoster, 2007.

Home, Brian. "Theology in the Narrative Mode." In *Companion Encyclopedia of Theology*, edited by Leslie Houlden, 958–75. London: Routledge, 1995.

Horan, Daniel P. "How Original Was Scotus on the Incarnation? Reconsidering the History of the Absolute Predestination of Christ in Light of Robert Grosseteste." *Heythrop Journal* 52 (2011) 374–91.

Horrobin, Peter. *Healing Though Deliverance.* Rev. ed. Vol. 2. Tonbridge, UK: Sovereign World, 2003.

———. *The Most Powerful Prayer on Earth: Pray the Prayer That Can Transform Your Life.* Ventura, CA: Regal, 2004.

Houlden, J. L. "Lord's Prayer." In *Anchor Bible Dictionary*, edited by D. N. Freedman, 356–62. New York: Doubleday, 1992.

Hubbard, Moyer V. *New Creation in Paul's Letters and Thought.* Cambridge: Cambridge University Press, 2002.

Hultgren, Arland. *Paul's Letter to the Romans: A Commentary.* Grand Rapids: Eerdmans, 2011.

Humphrey, Edith M. "New Creation." In *Dictionary for Theological Interpretation of the Bible*, edited by Kevin J. Vanhoozer, 536–37. London: SPCK, 2005.

Hunsinger, George. "Afterword: Hans Frei as Theologian." In *Theology and Narrative: Selected Essays of Hans Frei*, edited by George Hunsinger and William C. Placher, 235–70. New York: Oxford University Press, 1993.

Hvalvik, Reidar. "In Word and Deed: The Expansion of the Church in the Pre-Constantine Era." In *The Mission of the Early Church to Jews and Gentiles*, edited by Jostein Ådna and Hans Kvalbein, 265–87. Wissenschaftliche Untersuchungen zum Neuen Testament 127. Tübingen: Mohr/Siebeck, 2000.

Jackson, Bill. *The Eden Project: A Short Story.* Corona, CA: Radical Middle Press, 2012.

Jacobs, Louis et al. "Passover." In *Encyclopedia Judaica*, edited by Michael Berenbaum and Fred Skolnik, 15:678–83. Detroit: Macmillan Reference, 2007.

Janzen, J. Gerald. *Job.* Interpretation. Atlanta: John Knox, 1985.

Jenson, Robert W. *Systematic Theology.* Vol. 1. New York: Oxford University Press, 1997.

———. *Systematic Theology: The Works of God.* Vol. 2. New York: Oxford University Press, 1999.

Jeremias, Joachim. *The Eucharistic Words of Jesus.* Translated by Norman Perrin. London: SCM, 1966.

———. *The Lord's Prayer.* Translated by John Reumann. Philadelphia: Fortress, 1964.

———. *New Testament Theology.* Vol. 1, *The Proclamation of Jesus.* Translated by John Bowden. London: SCM, 1971.

Jewett, Robert. *Romans: A Commentary.* Hermeneia. Minneapolis: Fortress, 2007.

Jobes, Karen H. *1 Peter*. BECNT. Grand Rapids: Baker Academic, 2005.

Johnson, Adam J. *Atonement: A Guide for the Perplexed*. Guides for the Perplexed. New York: Bloomsbury T. & T. Clark, 2015.

Jones, L. Gregory. "Narrative Theology." In *The Blackwell Encyclopedia of Modern Christian Thought*, edited by Alister E. McGrath, 395–98. Malden, MA: Blackwell, 1993.

Keener, Craig S. *The Gospel of Matthew: A Socio-Rhetorical Commentary*. New ed. Grand Rapids: Eerdmans, 2009.

———. *Romans*. New Covenant Commentary Series 6. Eugene, OR: Cascade Books, 2009.

Kelly, Henry Ansgar. *Satan: A Biography*. Cambridge: Cambridge University Press, 2006.

Kelly, J. N. D. *Early Christian Doctrines*. 5th ed. London: A & C Black, 1977.

———. *The Epistles of Peter and of Jude*. Black's New Testament Commentary. 1969. Reprinted, London: Continuum, 1990.

Kelsey, David H. "The Doctrine of Creation from Nothing." In *Creation and Humanity: The Sources of Christian Theology*, edited by Ian A. McFarland, 47–65. 1985. Reprinted, Louisville: Westminster John Knox, 2009.

Kendall, R. T. *The Lord's Prayer*. London: Hodder & Stoughton, 2010.

Kidner, Derek. *Genesis: An Introduction and Commentary*. Tyndale Old Testament Commentaries 1. 1967. Reprint, Nottingham, UK: Inter-Varsity, 2008.

Klitsner, Judy. *Subversive Sequels in the Bible: How Biblical Stories Mine and Undermine Each Other*. Philadelphia: Jewish Publication Society, 2009.

Kuhn, Karl Georg. "New Light on Temptation, Sin, and Flesh in the New Testament." In *The Scrolls and the New Testament*, edited by Krister Stendahl, 94–113. London: SCM, 1958.

Kurz, William S. *Reading the Bible as God's Own Story: A Catholic Approach for Bringing Scripture to Life*. Ijamswille, MD: The Word among Us Press, 2007.

Kushner, Harold S. *The Book of Job: When Bad Things Happened to Good People*. New York: Nextbook and Schocken, 2012.

Ladd, George Eldon. *A Theology of the New Testament*. Grand Rapids: Eerdmans, 1974.

———. *A Theology of the New Testament*. Rev. ed. Grand Rapids: Eerdmans, 1993.

Lang, T. J. *Mystery and the Making of a Christian Historical Consciousness: From Paul to the Second Century*. BZNW 219. Berlin: de Gruyter, 2015.

Lapsley, Daniel, and Gustavo Carlo. "Moral Development at the Crossroads: New Trends and Possible Futures." *Developmental Psychology* 50 (2014) 1–7.

Laws, Sophie. *The Epistle of James*. Black's New Testament Commentaries. London: A & C Black, 1980.

Lenski, R. C. H. *The Interpretation of St. Matthew's Gospel*. Minneapolis: Augsburg, 1961.

Leonhard, Clemens. *Jewish Pesach and the Origins of the Christian Easter: Open Questions in Current Research*. Studia Judaica 35. Berlin: de Gruyter, 2006.

Levenson, Jon D. *Creation and the Persistence of Evil: The Jewish Drama of Divine Omnipotence*. 2nd ed. Princeton: Princeton University Press, 1994.

Liefeld, W. L. "Prayer." In *The International Standard Bible Encyclopedia, Revised*, edited by Geoffrey W. Bromiley, 3:931–39. Grand Rapids: Eerdmans, 1988.

Lincoln, Andrew T. *Ephesians*. WBC 42. Nashville: Nelson, 1990.

Lindars, Barnabas. *The Gospel of John*. New Century Bible. London: Oliphants, 1972.

Lindbeck, George A. *The Nature of Doctrine: Religion and Theology in a Postliberal Age.* Louisville: Westminster John Knox, 1984.

Link, Christian. "Creatio Continua." In *Religion Past and Present Online*, edited by Hans Dieter Betz et al., Leiden: Brill, 2011.

Lochman, Jan M. *The Lord's Prayer.* Translated by Geoffrey W. Bromiley. Grand Rapids: Eerdmans, 1990.

Lohmeyer, Ernst. *The Lord's Prayer.* Translated by John Bowden. London: Collins, 1965.

Löning, Karl, and Erich Zenger. *To Begin With, God Created . . . Biblical Theologies of Creation.* Translated by Omar Kaste. Collegeville, MN: Liturgical, 2000.

Lorenz, Hendrik. "Ancient Theories of the Soul." In *The Stanford Encyclopedia of Philosophy (on-line)*, edited by Edward N. Zalta, <http://plato.stanford.edu/archives/sum2009/entries/ancient-soul/>, 2009.

Lossky, Vladimir. *In the Image and Likeness of God.* New York: St Vladimir's Seminary Press, 1974.

————. *The Mystical Theology of the Eastern Church.* London: James Clarke, 1957.

Luz, Ulrich. *Matthew 1–7: A Commentary.* Translated by James E. Crouch. Rev. ed. Hermeneia. Minneapolis: Fortress, 2007.

Mann, William E. "Augustine on Evil and Original Sin." In *The Cambridge Companion to Augustine*, edited by Eleonore Stump and Norman Kretzmann, 40–48. Cambridge: Cambridge University Press, 2001.

Marcus, Joel. *Mark 8–16: A New Translation with Introduction and Commentary.* AB 27B. New Haven: Yale University Press, 2009.

Marshall, I. Howard. *A Concise New Testament Theology.* Downers Grove, IL: InterVarsity, 2008.

————. "The Development of the Doctrine of Redemption in the New Testament." In *Reconciliation and Hope: New Testament Essays on Atonement and Eschatology*, edited by Robert Banks, 153–69. Carlisle, UK: Paternoster, 1974.

————. *The Gospel of Luke: A Commentary on the Greek Text.* NIGTC. Exeter, UK: Paternoster, 1978.

————. "Jesus: Example and Teacher of Prayer in the Synoptic Gospels." In *Into God's Presence: Prayer in the New Testament*, edited by R. N. Longenecker, 113–31. Grand Rapids: Eerdmans, 2001.

————. *Last Supper and Lord's Supper.* Milton Keynes, UK: Paternoster, 1980.

————. *New Testament Theology.* Downers Grove, IL: InterVarsity, 2004.

Martin, Ralph P. *James.* WBC 48. Dallas, Tex: Word Books, 1998.

Matera, Frank J. *II Corinthians: A Commentary.* New Testament Library. Louisville: Westminster John Knox, 2003.

————. *Galatians.* Sacra Pagina. Collegeville, MN: Liturgical, 2007.

Matthews, Gerald, and Moshe Zeidner. "Traits, States, and the Trilogy of the Mind: An Adaptive Perspective on Intellectual Functioning." In *Motivation, Emotion, and Cognition: Integrative Perspectives on Intellectual Functioning and Development*, edited by D. Y. Dai and R. J. Sternberg' 143–74. Mahwah, NJ: Lawrence Erlbaum, 2004.

May, Gerhard. *Creatio ex Nihilo: The Doctrine of 'Creation out of Nothing' in Early Christian Thought.* Translated by A. S. Worrall. Edinburgh: T. & T. Clark, 1994.

Mayer, John D., Heather Frasier Chabot, and Kevin M. Carlsmith. "Conation, Affect, and Cognition in Personality." In *Cognitive Science Perspectives on Personality and Emotion*, edited by G. Matthews, 31–63. Amsterdam: Elsevier, 1997.

McBrayer, Justin P., and Daniel Howard-Snyder, eds. *The Blackwell Companion to the Problem of Evil*. Chichester, UK: Wiley Blackwell, 2013.

McCartney, Dan G. *James*. BECNT. Grand Rapids: Baker Academic, 2009.

McDonough, Sean M. *Creation and New Creation: Understanding God's Creation Project*. Milton Keynes, UK: Paternoster, 2016.

McFarland, Ian A. "The Fall and Sin." In *The Oxford Handbook of Systematic Theology*, edited by John Webster et al., 140–59. Oxford Handbooks. New York: Oxford University Press, 2007.

———. *From Nothing: A Theology of Creation*. Louisville: Westminster John Knox, 2014.

McGrath, Alister E. *Christian Theology: An Introduction*. 4th ed. Oxford: Blackwell, 2007.

McGuckin, John Anthony. *The Orthodox Church: An Introduction to Its History, Doctrine, and Spiritual Culture*. Malden, MA: Wiley-Blackwell, 2008.

McKeown, James. *Genesis*. Two Horizons Old Testament Commentary. Grand Rapids: Eerdmans, 2008.

McKinley, John E. *Tempted for Us: Theological Models and the Practical Relevance of Christ's Impeccability and Temptation*. Milton Keynes, UK: Paternoster, 2009.

McKnight, Scot. *Jesus and His Death: Historiography, the Historical Jesus, and Atonement Theory*. Waco, TX: Baylor University Press, 2005.

McMullin, Ernan. "Creation *Ex Nihilo*: Early History." In *Creation and the God of Abraham*, edited by David B. Burrell et al., 11–23. Cambridge: Cambridge University Press, 2010.

Meier, John P. *A Marginal Jew: Rethinking the Historical Jesus*. Vol. 2: *Mentor, Message, and Miracles*. ABRL. New York: Doubleday, 1994.

Méndez Montoya, Angel F. *Theology of Food: Eating and the Eucharist*. Illuminations—Theory and Religion. Chichester, UK: Wiley-Blackwell, 2009.

Metzger, Bruce M. "Seventy or Seventy-Two Disciples." *NTS* 5 (1959) 306–17.

Meyendorff, John. *Byzantine Theology: Historical Trends and Doctrinal Themes*. 2nd ed. New York: Fordham University Press, 1979.

Michaels, J. Ramsey. *1 Peter*. WBC 49. Dallas: Word, 1998.

———. *The Gospel of John*. NICNT. Grand Rapids: Eerdmans, 2010.

Miller, Timothy D. "On the Distinction between Creation and Conservation: A Partial Defence of Continuous Creation." *Religious Studies* 45 (2009) 471–85.

Moberly, R. W. L. "Did the Serpent Get It Right?" *Journal of Theological Studies* n.s. 391 (1988) 1–27.

———. *The Theology of the Book of Genesis*. Old Testament Theology. Cambridge: Cambridge University Press, 2009.

———. "What Is Theological Interpretation of Scripture?" *Journal of Theological Interpretation* 3 (2009) 161–78.

Moltmann, Jürgen. "Creation and Redemption." In *Creation, Christ and Culture: Studies in Honour of T. F. Torrance*, edited by Richard W. A. McKinney, 119–34. Edinburgh: T. & T. Clark, 1976.

———. *The Future of Creation*. London: SCM, 1979.

———. *God in Creation: An Ecological Doctrine of Creation*. London: SCM, 1985.

———. "Reflections on Chaos and God's Interaction with the World from a Trinitarian Perspective." In *Chaos and Complexity: Scientific Perspectives on Divine Action*, edited by Robert John Russell et al., 205–10. Vatican: Vatican Observatory, 1995.

———. "The Spirit of Life." In *The Spirit in Creation and New Creation*, edited by Michael Welker, 65–78. Grand Rapids: Eerdmans, 2012.

Moo, Douglas J. *2 Peter and Jude*. NIVAC. Grand Rapids: Zondervan, 1996.

———. "Creation and New Creation." *Bulletin for Biblical Research* 20 (2010) 39–60.

———. *The Epistle to the Romans*. NICNT. Grand Rapids: Eerdmans, 1996.

———. *The Letter of James*. PNTC. Grand Rapids: Eerdmans, 2000.

———. *The Letters to the Colossians and to Philemon*. PNTC. Grand Rapids: Eerdmans, 2008.

Morris, Leon. *The Gospel according to John*. NICNT. Grand Rapids: Eerdmans, 1995.

———. *Luke: An Introduction and Commentary*. Tyndale New Testament Commentaries 3. Downers Grove, IL: IVP Academic, 1988.

Moses, Robert Ewusie. *Practices of Power: Revisiting the Principalities and Powers in the Pauline Letters*. Minneapolis: Fortress, 2014.

———. "'The Satan' in Light of the Creation Theology of Job." *Horizons in Biblical Theology* 34 (2012) 19–34.

Motyer, Steve. "New, Newness." In *Evangelical Dictionary of Theology*, edited by Walter A. Elwell, 824. Grand Rapids: Baker Academic, 2001.

Murphy, Ed. *The Handbook for Spiritual Warfare*. 3rd ed. Nashville: Nelson, 2003.

Murphy, Roland E. *Proverbs*. WBC 22. Nashville: Nelson, 1998.

Myers, Allen C., ed. *The Eerdmans Bible Dictionary*. Grand Rapids: Eerdmans, 1987.

Nelson, Derek R. *Sin: A Guide for the Perplexed*. London: T. & T. Clark, 2011.

Neufeld, Thomas R. Yoder. *Recovering Jesus: The Witness of the New Testament*. Grand Rapids: Brazos, 2007.

Newsom, Carol A. "The Book of Job: Introduction, Commentary, and Reflections." In *The New Interpreter's Bible*, edited by Leander E. Keck, 4:319–637. Nashville: Abingdon, 1996.

Newsom, Carol A. *The Book of Job: A Contest of Moral Imaginations*. Oxford: Oxford University Press, 2003.

Neyrey, Jerome H. *The Gospel of John*. New Cambridge Bible Commentary. Cambridge: Cambridge University Press, 2007.

Nicholl, Desmond S. T. *An Introduction to Genetic Engineering*. 3rd ed. Cambridge: Cambridge University Press, 2008.

Nijman, M., and K. A. Worp. "'Ἐπιούσιοσ' in a Documentary Papyrus?" *Novum Testamentum* 41 (1999) 231–34.

Nolland, John. *The Gospel of Matthew: A Commentary on the Greek Text*. NIGTC. Grand Rapids: Eerdmans, 2005.

———. *Luke 1—9:20*. WBC 35A. Dallas: Word, 1989.

———. *Luke 9:21—18:34*. WBC 35B. Dallas: Word, 1993.

O'Brien, Peter T. *Colossians, Philemon*. WBC 44. Dallas: Word, 1998.

———. *The Letter to the Ephesians*. PNTC. Grand Rapids: Eerdmans, 1999.

O'Collins, Gerald. *The Lord's Prayer*. London: Darton, Longman and Todd, 2006.

O'Loughlin, Thomas. *The Eucharist: Origins and Contemporary Understandings*. London: Bloomsbury T. & T. Clark, 2015.

Oates, Wayne E. *Temptation: A Biblical and Psychological Approach*. Louisville: Westminster John Knox, 1991.

Och, Bernard. "Creation and Redemption: Toward a Theology of Creation." *Judaism* 44 (1995) 226–43.

Osborn, Lawrence H. "Creation." In *New Dictionary of Biblical Theology*, edited by T. Desmond Alexander and Brian S. Rosner, 429–35. Leicester, UK: Inter-Varsity, 2000.

Osborne, Grant R. *Revelation*. BECNT. Grand Rapids: Baker Academic, 2002.

Oswalt, John N. *The Book of Isaiah Chapters 1–39*. Grand Rapids: Eerdmans, 1986.

Packer, J. I. *Praying the Lord's Prayer*. Wheaton, IL: Crossway, 2007.

Page, Sydney H. T. *Powers of Evil: A Biblical Study of Satan and Demons*. Grand Rapids: Baker Books, 1995.

Pannenberg, Wolfhart. "The Doctrine of Creation and Modern Science." *Zygon* 23 (1988) 3–21.

———. "Faith in God the Creator and Scientific Cosmology." *Communio: International Catholic Review* 28 (2001) 450–62.

———. "Problems between Science and Theology in the Course of Their Modern History." *Zygon* 41 (2006) 105–12.

———. *Systematic Theology*. Translated by Geoffrey W. Bromiley. Vol. 2, Edinburgh: T. & T. Clark, 1994.

———. *Systematic Theology*. Translated by Geoffrey W. Bromiley. Vol. 3, Edinburgh: T. & T. Clark, 1998.

Parker, D. C. *The Living Text of the Gospels*. Cambridge: Cambridge University Press, 1997.

Patmore, Hector M. *Adam, Satan, and the King of Tyre: The Interpretation of Ezekiel 28:11–19 in Late Antiquity* Leiden: Brill, 2012.

Patrick, Dale. "The Kingdom of God in the Old Testament." In *The Kingdom of God in 20th-Century Interpretation*, edited by Wendell Willis, 67–79. Peabody, MA: Hendrickson, 1987.

Patterson, David. *Open Wounds: The Crisis of Jewish Thought in the Aftermath of Auschwitz*. Seattle, WA: University of Washington Press, 2006.

Paul, Mart-Jan. "The Disturbing Experience of Eliphaz in Job 4: Divine or Demonic Manifestation?" In *Goochem in Mokum, Wisdom in Amsterdam: Papers on Biblical and Related Wisdom Read at the Fifteenth Joint Meeting of the Society for Old Testament Study and the Oudtestamentisch Werkgezelschap, Amsterdam July 2012*, edited by George J. Brooke and Pierre van Hecke, 108–20. Old Testament Studies 68. Leiden: Brill, 2016.

Paul, Shalom M. et al. "Creation and Cosmogony in the Bible." In *Encyclopedia Judaica*, edited by Michael Berenbaum and Fred Skolnik, 273–80. Detroit: Macmillan Reference, 2007.

Peacocke, Arthur R. *Creation and the World of Science*. Oxford: Clarendon, 1979.

———. *Evolution: The Disguised Friend of Faith. Selected Essays*. Philadelphia: Templeton Foundation Press, 2004.

———. *Theology for a Scientific Age: Being and Becoming—Natural, Divine, and Human*. Theology and the Sciences. Minneapolis: Fortress, 1993.

Peckham, John C. *Canonical Theology: The Biblical Canon, Sola Scriptura, and Theological Method*. Grand Rapids: Eerdmans, 2016.

Peters, Ted. "On Creating the Cosmos." In *Physics, Philosophy and Theology: A Common Quest for Understanding*, edited by Robert John Russell et al., 273–96. Vatican: Vatican Observatory, 1988.

Petuchowski, Jakob J. "Jewish Prayer Texts of the Rabbinic Period." In *The Lord's Prayer and Jewish Liturgy*, edited by Jakob J. Petuchowski, 21–44. New York: Seabury, 1978.

Pfleiderer, Georg. "The Atonement." In *Trinitarian Soundings in Systematic Theology*, edited by Paul Louis Metzger, 127–38. London: Continuum, 2010.

Pope, Marvin H. *Job: Introduction, Translation, and Notes*. 3rd ed. AB 15. Garden City, NY: Doubleday, 1973.

Powlison, David. "The Classical Model." In *Understanding Spiritual Warfare: Four Views*, edited by James K. Beilby and Paul Rhodes Eddy, 89–111. Grand Rapids: Baker Academic, 2012.

———. "Response to C. Peter Wagner and Rebecca Greenwood." In *Understanding Spiritual Warfare: Four Views*, edited by James K. Beilby and Paul Rhodes Eddy, 204–09. Grand Rapids: Baker Academic, 2012.

Rad, Gerhard von. *Genesis: A Commentary*. Translated by John H. Marks. Rev. ed. Old Testament Library. Philadelphia: Westminster, 1972.

Raquel, Sylvie T. " Canon, Old Testament." In *The Lexham Bible Dictionary*, edited by John D. Barry et al., Bellingham, WA: Lexham, 2015.

Rengstorf, Karl Heinrich. "Μαθητής." In *TDNT* 4:415–61. Grand Rapids: Eerdmans, 1967.

Reno, R. R. *Genesis*. Brazos Theological Commentary on the Bible. Grand Rapids: Brazos, 2010.

Robinson, Robert B. "Narrative Theology." In *The Encyclopedia of Christianity*, edited by Erwin Fahlbusch et al., Grand Rapids: Eerdmans, 2003.

Rowe, William L., ed. *God and the Problem of Evil*. Blackwell Readings in Theology 1. Oxford: Blackwell, 2001.

Russell, Robert John. "Quantum Physics in Philosophical and Theological Perspective." In *Physics, Philosophy and Theology: A Common Quest for Understanding*, edited by Robert John Russell et al., 343–74. Vatican: Vatican Observatory, 1988.

———. "Recent Theological Interpretations of Evolution." *Theology and Science* 11 (2013) 169–84.

Samuelson, Norbert M. *Judaism and the Doctrine of Creation*. Cambridge: Cambridge University Press, 1994.

Sasse, Hermann. "Κοσμέω, Κόσμος, Κόσμιος, Κοσμικός." In *TDNT* 3:868–98. Grand Rapids: Eerdmans, 1965.

Scherer, K, R. "Plato's Legacy: Relationships between Cognition, Emotion, and Motivation." *Geneva Studies in Emotion and Communication* 9 (1995) 1–7. http://www.unige.ch/fapse/emotion/publications/pdf/plato.pdf.

Schloss, Jeffrey. "Hovering over Waters: Spirit And the Ordering of Creation." In *The Spirit in Creation and New Creation*, edited by Michael Welker, 26–49. Grand Rapids: Eerdmans, 2012.

Schnabel, Eckhard J. *Early Christian Mission*. 2 vols. Vol. 2: *Paul and the Early Church*. Downers Grove, IL: InterVarsity, 2004.

Schnackenburg, Rudolf. *The Gospel according to St. John*. Vol. 2. Translated by Cecily Hastings et al. London: Burns & Oates, 1980.

Schreiner, Thomas R. "Penal Substitution View." In *The Nature of the Atonement: Four Views*, edited by James Beilby and Paul Rhodes Eddy, 67–98. Downers Grove, IL: IVP Academic, 2006.

———. *Romans*. BECNT. Grand Rapids: Baker Academic, 1998.

Schweizer, Eduard et al. "Σάρξ, Σαρκικός, Σάρκινος." In *TDNT* 7:98–151. Grand Rapids: Eerdmans, 1971.

Segal, Alan F. *Paul the Convert: The Apostolate and Apostasy of Saul the Pharisee.* New Haven: Yale University Press, 1990.

Singer, Simeon, ed. *The Authorised Daily Prayer Book of the United Hebrew Congregations of the Commonwealth.* 4th ed. London: Collins, 2006.

Smith, Gary V. "Job IV 12–21: Is It Eliphaz's Vision?" *Vetus Testamentum* 40 (1990) 453–63.

Snodgrass, Klyne. *Ephesians.* NIVAC. Grand Rapids: Zondervan, 1996.

Soulen, R. Kendall. *The Divine Name(s) and the Holy Trinity: Distinguishing the Voices.* Vol. 1. Louisville: Westminster John Knox, 2011.

———. *The God of Israel and Christian Theology.* Minneapolis: Fortress, 1996.

Southgate, Christopher. *The Groaning Creation: God, Evolution and the Problem of Sin.* Louisville: Westminster John Knox, 2008.

Speiser, E. A. *Genesis.* AB 1. New York: Doubleday, 1964.

Spinks, Bryan D. *Do This in Remembrance of Me: The Eucharist from the Early Church to the Present Day.* London: SCM, 2013.

Starr, James. "Does 2 Peter 1:4 Speak of Deification?" In *Partakers of the Divine Nature: The History and Development of Deification in the Christian Traditions,* edited by Michael J. Christensen and Jeffery A. Wittung, 81–92. Grand Rapids: Baker Academic, 2007.

Stephens, Mark B. *Annihilation or Renewal? The Meaning and Function of New Creation in the Book of Revelation.* Wissenschaftliche Untersuchungen zum Neuen Testament 2/307. Tübingen: Mohr/Siebeck, 2011.

Stevenson, Kenneth W. *The Lord's Prayer: A Text in Tradition.* London: SCM, 2004

Stewart-Sykes, Alistair. "Catechumenate and Contra-Culture: The Social Process of Catechumenate in Third-Century Africa and Its Development." *St Vladimir's Theological Quarterly* 47 (2003) 289–306.

Stott, John R. W. *The Message of Ephesians: God's New Society.* 2nd ed. The Bible Speaks Today. Nottingham, UK: Inter-Varsity Press, 1981.

Strelan, Rick. "Recognizing the Gods (Acts 14.8–10)." *NTS* 46 (2000) 488–503.

Stump, Eleonore. "Petitionary Prayer." *American Philosophical Quarterly* 16 (1979) 81–91.

Subramanian, J. Samuel. "The Lord's Prayer in the Gospel of Matthew." In *Resourcing New Testament Studies: Literary, Historical, and Theological Essays in Honor of David L. Dungan* edited by Allan J. McNicol et al., 107–22. New York: T. & T. Clark International, 2009.

Theron, Johann. "Trinity in the Temptation Narrative and the Interpretation of Noordmans, Dostoyevski, and Mbeki." *Journal of Reformed Theology* 1 (2007) 204–22.

Thielman, Frank. *Ephesians.* BECNT. Grand Rapids: Baker Academic, 2010.

Thiselton, Anthony C. *The SPCK Dictionary of Theology and Hermeneutics.* London: SPCK, 2015.

———. *Systematic Theology.* London: SPCK, 2015.

Tidball, Derek et al., eds. *The Atonement Debate: Papers from the London Symposium on the Theology of Atonement.* Grand Rapids: Zondervan, 2009.

Travis, Stephen H. *Christ and the Judgement of God: The Limits of Divine Retribution in New Testament Thought.* Milton Keynes, UK: Paternoster, 2009.

———. *I Believe in the Second Coming of Jesus.* London: Hodder & Stoughton, 1982.

Turner, David L. *Matthew*. BECNT. Grand Rapids: Baker Academic, 2008.

Turner, Max. "Book of Ephesians." In *Dictionary for Theological Interpretation of the Bible*, edited by Kevin J. Vanhoozer, 186–91. London: SPCK, 2005.

van der Watt, Jan G. "Conclusion: Soteriology of the New Testament—Some Tentative Remarks." In *Salvation in the New Testament: Perspectives on Soteriology*, edited by Jan G. van der Watt, 505–22. Novum Testamentum Supplements 121. Leiden: Brill, 2005.

Van Driel, Edwin Chr. *Incarnation Anyway: Arguments for Supralapsarian Christology*. American Academy of Religion Academy Series. Oxford: Oxford University Press, 2008.

VanDrunen, David. *Divine Covenants and Moral Order: A Biblical Theology of Natural Law*. Grand Rapids: Eerdmans, 2014.

Vanhoozer, Kevin J. *Biblical Authority after Babel: Retrieving the Solas in the Spirit of Mere Protestant Christianity*. Grand Rapids: Brazos, 2016.

———. *The Drama of Doctrine: A Canonical Linguistic Approach to Christian Theology*. Louisville: Westminster John Knox, 2005.

———. "Imprisoned or Free: Text, Status and Theological Interpretation in the Master/ Slave Discourse of Philemon." In *Reading Scripture with the Church: Toward a Hermeneutic for Theological Interpretation*, edited by A. K. M. Adam et al., 51–93. Grand Rapids: Baker Academic, 2006.

———. *Pictures at a Theological Exhibition: Scenes of the Church's Worship, Witness and Wisdom*. Downers Grove, IL: IVP Academic, 2016.

———. *Remythologizing Theology: Divine Action, Passion, and Authorship*. Cambridge Studies in Christian Doctrine 18. Cambridge: Cambridge University Press, 2010.

———. "What Is Theological Interpretation of the Bible?" In *Dictionary for Theological Interpretation of the Bible*, edited by Kevin J. Vanhoozer, 19–25. London: SPCK, 2005.

Vanhoozer, Kevin J., and Daniel J. Treier. *Theology and the Mirror of Scripture: A Mere Evangelical Account*. Studies in Christian Doctrine and Scripture. London: Apollos, 2016.

Varner, William. *The Book of James: A New Perspective*. Woodlands, TX: Kress, 2010.

Vlachos, Hireotheos. *Orthodox Psychotherapy*. Levadia, Greece: Birth of the Theotokos Monastery, 1994.

Wagner, C. Peter, and Rebecca Greenwood. "The Strategic-Level Deliverance Model." In *Understanding Spiritual Warfare: Four Views*, edited by James K. Beilby and Paul Rhodes Eddy, 173–98. Grand Rapids: Baker Academic, 2012.

Waltke, Bruce K. "The Creation Account in Genesis 1:1–3. Part I: Introduction to Biblical Cosmogony." *Bibliotheca Sacra* 132 (1975) 25–36.

———. "The Creation Account in Genesis 1:1–3. Part IV: The Theology of Genesis 1." *Bibliotheca Sacra* 132 (1975) 327–42.

———. *Genesis: A Commentary*. Grand Rapids: Zondervan, 2001.

Walton, John H. *Genesis*. NIVAC. Grand Rapids: Zondervan, 2001.

Wangerin, Walter. *The Book of God: The Bible as a Novel*. Oxford: Lion, 1996.

Ward, Benedicta. "Introduction." In *The Lives of the Desert Fathers: The Historia Monachorum in Aegypto*. 1–46. Kalamzoo, MI: Cistercian Publications, 1980.

Ware, Kallistos. "God Hidden and Revealed: The Apophatic Way and the Essence-Energies Distinction." *Eastern Churches Review* 7 (1975) 125–36.

Watson, Francis. "The Fourfold Gospel." In *The Cambridge Companion to the Gospels*, edited by Stephen C. Barton, 34–52. Cambridge Companions to Religion. Cambridge: Cambridge University Press, 2006.

Watts, John D. *Isaiah 34–66*. Rev. ed. WBC 25. Nashville: Nelson, 2005.

Weaver, Dorothy Jean. *Matthew's Missionary Discourse: A Literary Critical Analysis*. Journal for the Study of the New Testament Supplements 38. Sheffield, UK: JSOT Press, 1990.

Webster, John. "Canon." In *Dictionary for Theological Interpretation of the Bible*, edited by Kevin J. Vanhoozer, 97–100. London: SPCK, 2005.

Wellum, Stephen J. "Editorial: Reflecting upon the 'Theological Interpretation of Scripture.'" *Southern Baptist Journal of Theology* 14 (2010): 2–3.

Wenham, David. "The Christian Life: A Life of Tension? A Consideration of the Nature of Christian Experience in Paul." In *Pauline Studies: Essays Presented to Professor F. F. Bruce on His 70th Birthday*, edited by Donald A. Hagner and Murray J. Harris, 80–94. Exeter, UK: Paternoster, 1980.

———. "How Jesus Understood the Last Supper: A Parable in Action." *Themelios* 20 (1995) 11–15.

Wenham, Gordon J. "Flood." In *New International Dictionary of Old Testament Theology and Exegesis*, edited by Willem A. VanGemeren, 640–42. Carlisle, UK: Paternoster, 1996.

———. *Genesis 1–15*. WBC 1. Waco, TX: Word, 1987.

Westermann, Claus. *Genesis 1–11: A Commentary*. Continental Commentaries. Translated by John J. Scullion. Minneapolis: Fortress, 1994.

White, Ellen. *Yahweh's Council: Its Structure and Membership*. Forschungen zum Alten Testament 2/65. Tübingen: Mohr/Siebeck, 2014.

Whybray, R. Norman. *Job*. Readings. Sheffield: Sheffield Academic, 1998.

Wiles, Maurice. *The Remaking of Christian Doctrine*. London: SCM, 1974.

———. "Scriptural Authority and Theological Construction: The Limitations of Narrative Interpretation." In *Scriptural Authority and Narrative Interpretation*, edited by Garrett Green, 42–58. Philadelphia: Fortress, 1987.

Wilkin, Robert N. et al. *Four Views on the Role of Works at the Final Judgment*. Counterpoints. Grand Rapids: Zondervan, 2013.

Wilkins, M. J. "Disciples and Discipleship." In *Dictionary of Jesus and the Gospels; Second Edition* edited by Joel B. Green et al., 202–12. Downers Grove, IL: InterVarsity, 2013.

Wilkinson, David. *The Message of Creation: Encountering the Lord of the Universe*. Leicester, UK: Inter-Varsity, 2002.

Williams, Anna N. *The Ground of Union: Deification in Aquinas and Palamas*. New York: Oxford University Press, 1999.

Williams, Rowan. *Where God Happens: Discovering Christ in One Another*. Boston: New Seeds, 2005.

Wilson, Lindsay. "Book of Job." In *Dictionary for Theological Interpretation of the Bible*, edited by Kevin J. Vanhoozer, 384–89. London: SPCK, 2005.

Wink, Walter. *Engaging the Powers: Discernment and Resistance in a World of Domination*. Philadelphia: Fortress, 1992.

———. *Naming the Powers: The Language of Power in the New Testament* Philadelphia: Fortress, 1984.

———. *Unmasking the Powers: The Invisible Forces That Determine Human Existence.* Philadelphia: Fortress, 1986.

———. "The World Systems Model." In *Understanding Spiritual Warfare: Four Views,* edited by James K. Beilby and Paul Rhodes Eddy, 47–71. Grand Rapids: Baker Academic, 2012.

Wink, Walter, and Michael Hardin. "Response to Gregory Boyd." In *Understanding Spiritual Warfare: Four Views,* edited by James K. Beilby and Paul Rhodes Eddy, 158–62. Grand Rapids: Baker Academic, 2012.

Witherington, Ben III. *Imminent Domain: The Story of the Kingdom of God and Its Celebration.* Grand Rapids: Eerdmans, 2009.

Wolterstorff, Nicholas. "The Unity behind the Canon." In *One Scripture or Many? Canon from Biblical, Theological, and Philosophical Perspectives,* edited by Christine Helmer and Christof Landmesser, 217–32. New York: Oxford University Press, 2004.

Wood, Charles M. *The Formation of Christian Understanding: Theological Hermeneutics.* 2nd ed. 1993. Reprinted, Eugene, OR: Wipf & Stock, 2000.

Wright, Christopher J. H. *The Mission of God: Unlocking the Bible's Grand Narrative.* Nottingham, UK: Inter-Varsity Press, 2006.

Wright, N. T. *Colossians and Philemon: An Introduction and Commentary.* Tyndale New Testament Commentaries 12. Downers Grove, IL: IVP Academic, 1986.

———. *Jesus and the Victory of God.* London: SPCK, 1996.

———. "The Letter to the Romans: Introduction, Commentary, and Reflections." In *The New Interpreter's Bible: A Commentary in Twelve Volumes,* edited by Leander E. Keck, 395–770. Nashville: Abingdon, 2002.

———. *The Lord and His Prayer.* London: SPCK, 1996.

———. "The Lord's Prayer as a Paradigm of Christian Prayer." In *Into God's Presence: Prayer in the New Testament,* edited by R. N. Longenecker, 132–54. Grand Rapids: Eerdmans, 2001.

Wright, W. "Some Apocryphal Psalms in Syriac." *Proceedings of the Society of Biblical Archaeology* 9 (1886/7): 257–58, 64–66.

Young, Brad H. *The Jewish Background to the Lord's Prayer.* Tulsa, OK: Gospel Research Foundation, 1984.

Ziesler, John. *Paul's Letter to the Romans.* New Testament Commentaries. London: SCM, 1989.

Subject Index

Author Index

Lightning Source UK Ltd.
Milton Keynes UK
UKHW020356250319
339732UK00005B/77/P

9 781532 633898